From C *to* C :

an

introduction

to ANSI

Standard C

JAMES GARDNER

Library Routines

```
<stdlib.h>   void     abort(void);
<stdlib.h>   int      abs(int i);
<math.h>     double   acos(double x);
<time.h>     char *   asctime(const struct tm *loctim);
<math.h>     double   asin(double x);
<assert.h>   void     assert(int expression);
<math.h>     double   atan(double x);
<math.h>     double   atan2(double y,double x);
<stdlib.h>   int      atexit(void (*wrapfunc)(void));
<stdlib.h>   double   atof(const char *s);
<stdlib.h>   int      atoi(const char *s);
<stdlib.h>   long     atol(const char *s);
<stdlib.h>   void *   bsearch(const void *key,const void *table,
                         size_t N,size_t keysize,
                         int (*compar)(const void *,const void *));
<stdlib.h>   void *   calloc(size_t N,size_t size);
<math.h>     double   ceil(double x);
<stdio.h>    void     clearerr(FILE *stream);
<time.h>     clock_t  clock(void);
<math.h>     double   cos(double x);
<math.h>     double   cosh(double x);
<time.h>     char *   ctime(const time_t *time_num);
<time.h>     double   difftime(time_t time2,time_t time1);
<stdlib.h>   div_t    div(int top,int bottom);
<stdlib.h>   void     exit(int status);
<math.h>     double   exp(double x);
<math.h>     double   fabs(double x);
<stdio.h>    int      fclose(FILE *stream);
<stdio.h>    int      feof(FILE *stream);
<stdio.h>    int      ferror(FILE *stream);
<stdio.h>    int      fflush(FILE *stream);
<stdio.h>    int      fgetc(FILE *stream);
<stdio.h>    int      fgetpos(FILE *stream,fpos_t *pos);
<stdio.h>    char *   fgets(char *string,int n,FILE *stream);
<math.h>     double   floor(double x);
<math.h>     double   fmod(double x,double y);
<stdio.h>    FILE *   fopen(const char *name,const char *options);
<stdio.h>    int      fprintf(FILE *stream,const char *format, ...);
<stdio.h>    int      fputc(int c,FILE *stream);
<stdio.h>    int      fputs(const char *string,FILE *stream);
<stdio.h>    size_t   fread(void *ptr,size_t size,size_t count,
                         FILE *stream);
<stdlib.h>   void     free(void *ptr);
<stdio.h>    FILE *   freopen(const char *name,const char *options,
                         FILE *stream);
<math.h>     double   frexp(double x,int *expptr);
<stdio.h>    int      fscanf(FILE *stream,const char *format, ...);
<stdio.h>    int      fseek(FILE *stream,long offset,int origin);
<stdio.h>    int      fsetpos(FILE *stream,const fpos_t *pos);
<stdio.h>    long     ftell(FILE *stream);
<stdio.h>    size_t   fwrite(const void *ptr,size_t size,size_t count,
                         FILE *stream);
<stdio.h>    int      getc(FILE *stream);
<stdio.h>    int      getchar(void);
<stdlib.h>   char *   getenv(const char *name);
```

```
<stdio.h>    char *  gets(char *string);
<time.h>     struct tm *gmtime(const time_t *time_num);
<ctype.h>    int     isalnum(int c);
<ctype.h>    int     isalpha(int c);
<ctype.h>    int     iscntrl(int c);
<ctype.h>    int     isdigit(int c);
<ctype.h>    int     isgraph(int c);
<ctype.h>    int     islower(int c);
<ctype.h>    int     isprint(int c);
<ctype.h>    int     ispunct(int c);
<ctype.h>    int     isspace(int c);
<ctype.h>    int     isupper(int c);
<ctype.h>    int     isxdigit(int c);
<stdlib.h>   long    labs(long n);
<math.h>     double  ldexp(double x,int N);
<stdlib.h>   ldiv_t  ldiv(long top,long bottom);
<locale.h>   struct lconv *localeconv(void);
<time.h>     struct tm *localtime(const time_t *time_num);
<math.h>     double  log(double x);
<math.h>     double  log10(double x);
<setjmp.h>   void    longjmp(jmp_buf snapshot,int value);
<stdlib.h>   void *  malloc(size_t size);
<stdlib.h>   int     mblen(const char *mb,size_t N);
<stdlib.h>   size_t  mbstowcs(wchar_t *wcstr,const char *mbstr,size_t N);
<stdlib.h>   int     mbtowc(wchar_t *wc,const char *mb,size_t N);
<string.h>   void *  memchr(const void *obj,int c,size_t N);
<string.h>   int     memcmp(const void *obj1,const void *obj2,size_t N);
<string.h>   void *  memcpy(void *dest,const void *src,size_t N);
<string.h>   void *  memmove(void *dest,const void *src,size_t N);
<string.h>   void *  memset(void *mem,int c,size_t N);
<time.h>     time_t  mktime(struct tm *timestruct);
<math.h>     double  modf(double x,double *yp);
<stddef.h>   size_t  offsetof(type,structure_member);
<stdio.h>    void    perror(const char *usermsg);
<math.h>     double  pow(double x,double y);
<stdio.h>    int     printf(const char *format, ...);
<stdio.h>    int     putc(int c,FILE *stream);
<stdio.h>    int     putchar(int c);
<stdio.h>    int     puts(const char *string);
<stdlib.h>   void    qsort(void *table,size_t N,size_t size,
                          int (*compar)(const void *,const void *));
<signal.h>   int     raise(int sig);
<stdlib.h>   int     rand(void);
<stdlib.h>   void *  realloc(void *oldp,size_t size);
<stdio.h>    int     remove(const char *filename);
<stdio.h>    int     rename(const char *oldname,const char *newname);
<stdio.h>    void    rewind(FILE *stream);
<stdio.h>    int     scanf(const char *format, ...);
<stdio.h>    void    setbuf(FILE *stream,char *buf);
<setjmp.h>   int     setjmp(jmp_buf snapshot);
<locale.h>   char *  setlocale(int class,const char *locale);
<stdio.h>    int     setvbuf(FILE *stream,char *buf,int type,size_t size);
<signal.h>   void (* signal(int sig,void (*newfunc)(int)))(int);
<math.h>     double  sin(double x);
<math.h>     double  sinh(double x);
<stdio.h>    int     sprintf(char *string,const char *format, ...);
<math.h>     double  sqrt(double x);
<stdlib.h>   void    srand(unsigned seed);
```

From **C** *to* **C** *:*

an

introduction

to ANSI

Standard C

with Reference Manual

JAMES GARDNER

with the
Software Development
Group
University of Waterloo

HARCOURT BRACE JOVANOVICH, PUBLISHERS
AND ITS SUBSIDIARY, ACADEMIC PRESS

SAN DIEGO   NEW YORK   CHICAGO   AUSTIN   WASHINGTON, D.C.
LONDON   SYDNEY   TOKYO   TORONTO

Preface

C was developed in the late 1960s by researchers at AT&T's Bell Laboratories, Murray Hill, New Jersey. The first major programs written in C were related to the UNIX[1] operating system. Most of UNIX itself is written in C, and the majority of programs running on UNIX machines are also written in C.

UNIX and C proved to be popular with many programmers, especially in research facilities, colleges, and universities. As a result, many of the more innovative programs of the 70s and 80s were written in C. In order to run these programs on other systems, versions of C have been created for almost every type of computer on the market today.

The drive to make C available for almost every computer was helped by C's simplicity and versatility. Some programming languages (for example, Cobol and PL/I) are too complex to run on small machines like microcomputers, but most machines have enough capacity to run C (or simplified versions of C). Other languages (notably assemblers) are simple enough, but are too strongly linked to the abilities of a particular machine or operating system; such languages are difficult to transfer to other systems.

Today, C has spread far beyond its roots in UNIX, although it continues to be affected by developments in the UNIX-based world. In North America, the POSIX committee of IEEE (the Institute of Electrical and Electronics Engineers) is currently developing a standard for UNIX-like operating systems, and the requirements of this POSIX standard will undoubtedly influence what programmers will expect to see in any version of C. In Europe, the X/OPEN committee of ISO (the International Standards Organization) is engaged in similar activity, and this too will have its effect on the future of C.

Meanwhile, C has inspired offshoot programming languages, most notably C++ from Bell Laboratories. C++ is similar to C, but contains a number of additional features that tend to change the way in which programmers think of their programs. In time, some of the extra features of C++ will probably be incorporated into C itself, although it remains to be seen how extensive this cross-fertilization will be.

The ANSI Standard for C

From the foregoing discussion, you can see that there has been a gradual evolution in our ideas of what C is and what it should be. It was only natural that standards organizations around the world would attempt to unify the different directions of this evolution. The standard described in this book is the **ANSI Standard**, created by the American National Standards Institute (ANSI) in consultation with committees of the International Standards Organization (ISO) and the standards organizations of many other countries. We expect that the ANSI standard will soon become the international standard for C.

---

1. UNIX is a trademark of AT&T Bell Laboratories, Murray Hill, New Jersey.

This book is based on the draft version of the ANSI standard prepared by the ANSI X3J11 committee, dated May 13, 1988. The only changes made to the standard since that time have been clarifications to the wording (called "editorial changes"). At the time of writing no further changes were expected, and it is expected that the final version of the standard will be officially recognized in the near future.

Versions of C that predate the standard may be substantially different. These older versions of C will disappear in the course of time, but for now, readers should be warned:

☞   Many widely used versions of C were developed before the ANSI standard, and therefore will not provide some of the features that the standard requires.

Appendix B briefly describes how older versions of C differ from the standard. Appendix G provides documentation for the **C2C** from the Software Development Group at the University of Waterloo. This implementation of C reflects the latest draft of the full ANSI standard. It is available for the IBM PC or PS/2 and compatible computers, and is available to adapters.

Overview of ANSI C

The list below outlines the most important features of ANSI C, and what distinguishes C from other languages. Many of the terms we will use will only be meaningful to people who already have some programming experience. New programmers can look up the terms in the glossary (Appendix A), or simply wait until the terms are explained in later chapters of the book.

- C is a *free-form* language. This means that C programs do not have to be arranged on the page in any particular way. You may break up a single instruction over several lines, or put several instructions on the same line. Lines may be indented freely.

- Comments may be placed anywhere in a program.

- Programs are made up of smaller "subprograms" called *functions*. A function typically performs a single task, large or small. For example, you might have a short function that puts the letters of a word into uppercase, or a long one that searches through a file to find a particular piece of information.

- A function that performs a large task often calls on other functions to perform smaller parts of the task. Usually, any function can call any other function (although there are ways to create functions that can only be called by a few of the other functions in the program). Functions can even call themselves, a process called *recursion*.

- A hosted implementation of C comes with a standard *library* of supplied functions. These save you time and effort. For example, you don't have to write your own functions to calculate sines or logarithms—such functions are supplied as part of the implementation. C uses library functions to perform many operations that other languages build right into the language itself: reading and writing files, working with character strings, handling unusual events, and so on.

- When a function is called, the caller may pass *arguments*. Arguments are pieces of information that the function will use in its work. For example, a function that calculates square roots would be passed a number whose square root you want to find. All C arguments are passed *by value*; this term is described in a later chapter.

- Often, a function is called to calculate a particular value. This value, called the *result* of the function, is returned for the caller's use.

- Each function is made up of *declarations* and *statements*. Declarations are descriptive: they describe the pieces of information that will be used by the function and can also specify initial values for data objects. Statements are active: they work with information to achieve results.

- Many different types of information can be declared:

  > *integers and floating point numbers of varying lengths*
  > *single characters and character strings*
  > *arrays (lists of information)*
  > *pointers (giving the location of other pieces of information)*
  > *structures (records made up of different kinds of information)*
  > *user-defined types*

- Statements can be loosely broken into two types: expressions (which perform various kinds of calculations) and control statements (which dictate the order in which actions are performed). C's control statements include looping constructs (**while, do-while, for**), conditional constructs (**if, else, switch**), and transfers (**goto, return, break, continue**).

- Operations that can be performed in expressions include:

  > *addition, subtraction, multiplication, real division, integer division, remainder*
  > *increment and decrement operations*
  > *pointer arithmetic*
  > *type conversion*
  > *comparisons*
  > *assignments*
  > *function calls*
  > *bit operations (shifting, complementing, AND, inclusive and exclusive OR)*
  > *logical operations (AND, OR)*
  > *finding addresses*
  > *indirecting through pointers*
  > *array subscripting*

- C programs pass through a *preprocessor* which can be used to modify the text of the program. Preprocessing facilities include:

  conditional compilation
  macro definition
  inclusion of code from other source files

Organization of this Book

This book is divided into several parts. Part I, the Learner's Guide, presents the fundamental concepts of ANSI C, giving examples of how the language can be used in simple programs. Those who are already familiar with some version of C may choose to skip this part. For new C programmers, however, it provides a step-by-step introduction to programming in general, and the ANSI C language in particular.

Part II, Programming Strategies, offers hints for writing C programs. Its purpose is to discuss the philosophy of writing programs in C, as opposed to the bare rules of the C language.

Part III, the User's Guide, provides a complete technical description of the language. This part of the book is mainly intended as a reference aid. However, it also provides detailed explanations of features glossed over in the tutorial.

Part IV describes the standard library functions of the ANSI standard. This information supplements information found in the other parts of the book.

There is a great deal of duplication between parts. This is an outgrowth of our experience with other books on C. Books that are aimed at *teaching* C are usually not organized in a way that makes for convenient reference; because they explain a bit at a time, readers must read small passages from several different chapters to get a complete description of any language feature. Books that serve as *reference manuals* for working C programmers are entirely inappropriate for novices trying to learn the language. One reason that we wrote *From C to C* is because we saw a need for a book that would be useful both to those who were learning the language and to those who were actively programming in it.

Acknowledgments

This book would not be possible without the advice and support I have received from Peter Fraser, Director of the Software Development Group at the University of Waterloo. Peter has patiently read draft after draft, pointed out numerous oversights and overstatements, tidied up programming examples, and generally pushed me to make this book the best it could be. He has also made sure that I had the time and resources to see this book to completion. If a book can be likened to a child, Peter was the doctor who made sure this one was born healthy.

I would also like to thank the many people at Harcourt Brace Jovanovich who have helped make this book what it is: Richard Bonacci, acquisitions editor; Julia Ross, manuscript editor; Linda Wild, designer; and Diane Southworth, production manager. I owe them gratitude and apologies for their time and patience on a project that has taken much longer than a naive author ever expected.

A word of appreciation is due to the X3J11 committee that created the ANSI standard for C. It was a difficult task, and one where I'm sure adverse criticism far outweighs praise. I for one would like to congratulate them on a job well done.

I would also like to thank the reviewers who provided suggestions at various stages of development: William E. Clark, Texas A&M University; Henry Etlinger, Rochester Institute of Technology; Bill Walker, East Central University, Ada, Oklahoma; John Kapenga, Western Michigan University; Grady Early, Southwest Texas State University; James F. Peters, III, Kansas State University; Gerald W. Adkins, Georgia State College; Frank Burke, Middlesex County College, Edison, New Jersey; Paul M. Johns, Lansing Community College; Robert C. Baker, BDM Software; Larry Cottrell, University of Central Florida; and John H. Halton, University of North Carolina.

Finally, my thanks go to Honeywell Bull and to the University of Waterloo who funded some of the work, to the Software Development Group who told me what they hated in text books, to Chris Redmond who read early drafts with fresh eyes, to Lorne Grossman who was my first guinea pig, and to my wife Linda Carson who told me what a pica was.

Short Table of Contents

Full Table of Contents

Part I
Learner's Guide

Part III
User's Guide

Part IV
The Standard Library

PART I
ANSI C: The Learner's Guide

The Learner's Guide explains the basic features of the C programming language. We will not cover all the fine details; that is done in the User's Guide, Part III of this book. However, we will touch on most of the major features of the language, so you should have little difficulty with the manual once you have worked through the Learner's Guide.

The Learner's Guide is aimed at people who do not know C and who have little experience with programming in general. We do assume that you know some of the basics of computing (for example, that you've heard of a "file"), but we explain most of the terms we use. Appendix A provides a glossary for terms used in this book.

The ANSI Standard

A programming language standard like the ANSI standard might be compared to an architect's first sketches of a building; the standard shows what the language should "look like" and what its major features should be, but it's really only a picture of something that doesn't yet exist.

After an architect produces initial sketches of a building, someone must make detailed blueprints and then actually construct the building. In the same way, a standard is only the beginning of making a computer language: someone must figure out how to make a computer do the things that the standard requires and must then construct a working version of the language. This produces an **implementation** of the language: a set of one or more programs that let you prepare and run C programs in the way that the standard describes.

Implementations on different types of computers may be slightly different. To continue our analogy with buildings, different computers are like different kinds of terrain, and language builders must make allowances for the "lay of the land."

The ANSI standard recognizes that different types of computers work in slightly different ways, so implementations are given some freedom in how they handle certain features of the C language. In situations where individual implementations are allowed to choose how they behave, we say that the behavior is **implementation-defined**. The Learner's Guide will always point out when program behavior is implementation-defined; whenever possible, we will list the alternative ways in which programs may behave.

One of the most important distinctions between implementations of C is whether they are **hosted** or **free-standing**. A hosted implementation runs programs with the aid of an **operating system**; an operating system can be thought of as a collection of "servant" programs which help other programs perform common operations like reading and writing information. A free-standing implementation runs programs without an operating system;

this means that free-standing C programs must do everything "from scratch." Most implementations of C are hosted, so this book will say little about free-standing implementations.

Exercises

The Learner's Guide contains many exercises to help you become familiar with how C works. In addition, we strongly recommend that you experiment with the language by writing your own programs.

The ANSI standard for C is an abstraction. In order to write and run your own C programs, you must work with an actual implementation. The implementation provided with this book is called **C2C**, a version of ANSI C for the IBM PC and truly compatible machines running MS-DOS version 3.0 or later.

Details of how to prepare and run programs with **C2C** are given in boxes throughout the book. These details have been separated from the main body of the text for two reasons:

(a)   This text describes the ANSI standard. We want to avoid confusing the standard in its "pure" state with the technical details associated with **C2C** itself. Our book should be applicable to any C implementation conforming to the standard.

(b)   The standard will not change in the near future; a lengthy review process is required before any change can be made. On the other hand, implementations are constantly changing: the implementers devise ways to make the implementation work faster and more efficiently, with enhanced options and features. By separating the descriptions of the standard and the implementation, we make it easier to improve how the implementation works, without changing what we say about the standard.

If you do not have access to a PC where you can run **C2C**, you may have a problem. As we have stressed, many widely used C implementations do not follow the standard as yet. Since we will be describing how to write programs for ANSI C, you will probably find that the programs will not run using earlier implementations. However, manufacturers are hurrying to provide ANSI implementations for their machines, so the problem is only a short-term one.

chapter 1   Elements of Programming

Before we begin describing the details of the C programming language, we should discuss programming in general: how it works and how you should approach it.

1.1 Basic Terminology

A **program** is a sequence of instructions telling a computer how to perform a particular job. Programs are often called **software** to distinguish them from **hardware**, the actual machinery of a computer. Together, software and hardware make a computer run.

Computer hardware can follow instructions only when they are presented in a form called **machine code**. Machine code instructions are often quite complicated and difficult for humans to understand. For this reason, people usually write programs in a **programming language** like C. A programming language lets you write instructions in a form that is easier to understand and more versatile than machine code.

A program written in a programming language is called **source code**. Once a source code version of a program has been written, facilities inside a computer can *translate* this source program into machine code instructions that the machine itself can understand.

This means that every C program you write goes through two different stages inside the computer:

(a)   a translation stage, where the source code of the program is converted to a form that is easier for the computer to understand;

(b)   an execution stage, where the translated instructions of the program are actually carried out.

With some implementations of C, these two stages are widely separated. In fact, some implementations are designed to translate a program on one type of computer, but run the program on an entirely different type. (This is called **cross-compiling**.) With other implementations, the stages happen almost simultaneously. For example, a C **interpreter** works by reading an instruction, translating it, executing it, reading another instruction, translating it, executing it, and so on.

The most common approach to preparing a C program is **compiling**. A program called a **compiler** translates source code into a form called **object code**. Object code is an intermediate stage between source code and full machine code. It is not necessary to translate the program all at once; programs are often divided into parts and the parts compiled separately. When all parts have been compiled, the object code for each part is **linked** together to produce a complete executable program.

Every program ought to produce **output**, a record of the results of the program's work. If a program produces no output, you have no way of knowing what the results of the work were—the work is wasted. Output can be written on paper, on the display screen of a computer terminal, to information storage devices like disks and tapes, or even to other computers. Output may be text that can be read by people or information in a form that is only meaningful to another computer.

Many programs also make use of **input**. Input is information that originates outside the program. It may be entered from a keyboard, from disks and tapes, or from other machines. A program "processes" input information to obtain output results.

1.2 Stages of Program Preparation

The translation and execution stages are the parts of program preparation that are performed by the computer. However, the work that the machine does is only a small part of the total programming process. Below we list *all* the stages of program preparation, from first to last.

Problem Analysis

The first step in writing a program is defining the job that the program should do. If you want the program to solve a particular problem, you must make sure that you *understand* the problem. What are the goals you want to reach? How will the computer help you reach them? Is using a computer really the best approach? There is no point in writing a program if it is not going to be useful, or if there is a better way to do the same job.

System Design

Once you have clearly identified your goals, you must *design* a program or set of programs that accomplish those goals. This means describing what you want the program(s) to do: what kind of input information is needed, how this input should be processed, what sort of output is expected. If the project involves more than one program, the design stage also determines how these programs will interact.

Logic Design

Once you know how a program should behave, you must figure out how to make it work that way. This means you must design the *logic* of the program: the steps that the program will take in order to achieve its results. One of the best approaches to logic design is called **Stepwise Refinement** or **Topdown Decomposition**. This will be discussed in the next section.

Coding

The logic design tells you in general terms what actions a program should take. In the coding stage, you express those general terms as specific instructions in a programming language. In other words, you write the source code for the program.

When coding a large program, many programmers start by making small **prototype** programs to test parts of the logic design. Such programs give you a quick way to try various approaches to implementing the design, so that you can evaluate the correctness and efficiency of each approach without investing a lot of effort. Prototype programs often help to reveal any flaws your logic design might have. It is better to take a bit of time experimenting with your design when you begin coding than to spend a lot of time correcting problems later on.

Debugging

The first draft of any program almost always contains errors (known as **bugs**). In the debugging stage, you identify the bugs (usually by running the program to see how it behaves), and then correct them.

Bugs fall into three general classes. **Translation errors** are problems found when the program is translated to machine language; for example, typing mistakes in the source code can confuse instructions so that the translator doesn't understand what you're trying to say. **Execution errors** are problems found while the program is executing; for example, the program may attempt some invalid operation, like dividing by zero. **Logic errors** are problems found after the program finishes execution; the computer was able to carry out all the instructions you specified, but some mistake in those instructions meant that your program didn't do what you wanted it to.

Debugging requires patience: errors can be subtle and hard to identify, especially in a large program. Being careful in the logic design and coding stages can save a lot of effort when you reach the debugging stage.

Testing

Testing is an extension of debugging. After correcting the obvious bugs, you must make sure that the program behaves properly in all possible cases. This means checking to make sure that the program handles complicated or unexpected kinds of input, that it has some way of dealing with input errors, that it works efficiently, and so on. Ideally, people who will eventually be using the program should be involved in some stage of the testing process; a program is not finished until it is acceptable to the user.

Documentation

In the documentation stage, you write explanations of how your program works and how it is used. Most of the time, the documentation for a program will be written earlier in the programming process (for example, during testing, so that people testing the program understand how to use it). However, changes to documentation are often required *after* testing, because the testing process reveals changes that should be made to the program.

Production

When the program has been thoroughly tested and documented, it is ready to go into "production." This means that it is used for its intended purpose.

Maintenance

Even after the program goes into production, it should not be considered finished. New bugs may be found through extensive use. It is also common for small changes to be required. If, for example, your program produces some kind of report, users may decide they want a different format for the report, or new information added to the report. The ongoing work of correcting bugs and making minor changes is called **program maintenance**.

Updates and Revision

Even maintenance is not the end. Experience shows that most programs need major overhauls from time to time, in response to changes in a company's business situation or to improvements in competitive products. Major revisions are often called **program updates**.

With simple programs (like the exercises in the Learner's Guide), the stages of the programming process tend to merge with each other. For example, it can be hard to separate logic design from coding—the design stage may just be a moment's thought before you start writing code. In larger programs, however, it is useful to separate the two stages. If you start coding before you have a clear picture of how your program will work, you usually end up with something that is messy and inefficient.

We will not say much more about some of the stages we have just mentioned, even though we have only scratched the surface. For example, there is a vast amount that could be said about making a program acceptable to the user (what sales people call "user-friendly"), but we do not have the space to give this topic the treatment it deserves.

Similarly, our Learner's Guide says little about documenting programs, even though documentation is one of the most important and neglected aspects of the programming process. Our primary goal is to teach the C language, not English. However, we strongly recommend that you write a paragraph or two about every program you create, explaining what it does and how it is used.

1.3 Stepwise Refinement

The stepwise refinement approach to program logic divides the program's work into a sequence of general steps, then divides each step into slightly more detailed actions, and so on. As an example of this process, we'll leave the computer field for a moment and concentrate on a more mundane job: getting a cup of coffee. We can break this job into the following general steps.

(1)   Get a coffee pot.

(2)   Put some water in the coffee pot.

(3)   Get some coffee.

(4)   Put the coffee in the coffee pot.

(5)   Heat the pot until the coffee percolates.

(6)   Get a cup.

(7)   Pour the brewed coffee into the cup.

In writing these steps, we made no effort to provide details (for example, how much coffee to put in the pot, how much water to use, and so on). All we wanted was a general outline of what you have to do.

Once we have drawn up this general outline, *then* we can begin to get more specific, by breaking each general step into more detailed steps. For example, step (3) might be divided into the following.

(3a)   Get coffee beans.

(3b)   Put the coffee beans into a coffee grinder.

(3c)   Grind the beans to make coffee.

Each of these steps can also be divided into more detailed actions. For example, we can divide (3a) into the following:

(3a-1)   Go to the refrigerator.

(3a-2)   Look for a can of coffee beans.

(3a-3)   If the can is empty, buy more beans.

(3a-4)   Otherwise, use the coffee beans from the can.

And of course, these can be divided again; for example, (3a-3) could be divided into steps explaining how to go to the grocery store, find the aisle where coffee beans are located, and so on.

It may sound as if we're making a simple job more complicated by splitting it up into all these steps. Notice, however, that we are not *inventing* complications. All these actions are things someone might reasonably do when making coffee.

☞ The stepwise refinement process doesn't invent complexity—it just reveals complexity that we don't usually think about.

(If you don't believe making coffee is a complex job, just consider for a moment how difficult it would be to train a dog to do it.)

At every stage of stepwise refinement, a job gets simpler. We begin with the entire job of making a cup of coffee, then break it into steps. Next we simplify our goal by looking at a single step (getting coffee). We break that into steps, and simplify the task again by looking at one of these smaller steps. The jobs we are trying to describe get smaller and smaller, so the task of describing them gets easier and easier.

This same process carries over into the art and craft of programming. To design the logic of a program, you can divide the program's work into very general steps, then divide each step into smaller steps, and so on. If you go into full detail immediately, you are continually dealing with a job at the level of maximum complexity; if you work into a job bit by bit, you will find it much easier to grasp what your program has to do and how it can go about doing it.

1.3.1 General Routines

Some of the steps in solving a problem may be easier than others. For example, step (7) in our breakdown of the coffee problem is very simple: pour the coffee into the coffee cup. On the other hand, we have already pointed out that step (3) (getting coffee) can be complicated, especially if it involves a trip to the grocery store.

One way we simplify complicated actions is to build up a collection of general routines that we are ready to perform when a specific occasion requires it. For example, children are taught how to "buy something at a store." Once they know how to do this general operation, they are able to buy any specific thing that's needed: coffee, milk, bread, and so on. They do not have to be taught "buying coffee" and "buying milk" as separate skills.

Computer programs often work the same way. Parts of the program are written to perform general operations like printing out a value. Once this is done, you can use the same routine for printing out many different values. By writing a single general routine that can be applied to a number of similar situations, you save a lot of work.

1.3.2 Multiple Solutions

☞   There is never a unique solution to a given problem.

For example, the steps we gave for "getting a cup of coffee" were certainly not the only way we could reach our goal. We could have given steps for making instant coffee, or for making filter coffee, or for going to a restaurant and buying a cup of coffee, or for persuading someone else to go get coffee. To choose the best solution, you have to weigh several factors: which approach is most convenient, which gives the most desirable results, and so on.

In the same way, there is usually more than one way to write a program. This means that you should not immediately use the first approach that occurs to you. Think a bit longer to see if there is another way that turns out to be better than what first came to mind. Your first approach may indeed be the one you finally choose, but taking time to consider alternatives will make you more confident that you really have picked the best solution.

Finally, don't be afraid to change your mind part way through program development. If you think of a better approach, or if the approach you have chosen turns out to have significant problems, reconsider the situation. It is far better to rework all or part of a program than to press on with something that will not do the job properly.

1.4 Programming Style

Learning to write good programs means more than just learning the rules of a particular programming language. It means learning to write programs that are *clean*: easy to read, easy to understand, and easy to modify when the need arises.

A major factor in achieving these goals is programming "style." This is so important that we want to talk about it before we show any examples of C programs. Style is partly an art, learned through programming experience and by examining programs written by other people (such as the examples in this book). Style is also a craft that can be learned by paying attention to a few basic principles.

Later chapters of this book offer many tips for improving your programming style. In this section, we will only discuss two simple aspects of style: indentation and commenting.

1.4.1 Indentation

The instructions in a C program combine English words with mathematical expressions. Words and parts of expressions are usually separated by spaces, just as in an English sentence.

Anywhere that you may put a space character in C source code, you may put any number of spaces. Instead of spaces, you may also use tab characters or start a new line. This means that the C instructions

```
a = b + c;
```

and

```
a =
b   +   c;
```

are equally valid and have exactly the same meaning. Tabs and spaces are called **whitespace** characters. Another common whitespace character is the **new-line**: this is a character that tells C to end one line and start a new one.

☞ Anywhere that you may use one whitespace character, you may use any combination of whitespace characters.

Because C lets you put in extra whitespace, you are free to indent lines or sets of lines in your program. Proper indentation will make your program more readable. For example, if a group of related instructions all have the same indentation, you will be able to *see* that the instructions are related. Good indentation style often helps you catch programming errors, even before you test your program.

1.4.2 Comments

Comments are another important aspect of programming style. Beginners frequently say, "I know what my program does, so comments aren't necessary." This may be true at the time you write the program, but as the months pass, the clarity of your memory will fade. Furthermore, it often happens that someone else has to figure out how the program works when you are no longer available. In many businesses, the person who *maintains* a program is often not the person who originally wrote it. You have an obligation to make your programs easy to understand, and nothing contributes more to understanding than clear and readable comments.

In C, comments begin with the characters /* and end with */. A comment may be split over several lines, as in

```
/*
 *   This
 *   is
 *   a
 *   comment.
 */
```

Notice how we used stars on the comment lines to make them stand out. This is not necessary, but it makes your comments more noticeable.

For good style, every program should contain a comment explaining what the program does and how the program is used.

☞ Comments should be added wherever they can help clarify what the code of the program is doing.

A comment may appear anywhere a whitespace character is allowed: at the end of lines, as in

```
n = i * 2; /* "n" is now even */
```

at the beginning of lines, as in

```
/* Now we capitalize "c" */ c = c + 'A' - 'a';
```

or even in the middle of lines, as in

```
Angle1 = Angle2 + /* 2 pi */ 6.28318;
```

However, you should bear in mind that comments are intended to help others read and understand the program. Comments may be allowed in the middle of lines, but a comment in the wrong place may make a program more cluttered and hard to read. For best readability, a comment should usually be put on a line of its own, perhaps surrounded by blank lines to make the comment stand out more clearly.

1.4.3 A Note About Examples

Readers should view the examples in this book as models of one good programming style. Ultimately, you may decide that a different style is more in keeping with your personal tastes. However, the style that we present here is a good starting point and imitating it is a good way to begin programming in C.

While the examples are always written in good style (or at least we hope so), they do not always show the "best" way to write a piece of code. Every example is limited by the features of C that we have described up to that point in the book. This means that early examples are often rather crude: there are more elegant ways to write these programs, but we will not have discussed the required features of the language. Even in later programs, there are places where we might have taken programming "short cuts," but did not. Some programs are difficult enough to understand when they are written in the most straightforward manner; taking short cuts would only risk more confusion.

We have tried to keep our examples as short as possible. However, certain features of C only arise naturally in large programs. To avoid long examples, we have sometimes resorted to blatantly contrived situations.

For all these reasons, readers will find it worthwhile to examine our examples and to think about ways in which they can be improved. For example, once you have finished working your way through the Learner's Guide, you may find it useful to go back through the book and try rewriting the examples in early chapters using more sophisticated features of C.

We also recommend that users run all the sample programs we discuss in this book. This gives you practice using C and "hands on" knowledge of how these programs work. Everyone learns better by doing. Practice and experimentation are crucial to learning about C.

chapter 2   Functions

A C program is made up of **functions**. Every function specifies one or more actions for your program to perform. In this chapter, we will examine the simplest characteristics of functions: what they look like and how they are used.

2.1. *Function Names*

All functions have names.

☞ The name of a function can be made up of uppercase letters, lowercase letters, digits, and the underscore character (`'_'`). The first character of the name cannot be a digit.

When you name the functions of your program, you should not use names that begin with an underscore. Such names are reserved for the use of the *C library* (which we will discuss later in this chapter).

The following are all valid names for functions:

```
Func2    abc    MY_FUNC    Make_Graph
```

The following are both invalid names, for the reasons given by the comments:

```
2func   /* can't start with digit */
pl$s    /* can't have $ character */
```

Uppercase letters are not equivalent to lowercase ones in function names. For example, FUNC, Func, and func are all *different* names, referring to different functions. In general, however, you should avoid having different functions with names that only differ in the case of their letters. There are two reasons for this:

(a)   It is easy to confuse one name with the other when you are reading and writing the program. The difference between names like Func and func is easy to overlook.

(b)   Technical limitations on some types of computer systems may make it impossible for those systems to distinguish between upper- and lowercase letters at some points in the process of translating and executing programs. Usually, the problem comes when these systems try to *link* compiled programs. On some systems, the software that does the linking is too primitive to distinguish upper- and lowercase letters. For this reason, you cannot rely on case distinction to differentiate between function names.

Box 2.1: Length of Function Names

In all implementations of **ANSI** C, function names can contain up to 31 characters. Some implementations accept even longer names. However, on some machines, technical limitations make it necessary for function names to be *truncated* (chopped down) to their first **six** characters. For this reason, it is a good idea to make sure that all the functions in your program have names that are unique in the first six characters.

2.1.1. Reserved Words

As you will see in the rest of this book, some words and names have special meaning in C. For example, the word **while** is used to start a particular type of action. Since these words already have a meaning in C, you cannot give them new meanings—you cannot use these words as names for functions or other parts of your program. We say that these are **reserved words** because you cannot use them as names. The reserved words of C are

```
auto        double      int         struct
break       else        long        switch
case        enum        register    typedef
char        extern      return      union
const       float       short       unsigned
continue    for         signed      void
default     goto        sizeof      volatile
do          if          static      while
```

Reserved words are also called **keywords**.

We won't explain what any of these words mean at the moment; we will just point out that you can't use any of them as function names. If you try to use them as names, you will receive error messages when you try to translate the program.

2.2. *Arguments and Results*

A function is a program in miniature. It is (often) given input to work with, and it (usually) produces output. As examples, consider a few functions from mathematics:

(a) The square root function is given a number (x) as input and produces another number (the square root of x) as output.

(b) The sine function is given an angle as input and produces a number (the sine of the angle) as output.

(c)   A function based on the Pythagorean theorem might take two numbers as input (the lengths of the two shorter sides of a right triangle) and produce another number as output (the length of the hypotenuse).

In C, input values given to a function are called the **arguments** of the function. An output value is called the **result** or *return value* of the function. Functions may take any number of arguments, but they have at most one result.

The examples of functions that we gave above all had numeric arguments and results. In C, functions can work with other kinds of values too. For example, in the next chapter, we will write a function that takes a lowercase letter as its argument and produces the corresponding uppercase letter as its result. We could also write a function that took a list of words as its argument and returned the same list, sorted into alphabetical order. The idea of a function is a versatile one.

2.3. Function Definitions

A **function definition** describes what a function does and how it is used. The definition has two parts: the **prototype** and the **body**.

2.3.1. Function Prototypes

A function prototype tells the name of the function, and describes the arguments and result of the function. For example, here is a simple function prototype.

```
int plus(int a,int b)
```

We'll explain this prototype by breaking it into parts.

int plus(int a,int b)
> The beginning of the prototype tells the **type** of value that will be returned as the result of the function. In our example, this is the keyword **int**. It indicates that the function returns an **integer** value.

☞   An **integer** is a number (positive, negative, or zero) without a fractional part or decimal point.

> 1 is an integer; 1.5 and 1.0 are not. In later chapters, we will discuss other types of values that functions may return.

int **plus**(int a,int b)
> The next part of the function prototype is the name of the function. In our example, this name is plus. The function name in a prototype is followed by an opening parenthesis ' ('.

```
int plus(int a,int b)
```
Next comes a list describing the arguments for the function. This is called the **parameter list** of the prototype. Items in the list are separated by commas, and the end is marked by a closing parenthesis ') ' . Extra white space may be added, as in

```
int plus( int a , int b )
```

For each function argument, the parameter list gives the type of value that the function expects as input and a name that the function will use to refer to the argument value. This kind of name is known as a **formal parameter**. In our example, plus has two formal parameters (and therefore takes two argument values). Both are integers; the first argument is associated with a parameter named a and the second is associated with a parameter named b.

Formal parameter names must follow the same rules we gave for function names: they may contain letters, digits, and underscore characters, they may not begin with a digit, and so on. Inside the function definition, the formal parameters stand for the argument values that the function receives as input.

2.3.2. The Function Body

The body of a function follows the function prototype in a function definition. The body is always enclosed in **brace brackets**. An **opening brace bracket** is ' { ' and a **closing brace bracket** is ' } ' .

The body of a function is made up of **declarations** and **statements**. A declaration lists one or more names that appear in the function and tells how those names will be used. Names declared inside a function often refer to **data objects**: the pieces of information that the function uses in its calculations. For example, you might have a declaration saying that x, y, and z are going to be the names of data objects that have integer values. This would be written

```
int x,y,z;
```

A statement describes an action that your function should perform. For example, the statement

```
x = 1;
```

says that x should be given the value 1.

In the above examples, both the declaration and the statement end in a semicolon (;). You will see that most statements and all declarations end in a semicolon.

As a trivial example of a function body, consider the function plus whose prototype we discussed in the last section. Let's say that plus takes two integers as arguments and returns the sum of those two integers. The definition of plus looks like this:

```
int plus(int a,int b)
{
        return a+b ;
}
```

This definition consists of the prototype followed by brace brackets enclosing the body of the function.

We could have compressed this function to

```
int plus(int a,int b) { return a+b; }
```

because it doesn't matter how the instructions in a C program are broken up into lines. However, you will find that larger functions are more readable if they are well spread out, so we will spread out short functions too. In fact, many programmers would find it convenient to spread out the declaration to

```
        int
plus( int a,  int b)
{
        return a+b ;
}
```

With this format, the name of the function begins a line, and that can make it easier to find when you are reading a printout of a program or searching through a file containing the program.

2.3.3. The Return Statement

The body of our `plus` function is the single statement

```
return a+b ;
```

This is a **return** statement.

☞   A **return** statement consists of the word **return** followed by an **expression**. An expression is a sequence of operations that yield a value.

To understand what a **return** statement does in a C function, we'll again examine mathematical functions like the square root function. You give the square root function a value (x) and it gives back another value (the square root of x). In the same way, we give our `plus` function two values (named a and b) and it is supposed to return the sum of those values. The **return** statement specifies the result that the function returns.

To put it another way, a function is a set of instructions designed to produce the answer to some problem. When the function has calculated the answer, it executes a **return** statement. In effect, the **return** statement says, "Here is the answer I was asked to find." This answer is the value of the expression that appears in the **return** statement.

A complicated function may have many instructions before the **return** statement that calculates the function's final answer. However, our plus function is simple enough that it doesn't need any extra instructions. It can go directly to the **return** statement that calculates the function's result:

```
return a+b ;
```

This says that the return value for the function is the result of the expression a+b. The formal parameters of plus are a and b, so C will add the argument values associated with a and b and return the sum as the "answer" the function was asked to find.

2.3.4. Other Operators

Our plus function used the addition operator + in an obvious way. The other arithmetic operators in C are equally easy to use.

Table 2.1
Simple Arithmetic Operations

Addition	A+B
Subtraction	A−B
Multiplication	A*B
Division	A/B
Remainder	A%B
Negation	−A
Plus	+A

Subtraction is denoted by the minus operator (−). The value of the expression

```
A - B
```

is the value of A minus the value of B.

The minus operator can also be used to change the sign of a number. If A is a number, −A is the number with the opposite sign.

The plus operator can also be used as a sign, as in +A. The value of +A is equal to A.

Multiplication is denoted by the asterisk (*). The expression

```
A * B
```

is read "A times B." Its value is the value of A times the value of B.

Division is denoted by the slash (/). The expression

```
A / B
```

is read "A divided by B." Its value is the value of A divided by the value of B. It is an error for B to be zero.

If A and B are both positive integers, the value of A/B is the integer that results when you divide A by B and throw away any remainder. For example, 9/5 has the value 1 because the remainder (4) is discarded.

If A and B are not both positive, the value of A/B may vary from one implementation of C to another. For this reason, you should try to avoid integer division that uses negative numbers.

The "remainder" or "modulo" operation is denoted by the percent character (%). The expression

```
A % B
```

is read "A mod B." Its value is the remainder obtained when you divide A by B. For example, 9%4 has the value 1. If A%B is zero, A is a multiple of B because when you divide A by B there is no remainder.

A%B is always equal to

```
A - ((A/B)*B)
```

Since the remainder operation is defined in terms of the division A/B, B cannot be zero. In addition, different implementations will return different values for A%B when one operand is negative and the other is positive.

Box 2.2: Integer Division and Remainder

With **C2C**, integer division always "truncates towards zero." For example, the **ANSI** standard allows the result of 9/-5 to be either -1 or -2. Our version of C always chooses the alternative that is closer to zero; in this case, the result will be -1. This means that the remainder operation always returns a non-negative value. For example, the value of 9%-5 is 4.

C performs multiplication, division, and remainder operations before addition and subtraction. The result of

```
3 + 2 * 2
```

is 7. Parentheses may be used to change the order of evaluation. In

```
(3 + 2) * 2
```

the addition is performed first, so the result is 10.

2.3.5. Exercises

1. What does the following function do?

```
int ex1(int a,int b)
{
        return a-b ;
}
```

2. What does the following function do?

```
int ex2(int i)
{
        return 2+3*i ;
}
```

3. What does the following function do?

```
int ex3(int a,int b)
{
        return (a/b)*b ;
}
```

4. Write a function named `neg` that takes one integer argument and returns the value with the opposite sign of the argument.

5. Write a function named `square` that returns the square of an integer argument (that is, the number times itself).

6. Write a function named `cube` that returns the cube of an integer argument (that is, the number times itself times itself).

2.4. Calling a Function

To use a function, you must "call" it. The simplest way to call a function is to give the function's name, followed by a list of argument values enclosed in parentheses. Arguments are given in the same left-to-right order as the corresponding parameters. For example,

```
plus(2,3)
```

calls our `plus` function. The argument associated with the parameter a is 2; the argument associated with the parameter b is 3. The `plus` function will add the two argument values to get 5. Therefore, the number 5 is the *result* of the `plus` function.

Now suppose we see `plus` used in an expression, as in

        7 + plus(2,3)

To evaluate this expression, C must first find a value for `plus(2,3)`. As we have already discussed, the result is 5. C can then go back and use this result in the expression that contained the reference to `plus`. This means that the value of

        7 + plus(2,3)

is 12 (7+5).

2.4.1. Decimal Integer Constants

The arguments we gave in the above function call are **decimal integer constants**. "Decimal" means that they are written base 10, using the digits `'0'` to `'9'`. For negative numbers, put a minus sign in front of a decimal integer constant. (You can also put a plus sign in front of such a constant. The result has the same value as the original constant.)

When you write an integer constant, you may not put commas in the middle. For example, `10,000` is not a valid integer constant; you must write `10000`.

The "decimal" form is only one way of writing integer values. Other forms will be discussed in Section 3.4.

2.4.2. Expressions as Function Arguments

The arguments in a function call do not have to be single values. They can be expressions, as in

        plus(15%9,4)

To perform this function call, C first obtains the remainder when 15 is divided by 9, that is, the number 6. It then calls `plus` with the arguments 6 and 4. The result of this call is therefore 10. As another example,

        plus(plus(2,3),4)

contains two calls to `plus`. The first to be executed is the call inside the parentheses. This adds 2 and 3 and returns 5. The result value 5 is then used in a second call to `plus`. The steps in the evaluation process are therefore:

$$plus(plus(2,3),4)$$
$$\Downarrow$$
$$plus(5,4)$$
$$\Downarrow$$
$$9$$

2.5. *The main Function* _____

Every working C program[1] has a function named `main`. This is always the first function to be executed. Other functions in the program are only executed if they are called by `main` (or if they are called by a function called by `main`, and so on).

Program execution ends when `main` finishes execution: `main` can end because it executes a **return** statement or because the last statement in `main` has been executed. (There are also ways to end a program prematurely, before `main` finishes. One of these is discussed in Section 8.5.1.)

The definition of `main` is written in the same way as any other function definition: a prototype followed by a body enclosed in brace brackets. A typical prototype for `main` is

```
int main(void)
```

The **int** at the beginning says that `main` returns an integer. Our `main` function does not need any argument values, so we put the keyword **void** in place of the parameter list.

☞ If a function does not take any arguments, put **void** in place of the parameter list.

We are now ready to show the complete definition of `main` for our first program. After the definition, we will work backwards through the definition to explain what each part means.

```
int main(void)
{
    printf("The sum of 2 and 3 is %d",plus(2,3));
    return EXIT_SUCCESS ;
}
```

2.5.1. EXIT_SUCCESS

First, let's look at the **return** statement. The expression that follows the keyword **return** is `EXIT_SUCCESS`. This is a special expression that the `main` function of a program can return to indicate that the program successfully completed its job. `EXIT_SUCCESS` stands for an integer, which is why the prototype for `main` says that `main` returns an **int**.

`EXIT_SUCCESS` is a "standard" symbol. The implementation of C that you are using contains its own definition for `EXIT_SUCCESS`. In a few sections, we will discuss where that definition comes from.

Almost every program we show in this book will have `main` returning the `EXIT_SUCCESS` value. There is a corresponding value called `EXIT_FAILURE`. The `main` function can return this value if it decides that something has gone wrong.

_____

1. That is, when using a hosted implementation. A free-standing implementation can set up programs differently.

2.5.2. The printf Function

The first statement of our sample `main` is

```
printf("The sum of 2 and 3 is %d",plus(2,3));
```

We recognize the `plus(2,3)`. It is a name followed by a list of values enclosed by parentheses, so it is a function call. But what does the rest of the statement mean?

If you look at the format of the statement, it is the name `printf` followed by a list of things in parentheses. This means that it has to be another function call. The name of the function is `printf`. The two arguments being passed to the function are

```
"The sum of 2 and 3 is %d"
plus(2,3)
```

The `printf` function is a **library function**. Like `EXIT_SUCCESS`, it is a standard symbol that is (in a loose sense) "built into" the implementation of C. It works like any other function, but it has been written for you by the people who created the version of C on your computer.

☞ Every implementation of C has a large collection of library functions. Library functions perform operations that are frequently used in programs.

Some of these operations can *only* be performed using library functions; for example, the only way to perform input or output in C is with library functions. Other library functions are just supplied to make things easier for the programmer; for example, it is possible to write your own code to calculate the square root of a number, but it's much easier to call the library function that does this. (The name of the square root function is `sqrt`.)

The function `printf` prints out values according to a **format string**. This format string is given as the first argument to `printf`. In

```
printf("The sum of 2 and 3 is %d",plus(2,3));
```

the format string is `"The sum of 2 and 3 is %d"`. We'll discuss what this means in a moment.

Any values that you want `printf` to print out are listed after the format string. In our example, there is only one value: `plus(2,3)`. To obtain this value, C calls the `plus` function we defined in Section 2.3.2. The result of this call to `plus` is 5, so `printf` is being asked to print out the value 5.

Our `printf` format string is written as a number of characters enclosed in double quotes (").

☞ Strings are always enclosed in double quotes.

The format string is made up of normal characters and **placeholders**. When `printf` prints output, it prints all the normal characters as they are given and replaces the placeholders with the argument values that are listed after the format string.

Placeholders in format strings always begin with the '%' character. The '%' is followed by one or more characters indicating the sort of value that is associated with the placeholder and how this value should be printed. In our example, we have the placeholder %d. This indicates that the value to be printed out is an integer and that it should be printed in "decimal" (base 10) format. (Other formats are possible, and we will discuss some of them in Section 3.)

Putting all this together, we see that

```
printf("The sum of 2 and 3 is %d",plus(2,3));
```

prints the message

```
The sum of 2 and 3 is 5
```

The normal characters are printed out, and the placeholder is replaced with the argument value plus(2,3), or 5.

The format string for printf can have more than one placeholder. For example,

```
printf("The sum of %d and %d is %d",4,5,plus(4,5));
```

has three placeholders in the format string. The first is replaced by the first argument after the format string, the second by the second argument, and so on. As a result, the function call prints out

```
The sum of 4 and 5 is 9
```

You can call printf with only a format string, as in

```
printf("Hello there!");
```

This just prints out the characters in the string. The format string cannot contain placeholders in this case, because we haven't specified any values to fill in the placeholders.

Whenever you call printf, you should make sure that the number of placeholders in the format string equals the number of argument values following the string. There are ways to use printf in which the two numbers will be different, but we will not discuss those in the Learner's Guide. (See the full description of printf in the Standard Library.)

2.5.3. Exercises

1. What does the following printf function call print out?

```
printf("The sum of 2 and %d is %d",3,2+3);
```

2. What does the following print out?

```
printf("%d * %d = %d",plus(2,3),2,plus(6,4));
```

3. What does the following function do?

```
int plus_and_print(int a,int b)
{
    printf("%d + %d = %d",a,b,a+b);
    return a+b ;
}
```

4. Write a function `times_and_print` that works like `plus_and_print` but multiplies its arguments instead of adding them.

2.6. A Complete Program

We are now ready to present a complete program based on the `main` function that we showed in Section 2.5. This program will contain several features that we have not yet explained, but we will discuss them shortly.

```
/*
 * This program performs a trivial calculation.
 */

#include <stdio.h>
#include <stdlib.h>

extern int plus(int a,int b);

int main(void)
{
    printf("The sum of 2 and 3 is %d",plus(2,3));
    return EXIT_SUCCESS ;
}

/*
 * "plus" returns the sum of its arguments.
 */

int plus(int a,int b)
{
    return a+b ;
}
```

The major parts of this program are the definition of `main` (which is always necessary) and the definition of `plus` (which is necessary because it is called by `main`). It is traditional to have `main` appear before other functions in the program, but it is not necessary. It would be perfectly valid to put `plus` before `main`.

In addition to the function definitions, we have some comments and the three lines:

```
#include <stdio.h>
#include <stdlib.h>
extern int plus(int a,int b);
```

The comments were included for good style. A program this simple can be understood without comments, but we may as well begin developing good habits. The other lines are explained in the sections that follow.

2.6.1. Inclusion Directives

The lines

```
#include <stdio.h>
#include <stdlib.h>
```

are called **inclusion directives** or simply **#include**s: ′ **#** ′ is called the "number sign", so **#include** is often pronounced "number-include."

You need **#include** directives whenever your program uses standard symbols like EXIT_SUCCESS and the printf library function. The C translator doesn't immediately recognize these symbols the way it recognizes a keyword like **return**. The translator has to be told to look up the meanings of these names.

☞   **#include** directives tell the C translator where to look up the meanings of standard symbols.

The meanings are stored in **standard headers**. A standard header is a collection of descriptions of standard symbols like printf and EXIT_SUCCESS. The line

```
#include <stdio.h>
```

tells the C translator to read the standard header called <stdio.h>. This header contains descriptions of standard symbols related to input and output, including a description of printf.

The following

```
#include <stdlib.h>
```

tells the C translator to read the standard header called <stdlib.h>, which contains definitions of EXIT_SUCCESS and EXIT_FAILURE, as well as a variety of other symbols that will be discussed throughout the rest of this book. Appendix E summarizes the contents of most standard headers.

The **#include** directives for a standard header must appear outside all function definitions and before the first use of any of the standard symbols that the header describes. This means that the best place for such **#include** directives is usually at the beginning of your source code, immediately after any comments that describe what the source code does.

A standard header tells the C translator what standard symbols mean; without the header, the C translator won't know what you're talking about.

☞ Whenever you use a standard symbol, you should make sure that the source code contains an **#include** directive for the appropriate standard header.

2.6.2. External Prototype Declarations

After the **#include** directives, our program example contained the line:

```
extern int plus(int a,int b);
```

This is called an **external function prototype declaration**. It describes the result and the arguments of the plus function before plus is called by main. This tells C the *form* that will be used when plus is called: an integer result and two integer arguments. The word **extern** at the beginning indicates that this is not the actual definition of the plus function; this is just a description or **declaration** of the function.

If our program did not have this declaration, C would begin reading through the program and would find the reference to plus inside main. This would be the first time the name plus was encountered and the computer would have to try to guess what the name stood for.

The external prototype declaration avoids this guessing game. Before plus is used, the prototype tells C all the important information about the function (the type of the arguments and the type of the result). When plus is finally used in main, the computer knows exactly how the function call behaves.

For good style, every program should have an external prototype declaration for each function that is called. This declaration should appear *before* the function is called. The easiest way to do this is to put external prototype declarations for all called functions at the beginning of your program. An external prototype declaration always ends in a semicolon (;).

Notice that we didn't put in an external prototype declaration for main. We don't need one because the program itself doesn't call main.

Notice also that we didn't put in an external prototype declaration for printf. The standard header <stdio.h> supplies a complete description of printf, including an external prototype, so you shouldn't write the prototype yourself.

2.6.3. Running the Program

Now that you have seen a complete program, you should try running it to see how it works. Box 2.3 tells how to do this with **C2C**. Because implementations work in such a variety of ways, we cannot give exact details of how to prepare your source code, translate it, and execute it using a different version of C. The best way to learn how to use your version of C is to ask a more experienced programmer, or to read the manuals that come with your implementation.

Box 2.3: Simple Programs and C2C

This box describes how to translate and execute a simple program with **C2C**. For our purposes, a simple program is one whose source code is contained in a single file.

Before you can run your first program with **C2C**, you must install **C2C** on your computer. The installation process is described in Appendix G.

After this, you must create a text file containing the source code of your program. To do this, you must use a program called a **text editor**. The most common text editor for IBM PCs and compatibles is called EDLIN, but there are many other text editors available. Using a text editor is an art in itself, and beyond the scope of this book. However, most text editors are easy to use for simple tasks like entering the source code of a program. It is a common convention to save C source code in files whose names end in .c, as in myfile.c.

Once you have your source code in a file, enter the command

    c2c *srcfile.c*

(where *srcfile.c* is the name of the file that contains your source code). This compiles (translates) your program and stores the result in a file named a.exe. You can then execute the program just by typing the command

    a

(without the .exe ending), provided that your search rules are set up appropriately. See the description of **PATH** in your MS-DOS documentation for more on search rules.

As an alternative, you can use the command

    c2c *srcfile.c* output=*exefile.exe*

This compiles the source code and stores the translated result in the file you specify in place of *exefile.exe*. As shown, this file name should end in .exe. To execute this file, type in a command line that just consists of the name of the file, without the .exe. For example, if you compile a program with

    c2c prog.c output=prog.exe

you can execute the program with

    prog

Appendix G discusses further aspects of using the **C2C** compiler, including descriptions of command line options that **C2C** supports. At this point, students may want to restrict their attention to Sections G.1 and G.2.

2.6.4. Exercises

1. Write a program that multiplies two times three and prints out the answer. Use the `times` function you wrote in a previous exercise.

2. Write a program that multiplies two times three and prints out the answer. Do *not* use `times`.

2.7. Review

The instructions of a C program are grouped together in *functions*. The most important characteristics of a function are:

(a)   its name;
(b)   its arguments (the values that it takes as input);
(c)   its result (the value that it produces as its "answer").

A function *prototype* provides all this information in a simple form:

> *type name(type name, type name, ...)*

The first *type* is the type of result returned by the function. After that comes the *name* of the function. The entries inside the parentheses describe the arguments of the function, telling the type of each argument and giving a *formal parameter name* that will be used to refer to the argument value. The only *type* we have discussed as yet is the **int** type, used for integers (numbers without fractional parts or decimal points).

A function *definition* is written as a function prototype followed by a function *body*. The function body consists of one or more instructions enclosed in brace brackets. Every function we have discussed so far has used a **return** statement to calculate and return the function's result. The operations used in **return** statements have been:

```
-A   /* minus A          */
+A   /* plus A           */
A+B  /* A plus B         */
A-B  /* A minus B        */
A*B  /* A times B        */
A/B  /* A divided by B   */
A%B  /* A modulo B       */
```

Every program must have a function called `main`. When you run a program, it begins execution with the first instruction of `main`. To indicate success, `main` may contain a **return** statement that uses the standard symbol EXIT_SUCCESS.

A *library function* is a function that is provided as part of a C implementation. In order to use a library function or a standard symbol, you **#include** a *standard header* that contains a description of the function or symbol.

The `printf` library function is used to print out values. You tell it what kind of values to print out with a *format string*. A format string consists of normal characters and *placeholders*. The only placeholder we have discussed is `%d`, telling `printf` to print out an integer in decimal format.

Any program that uses `printf` should have

```
#include <stdio.h>
```

before `printf` is called. Any program that uses `EXIT_SUCCESS` should have

```
#include <stdlib.h>
```

before `EXIT_SUCCESS` is used.

Good style dictates that every program should include an *external function prototype declaration* for every function called by the program. This kind of declaration consists of **extern** followed by a normal function prototype. External prototype declarations should appear after any **#include** directives, but before other functions in your program. You do not have to specify external prototype declaration for a library function; the declaration is provided as part of the standard header that you **#include** when you want to use the function.

chapter 3   Simple Data

So far, our programs and functions have only dealt with the **int** (integer) type. C can deal with many other types of data, and in this chapter, we'll look at some of them. First, however, we'll discuss some principles of how C handles data.

3.1 What Is Data?

We use the term "data" for any type of information that can be manipulated by a computer. **Data objects** are pieces of information inside the computer. For example, an **int** value is a data object.

The simplest piece of data in a computer is called a **bit**. Conceptually, it is like a light switch: it has two settings, *on* and *off*. The *on* setting represents the number 1 and the *off* setting represents the number 0.

All other kinds of information are represented by groups of bits. For example, a single bit can represent the two numbers 0 and 1. With two bits, you can represent four numbers:

> 00 is zero
> 01 is one
> 10 is two
> 11 is three

In a similar way, three bits can represent eight numbers, four bits can represent sixteen numbers, and so on. This is called the **binary number system**. (To be more precise, the binary number system is a specific way of representing positive integers using only the digits 0 and 1.) In general, N bits can represent a range of 2^N values.

Inside the computer, bits are organized in groups called **bytes**. Different computers have bytes of different sizes. In computers that run **ANSI** standard C, a byte must have at least eight bits. Many machines use larger bytes.

Bytes themselves are grouped into **words**. A word contains the number of bits used to represent an **int** value. In computers that run **ANSI** C, a word must contain at least sixteen bits, and again, many machines have much larger words. The range of integers that a computer can represent is dictated by the number of bits used to make up a word. A machine with many bits in a word can represent a wider range of integers than a machine that has relatively small words.

The information in a computer is therefore made up of bits, which go together to make up bytes, which go together to make up words. The words inside the computer are the computer's **memory**. Generally, we picture memory as one long string of bytes.

☞ In C, the byte is the basic unit for measuring the amount of memory needed to hold pieces of data.

Sets of bytes in the computer's memory are called **memory locations**. When we say that a piece of data is stored in a particular memory location, we mean that the computer is using a particular set of one or more bytes to hold that piece of information.

Memory locations are numbered. Some types of computers just number the words in memory, while others number every byte. The number attached to a memory location is called the **memory address** of that location.

If you could look at a memory location, all you would see would be a collection of bits: ones and zeros. We've indicated how these could be used to represent positive integers, but how do you represent other kinds of data?

(a)   Negative integers are represented by dividing all the possible bit patterns in two, and saying that half of them represent positive numbers and the other half negative numbers. For example, it is common for the set of negative numbers to be the set of all numbers with the leftmost bit on, while the positive numbers are the numbers with that bit off. Such a bit is usually called the **sign bit** because it tells whether a number is positive or negative.

(b)   To represent text characters, the computer just numbers all the characters it wants to represent. To represent a character in memory, the computer uses the character's number. For example, the computer could give ′a′ the number 1, ′b′ the number 2, and so on to 26. After this, we could begin uppercase letters, giving ′A′ the value 27, ′B′ the value 28, and so on up to 52.

Next we could give numbers to the digit characters: 53 to the digit ′0′, 54 to the digit ′1′, and so on. Notice that we're distinguishing between *numbers* and the digit characters we use to write numbers. Humans may think of numbers in terms of digit characters, but computers "think" of numbers in terms of bits. In later sections, we will see that it is important to know when we are discussing a number expressed as bits and a number expressed as one or more digit characters.

After the digit characters, we can number punctuation and other special characters. Since there is no obvious way of ordering these characters, the order we choose is arbitrary.

As it turns out, computers do not actually number characters in the simple way we've just described, but the principle is the same. Upper- and lowercase letters are numbered in ascending order, although they are not always consecutive. For example, one popular method of numbering characters numbers ′A′ through ′I′ consecutively, then leaves a gap before starting again at ′J′. However, you can always be sure that all the digits ′0′ through ′9′ are numbered consecutively, and that the distance from a lowercase letter to the corresponding uppercase letter is always the same (so that the distance from ′a′ to ′A′ is equal to the distance from ′b′ to ′B′ or from ′z′ to ′Z′).

(c)   In order to understand how computers represent numbers that have fractions, it's helpful to think of the way numbers are represented in "scientific notation." For example, 145×10^{-2} represents the number 1.45. The important numbers in this expression are the **exponent** (the power to which 10 is raised) and the **mantissa** (the 145 in our example). The two integers -2 and 145 determine the single number 1.45. The way that computers represent numbers with fractions is more complicated than our example, but conceptually similar: each number is represented as two groups of bits, one giving an exponent and one giving a mantissa. Numbers represented in this way are called **floating point numbers**.

The more bits there are in the mantissa part of a floating point number, the greater the **precision** of the number. Speaking loosely, a bigger mantissa means "more digits after the decimal point" in the fractional part of the number and therefore a more precise fraction. Many computers have several sizes of floating point numbers: ones with a lot of bits in the mantissa for very precise calculations, and ones with fewer bits in the mantissa, for normal calculations.

(d)   Machine language instructions for the computer can also be stored in memory. An instruction is usually broken up into several groups of bits. One group indicates what kind of instruction this is: an add instruction, a subtract instruction, and so on. Other groups give numbers representing the addresses of memory locations that should be used by the instruction. For example, an addition instruction might contain three groups of bits: one to indicate that this is an addition instruction, and two giving the memory locations of the numbers to be added.

(e)   Other types of data are expressed in terms of the data objects we have discussed: bits, integers, characters, and floating point numbers.

The above discussion shows that a memory location can contain many different kinds of data. Just "looking" at a memory location, you cannot tell what kind of data it contains: it's all just ones and zeros. The C language therefore associates a **type** with each memory location the program uses.

☞ Types tell the program how to interpret the contents of each memory location.

Every type has its own number of bits. The number of values that a type can represent is dictated by the number of bits. Every type has a **range** of values that it can represent.

We have already discussed **int**, the type C uses for the integer values we talked about in Section 2. In the rest of this chapter, we will talk about other simple data types.

3.2 Characters

The **char** data type is used for single characters. Every **char** value occupies a single byte in memory. Since a byte is at least eight bits long (in **ANSI** C), a **char** value is also at least eight bits long.

When a single character is used as data, it is enclosed in single quote marks (apostrophes), as in

```
'A'     'b'     '1'     ';'
```

These are called **character constants**. Be sure to note the difference between 1 and '1'. Without quotes, 1 is an integer number expressed in bits. With quotes, '1' is a character, like 'A' or 'b'. Also be sure to distinguish between single quotes and double quotes. In C, 'A' is a character constant; "A" is a *string literal*, which we will discuss in Section 7.4.1.

When you want to use printf to write out a character, the format string should contain a placeholder of the form %c. This works like the %d placeholder, except that it indicates a character instead of a decimal integer. For example,

```
printf("%c is the uppercase form of %c",'A','a');
```

prints out

```
A is the uppercase form of a
```

Function arguments and function results may have the **char** type. For example, consider the function

```
char next(char ch)
{
    return ch+1 ;
}
```

The function prototype says that next returns a **char** result. The single argument of next is also a **char** value, referred to by the formal parameter ch. (As always, we could have used any name for the formal parameter. We used ch because it is simple and suggests a "character.")

The value that next returns is the value of its argument plus 1. What does it mean to add 1 to a **char** value? In the last section, we noted that the computer numbers all the possible characters, then uses numbers to represent characters. When a C instruction adds 1 to a **char** value, C adds 1 to the number in the memory location that holds the **char** value. The result is the number associated with the *next* character. For example, the result of

```
next('a')
```

is the character 'b'. Similarly, the result of

```
next('B')
```

is the character 'C'.

In the same way, we could write another function

```
char previous(char ch)
{
    return ch-1 ;
}
```

The result of `previous` is the character that comes before its argument character.

```
previous('b')
```

is `'a'`. Notice that

```
previous( next('a') )
```

is the letter `'a'` itself.

Any arithmetic operation that can be performed on integers can be performed on characters. However, arithmetic with **char** data can give integer results. The value of

```
'b' - 'a'
```

is the **int** 1 because the two letters are one apart. This means that

```
'b' - 'a' + 'A'
```

is equivalent to

```
1 + 'A'
```

so the result of the expression is `'B'`. If we start with a lowercase `'b'`, subtract `'a'` and add `'A'`, we get an uppercase `'B'`. The same sort of thing happens if we start with any lowercase letter.

$$'c' - 'a' + 'A'$$
$$\Downarrow$$
$$2 + 'A'$$
$$\Downarrow$$
$$'C'$$

This suggests that we can define

```
char upper(char ch)
{
    return ch - 'a' + 'A' ;
}
```

as a function that can change any lowercase letter into its uppercase equivalent.

The same sort of trick can be used to convert a digit character into an actual integer. Remember that a digit character is not the same as an integer (expressed in bits). If you recall the sample way we numbered characters in Section 3.1, the digit character ' 0 ' (zero) was actually represented by the number 53. On your computer, the digit ' 0 ' is probably represented by some other nonzero number, but that's not relevant. The important point is this:

☞   The *character* ' 0 ' (in single quotes) is not the same as the *integer* 0 (no quotes).

So how do we turn the *character* ' 0 ' into the number 0? We have already seen that when we subtract one character from another, we get an integer. Also, if we subtract the digit ' 0 ' from itself, we know we'll have to get the integer zero (since anything minus itself is zero). What do we get if we subtract the digit ' 0 ' from the digit ' 1 '? We get the *integer* 1, because the two characters are one apart. Similarly, the digit character ' 2 ' minus the digit character ' 0 ' is the *integer* 2.

Putting all this together, we can write the following function:

```
int char_to_int(char ch)
{
       return ch - '0';
}
```

In this function, the parameter name ch stands for the digit character we want to change into an integer. When we subtract ' 0 ' from the digit character represented by ch, we get the integer that corresponds to this digit. The **return** statement returns this integer as the result of char_to_int. For example,

```
char_to_int('4')
```

is the **int** value 4.

3.2.1 Character Sets

We have said that computers represent characters with numbers. There are several different conventions dictating which number represents which character. Thus we cannot say that a letter like ' A ' is represented by the same number in every implementation of C.

In addition, different machines have different collections of characters that *can* be represented. For example, a non-English version of C might need to represent non-English letters and punctuation symbols.

☞   The collection of characters that can be represented on a computer, together with the numbers that represent those characters, is called the **character set** of the computer.

The **ANSI** standard was written to allow C programs to use any character set that follows certain rules (for example, the rule that lowercase letters can be distinguished from uppercase).

The most common character sets for implementations of C are known by the names ASCII, EBCDIC, and ISO 646. At a few points in the Learner's Guide, we say things about the **char** type that are true of these three character sets but may not be true of other character sets. This should cause no problems, since we do not expect to see any **ANSI** implementations of C that do not use one of these three sets or minor variants of them (for example, slightly changed for different countries or alphabets).

In the last section, some of you may have been wondering what you get when you add 1 to the letter ′Z′, or subtract 1 from the letter ′A′. The answer depends on the character set that your machine uses, since the character set dictates the numbers that are associated with each letter. For example, the character before ′A′ in the ASCII character set is the at-sign ′@′. The character before ′A′ in the EBCDIC character set is the opening brace ′{′. As you can see, the way that characters are arranged in character sets is largely arbitrary.

Box 3.1: The C2C Character Set

C2C uses the eight-bit ASCII character set. Each character is eight bits long. Appendix H lists the characters of the eight-bit ASCII character set and their numeric equivalents.

3.2.2 Special Characters and Escape Sequences

In addition to the normal letters, digits, and punctuation characters, character sets for **ANSI** C must have several special characters that are often used when printing out lines of text. For example, the backspace character moves backwards one character on the line. If you print a letter ′A′ followed by a backspace character followed by an underscore, the underscore will be printed in the same position as the ′A′. Printed on paper, this would underline the ′A′.

Now how could you write a printf instruction to do this underlining? You need some way to represent the backspace character inside the printf format string. This is done using an **escape sequence**.

☞ An escape sequence is a combination of two or more characters representing a single character. The first character is always the backslash (\). The characters that follow are usually letters or numbers.

For example, a backspace is represented by ′\b′. This represents a single character, even though it is written with two characters.

Below we list a number of escape sequences recognized by the **ANSI** standard and describe the special characters they represent.

\a   *alert*   Typically, causes a beep sound on the computer or computer terminal.

\b   *backspace*   Moves the cursor backwards one position.

\f	*formfeed*	If this character appears when writing output on paper, output will skip to the start of the next page. On many computers and computer terminals, the formfeed clears the display screen.
\n	*new-line*	When this is written as output, printing will jump to the start of a new line.
\r	*return*	When this is written as output, printing will go back to the start of the same line.
\t	*horizontal tab*	Moves the cursor to the next horizontal tab stop.
\v	*vertical tab*	Moves the cursor to the next vertical tab stop.
\'	*single quote*	Used when you want a character constant that contains a single quote character, as in ' \' ' . If you just wrote ' ' ' , C would see the first two quotes and think you were trying to use a character constant that didn't contain a character.
\0	*NUL*	We will discuss this when we begin to talk about strings (in 6.3.2).

The most frequently used escape sequence is probably ' \n' . When used in a printf call, it indicates where you want to start (or end) a line of output. The following:

```
printf("This prints\ntwo lines");
```

gives the output

```
This prints
two lines
```

The new-line character is useful when you are making several successive calls to printf. If you say

```
printf("How are you?");
printf("I am fine.");
```

the output will be

```
How are you?I am fine.
```

The output from the second printf call immediately follows the output from the first. If you want two separate lines, you must put in the new-line character explicitly, as in

```
printf("How are you?\n");
printf("I am fine.\n");
```

We added '\n' to the second printf so it would end in a new-line character too. Sometimes you want all the output from several printf calls to appear on the same line, but most of the time you will find that each printf format string should end in '\n'.

3.2.3 Exercises

1. Write a function named lower that takes an uppercase letter as an argument and returns the lowercase equivalent.

2. Write a program that prints the following two lines of text:

   ```
   Write a program that prints the
   following two lines of text.
   ```

3. Write a function with the prototype

   ```
   char under(char ch)
   ```

   The function takes a character as its argument and writes out that character, underlined. Once the function has written this out, it should return the same value as it was passed; in other words, the function's result will be equal to its argument.

4. What does this program print out?

   ```
   #include <stdio.h>
   #include <stdlib.h>
   extern char next(char ch);

   int main(void)
   {
       printf("%c\n%c\n%c\n",'a',next('a'),
              next(next('a')));
       return EXIT_SUCCESS;
   }

   char next(char ch)
   {
       return ch+1 ;
   }
   ```

3.3 Floating Point Numbers

Floating point constants have a decimal point, an exponent, or both, as in

```
1.5     1.     .5     2.7e4     3E-2
```

As shown above, an exponent is written as an 'e' or 'E' followed by a positive or negative number. When a floating point constant contains an exponent, the value of the constant is the value before the exponent multiplied by 10 to the power given by the exponent. For example, 2.7e4 is 2.7 times 10 to the fourth power, or 27000.0. Similarly, 3E-2 is 0.003.

There are three types of floating point numbers: **float**, **double**, and **long double**. Historically, these names refer to floating point numbers with different precisions: **float** has the lowest precision and **long double** has the highest. However, many machines do not have three separate degrees of precision, so **long double** may be the same precision as **double** and/or **double** may be the same as **float**.

☞ By default, floating point constants have the type **double**.

Thus 3.0 is **double**. If you want a **float** constant, add an 'f' on the end, as in 3.0f. If you want a **long double** constant, add an 'L' on the end, as in 3.0L. When an 'f' or 'L' is used in this way, it is called a **suffix**.

Arithmetic with floating point numbers uses the same operators as integer arithmetic. For example, you might have expressions like

```
4.5 + 6.987
1.2 - 5.8
7.888 * 6.0
12.5 / 2.5
```

The result of floating point arithmetic is a floating point number with the same type as the operand with the greatest precision, as shown below:

```
float + float          ⇒ float
float + double         ⇒ double
float + long double    ⇒ long double
double + double        ⇒ double
double + long double   ⇒ long double
```

The remainder operation (%) may not be used with floating point arguments. If you try, the C translator will print a message saying that the operation is not allowed. If you try to run a program that contains such an operation, you will probably be told that your program is in error and the operation will not give you a meaningful result.

3.3.1 Printing Floating Point Numbers

When printing out floating point values with printf, you may use any of the following placeholders in the format string:

%e   prints a **float** or **double** value using an exponent that has a lowercase 'e'. For example, printf("%e\n",100.0) prints 1.0e2.

%E   is the same as %e except that it uses an uppercase 'E'.

%f   prints a **float** or **double** value without resorting to an exponent, if possible. For
      example, `printf("%f\n",1e2)` prints `100.000000`.

%g   uses either %e or %f—whichever gives the nicer-looking representation of the
      number. (For a more technical explanation of %g, see the description of `printf` in
      Section IV.4.)

%G   uses either %E or %f.

In all cases, the argument value that will be filled into the placeholder should have the
float or **double** type. To print **long double** values, put an 'l' in front of the letter
used in ordinary placeholders. Thus %lf would print a **long double** value in a normal
format.

Often, you will want to have more control over the format of floating point numbers
that you print out. For example, if a floating point number represents a money value, you
will want to have precisely two digits after the decimal point. You can get this effect by
changing the form of the placeholder in the format string.

If you want `printf` to write a floating point value with precisely N digits after the
decimal point, use the %g placeholder but put .N before the 'g'. The .N is called a
precision. For example,

```
printf("%.2g\n",10.289);
```

prints

```
10.29
```

As requested, you get two digits after the decimal point. Notice that the value printed out
has been rounded appropriately.

```
printf("%.5g\n",10.289);
```

prints

```
10.28900
```

Extra zeros are added as padding to get five digits after the decimal point.

A precision dictates the number of characters that should follow the decimal point.
You can also specify the number of characters that should be used for the entire number.
You do this by putting an integer (called a **width**) after the '%'. For example,

```
printf("%8g\n",1.5);
```

has a placeholder that tells `printf` to print the given value using a total width of eight characters. If the number doesn't need that many characters, `printf` will pad it on the left with blanks. This can be combined with the `.N` construction, as in

```
printf("%8.2g\n",2000.);
printf("%8.2g\n",10000.);
```

which prints

```
 2000.00
10000.00
```

The `.2` in both placeholders indicates two digits after the decimal point. The 8 indicates a total width of eight characters (including the decimal point) when the number is printed out. The `printf` function writes a blank before writing the `2000.00` so that the number is printed with the full eight characters. As shown above, width values can be used to line up decimal points when you are printing columns of numbers.

Width values can appear in other types of placeholders.

```
printf("%5d\n",1);
printf("%5d\n",10000);
```

prints out

```
    1
10000
```

Both numbers are printed with a width of five characters. Leading blanks are used to pad numbers to the correct width.

If the width you specify is not large enough to display the proper value of the number, `printf` will use as many characters as necessary. For example,

```
printf("%2d\n",100);
```

prints

```
100
```

Even though you only gave a width of 2, `printf` needed three characters, so it used three characters.

As a final note, we should point out that you cannot use floating point placeholders to print out integer values, and vice versa. For example,

```
printf("%d\n",2.1);
printf("%f\n",2);
```

are both invalid. Argument values must have the type that is expected by the corresponding placeholder. (Note that the above calls to `printf` may still print out values, but the printed values will be incorrect.)

3.3.2 Exercises

1. What is the output of

   ```
   printf("%5d %8.2g\n",1,1.5);
   printf("%5d %8.2g\n",10,10.5);
   printf("%5d %8.2g\n",100,100.5);
   printf("%5d %8.2g\n",1000,1000.5);
   printf("%5d %8.2g\n",10000,10000.5);
   ```

2. What is the output of

   ```
   printf("%e = %E = %f\n",1.4,1.4,1.4);
   ```

3. What is the output of

   ```
   printf("%.5g\n",3.14159);
   printf("%.4g\n",3.14159);
   printf("%.3g\n",3.14159);
   printf("%.2g\n",3.14159);
   printf("%.1g\n",3.14159);
   ```

4. Assume that the local sales tax is 4 percent. Write a function named `tax` that takes a **double** argument representing the price of a taxable item. The result of the function is a **double** value giving the amount of tax on this price. The function should also print out lines of the following form:

   ```
   The price of the item is $NNNN.NN.
   The tax on the item is $NNNN.NN.
   ```

5. Write a function named `tax2` that is similar to the previous sales tax function. However, `tax2` takes two arguments: the first is a **double** value representing the percentage tax on an item and the second gives the price of the item. For example,

   ```
   tax2(.05,1.00)
   ```

   returns the tax on a dollar item if the local sales tax is 5 percent.

3.4 Additional Integer Types

So far, all the integers we have discussed have had the type **int** and have been written in decimal (%d) form. In this section, we will look at other ways to represent integers.

3.4.1 Long and Short Integers

Some machines use the same number of bits to hold every integer value. On other machines, integers can come in different "sizes." Short integer types take up less room in memory, but can only hold integer values that fall within a small numeric range. Longer types require more memory but can hold a much wider range of values.

In order to accommodate machines with different integer sizes, C recognizes the types **long int** and **short int** in addition to the ordinary **int**. These types are usually just written **long** and **short**. For example, you might write

```
long power(short base,short exponent)
```

as the prototype for a function named power that took two **short int** arguments and returned a **long int** result.

The size of **short**, **int**, and **long** values will vary from machine to machine. If a machine only has one size for integers, **short**, **int**, and **long** will all be the same length. If a machine only has two integer sizes, **int** will be the same as **short** or the same as **long**—the choice is up to the individual implementation.

A **short** is guaranteed to be at least 16 bits long, which means it can store numbers between −32767 and +32767. A **long** is guaranteed to be at least 32 bits long, which means it can store numbers between −2147483647 and +2147483647. A plain **int** is at least as long as a **short**, so it has at least the same range as **short**. On some machines, the range of values that can be taken by these types may be wider than we have just stated.

If you try to force an integer type to hold a number that is too big, you have a problem called an **overflow**. For example, suppose your computer can have **short** numbers up to +32767 and you try to store +40000 in a memory location with the **short** type. The computer can't do this: +40000 is too big for the number of bits in a **short**. Some implementations of C will print an error message when an overflow occurs. Others just start giving incorrect results. Either way, if you are using numbers that are this big, you will have to use **long** integers.

You can create a **long** integer constant by putting 'L' or 'l' as a suffix after an ordinary integer constant. For example, 1L is the **long** version of 1. There is no suffix to create a **short int** constant.

A constant without a suffix will still be **long** if it has to be. For example, if the largest **int** value on a particular machine is 32767, the constant 40000 will have the **long** type, even though it has no 'L' or 'l' suffix. If C didn't use the **long** type, your program would get an overflow error. Constants that do not need to be **long** will be **int**.

To print out a long integer value in decimal format, use the printf placeholder %ld. This is similar to %d, except that it is used for **long** values instead of ordinary **int**. You do not need special placeholders for **short** values.

3.4.2 Unsigned Integers

With the **int**, **long**, and **short** types, half the range of values will be positive and half will be negative (zero will be in one half or the other). C also has **unsigned** integer types. These do not try to represent negative values; instead, they give twice the range of positive numbers.

There are four unsigned types: **unsigned char**, **unsigned int**, **unsigned long int**, and **unsigned short int**. The last three are often abbreviated **unsigned**, **unsigned long**, and **unsigned short**. Each unsigned type has the same number of bits as the corresponding signed type.

The unsigned types can never be negative. This means that the lowest unsigned value is always 0. The **unsigned char** type goes up to at least 255. The **unsigned short** and **unsigned int** types go up to at least 65535. The **unsigned long** type goes up to at least 4294967295.

You may perform normal integer arithmetic operations with unsigned values. Unsigned arithmetic *never* overflows. If you add 1 to the highest value in an unsigned type, the addition just wraps around to zero again. Mathematically, we say that unsigned arithmetic is carried out *modulo* the highest value of the type, plus one.

You may turn decimal constants into unsigned constants by using U or u as a suffix. For example, 1U has the type **unsigned int**. You can use both an unsigned suffix and a long suffix; 1UL and 1LU are equivalent and have the type **unsigned long**. As with ordinary integers, an unsigned constant will be **unsigned long** if it is too big to fit into an **unsigned int**.

To print out a normal **unsigned int** value, use the placeholder %u in a printf format string. To print out an **unsigned long** value, use %lu.

The keyword **signed** can be used to distinguish normal integer types from unsigned types. For example, you can write **signed long** instead of just **long**; however, the two mean the same thing.

The two character types are **signed char** and **unsigned char**. The plain **char** type will be similar to one of these, but some implementations say that **char** is like **signed char** while others say **char** is like **unsigned char**. In Part II of this book, we will discuss instances where the difference between **signed char** and **unsigned char** is significant.

3.4.3 Octal and Hexadecimal Integers

The number system we use in everyday life is the decimal (base 10) system. Digits run from ' 0 ' to ' 9 '; a number like 325 represents 3 hundreds, 2 tens, and 5 ones.

In computer programs, it is sometimes more practical to use the octal (base 8) or hexadecimal (base 16) number systems. These two number systems are closely related to the bits that represent integers inside the computer, so they are a more "natural" way of printing some types of integer data.

(NOTE: Inside the computer, **int** values are always represented in binary form, as a sequence of bits. It is only when we are reading or writing numbers in human-readable form that we can choose to print numbers in decimal, octal, or hexadecimal formats.)

The octal system uses the digits from ′0′ to ′7′. These correspond to all the possible combinations of three bits:

```
octal 0 = bits 000
octal 1 = bits 001
octal 2 = bits 010
octal 3 = bits 011
octal 4 = bits 100
octal 5 = bits 101
octal 6 = bits 110
octal 7 = bits 111
```

The octal number 077 is therefore represented by the bits

```
000111111
```

In C programs, an integer that begins with a zero is treated as an octal integer; without the zero, it would be a decimal integer. For example, 10 is a decimal integer equal to ten; 010 is an octal integer equal to eight. Just as the digits in a decimal number indicate ones, tens, hundreds, and so on, the digits in an octal number indicate ones, eights, sixty-fours, and so on. This means that octal number 077 is 7 eights and 7 ones, equal to the decimal number 63.

The hexadecimal or "hex" system uses the digits from ′0′ to ′9′ plus the letters from ′A′ to ′F′. These correspond to all the possible combinations of four bits:

```
hex 0 = bits 0000 = decimal 0  = octal 000
hex 1 = bits 0001 = decimal 1  = octal 001
hex 2 = bits 0010 = decimal 2  = octal 002
hex 3 = bits 0011 = decimal 3  = octal 003
hex 4 = bits 0100 = decimal 4  = octal 004
hex 5 = bits 0101 = decimal 5  = octal 005
hex 6 = bits 0110 = decimal 6  = octal 006
hex 7 = bits 0111 = decimal 7  = octal 007
hex 8 = bits 1000 = decimal 8  = octal 010
hex 9 = bits 1001 = decimal 9  = octal 011
hex A = bits 1010 = decimal 10 = octal 012
hex B = bits 1011 = decimal 11 = octal 013
hex C = bits 1100 = decimal 12 = octal 014
hex D = bits 1101 = decimal 13 = octal 015
hex E = bits 1110 = decimal 14 = octal 016
hex F = bits 1111 = decimal 15 = octal 017
```

Thus the hexadecimal constant 3F is represented by the bits

```
00111111
```

which is almost the same as the octal constant 077 (the hex constant is missing one zero bit).

Hexadecimal constants begin with 0X or 0x. Letters in a hexadecimal constant can be upper- or lowercase, so 0Xa1 is the same as 0xA1. The columns in a hexadecimal constant represent ones, 16s, 256s, and so on. The following are different ways of writing the same value:

    0x0f   0X0F   0x0F   15   017

Octal and hexadecimal constants normally have the **unsigned int** type. If they don't fit into the appropriate range, they will be **long**, or **unsigned long**. Suffixes can also be used to get a specific type, as in 0x0FUL.

The printf function can write **int** values in octal and hexadecimal form.

%o   is a placeholder indicating that the associated argument is an **int** that should be written in octal form. This means that it will be written using octal digits. By default, printf does *not* put a leading zero on octal numbers—it just uses the octal digits.

%x   is a placeholder indicating that the associated argument is an **int** that should be written in hexadecimal form. Lowercase letters are used for hexadecimal digits greater than '9'.

%X   is the same as %x except that uppercase letters are used for hexadecimal digits greater than '9'.

Similarly, printf uses the placeholders %lo, %lx, and %LX for **long** values.

Box 3.2: What Length of Integer Should You Use?

Machines that have different lengths of integers are usually constructed so that one length is "preferred." This means that arithmetic and other operations using the preferred integer length are more efficient than operations using other integer lengths. C implementations are written so that the plain **int** type corresponds to the preferred length. This means that your programs should use **int** instead of **short** or **long** wherever this is feasible.

3.4.4 Exercises

In these exercises, assume the maximum **short** and **int** value is 32767, assume the maximum **unsigned short** and **unsigned int** value is 65535, assume the maximum **long** value is 2147483647, and assume the maximum **unsigned long** value is 4294967295.

1. What does the following print out?

```
printf("%lo = %lx = %ld\n",15L,15L,15L);
```

2. What does the following print out?

```
printf("%lo = %lx = %ld\n",0X0FL,0X0FL,0X0FL);
```

3. What does the following print out?

```
printf("%u %lu\n",32767U+1U,32767LU+1LU);
```

3.5 Arithmetic with Mixed Types

When the operands of an arithmetic operation have different types, C must convert them to the same type before it can evaluate the expression. This happens automatically. For example, if you add an integer to a floating point number, the integer is automatically converted to floating point; you do not have to use some special notation to perform the conversion. In this section, we describe the two basic automatic conversion schemes.

☞ In general, before an operation (addition, multiplication, and so on) can happen, both operands must have the same type. C converts one or both operands to the type that is "best" able to represent the full range of values for both of the original operand types.

It turns out to be quite tricky to come up with a formula that lets you decide the "best" type for some mixed-type arithmetic operations. The **ANSI** standard was written to deal with many different kinds of computers, each of which may have different sizes for characters, integers, and floating point numbers. In order to define how C should behave on so many different machines, the rules for conversion must be phrased in a rather complicated way. Don't be dismayed if you are confused the first time you read the sections that follow. If you don't understand everything right now, come back to this section after you have more experience with C; this material *is* complicated, and may be best learned a little at a time.

3.5.1 The Integral Promotions

Some types of values are always converted when they appear in expressions. The goal is to convert the shorter integer-like types into **int** or **unsigned int**, making sure to preserve the value of the original type (including the sign). These automatic conversions are called the **integral promotions**.

Values of the **signed char** and **short** types are automatically converted to **int**; **unsigned char** and **unsigned short** will also be converted to **int**, provided that the **int** type is capable of representing all the values of the original type. If there are some values that **int** cannot represent, **unsigned char** and/or **unsigned short** will be converted to **unsigned int** instead of the usual signed **int**.

To show how all this works, suppose that on a particular machine,

char has 8 bits
short has 16 bits
int has 32 bits

Then the integral promotions have the following effect:

```
char           ⇒ signed int
signed char    ⇒ signed int
unsigned char  ⇒ signed int
signed short   ⇒ signed int
unsigned short ⇒ signed int
```

since a 32-bit **signed int** can represent all the signed or unsigned 8-bit and 16-bit values.

On another machine, however, suppose

char has 8 bits
short has 16 bits
int has 16 bits

Then the integral promotions have the following effect:

```
char           ⇒ signed int
signed char    ⇒ signed int
unsigned char  ⇒ signed int
signed short   ⇒ signed int
unsigned short ⇒ unsigned int
```

Both **int** and **unsigned short** have 16 bits. The range of **unsigned short** values will be 0 to 65535, while the range of **int** values goes from negative values to 32767 (on most machines with 16-bit integers). On such a machine, the integral promotions will convert **unsigned short** values to **unsigned int** instead of just **int**, because there are some **unsigned short** values outside the range of the **int** type.

Partly because of the integral promotions, character constants like 'A' are always interpreted as **int** values. This may surprise you: at first glance, it seems as if they should have the **char** type. However, the integral promotions say that **char** values are converted whenever they are used in an expression; thus, if character constants had the **char** type, they would have to be converted any time they were used. Since they would have to be converted anyway, the **ANSI** standard simplifies the situation by saying that character constants start out with the **int** type.

3.5.2 The Usual Arithmetic Conversions

When two operands have different types, C also converts the operands to the type of the operand that can represent the largest range of values. This means that conversion of operands obeys the following list of rules. These rules are known as the **usual arithmetic conversions**.

(1)   If either operand is **long double**, the other is converted to **long double**.

(2)   Otherwise, if either operand is **double**, the other is converted to **double**.

(3)   Otherwise, if either operand is **float**, the other is converted to **float**.

(4)   Otherwise, the integral promotions take place on both operands if necessary. Then:

    (a)   If either operand is **unsigned long**, the other is converted to **unsigned long**.

    (b)   Otherwise, if one operand is **long** and the other is **unsigned**, the **unsigned** is converted to **long** if the **long** type can represent the whole range of values that an **unsigned** might have. If there are some **unsigned** values that cannot be represented as a **long**, both operands are converted to **unsigned long**.

    (c)   Otherwise, if either operand is **long**, the other is converted to **long**.

    (d)   Otherwise, if either operand is **unsigned int**, the other is converted to **unsigned int**.

    (e)   Otherwise, both operands will have type **int**.

The result of any arithmetic expression has the same type that the two operands had. For example, if an expression involves an **int** and a **double**, the **int** is converted to **double**, and the result is **double**.

Remember that any floating point constant has the **double** type. Decimal constants will normally be **int** unless they are too large or have a suffix. Octal and hexadecimal constants are normally **unsigned**.

Since an expression may be made up of several sub-expressions, the usual arithmetic conversions may be applied several times to the same expression. For example, consider

```
2.0 + 3 * 2L
```

The first operation performed is the multiplication. The 3 is **int** and the 2L is **long**, so the two operands are converted to **long** (by rule (c) above) and the result is **long**. The addition therefore adds a **double** to a **long**. The **long** is converted to **double** (by rule 2) and the result is **double**.

3.5.3 Explicit Conversions

In addition to the automatic conversions described above, programs can explicitly convert a value of one type to another type. Converting from one type to another is called a **cast operation**. To convert a value to a particular type, put the name of the desired type in parentheses immediately before the value. For example,

```
(int) 4.0
```

converts a **double** constant to **int**.

```
(long double) (5+3)
```

converts the **int** result of the addition to **long double**.

The mechanics of converting one type to another type can be complicated, since there are so many types and so many different ways that different machines can represent these types. For full details, see III.2. At the moment, we will only make note of the points that are most important to new programmers.

Floating Point Type to Integral Type
The floating point type is truncated towards zero, not rounded. This means that the fractional part of the floating type is just discarded. For example, 4.7 becomes 4 and –2.6 becomes –2.

Unsigned Integer to Signed Integer
If the range of the unsigned type fits in the range of the signed type, the result of the cast is the signed integer that is equal to the unsigned value. If the range of the unsigned type does not fit in the range of the signed type, the result of the conversion may be negative. This surprising result occurs because of the way integers are stored as collections of bits inside the computer.

Integer to Character
If a signed or unsigned integer is converted to **unsigned char**, the result is the integer value modulo the largest **unsigned char** value, plus one. In most implementations, this just means throwing away all but one byte of the integer (this byte is technically known as the *low order* byte). If a signed or unsigned integer is converted to **signed char**, the value of the integer should fit in the range of **signed char** values; if it does not, the result depends on the individual implementation. Since the **char** type is signed on some machines and unsigned on others, converting integer values to the plain **char** type will work like one of the above cases. If you want your programs to be system-independent, avoid using the **char** type whenever possible; use **unsigned char** except in instances where the sign is important, in which case use **signed char**.

3.5.4 Passing Arguments to Functions

When one function calls another, the types of the arguments passed by the caller must be the same as the types expected by the callee. For example, problems will result if the caller passes a floating point number, but the callee expects an **int**.

When you supply an external prototype declaration, you tell C the type of arguments that a function expects. Using the information in the prototype, C will automatically convert each argument value to the expected type. For example, consider

```
extern float f(float x);
        ...
f(3.0)
```

The prototype says that f takes a **float** argument. In the call to f the argument is the constant 3.0, and we have noted that all such constants have the **double** type. However, C automatically converts this **double** value to **float** when f is called: the external prototype tells what type the argument has to be and C converts the given value to that type. In the same way, we could say

```
f(3)
```

and C will convert the **int** value 3 to **float**.

Similarly, suppose we have

```
extern int g(int arg);
        ...
g(4.9)
```

The prototype says that the argument for g should be an integer, so the 4.9 is converted to the **int** 4 before being passed to g.

3.5.5 Exercises

1. Give the result of each of the following expressions, and tell what type it has. Assume that the plus function returns an **int**.

```
1 + 1.0
1U + 1.0
1L + 1UL
1L + 1U
1.0L + 1U
(float) (1L + 1U)
1 + 2 + 3.0
(int) (1 + 2 + 3.0)
1 + (float) 2
'c' + 1
1.5f +2.0
1 + 1.4f
1.4f + 1.5L
(double) 'c' - 'a'
(short) 1 + (short) 2
(unsigned) ( (2 + 3) * (short) 4 )
(double) plus(2,3)
plus( (int) 2.0, 3)
plus(2,3) + 5U
```

2. For each of the results in the previous question, give a `printf` placeholder that could be used to print out the value.

3. Consider the function

```
double guess(double x)
{
    return (x - (int) x) ;
}
```

What is `guess(1.4); guess(-1.4)`? Write a program that calls `guess` with these values and see if your predictions are correct.

4. Write a function `low_int` that takes a positive **double** argument and returns the first **int** value less than or equal to the argument. For example, `low_int(4.2)` has the **int** value 4; `low_int(3.0)` is 3. Does your `low_int` function work for negative numbers too? (NOTE: Your function only has to work for **double** values within the range of values that **int** can represent.)

5. With the concepts we have discussed this far, can you write a function `high_int` that takes a positive **double** argument and returns the first **int** value greater than or equal to the argument? If so, write the function. If not, why not?

3.6 The Void Type

We have already seen that the word **void** is used in prototypes for functions that do not take any arguments (for example, `main` in the programs we have written so far). The word **void** is also used when a function does not return a value. For example,

```
void printint(int i)
{
    printf("%d\n",i);
    return;
}
```

does not return a value. It just prints out the value of its argument. Because it does not return a value, there is no expression specified on the **return** statement. The **return** statement could even be omitted, since the function will automatically return to its caller when it reaches the end of the function body.

An external prototype declaration of a **void** function is just like any other external prototype. For example,

```
extern void printint(int i);
```

would be a suitable external prototype for `printint`.

3.6.1 Exercises

1. Write a function named `newline` that takes no arguments and returns no value. All it does is print out a new-line (`'\n'`) character using `printf`.

3.7 Review

Each piece of information in a computer is represented as a *binary* value (a sequence of ones and zeros). Various "tricks" let the computer represent characters, fractions, machine instructions, and other types of data.

In C, characters have the **char** type. A *character constant* is written as a character enclosed in single quotes. Character constants actually have the **int** type and can be used in arithmetic expressions. When a character is used in an arithmetic expression, its numeric value is based on the *character set* used by the implementation of C.

Special characters in character constants can be represented by *escape sequences* which consist of a backslash (\) followed by one or more other characters. One of the most commonly used escape sequences is `'\n'`, standing for a *new-line* character.

Floating point numbers have a decimal point and/or an exponent. There are three floating point types: **float**, **double**, and **long double**. Floating point constants always have the **double** type.

Integer constants can be written in octal and hexadecimal formats, as well as the decimal format discussed in Section 2.4.1. Integer data can be **long**, **short**, or **int**, and can be **signed** or **unsigned**. Unsigned values can never be negative.

The `printf` function has placeholders corresponding to all the data types we have discussed. They are:

```
%c        — character format, int value
%d        — decimal format, int value
%e,%E     — scientific notation, double value
%f        — normal representation, double value
%g,%G     — "best" representation, double value
%i        — decimal format, int value
%o        — octal format, int value
%u        — decimal format, unsigned int value
%x,%X     — hexadecimal format, int value
%ld       — decimal format, long int value
%Le,%LE   — scientific notation, long double
%Lf       — normal representation, long double
%Lg,%LG   — "best" representation, long double
%li       — decimal format, long int value
%lo       — octal format, long int value
%lu       — decimal format, unsigned long
%lx,%LX   — hexadecimal format, long int value
```

When any of the shorter integer-like types are used in an expression, they are converted to **int** or **unsigned int** through the *integral promotions*. When an expression contains values of different types, the values are automatically converted to a common type according to rules called the *usual arithmetic conversions*.

Values may also be converted explicitly using the *cast* operation, but this is seldom necessary in C. When a value is passed to a function, it is converted to the type indicated by the function's prototype or external prototype declaration.

The **void** type is used in a function prototype when the function takes no arguments or returns no value.

chapter 4   Statements

The programs that we have written so far have only used two types of statements: the **return** statement (which returns a value from a function) and the function call (for example, calls to printf). In this chapter, we will discuss most of the other statements recognized by C.

4.1 Assignments

Assignment is one of the most common actions in any programming language. An assignment operation stores a value in a particular memory location. There are several ways to indicate the location where you want the value stored, but the easiest is to use a **variable name**.

4.1.1 Declaring Variables

In C, **variables** are created by declarations. The declaration gives the variable's type and name. For example,

```
float x;
```

is a declaration for a variable named x. The declaration says that x will be used to hold **float** values. When C sees the declaration, it will allocate a piece of memory for x that is big enough to hold a **float** value.

One declaration can declare several variables. For example,

```
char a, b, c;
```

declares three **char** variables. The variable names are separated by commas. The end of the declaration is again indicated by a semicolon.

Any function body may begin with declarations. For example,

```
/*
 * This function figures out sales tax.
 * The first argument is an integer giving
 * percent for tax.  The second is the
 * price of an article.  Result is total
 * tax on item.
 */
```

```
double sales_tax(int tax_percent,double price)
{
    double taxrate, tax;
    taxrate = tax_percent / 100.00;
    tax = price * taxrate;
    printf("The tax is %8.2f.\n",tax);
    return tax ;
}
```

shows a function in which variables named `taxrate` and `tax` are declared to hold **double** values.

4.1.2 The Assignment Action

As seen above, values are assigned to variables with statements of the form

name = *expression*;

The value of the expression is stored in the memory location associated with the variable. Later on, the value stored in the variable can be used in another expression or function by using the variable's name. For example, we used the value stored in `taxrate` in the assignment

```
tax = price * taxrate;
```

After this assignment, we used the value of `tax` in the call to `printf`.

To perform an assignment, the right side of the assignment is evaluated and the result is assigned to the name on the left side. With a statement like

```
i = i + 1;
```

the right side is evaluated by adding 1 plus the current value of `i`. The result of this addition is then stored in `i`. The assignment therefore increments the current value of `i` by 1.

Notice that C does not use the equals sign = in the same way that mathematics does. In mathematics, A=B describes a *relationship* between two values. In a C program, A=B tells the computer to perform an *action*.

If the variable on the left of an assignment is not the same type as the expression on the right, but both are arithmetic types (that is, character, integer, or floating point types), the assignment converts the result of the expression to the type of the variable. For example,

```
float x;
x = 3;
```

is valid. The integer 3 is converted to **float** before it is assigned to `x`. Similarly, you can say things like

```
int i;
char ch;
i = 'a';
ch = i;
```

This begins by assigning `'a'` to the **int** variable i. This will be the (effectively arbitrary) number that represents `'a'` internally. (Remember that character constants like `'a'` have the **int** type, so no conversion is necessary for this assignment.) In the second assignment, the value of i is converted to **char** before being assigned to ch. The variable ch ends up with the value `'a'`.

4.1.3 Passing Variables as Function Arguments

A variable may be given as an argument to a function. For example, you might say

```
int i, j, k;
i = 2;
j = 3;
k = plus(i,j);
```

As you might guess, the values of i and j are passed to the plus function; plus adds these to get 5, so k is assigned the value 5.

☞   When a variable is used as a function argument, the function receives a *copy* of the variable's value.

The function can do whatever it likes with its copy of the value; but because it is only a copy, the actions of the function have no effect on the variable given in the function call.

For example, suppose we have a function

```
double twice(double x)
{
    x = 2 * x;
    return x;
}
```

and we use it with

```
double y;
y = 3.0;
printf("%g    %g\n",y,twice(y));
```

The twice function changes the value of the parameter x, but this has no effect on the argument y; x just holds a copy of the value of y and y is unchanged by anything the function does to x. Thus the output of the above printf statement is

```
3.000000    6.000000
```

4.1.4 Compound Assignments

As some examples have already shown, programs often change the current contents of a variable by adding some value. For this reason, C provides a shorthand notation for this operation.

name += *expression*;

means that the current contents of *name* should be changed by adding the result of the *expression*. For example,

```
i += 2;
```

is equivalent to

```
i = i + 2;
```

This sort of operation is called a **compound assignment** because it combines assignment with another operation (in this case, addition).

There are several other compound assignment operators.

name −= *expression*;

subtracts the given value from the current contents of *name*. Similarly,

name *= *expression*;
name /= *expression*;
name %= *expression*;

combine assignment with multiplication, division, and the remainder operation.

4.1.5 Assignments as Expressions

In C, the assignment operation is treated as an expression. This means that the operation has a *result*, in the same way that addition or subtraction has a result. The result of an assignment is the value that was assigned. You can use this result in other expressions. For example, in

```
y = z = 0.0;
```

the assignments are evaluated from right to left; 0.0 is assigned to z. The result of this assignment is 0.0, and this result value is assigned to y. The above statement therefore assigns 0.0 to both y and z. For a more complicated example,

```
a = 1 + (b=2);
```

assigns 2 to b, then takes the result of the assignment (2), adds 1, and assigns the result to a. As you might guess, the above statement is written in poor style; it would be much easier to understand if we wrote it as the two statements

```
b = 2;
a = 1 + b;
```

4.1.6 Exercises

1. What does the following print out?

```
#include <stdio.h>
#include <stdlib.h>
int main(void)
{
    char ch;
    ch = 'x';
    printf("%c\n",ch);
    ch = ch - 'a' + 'A';
    printf("%c\n",ch);
    return EXIT_SUCCESS;
}
```

2. What does the following print out?

```
#include <stdio.h>
#include <stdlib.h>
extern int incr(int i);
int main(void)
{
    int j;
    j = incr(1);
    printf("%d\n",j);
    j = incr(j);
    printf("%d\n",j);
    j += incr(j);
    printf("%d\n",j);
    printf("%d %d\n",incr(j),j);
    return EXIT_SUCCESS;
}
int incr(int i)
{
    return i+1 ;
}
```

4.2 While Loops

A **looping statement** can execute one or more other statements several times. C has three kinds of looping statements: **while** loops, **do-while** loops, and **for** loops.

A **while** loop repeats one or more statements as long as a specified condition is true. The following program shows a typical use of the **while** loop:

```
/*
 * This program calculates compound interest
 * on $1000 over years 1987 - 1997, at 8%.
 */
#include <stdio.h>
#include <stdlib.h>
int main(void)
{
    int Year;
    double Amount;
    Amount = 1000.00;
    Year = 1987;
    while (Year < 1997) {
        printf("%4d: %9.2f\n",Year,Amount);
        Amount *= 1.08;
        Year += 1;
    }
    printf("%4d: %9.2f\n",Year,Amount);
    return EXIT_SUCCESS;
}
```

This will print out the following:

```
1987:    1000.00
1988:    1080.00
1989:    1166.40
1990:    1259.71
1991:    1360.49
1992:    1469.33
1993:    1586.87
1994:    1713.82
1995:    1850.93
1996:    1999.00
1997:    2158.92
```

Looking at the **while** loop more closely, you see that it begins with

```
while (Year < 1997)
```

A **while** loop always begins with the keyword **while** followed by an expression in parentheses. This expression is called the **condition** of the **while** loop. After the condition comes the **body** of the **while** loop. This is usually a number of statements enclosed in brace brackets (like the body of a function). If the body only has one statement, the brace brackets may be omitted.

When C executes a **while** loop, it begins by evaluating the condition. If the condition is true, C will execute the statements in the body of the loop. When it has finished the body, it goes back up to the top again, tests the condition, and so on. The body will be executed over and over until the condition becomes false.

4.2.1 The Condition of a While Loop

In our sample program, the condition was

```
(Year < 1997)
```

This is true as long as the value of Year is less than 1997. The commonly used condition expressions are summarized below:

Table 4.1
Common Condition Expressions

A<B   true when A is less than B
A>B   true when A is greater than B
A<=B   true when A is less than or equal to B
A>=B   true when A is greater than or equal to B
A==B   true when A is equal to B
A!=B   true when A is not equal to B

The operators >, <, and so on are known as **relational operators** because they test whether a given relation is true.

☞ The result of a relational operator is an **int** value: 1 if the relation is true and 0 if the relation is false.

When the condition of the **while** loop is tested, C actually determines whether or not the condition is zero. If the condition is nonzero, the body of the loop is executed. If the condition is zero, execution will go on to the statement that follows the **while** loop. This means that you could write

```
i = 5;
while (i) {
    printf("%d\n",i);
    i -= 1;
}
```

to print out the integers from 5 down to 1. When i reaches 0, the value of the condition is zero, so the body of the loop will not be executed again. Thus

```
while (i)
```

is equivalent to

```
while (i != 0)
```

Any integral expression can be used for the condition of a **while** loop, and this leads to one of the most common C programming errors. You may write

```
while (A = B)
```

when you mean

```
while (A == B)
```

A single = sign means assignment. A=B will assign the value of B to A. The value of this assignment expression is the value assigned, namely B. This means that

```
while (A = B)
```

will keep on looping as long as B is nonzero. If you write something like

```
while (A = 1)
```

the value of the assignment will always be nonzero (1), so the loop will keep looping forever. What you probably mean is

```
while (A == 1)
```

which will keep looping until A does not have the value 1. Be on the lookout for this mistake—it catches even the most experienced programmers.

Notice that C tests the condition of a **while** loop *before* executing the body of the loop. If the condition is not true the first time it is tested, the body of the loop will not be executed at all. For example, in

```
i = 5;
while (i < 4) {
    printf("Hello there!\n");
}
```

the body of the **while** is not executed at all.

4.2.2 Exercises

1. What does the following program print out?

```
#include <stdio.h>
#include <stdlib.h>
int main(void)
{
    char ch;
    ch = 'a';
    while (ch <= 'z') {
        printf("%c",ch);
        ch += 1;
    }
    printf("\n");
    return EXIT_SUCCESS;
}
```

2. Consider the following function:

```
int f(int n)
{
    int result;
    result = 1;
    while (n > 0) {
        result *= n;
        n -= 1;
    }
    return result ;
}
```

What value is returned for f(4)? f(1)? f(0)? f(-1)? In general, what does f return?

3. What does the following program print?

```
#include <stdio.h>
#include <stdlib.h>
int main(void)
{
    int i, j, k;
    i = j = 1;
    printf("%d,%d,",i,j);
```

```
while (j < 10) {
    k = i + j;
    printf("%d,",k);
    i = j;
    j = k;
}
printf("%d\n",i+j);
return EXIT_SUCCESS;
}
```

4. Write a program that writes out the squares of all positive integers less than 20.

5. Write a function int sum that takes a single positive integer argument and returns the sum of all positive integers less than or equal to the argument.

6. Write a function with the prototype

```
double interest(double rate,double principal,int years)
```

This function returns the total amount of interest on a sum of money after a given number of years. The principal argument is the amount of money you start with. The rate argument is the interest rate (so a rate of 0.05 indicates 5 percent interest). The years argument indicates how many years the money is allowed to accumulate interest. (Assume the interest is compounded annually.)

7. Write a program that uses the interest function from the previous question. The program should figure out the total amount of interest on a principal of $1000 over a period of 20 years. The interest rate starts at 7 percent. Every five years, the interest rate goes up a percentage point. Your program should print out the final interest rate, the final amount of accrued interest, and the total amount of money at the end of the 20 years (interest plus principal).

4.3 Other Looping Statements

C has two other statements that loop through a block of code repeatedly.

4.3.1 The Do-While Statement

A **do-while** loop is similar to a **while** loop. It has the form

```
do {
    statements
} while (expression);
```

The body of the loop is executed, then the *expression* is tested to see if it is true (nonzero). Looping continues until the *expression* is found to be false (zero).

Notice that the condition of the **do-while** is tested *after* the body of the loop has been executed. This means that the body of the loop will always be executed at least once. (Remember that the body of a **while** loop might not be executed at all—**while** tests its condition *before* executing the body, and if the condition starts off false, the body is not executed).

As an example of **do-while**, here is the compound interest program from Section 4.2 written with a **do-while** loop instead of **while**:

```
/*
 * Again, we calculate compound interest
 * on $1000 over years 1987 - 1997, at 8%.
 */
#include <stdio.h>
#include <stdlib.h>
int main(void)
{
    int Year;
    double Amount;
    Amount = 1000.00;
    Year = 1987;
    do {
        printf("%4d: %9.2f\n",Year,Amount);
        Amount *= 1.08;
        Year += 1;
    } while (Year <= 1997);
    return EXIT_SUCCESS ;
}
```

Compare this to the previous version of the program and identify what the differences are.

4.3.2 The For Statement

Many of the loops that we have looked at so far have used a variable to count how many times the loop should be executed. For example, in our first example of a **while** loop, we had

```
Year = 1987;
while (Year < 1997) {
    printf("%4d: %9.2f\n",Year,Amount);
    Amount *= 1.08;
    Year += 1;
}
```

Year was initialized to a value before the loop and incremented each time through the loop. When the value of Year passed a certain point, the **while** stopped looping.

The **for** loop is a short form for this kind of loop. It has the form

```
for (init; condition; incr) {
    statements
}
```

where *init*, *condition*, and *incr* are all expressions. The **for** loop is evaluated as

```
init;
while (condition) {
    statements
    incr;
}
```

For example, the above **while** loop could be written

```
for (Year = 1987; Year < 1997; Year += 1) {
    printf("%4d: %9.2f\n",Year,Amount);
    Amount *= 1.08;
}
```

The **for** loop version is more compact than the **while** loop. It is also a little easier to read—all the information about starting and stopping the loop appears on one line. With **while**, you have to look at both the beginning and the end of the loop to get this information.

Any of the three expressions inside the parentheses of a **for** loop can be omitted. For example, here is a function that calculates a **double** argument to a positive integer power:

```
double power(double base,int exponent)
{
    double result;
    result = 1;
    for ( ; exponent > 0; exponent -= 1)
        result *= base;
    return result ;
}
```

We omitted the *init* expression because exponent gets its value from the argument that is passed. Even though there was no *init* expression, notice that we still had to put in a semicolon before the *condition* expression.

If you omit the *condition* expression, the **for** loop will be equivalent to

```
init;
while (1) {
    statements
    incr;
}
```

Since the condition of the **while** loop is 1, it is always nonzero and the **while** will just keep looping. This may be an infinite loop (a loop that never stops). On the other hand, the body of the loop could contain a statement that "breaks out" of this continual looping. We will discuss this statement in Section 5.3.1.

With both **for** and **do-while**, you do not need brace brackets around the body of the loop if the body only has a single statement. For example,

```
for (i=1; i<=10; i+=1)
    printf("%2d %3d\n",i,i*i);
```

prints the squares of the first ten positive integers. In some cases, the body of the loop can be omitted entirely. We will see examples of this in later chapters.

The body of a loop can contain another loop. For example,

```
int x, xmax, y;
for (y = 4; y >= -4; y -= 1) {
    xmax = 16 - (y*y);
    for (x = 0; x <= xmax; x += 1)
        printf("*");
    printf("\n");
}
```

prints out

```
*
* * * * * * *
* * * * * * * * * * *
* * * * * * * * * * * * * *
* * * * * * * * * * * * * * * *
* * * * * * * * * * * * * * *
* * * * * * * * * * * *
* * * * * * *
*
```

This technique can be used to draw simple graphs.

4.3.3 Exercises

1. Rewrite your `interest` function from the last set of exercises so that it uses a **for** loop instead of a **while**.

2. Using a **for** loop, write a program that prints out the squares of the first 20 positive integers.

3. What does the following program write out?

```
#include <stdio.h>
#include <stdlib.h>
extern char upper(char lc);

int main(void)
{
    char ch;
    for (ch='a'; ch<='e'; ch+=1)
        printf("%c",upper(ch));
    printf("\n");
    return EXIT_SUCCESS;
}
char upper(char lc)
{
    return lc-'a'+'A';
}
```

4. Write a function `starline` that accepts a positive integer and writes out that number of asterisk characters (*). The value returned by `starline` is the number of characters printed (not counting the new-line character on the end of the line).

5. What does the following program write out?

```
#include <stdio.h>
#include <stdlib.h>
int main(void)
{
    int i,j;
    for (i=1; i<=5; i+=1) {
        for (j=1; j<=i; j+=1) {
            printf("%d ",j);
        }
        printf("\n");
    }
    return EXIT_SUCCESS;
}
```

6. What does the following program write out?

```
#include <stdio.h>
#include <stdlib.h>
```

```
int main(void)
{
    int i,j;
    for (i = 1; i <= 10; i += 1) {
        for (j = 1; j <= 10; j += 1)
            printf("%4d",i*j);
        printf("\n");
    }
    return EXIT_SUCCESS;
}
```

7. What does the following program write out?

```
#include <stdio.h>
#include <stdlib.h>
int main(void)
{
    int i,j;
    printf(" "); /* a single blank */
    for (i=1; i<=6; i+=1)
        printf(" %2d",i);
    printf("\n");
    for (j=1; j<=6; j+=1) {
        printf("%1d",j);
        for (i=1; i<=6; i+=1)
            printf(" %2d",i+j);
        printf("\n");
    }
    return EXIT_SUCCESS;
}
```

4.4 The If Statement _____

An **if** statement executes one or more other statements if a given condition is true. The format of the statement is

> **if** (*condition*) {
>   *statements*
> }

For example, consider

```
int iabs(int i)
{
    if (i < 0) {
        return -i ;
    }
    return i;
}
```

If the value of i is less than zero, the function executes

```
return -i;
```

This states that the result of the function is the negative of the value of i. As soon as this statement is executed, C says iabs has finished execution. A **return** statement gives the final result of a function, so there is no point in continuing execution of the function. C returns to whatever called the function.

If the value of i is not less than zero, the **return** statement inside the body of the **if** is not executed. Therefore C jumps to the statement

```
return i;
```

In this case, the function will return the value of i. Thus we see that if i is less than zero, iabs returns -i. Otherwise, it returns i.

This is the first function we have come across that has more than one **return** statement. A function can contain any number of **return** statements. However, only one **return** statement will ever be executed in a particular function call, because a **return** statement tells C to return the function's final result immediately to the function's caller.

The **if** statement handles condition expressions in the same way **while** does. A condition expression is true if its value is nonzero; it is false if its value is zero. Thus

```
if (i) {
    printf("i is nonzero\n");
}
```

calls printf only if i is nonzero.

As with looping statements, the brace brackets around the body of the **if** may be omitted if it holds only one statement. Thus we could have written

```
if (i)
    printf("i is nonzero\n");
```

An **if** statement may be followed by an **else** clause. This has the form

```
else {
    statements
}
```

For example,

```
if (i >= 0) {
    printf("i is not negative\n");
}
else {
    printf("i is negative\n");
}
```

works in the obvious way. The brace brackets may again be omitted if there is only one statement in the body of the **else** clause, so we could have written

```
if (i >= 0)
    printf("i is not negative\n");
else
    printf("i is negative\n");
```

Often, the body of an **if** or **else** contains another **if** or **if-else**. In this case, we say that one **if-else** is **nested** inside the other. For example, the following determines which of three values is largest:

```
if (A > B)
    if (A > C)
        printf("A is largest\n");
    else
        printf("C is largest\n");
else
    if (B > C)
        printf("B is largest\n");
    else
        printf("C is largest\n");
```

Each **else** clause is associated with the most recent **if** that doesn't already have an **else**. The way that **if**s and **else**s match up is shown by the indentation above. This example shows, by the way, that indentation is quite useful in helping a reader make sense of a program—it shows which **if-else** pairs are nested inside the others.

An **if** statement may have a looping statement in its body, and vice versa. For example, here is an (inefficient) program that prints the prime numbers in the range 2 through 50:

```
#include <stdio.h>
#include <stdlib.h>
```

```
int main(void)
{
    int i, j, is_prime;
    for (i = 2; i <= 50; i += 1) {
        is_prime = 1;
        for (j = 2; j < i; j += 1)
            if ( (i%j) == 0 )
                is_prime = 0;
        if (is_prime == 1)
            printf("%d is prime\n",i);
    }
    return EXIT_SUCCESS;
}
```

For each number i in the range 2 through 50, the program checks to see if any smaller number j divides i evenly (j divides i evenly if i%j is zero: that is, if there is no remainder when i is divided by j). If there is some j that divides i evenly, the is_prime variable is set to 0 (0 means "false", so the number is not prime). If is_prime is still 1 after all values of j have been tried, i has no divisors, so it is prime.

4.4.1 Logical Operators

Logical operators are often used in the condition expressions of **if** statements, **while** loops, **for** loops, and so on. There are three logical operators: logical negation, the logical AND, and the logical OR.

The logical negation operator is the exclamation point (!). A logical negation operation is written !A, where A is an integral type (signed or unsigned **char**, **short**, **int** or **long**). The result of the operation is an **int** 0 if A is nonzero, and an **int** 1 if A is zero. In other words, !A is false if A is true; !A is true if A is false.

```
if (!A)
    printf("A is zero\n");
else
    printf("A is nonzero\n");
```

shows how this works in an **if** statement.

The logical AND operator is a pair of ampersands (&&) (sometimes pronounced "amper-amper" or "andy-andy"). A&&B has the value 1 if both A and B are nonzero; otherwise, A&&B has the value 0. In other words, A&&B is true if both A and B are true; otherwise A&&B is false. For example,

```
int testrange(double x)
{
    if ( (x >= 3.0) && (x <= 4.0) ) {
        printf("%g is in range\n",x);
        return 1;
    }
```

```
    else {
        printf("%g is not in range\n",x);
        return 0;
    }
}
```

defines a function that determines if its argument is between `3.0` and `4.0`. It returns a 1 (true) if the argument is in the range, and 0 (false) if it is not.

The left operand of `&&` is always evaluated first. If the left operand is zero, the right operand is *not* evaluated. Since the left operand is false, the whole logical AND expression is false, and the value of the right operand is not needed. This can be an important point to remember in some cases. For example, consider

```
if ( (a != 0) && (b/a == 1) ) ...
```

In this expression, the left operand is evaluated first. If it is true (and `a` is not equal to zero), the right operand is evaluated. Since C does not evaluate the right operand if the left is false, there is no division when `a` is zero.

Using the `&&` operator, we can rewrite the nested **if-else** statements we showed in the last section, as the following:

```
if ( (A > B) && (A > C) )
    printf("A is largest\n");
else if (B > C)
    printf("B is largest\n");
else
    printf("C is largest\n");
```

This is more compact and easier to understand than the previous way we coded this operation.

The logical OR operator is a pair of OR-bars (`||`) (sometimes pronounced "orry-orry"). `A||B` is 0 if both `A` and `B` are zero; otherwise, `A||B` is 1. In other words, `A||B` is false if both `A` and `B` are false; if either operand is true, `A||B` is true. We might rewrite `testrange` as

```
int testrange(double x)
{
    if ( (x < 3.0) || (x > 4.0) ) {
        printf("%g is not in range\n",x);
        return 0;
    }
    else {
        printf("%g is in range\n",x);
        return 1;
    }
}
```

As with `&&`, the left operand of `||` is evaluated first. If it is found to be true (nonzero), the whole `||` expression is known to be true, so the right operand is not evaluated. Again, this is important if the right operand has side effects.

Logical operators can be combined into longer sequences. For example,

```
if ( (ch != ' ') && (ch != '\t') && (ch != '\n') )
    printf("%c is not white space\n",ch);
```

prints out the message if `ch` is not a space, a tab, or a new-line. The sequence is evaluated from left to right. Similarly,

```
if ( (ch == ' ') || (ch == '\t') || (ch == '\n') )
    printf("Found some white space\n");
```

prints out the message if `ch` is a space, a tab, or a new-line. Logical AND operations are carried out before logical OR operations (unless the OR is inside parentheses). Thus

```
if ((ch>='a')&&(ch<='z') || (ch>='A')&&(ch<='Z'))
    /* etc. */
```

tests to see if `ch` falls in the range `'a'` to `'z'`, or in the range `'A'` to `'Z'`. (As we noted earlier, with some character sets, the letters are not numbered consecutively, which means there are more characters between `'A'` and `'Z'` than just the uppercase letters.)

Logical negations take place before `&&` and `||` operations. Thus

```
!A && B
```

is true if `!A` and `B` are both true, that is, if `B` is nonzero (true) and `A` is zero (false).

4.4.2 Exercises

1. Write a function with the prototype

    ```
    int digit(char ch)
    ```

    If `ch` is a digit character (in the range `'0'` through `'9'`), the function returns a 1; otherwise, it returns 0. (Note that EBCDIC, ASCII, and ISO 646 all represent the digits with consecutive values—there are no gaps.)

2. Write a function `min3` that takes three **double** arguments and returns the value of the smallest one.

3. What does the following function do?

```
int mult_test(int a,int b)
{
      return !(a%b) ;
}
```

4. Write a function `high_int` that takes a **double** argument (positive or negative) and returns the first **int** value that is greater than or equal to the argument.

5. Write a function `vowel` that takes a single character as an argument. The function returns an **int** 1 if the character is an upper- or lowercase vowel, and 0 if the character is not a vowel.

6. Write a program that lists the various ways in which pennies, nickels, dimes, and quarters can be put together to make change for one dollar. A sample line of output might be

```
2 quarters, 3 dimes, 3 nickels, 5 pennies
```

(HINT: use a **for** loop for quarters, a **for** loop for dimes, and so on. Making the output read properly is one of the challenges.)

4.5 Reading Input

In previous sections of this chapter, we used assignment statements to give values to variables. Variables can also be given values using the `scanf` function.

The `scanf` function reads *input* values in much the same way that `printf` writes output values. Here's a simple example:

```
int i;
   ...
scanf("%d",&i);
```

This looks a lot like a `printf` statement. The first argument is a string containing a placeholder. Like `printf`, `scanf` uses the `%d` placeholder to represent an integer in decimal format. After the string comes the name of the variable that is to be given the input value. For reasons that we can't explain until Section 7, you have to put an ampersand (`&`) in front of variable names that you give for `scanf`.

As an example of how `scanf` works, here's a program that reads in integers and writes them out again, until one of the input values is negative. The negative number is not written out. After a negative number has been read, the program prints how many numbers were read in (not counting the final negative number).

```
#include <stdio.h>
#include <stdlib.h>
int main(void)
{
    int in;   /* number that is read in */
    int count; /* how many numbers */
    count = 0;
    scanf("%d",&in);
    while (in >= 0) {
        printf("%d\n",in);
        count = count + 1;
        scanf("%d",&in);
    }
    printf("We read %d numbers.\n",count);
    return EXIT_SUCCESS;
}
```

As input for this program, we might use the two lines

```
7   29   34
0   6789   -1 10
```

When scanf is asked to read a number, it skips over white space in input until it finds a number. This means that scanf will skip over the spaces that separate numbers on the same line. When scanf is asked to read a number and there is nothing left on the current line, scanf will go to the next line.

Notice that our input has a 10 after the −1. The 10 is never read because the program stops when it finds the first negative number. The output from the program will therefore be:

```
7
29
34
0
6789
We read 5 numbers.
```

Any program that uses scanf has to **#include** <stdio.h>. Usually, your program will already **#include** <stdio.h> because the program uses printf. You only have to **#include** the header once.

4.5.1 Other Placeholders

In the last section, scanf used the %d to read a decimal integer value into an **int** variable. Similar placeholders are used for other types of variables, as follows:

```
%c    — reading into char variables
%f    — reading into float variables
%lf   — reading into double variables
%Lf   — reading into long double variables
%ld   — reading into long variables
%hd   — reading into short variables
%u    — reading into unsigned variables
%lu   — reading into unsigned long variables
%hu   — reading into unsigned short variables
```

As an example, the following program reads in **double** numbers and prints out the square of each number, until a negative number is read:

```
#include <stdio.h>
#include <stdlib.h>
int main(void)
{
    double x;
    scanf("%lf",&x);
    while (x >= 0.0) {
        printf("%f\n",x*x);
        scanf("%lf",&x);
    }
    return EXIT_SUCCESS;
}
```

4.5.2 The Result of scanf

The scanf function returns a value, even though our previous examples have not made use of this value. The result of scanf is the number of items that have been read successfully. For example, suppose you try the function call

```
scanf("%d",&i)
```

but the input is

```
abcdef
```

The %d tells scanf that you want to read an integer, but the input doesn't match what is expected: it's a string of letters instead of a number. In this case, scanf returns the number 0 because it can't read a value into i. When a number can be read successfully, the above call to scanf would return a 1.

As an example of how the result of scanf can be used, we have rewritten the program from the last section so that it checks to make sure every call to scanf reads a number successfully.

```
#include <stdio.h>
#include <stdlib.h>
int main(void)
{
    double x;
    do {
        if ( 1 == scanf("%lf",&x) ) {
            /* number read successfully */
            if (x >= 0.0)
                printf("%f\n",x*x);
        }
        else {
            /* number not read successfully */
            x = -1.0;
        }
    } while (x >= 0.0);
    return EXIT_SUCCESS;
}
```

The **if** statement

```
if ( 1 == scanf("%lf",&x) )
```

tests to see if scanf read a value for x. If scanf does not return 1, a value was not read properly and the **else** clause assigns −1.0 to x. Since this is less than 0.0, the **do-while** loop will stop looping if a value cannot be read successfully.

4.5.3 Entering Input

So far, we have said that scanf reads input, but we haven't said where it gets this input: scanf reads input from the **standard input stream**, just as printf writes output to the **standard output stream**. Different implementations may have different defaults for these standard streams. In most C implementations, an interactive terminal serves as both the standard input and output stream. Other implementations, however, are designed to run programs that are *not* attached to terminals, and they would associate the standard input and output streams with other devices.

In addition, many implementations have facilities that let you specify standard input and output streams when you ask to run a C program. This means that the same program might be able to copy from the terminal to a disk file, from a disk file to the terminal, or from one file to another, depending on how the standard I/O streams are assigned when the program is invoked.

To find out how to enter input for scanf on your particular system, you will have to read the documentation for the system. Box 4.1 describes the standard input stream for **C2C**.

Box 4.1: Standard Input and Output Streams for C2C

By default, the standard input stream for **C2C** contains information entered from the PC keyboard, and the standard output stream sends data to the display screen.

To indicate the end of input for the standard input stream, you can enter a CTRL-Z character. You do this by holding down the Control key and pressing the ′Z′ key.

When you invoke a C program that has been compiled with **C2C**, you may put

       <filename

on the command line. This indicates that you want the given file to be used as the standard input stream instead of the PC keyboard. In this way, you can put input data in a file, and won't have to type it in each time you run the program.

You may also put

       >filename

on the command line for a C program. This indicates that you want the given file to be used as the standard output stream instead of the display screen. Data that would normally be shown on the screen will be written into the specified file. This data will write over anything the file currently contains, so the previous contents will be lost. Sending output to a file is useful whenever a program produces more output than can be displayed on a single screen.

The constructs *<filename* and *>filename* are called **redirection** constructs because they redirect the source of the standard input stream or the destination of the standard output stream.

4.5.4 Exercises

1. Write a function with the prototype

   ```
   long getlong(void);
   ```

   The function should use `scanf` to read a **long** integer. If a **long** value is read successfully, the function returns the value; if a value cannot be read successfully, the function prints out a message describing the program and returns −1L.

2. Write a program that reads in integers until it finds a −1. The program should then print out the average of the integers that were read.

3. Modify the program written for the previous exercise so that it works with **double** values instead of integers.

4. Write a program that reads in integers until it finds a −1. The program should then print out the largest integer that was read and the smallest.

5. Write a program that reads in pairs of floating point numbers and prints out the largest of each pair. The program should stop when it does not succeed in reading a pair of numbers, or when it reads in a pair of −1 values.

6. CONCORDANCE QUESTION: Throughout the Learner's Guide, we will give a series of exercises designed to build a program that can create a concordance of input text. (A concordance is a list of some or all of the words used in the text, usually giving the location(s) where each word appears and sometimes the context of each appearance, that is, a few of the surrounding words.) As a first step towards a concordance, write a program that reads 20 characters from the standard input and writes out all those characters that are upper- or lowercase letters. (In other words, it does not write out blanks, digits, punctuation characters, and so on.)

7. CONCORDANCE QUESTION: Change the program from the previous question so that it reads in 10 words and writes them out, one word per line. Words may be separated by any number of non-alphabetic characters, including punctuation characters and white space. (HINT: Write a function `get_word` which skips over any non-alphabetic characters in the input, then prints out a line containing a complete word. For future programs, you may find it convenient if `get_word` returns the number of characters that were in the word that it read.)

4.6 Review

A *variable* is created by a declaration that states the variable's type and name. Several variables may be declared in the same declaration. A function's variables are declared at the beginning of the function's body, before any of the "active" statements of the function.

Variables are given values with *assignment* expressions. There are two types of assignment.

(a)   *simple assignments* assign a variable the result of an expression.
(b)   *compound assignments* give a variable a new value by operating on the variable's old value.

Once a variable has been given a value, it may be used in other expressions. A variable's value may be passed as the argument to a function by giving the variable's name as an argument when a function is called.

A *looping statement* can execute a number of other statements repeatedly.

```
while (expression) {
    statements
}
```

repeats the given *statements* as long as the *expression* is nonzero (true).

```
do {
    statements
} while (expression);
```

repeats the given *statements* until the *expression* becomes zero (false).

```
for (init; condition; incr) {
    statements
}
```

is equivalent to

```
init;
while (condition) {
    statements
    incr ;
}
```

(where *init*, *condition*, and *incr* are all expressions).

```
if (expression) {
    statements
}
```

executes the given *statements* if the given *expression* is nonzero.

```
if (expression) {
    first_statements
}
else {
    second_statements
}
```

executes the *first_statements* if the *expression* is nonzero, and otherwise executes the *second_statements*.

Looping statements often use expressions that contain the following operations:

```
A >  B      — greater than
A >= B      — greater than or equal to
A <  B      — less than
A <= B      — less than or equal to
A == B      — equal to
A != B      — not equal to
A && B      — logical AND
A || B      — logical OR
!A          — logical negation
```

The result of each of these expressions is 1 if the given relationship is true, and 0 if it is false.

The scanf function reads input from the standard input stream. It is similar to printf, in that its first argument is a format string containing placeholders. After this comes the name of a variable into which a value should be read; the name should be preceded by an ampersand (&), as in

```
char ch;
    . . .
scanf("%c",&ch);
```

The result of scanf is the number of values that were read successfully.

chapter 5   Common Operations

We have now discussed the basic data types, statements, and operations of C. This leaves us with two major topics to discuss:

(a)   more complex data types (for example, pointers and arrays);
(b)   the most useful of the library functions (so far, we have only talked about `printf` and `scanf`).

Before we begin these major areas of discussion, it will be useful to cover a variety of lesser topics. Most of these are easier ways to do things we have already discussed, but we will introduce some new features of the language as well.

5.1 Auto-Increment/Auto-Decrement

Many of the functions and programs we have discussed contained expressions like

```
i += 1
```

This operation is so common that C has a special operator to do the job.

```
++i
```

is an expression that adds 1 to the variable i. The result of the expression is the new value of i. The ++ is known as the **auto-increment** operator.
The **auto-decrement** operator is --.

```
--i
```

is an expression that subtracts 1 from the variable i. The result of the expression is the new value of i.
These two operators can be used anywhere in a program. For example, suppose i is an integer variable.

```
i = 0;
while (i < 10) {
    printf("%d\n",i);
    ++i;
}
```

prints the integers from 0 to 9. We could also write

```
for (i = 0; i < 10; ++i)
    printf("%d\n",i);
```

to get the same result. We could even write

```
for ( i = -1; i < 9; printf("%d\n",++i) )
    /* nothing */;
```

combining the printf call and incrementing the variable i. This **for** loop does not need a body; everything is included in the three expressions on the **for** line.

Note, however, that this last example is harder to understand than the previous **for** loop. To get the same sequence of numbers, we had to start i at −1 instead of 0 this time, because ++i increments i *before* using the new value of i as an argument for printf. We also had to change the condition to i<9 instead of i<10. This is confusing: in the **for** loop, i runs from −1 to 9, but the output runs from 0 to 10.

To avoid such confusion, C lets you use the auto-increment operator in a second way.

```
i++
```

is an expression whose value is the current value of i. However, after this value is obtained, i is incremented by one. For example,

```
i = 0;
printf("%d\n",i++);
```

prints out the value 0, because the result of i++ is the value i has to begin with. However, i is incremented after its current value is obtained, so i has the value 1 after the printf.

```
for (i = 0; i < 10; printf("%d\n",i++) )
    /* nothing */;
```

prints the integers from 0 to 9. After the loop is finished, i has the value 10.

Similarly,

```
i--
```

is an expression whose result is the value of i. After this result is obtained, i is decremented by 1.

```
for (i = 10; i > 0; printf("%d\n",i--));
```

prints the integers from 10 down to 1.

The **for** loops we have been discussing for the past few paragraphs are written in a poor style. Putting the printf inside the *incr* expression is confusing. It is much better to say

```
for (i = 10; i > 0; i--)
    printf("%d\n",i);
```

This is clearer and easier to understand. We only used the bad style examples to show what C can do, if you really want.

Because ++ and -- operators assign new values to their operands, they can only be applied to operands that could appear on the left side of an assignment statement. Thus i++ is valid if i is a variable, but 10++ is not valid. It is also invalid to apply ++ or -- to a floating point operand.

5.1.1 The Condition Operator

The condition operator has the form

```
A ? B : C
```

where A is an expression with an integral type. There are a wide range of types that B and C can have, but for now, we will only use the types we have discussed so far.

The value of a conditional operation depends on the value of A. If A is nonzero (true), the value of the expression is the value of B; if A is zero (false), the value of the expression is the value of C. For example, the value of

```
(x > y) ? x : y
```

is x if x is greater than y; the value is y if x is not greater than y. In other words, the value of the expression is the value of the greater of x and y.

As another example, the following function returns the absolute value of its argument:

```
int iabs(int i)
{
    return ( (i >= 0) ? i : -i ) ;
}
```

If i is greater than or equal to zero, the result of the expression is just i; if i is less than zero, the result is -i. This result is returned by the **return** statement.

5.1.2 Order of Operations

We have mentioned that multiplication and division take place before addition and subtraction. This is because all of the operators in C have a ranking or **precedence** that dictates the order in which operations are carried out. Higher-precedence operations are evaluated before lower-precedence ones. C assigns multiplication and division a higher-precedence than addition and subtraction, so multiplication and division are evaluated before addition and subtraction. Parentheses may be used to change the order in which operations are evaluated.

Different operations may have the same precedence. For example, addition and subtraction have the same precedence. The operators of C can be divided into **precedence classes**. Each class is made up of all the operators that have a particular precedence.

When an expression contains a number of operators that are all in the same precedence class, the operations are usually carried out from left to right, as they appear on the source code line. The exceptions are the assignment expressions, which are carried out right to left.

The table below summarizes the precedence classes of the operations we have discussed so far, from highest precedence to lowest. Operations with equivalent precedence are all given on the same line. The letter E is used to stand for an expression and F for a function name. Notice that the table includes operations like function calls and cast conversions as well as the more obvious kinds of operations.

```
F(E,E,...)     E--     E++
--E     ++E     +E     -E     !E
(type)E
E*E     E/E     E%E
E+E     E-E
E<E     E>E     E<=E     E>=E
E==E     E!=E
E&&E
E||E
E?E:E
E=E     E+=E     E-=E     E*=E     etc.
```

As we encounter new operators, we will indicate where they belong on this list. The endpapers of this book include a complete list of C's operators and their precedence classes.

Precedence order is important to keep in mind for some common sorts of expressions. For example, consider:

```
A = F() && C == D
```

This expression consists of an assignment, a logical AND, and a test for equivalence. In C programs, you often want to use similar expressions, with the sense

```
(A = F()) && (C == D)
```

If you leave out the parentheses, however, precedence order says that the expression is evaluated as

```
A = (F() && (C == D))
```

which has a completely different meaning. Therefore, you must make sure you put in parentheses when they are needed. To avoid difficulty, put in parentheses whenever there is an element of doubt—they don't hurt.

5.1.3 Operand Evaluation

We have noted that `&&` and `||` expressions always have their first operand evaluated first and that the second operand is not evaluated if it is not necessary. It is important to note that most other expressions need not be evaluated in the order given in the source code. For example, in evaluating the sum of two expressions, C is free to evaluate either expression first. You may think this is unimportant, but consider the code:

```
i = 4;
j = (i) + (i++);
```

If the first operand in the addition is evaluated first, `j` is assigned the value 8. However, if the second operand is evaluated first, `j` is assigned the value 9 because `i` has been incremented to 5 by the time the first operand is evaluated. To prevent this kind of ambiguity, you should break up tricky expressions like these into more than one statement.

In the same way, C feels free to evaluate the arguments of a function call in any order. For example, suppose we have

```
i = 3;
f(i,(i=2));
```

This is valid because an assignment expression has a value just like any other kind of expression and this value can be passed as an argument to a function. However, this function call could be evaluated as

```
f(3,2)
```

if the first argument is evaluated first and

```
f(2,2)
```

if the second argument (and therefore the assignment) is evaluated first.

☞ There is no way to dictate the order in which C will evaluate function arguments or operands in most expressions.

If the order makes a difference, as in the above examples, you must rewrite the program to remove the ambiguity.

5.1.4 Exercises

1. What does the following loop print out?

```
for (i = 10; i != 0; i--)
    printf("%d %d\n",i,i*i);
```

2. What does the following loop print out?

```
for (i = 10; i-- != 0; printf("%d\n",i) );
```

3. What does the following loop print out?

```
for (ch = 'a'; ch <= 'e' ; printf("%c\n",ch++) );
```

4. Using auto-increment operators, write a program to print out the first 20 prime numbers.

5. Using a condition expression, write a function that returns the minimum of two **long** arguments.

6. What does the following function return?

```
float guess(float x,float y)
{
      return (y != 0.0) ? (x / y) : x ;
}
```

7. Give the value of each of the following expressions. Assume that A=0, B=1, and C=2.

```
A < B < C
A == 0 && B != 3
A = 0 && B != 3
B + C * C
B+-C
!B||C
B && A || C
B && C || A
A < B || C < B
A * B < C
A ? B : C
B ? A : C
```

5.2 Single Character Input

The getchar library routine is a very simple function for reading input from the standard input stream. In the last chapter, we described how scanf can do this, so you may be wondering why we need another function that does the same thing. There are several reasons:

(a)   The getchar function is more basic. It is less versatile than scanf, but it is simpler and faster.

(b)   The getchar function is used extensively in many existing C programs.

(c)   The getchar function has a number of features that demonstrate important aspects of the C library.

The getchar function takes no arguments. Its result is an **int** value representing a character. We will explain why it is **int** instead of **char** after a few examples.

```
int ch;
ch = getchar();
printf("%c",ch);
```

uses getchar to read a character, then uses printf to write the character. We could abbreviate this to

```
int ch;
printf("%c", ch=getchar() );
```

To evaluate the call to printf, C first evaluates the arguments. To evaluate the second argument, C calls getchar to read a character, assigns this character to ch, then passes the result of the assignment (the assigned character) to printf.

```
while ( ( ch=getchar() ) != '\n')
    printf("%c\n",ch);
```

is a common sort of loop. To evaluate the condition of the loop, the program reads a character with getchar, assigns the character to ch, and compares the assigned value to the new-line character. If the input character is not a new-line, the loop executes the printf. The effect of the loop is therefore to keep reading characters and printing them out until a new-line character is found.

The value returned by getchar is either a character in the character set that the implementation uses, or else a special **int** value known as EOF.

☞   The getchar function returns EOF when there is no more input to be read.

This condition is usually called "end-of-file", although it doesn't just happen when you are reading files.

```
while ( ( ch=getchar() ) != EOF )
    printf("%c",ch);
```

keeps reading in characters and printing them out until EOF is reached. This could be the basis of a simple copying program.

When using getchar, you should always take into consideration that you might reach end-of-file at any time. Therefore, we would write

```
while ( ((ch=getchar()) != EOF) && (ch!='\n') )
    printf("%c",ch);
```

to stop looping either when getchar reads a new-line or when getchar reaches end-of-file.

EOF is the reason that getchar returns an **int** value instead of a **char**. If getchar indicated end-of-file with some **char** value, your program couldn't tell when getchar was returning this character to indicate end-of-file and when getchar returned the character because that was what was read. For this reason, EOF is defined as *negative* **int** that does not match any **unsigned char** value. This way, getchar can return all possible **char** values, plus EOF.

Programs that use getchar must **#include** <stdio.h> before getchar is used; <stdio.h> provides an external prototype declaration for getchar, and also defines the EOF symbol.

Box 5.1: An Important Subtlety

EOF is a negative **int** value. Consider what happens in code of the form:

```
unsigned char ch;
ch = getchar();
if (ch == EOF) {
    /* and so on */
```

You can assign EOF to the **unsigned char** variable ch, but the EOF value will be converted to a positive number (since unsigned variables only hold positive values). In the operation that compares ch to EOF, the value of ch will be converted to a positive integer (because ch is always positive). Therefore the value of ch will *never* be equal to the negative EOF, even if ch was originally assigned the EOF value. Assigning EOF to ch "lost" the sign.

The same problem may happen if you declare ch to be a plain **char**. On some systems, **char** is equivalent to **unsigned char**, and the sign gets lost in some assignments.

To avoid this kind of problem, declare ch to be **int**, as in

```
int ch;
ch = getchar();
if (ch == EOF) {
    /* and so on */
```

This ensures that there is no loss of information.

5.2.1 Exercises _____

1. Write an external prototype declaration for getchar. (Note that programs should not specify such a prototype; it is part of the information that is included when you **#include** <stdio.h>.)

2. What does the following function do?

```
int getdigit(void)
{
    int ch;
    ch = getchar();
    if ( (ch >= '0') && (ch <= '9') )
        return ch - '0' ;
    else
        return ch;
}
```

3. Consider the following program:

```
#include <stdio.h>
#include <stdlib.h>
int main(void)
{
    int ch, i;
    i = 0;
    ch = getchar();
    while ( (ch >= '0') && (ch <= '9') ) {
        i = (ch - '0') + i*10;
        ch = getchar();
    }
    printf("%d\n",i);
    return EXIT_SUCCESS;
}
```

Tell what the program prints out, if each of the following lines is entered on the standard input stream:

```
12345
12345a
12b345
12,345
a12
34.5
```

4. Write a program that reads in lines of text (one character at a time) and prints them out with all alphabetic characters in uppercase. The program should stop when it reaches end-of-file.

5. Write a program that reads in lines of text and prints them out with all leading blanks removed. By "leading blanks", we mean one or more blank characters at the beginning of a line. A new line begins after every ' \n' character. The program should stop when it reaches end-of-file. For example, the program might read in

```
        Mary had a little lamb
            Its fleece was white as snow
    And everywhere that Mary went
        The lamb was sure to go
```

and print out

```
    Mary had a little lamb
    Its fleece was white as snow
    And everywhere that Mary went
    The lamb was sure to go
```

6. Write a program that reads in lines of text and prints them out with tab characters converted to an appropriate number of spaces. Assume that tab stops are set every eight columns. This means that if you read in a ' \t' character, you must put out at least one space, plus the number of spaces needed to reach column 8, column 16, column 24, or whatever multiple of eight comes next. (This forces you to keep track of how many characters you have written out on the current line.) The program stops when it reaches end-of-file. Assume the input text contains no backspace characters.

7. Modify the program written in the previous exercise so that it can handle input text that contains backspace characters.

8. CONCORDANCE QUESTION: Using getchar, write a program that reads in text and writes it all back out, one word per line. Blanks, punctuation characters, digits, and so on should not be written out.

9. CONCORDANCE QUESTION: Modify the program from the previous exercise so that all uppercase letters are converted to lowercase before being written out.

10. CONCORDANCE QUESTION: Modify the program from the previous exercise so that it keeps a count of how many lines, words, and characters are read. It should print out these counts when it reaches end-of-file.

5.3 Additional Statements _____

C has several kinds of statements we haven't discussed yet. These are not as common as loops and **if**s, but they can sometimes be useful.

5.3.1 Break

The **break** statement may appear in the body of a loop (and in the body of a **switch** statement, described shortly). The **break** statement tells C to jump out of the enclosing loop and to go on to whatever follows the loop. For example,

```
while ( ( ch=getchar() ) != '\n' )
    if (ch == EOF) {
        printf("\nUnexpected end of file\n");
        break;
    }
    if (ch != ' ')
        printf("%c",ch);
}
```

prints all the characters on the current line except blank characters. If getchar returns EOF before the end of the line, the **if** statement prints a warning message and uses **break** to stop the loop. The **break** statement is just the word "break" followed by a semicolon.

Consider the following loop:

```
int i, ch, count;
for ( i = 1; i <= 10; i++ ) {
    ch = getchar();
    count = 0;
    while (ch != '\n') {
        printf("%c",ch);
        if (++count >= 79)
            break;
        ch = getchar();
    }
    printf("\n");
}
```

This reads in text and writes it out, for a total output of ten lines. If any input line is longer than 79 characters, the output line is broken after the 79th character; the rest of the input line is printed on the next output line. Notice that the **break** statement is inside a **while** loop and the **while** loop is inside a **for** loop. A **break** statement only breaks out of the *smallest enclosing loop*. In this case, the smallest enclosing loop is the **while**.

5.3.2 Continue

The **continue** statement is similar to **break**; **continue** may only appear in the body of loops. While **break** jumps out of a looping statement completely, **continue** only ends one cycle of the loop. For example,

```
while ( ( ch=getchar() ) != EOF ) {
    if ( ch == ' ')
        continue;
    printf("%c",ch);
}
```

is a loop that reads in characters and prints out everything except blanks. If a blank is found, the **continue** tells C to skip the rest of the loop. However, C will go back to the top of the **while**, check the condition, and start executing the loop body again if the condition is true.

With **for** loops, **continue** jumps to the end of the loop body, but the *incr* expression is still executed. For example,

```
for ( ch = getchar(); ch != EOF; ch = getchar() ) {
    if (ch == ' ')
        continue;
    printf("%c",ch);
}
```

is a loop that reads in characters and prints out everything but blanks. The increment expression

```
ch = getchar()
```

is executed at the end of every loop, even if the **continue** statement skips the call to printf.

When a **continue** statement is enclosed by more than one loop, it ends a cycle of the smallest enclosing loop.

5.3.3 Switch

A **switch** statement is a shorthand for a series of **if** statements. The easiest way to understand how the statement works is to start with an example:

```
switch (op) {
  case '+':
    printf("Addition\n");
    break;
  case '-':
    printf("Subtraction\n");
    break;
```

```
    case '*':
        printf("Multiplication\n");
        break;
    case '/':
        printf("Division\n");
        break;
    default:
        printf("Unidentified operator\n");
}
```

The **switch** statement starts with the keyword **switch** followed by an expression in parentheses. This expression is known as the **control expression** of the **switch** statement. The control expression must have a (signed or unsigned) integer or character type.

After the control expression comes the body of the **switch**. This is almost always enclosed in brace brackets (although the braces can be omitted if the body of the **switch** only has one statement). The body of the **switch** statement consists of a number of **case clauses**. Case clauses begin with a line of the form

case *constant* :

This is called a **case label**.

Execution of the **switch** statement begins by evaluating the control expression. The value of this expression is then compared to the constants appearing in the case labels. If the control value matches a constant on one of the case labels, C will execute the code that follows the case label. Execution continues until it reaches the end of the **switch** body or a **break** statement. A **break** statement breaks out of the **switch** body and goes on to whatever follows the brace bracket that marks the end of the body.

default:

is a special case label. If the value of the control expression does not match any of the constants on the other case labels, C will execute the code that follows the **default** label. If the control expression doesn't match any of the case constants and there is no **default** label, C goes on to whatever follows the brace bracket that marks the end of the body. In other words, it skips the **switch** body entirely.

The **switch** statement at the beginning of this section has a control expression that only consists of a variable named op. If op is one of the characters '+', '-', '*', or '/', the program finds the matching case label and executes a printf call that prints out what kind of operator was found. If op is not one of these characters, the program executes the default case and prints out Unidentified operator.

A section of code inside the **switch** body may have more than one case label. For example,

```
switch (i%3) {
    case 0:
        printf("%d is divisible by 3\n",i);
        break;
```

```
      case 1:
      case 2:
        printf("%d is not divisible by 3\n",i);
   }
```

executes the second `printf` if `i%3` is either 1 or 2.

   The code after one case label can continue into the code after another case label. For example, the following function collects an integer from the standard input stream. If the first character is a zero, the number will be an unsigned octal integer. If it is a sign (`'+'` or `'-'`), the integer will be given in decimal form. If no sign appears, it will be positive and decimal.

```
int getint(void)
{
    int i, sign, base, ch;
    char maxdigit;
    i = 0;
    sign = 1;
    maxdigit = '9';
    while ( (ch=getchar()) == ' ')
        /* nothing */;
    switch (ch) {
      case '0':
        base = 8;
        maxdigit = '7';
        break;
      case '-':
        sign = -1;
      case '+':
        base = 10;
        break;
      default:
        /* number starts with digit */
        base = 10;
        i = ch - '0';
    }
    while (((ch=getchar()) >= '0')&&(ch <= maxdigit))
        i = (ch - '0') + (i * base);
    return i * sign ;
}
```

   Notice that the case clause for `'-'` continues on into the case clause for `'+'` because they both need to set `base` to `10`.

   This function skips over blanks, then assumes that the first character read is the first character of the integer being collected. It stops when it finds a character that cannot be part of the number being collected. Notice, for example, that the loop stops if it is collecting an octal number and finds one of the digits $'8'$ or $'9'$. You should examine the `getint` function carefully to make sure you understand how it works.

In **ANSI C**, wherever you can use a constant, you can also use a **constant expression**: an expression whose operands are constants. For example, you can have a case label of the form

```
case 2*3:
```

which is equivalent to

```
case 6:
```

5.3.4 Exercises

1. Consider the following function:

```
int calc(int a,int op,int b)
{
    switch (op) {
      case '+':
        return a + b ;
      case '-':
        return a - b ;
      case '*':
        return a * b ;
      case '/':
        return a / b ;
      case '%':
        return a % b ;
      default :
        printf("Unrecognized operator\n");
        return 0;
    }
}
```

Write a `main` function that uses `calc` to add 3 and 2.

2. Modify the `calc` function above so that it also lets you calculate a to the power b. Decide for yourself what `op` value will indicate this operation.

3. Modify `calc` so that it can also calculate the greatest common divisor of a and b (that is, the largest positive integer that divides evenly into both a and b). Decide for yourself what `op` value will indicate this operation.

4. Write a `main` routine that reads in an integer followed by an operator followed by another integer, and writes out the result of the operation. You should call both `getint` and `calc`.

5.4 Declaration Forms

So far, our functions and programs have used very simple declarations. In this section, we will widen our understanding of how declarations may be used.

5.4.1 Block Scope Variables

All the variables we have used so far have been declared at the beginning of function bodies. Such variables are said to have **block scope**, because they are defined inside a **block** (a section of code enclosed in brace brackets).

☞ The names of block scope variables are only recognized in the block where they are declared.

If a function declares a variable X and another function tries to use X, the second function will get an error; the only function that knows about the existence of X is the function that declares it.

Similarly, think about our two functions, `upper` and `lower`, defined in Section 3.2..

```
char upper(char ch)
{
    return ch - 'a' + 'A' ;
}
char lower(char ch)
{
    return ch - 'A' + 'a' ;
}
```

Both of these functions use a parameter named `ch`. This is valid in C, because `ch` has block scope in both `upper` and `lower`. The `upper` function doesn't know about the `ch` in `lower`, and vice versa, so there is no confusion about which `ch` the functions are working with.

☞ C lets different functions use parameters and variables that have the same name.

It is mere coincidence if this happens; a variable X in one function has no relationship to another X in a different function. An analogy may make this clearer: two different families may have sons named "John", but they are not the same boy. It happens that "John" is a popular name, just as some variable names happen to be popular (for example, `ch` for characters, `i` and `j` for integers).

Block scope variables can be declared at the beginning of any block. For example, if the body of a **while** statement is enclosed in brace brackets, you can have declarations at the beginning of the block. This is occasionally useful, but it is usually better to declare variables at the beginning of a function rather than somewhere in the middle.

All block scope variables are created when the block begins execution and are discarded when the block finishes. For example, when a function finishes execution, the program frees up all the memory that was occupied by the function's block scope variables. This memory is then available for other uses (for example, for block scope variables in the next function that is called).

5.4.2 File Scope Variables

If all variables had block scope, it would be difficult for functions to *share* information. The block scope variables of one function are entirely inaccessible to other functions, so they cannot be shared. In order to make information sharing possible, C also lets you define **file scope** variables.

Like block scope variables, file scope variables must be declared. Since declarations inside a function have block scope, the declaration of a file scope variable cannot be given inside a function. Instead, the declaration stands on its own, outside all functions. In

```
double pi;
int main(void)
{
    pi = 3.14159;
    /* etc. */
```

defines a file scope variable named `pi`. The `pi` variable can be used by all functions whose definitions follow the declaration of `pi` in the source file. For this reason, file scope variables are almost always declared at the beginning of a file, after **#include** directives but before any function definitions. You can, however, put file scope declarations between function definitions if you want.

Earlier, we said that a block scope variable was like the name "John": just as "John" refers to different people in different families, a block scope variable name refers to different memory locations in different functions. A file scope variable is like a well-known name that always refers to the same person, no matter who is talking, for example, "Shakespeare." When several people refer to "Shakespeare", they are all talking about the same man. Similarly, when several functions refer to a file scope variable named Y, they are all referring to the same data object.

A function can define a block scope variable with the same name as a file scope variable. Within the function, the name refers to the block scope variable; the existence of the file scope variable is ignored, as in the following example:

```
#include <stdio.h>
#include <stdlib.h>
int a;
extern double f(int i);
extern double g(double x);
```

```
int main(void)
{
    a = 2;
    printf("%g\n",f(a));
    return EXIT_SUCCESS;
}

double f(int i)
{
    double a;
    a = 3.0 * i;
    return g(a);
}

double g(double x)
{
    return a * x;
}
```

The block scope a inside f is entirely independent of the file scope a; it even has a different type. Inside g and main, however, a refers to the file scope a. As an exercise, examine the above program and predict what it prints out.

☞ A file scope variable exists from the start of program execution to the end. This means that file scope variables are "permanent," unlike block scope variables (which are created when their block begins execution and discarded when the block finishes).

5.4.3 File Scope Initializations

Variables can be given a value at the time they are declared. This process is called **initialization**.

File scope variables can be initialized with constants or constant expressions. To do this, put an equal sign (=) and the initialization value after the variable name in the variable declaration. This kind of construct is called an **initializer**. For example,

```
double pi = 3.14159;
double pi_by_2 = 3.14159 / 2.0;
int x = 3, y = 4;
```

are all legitimate file scope declarations that contain initializers. The declaration for x and y shows that one declaration can contain several initializers. If you want several variables initialized to the same value, you must state the initialization for each variable, as in

```
char ch1 = 'x', ch2 = 'x', ch3 = 'x';
```

You cannot say

```
char ch1 = ch2 = ch3 = 'x';    /* ERROR! */
```

If you say,

```
char ch1, ch2, ch3 = 'x';
```

the declaration only initializes ch3 to 'x'; ch1 and ch2 are not explicitly initialized.

File scope variables will already have their initialization values when the program begins execution. In other words, they behave as if they are initialized *before* the program starts to run.

If a file scope variable is not given an explicit initialization value, it is initialized as if it has been assigned the value zero. This means that a file scope declaration like

```
double z;
```

is equivalent to

```
double z = 0;
```

Since the 0 is converted to the correct type, z will start with the value 0.0.

Even though file scope variables are automatically initialized in this way, good style recommends that you do not depend on default initialization.

☞ Initialize file scope variables explicitly, or assume that they need to be assigned a value before they can be used.

Some older (non-**ANSI**) versions of C do not initialize file scope variables by default.

5.4.4 Block Scope Initializations

Declarations of block scope variables may also contain initializers, but the initialization process is slightly different. File scope initialization takes place before the program begins execution. Since a block scope variable doesn't exist until the block begins execution, block scope initialization cannot take place until the variable is created. Once the variable has been created, the initialization is performed as if it were a normal assignment operation. The initialization value can be any expression that would be acceptable in an assignment. For example, consider:

```
int a = 2;
double func(char ch)
{
    char nl = '\n';
    int i = ch;
    double x = 3.0 * a;
    int j = i - 'a';
    /* and so on */
```

This shows many different types of initializations. File scope variables must be initialized with a constant or constant expression. Block scope variables can have many different initialization expressions:

(a)   nl is initialized with a constant;

(b)   i is initialized using an argument value passed to the function;

(c)   x is initialized with an expression that refers to a file scope variable;

(d)   j is initialized with an expression that refers to a previously initialized block scope variable.

Block scope initializations are performed every time the block begins execution; file scope initializations are only performed once, before the program begins execution.

5.4.5 Exercises

1. What does the following program print out?

```
#include <stdio.h>
#include <stdlib.h>
extern int incr(int ch);
int a = 5;

int main(void)
{
    char a = 'A';
    printf("%c\n",incr(a));
    return EXIT_SUCCESS;
}

int incr(int ch)
{
    return ch + a;
}
```

2. What does the following program print out?

```
#include <stdio.h>
#include <stdlib.h>

int a = 2;

extern int incr2(int i,int j);
```

```
int main(void)
{
    int i = a;
    char a = 'A';
    printf("%c\n",incr2(a,i));
    return EXIT_SUCCESS;
}
int incr2(int i,int j)
{
    return i + j + a;
}
```

5.5 User-Defined Types

C lets programmers create their own data types, based on the standard data types. This is done with a **typedef** statement.

> **typedef** *type name*;

says that *name* will stand for the given *type* when it appears in declarations. For example, you might define

```
typedef float MONEY;
```

This says that MONEY will stand for the **float** type. You can then make declarations like the following:

```
MONEY salary;
```

This says that salary is a variable with the MONEY type, and is therefore a **float** object. There is no difference between the MONEY type and **float**; they can be used interchangeably.

You might ask, "If there is no difference between a user-defined type and the associated standard type, why bother to define new types?" There are two major reasons.

First, user-defined data types can have names that are more descriptive than **int**, **float**, and so on. For example, consider a program that handles personnel records for a company. Such records might use integers for both department and personal identification numbers. The program could therefore define

```
typedef int DEPT_ID;
typedef int PERSON_ID;
DEPT_ID i, j;
PERSON_ID k, l;
```

This makes it clear that `i` and `j` will be used to represent department IDs, while `k` and `l` will be used to represent personal IDs. If we just said,

```
int i, j, k, l;
```

it would be much more difficult to determine how each variable was being used. Thus the first justification for user-defined types is that they make programs more understandable.

Box 5.2: Style Note—Variable Names

In general, you should avoid using nondescriptive variable names like `i` and `j` to hold significant data. One-character names are fine for counters in **for** loops, but a variable should usually have a name that suggests what it holds. For example, it would be better to rewrite the nearby example as

```
DEPT_ID accounting, sales;
PERSON_ID manager, asst_manager;
```

to make it clear that the `DEPT_ID` variables hold ID numbers for the accounting department and the sales department, and the `PERSON_ID` variables hold ID numbers for a manager and assistant manager. Descriptive variable names make your programs much easier to understand.

The second justification for user-defined types is their flexibility. Going back to our previous example, suppose the company grows to the point where personal ID numbers are too big to fit in an **int** value, so it becomes necessary to use **long** values. All the programs that used **int** values will have to be changed. If the programs were written *without* user-defined types, someone would have to check every **int** declaration to see if the declared variable(s) refer to personal IDs, and change the appropriate declarations from **int** to **long**. However, if the programs were written *with* user-defined types, all you would have to do would be to change the **typedef** declaration to

```
typedef long PERSON_ID;
```

This automatically changes all the `PERSON_ID` declarations from **int** to **long**, without touching anything else in the program. The only other change you might have to make in your program is to change `printf` statements whose format strings still regard the `PERSON_ID` type as a normal **int**.

Type declarations using **typedef** may appear anywhere you would find a normal variable declaration. If a **typedef** declaration appears inside a block, the type name has block scope; if it is outside all functions, the name has file scope. Variable declarations that use the defined type name must appear within the name's scope.

User-defined types may be used to describe arguments or results in function prototypes. For example,

```
MONEY sales_tax(MONEY price)
```

is a prototype for a function that takes a MONEY argument and returns a MONEY value. (We assume that the program contains a previous **typedef** statement declaring MONEY.)

```
DEPT_ID find_department(PERSON_ID person)
```

is a prototype for a function that takes a PERSON_ID argument and returns a DEPT_ID value. This prototype might be used for a function that determines the department where a particular person works.

Defined type names may be used in cast operations. For example,

```
MONEY salary;
salary = (MONEY) 10000;
```

converts the integer 10000 into the MONEY type.

☞ User-defined type names encourage you to write programs in terms of what your data *means* instead of how the data is represented internally. In this way, your programs become more flexible and easier to understand.

Box 5.3: Style Note—Typedef Names

It is common programming practice to write all defined type names in uppercase (as demonstrated in our examples). This makes the names stand out in your source code.

5.5.1 Exercises

1. The following function accepts a temperature measured in Fahrenheit and converts it to Celsius.

```
int Fahr_to_Cel(int fahr)
{
      return (fahr-32) * 5 / 9 ;
}
```

Rewrite this function so that all arguments and the return value have a user-defined type named TEMPERATURE. Write the function in such a way that it works, regardless of whether TEMPERATURE is defined as **int**, **long**, **short**, **float**, or **double**.

2. Write a main function that prints out Fahrenheit temperatures and their Celsius equivalents, beginning at 0° F and going up by tens to 100° F. This function should use the Fahr_to_Cel function written for the previous exercise, and should work regardless of whether TEMPERATURE is defined as **int**, **long**, **short**, **float**, or **double**.

5.6 Enumerated Types

The **typedef** statement lets you define a type with a name of your choosing. An **enumerated type** is a data type with *values* of your own choosing. The easiest way to understand enumerated types is to look at an example.

```
enum days {
        Sunday, Monday, Tuesday, Wednesday,
        Thursday, Friday, Saturday
};
```

defines an enumerated type. The definition begins with the keyword **enum**. After this comes the **tag** of the enumerated type; this is a name that will be used to identify the type. Finally, the definition contains a list of identifiers (Sunday, Monday, and so on) enclosed in brace brackets. This is called the **enumeration list** and the identifiers in the list are the **enumerated values**.

The names inside the brace brackets stand for the values of the enumerated type. For the days enumerated type, there are seven possible values. In the example below, we create a variable that has the days type and we assign that variable a value.

```
enum days today;
today = Tuesday;
```

The declaration of the today variable consists of the keyword **enum** (to indicate an enumerated type), the tag days (to indicate the type to which we refer) and the name of the variable. After we have declared this variable, we can assign it one of the values that make up the type.

Enumerated types may be used in all the operations that we have discussed up to this point. For example, you can have statements like

```
if (today == Thursday) ...
while (today != Sunday) ...
for (today = Monday; today <= Friday; today++ ) ...
```

How does it all work? Enumerated types are actually special **int** types. The first name in the enumeration list is given the value 0. The rest of the names are numbered consecutively (Monday is 1, Tuesday is 2, and so on). In this way, the first names have low values and later names have higher ones. This means, for example, that

```
Sunday < Monday
Monday < Tuesday
/* and so on */
```

Since enumerated values are **int** values in disguise, you can do arithmetic with them:

```
today = Monday + 1;
```

assigns the value `Tuesday` to `today` (since `Tuesday` comes immediately after `Monday` in the original enumeration list). The **for** loop shown previously will have `today` run through the values from `Monday` to `Friday` (inclusive).

The definition of an enumerated type (the list giving the values of the type) should appear before any use of the type.

Because all enumerated types are **int** types in disguise, an expression like

```
Saturday + 1
```

is valid in C; the value of this expression is the integer 7. However, the result of the expression falls outside the range of values of the enumerated type. In most programs, it is an indication of some kind of logic error. The same applies to an expression like

```
Sunday - 1
```

Such expressions are valid, but illogical in most contexts.

5.6.1 Enumerated Values and Functions

Enumerated values may be used as the arguments and return values of functions. For example, here is a function that returns 1 if its argument is a weekday and 0 if the argument is a day of the weekend:

```
int weekday(enum days test_day)
{
    switch(test_day) {
      case Sunday:
      case Saturday:
        return 0;
      default:
        return 1;
    }
}
```

The argument in the prototype is declared with the form

```
enum days test_day
```

to indicate that it is a variable of the `days` enumerated type. The function itself is just a **switch** statement: if `test_day` is `Sunday` or `Saturday`, the function returns 0; otherwise, it returns 1.

As an example of a function that returns an enumerated value, consider this:

```
enum days getday(void)
{
    enum days in_day;
    printf("Enter the day of the week.\n");
```

```
            printf("0 for Sunday, 1 for Monday, etc.: ");
            scanf("%d",&in_day);
            return in_day;
        }
```

The `getday` function asks the user to enter a number standing for a day of the week, then uses `scanf` to read in the number. Notice that `scanf` can read the number directly into the `in_day` enumerated variable. An enumerated type is just **int** in disguise; data objects with an enumerated type can be used anywhere that **int** is valid.

5.6.2 Exercises

1. Rewrite the `weekday` function to use a conditional expression instead of a **switch** statement.

2. It is a fact of life that people make errors. Rewrite the `getday` function to check that the user enters a number between 0 and 6. If the user makes a mistake, the function should issue a message to this effect and give the user another chance to enter an appropriate number.

3. Write a program that calls `getday` to get a day of the week, then prints out the full name of that day, as in

   ```
   printf("Sunday\n");
   ```

4. Suppose we associate each day of the week with a unique single letter, as in

   ```
   Sunday      ⇒   'S'
   Monday      ⇒   'M'
   Tuesday     ⇒   'T'
   Wednesday   ⇒   'W'
   Thursday    ⇒   'R'
   Friday      ⇒   'F'
   Saturday    ⇒   'A'
   ```

   Write a function `char_to_day` that takes a single character as an argument and returns the corresponding value of the `days` enumerated type.

5. Write a function named `day_to_char`, the reverse of `char_to_day`. It takes an argument of the `days` enumerated type and returns the corresponding **char** value.

6. Rewrite `getday` so that it reads in one of the single characters instead of a number. Run the program from Exercise 3 with this version of `getday` instead of the previous one. Notice that you do not have to change `main` at all, since the prototype for `getday` does not change.

7. Rewrite `getday` so that it asks the user to enter the first three characters of a day of the week ("Sun", "Mon", and so on). Make sure you take into account that the user may make typing errors. Run the program from Exercise 3 with this version of `getday`.

5.7 Review

The expressions `++i` and `i++` are called *auto-increment* expressions; `++i` adds 1 to i and uses the resulting value as the result of the expression. The value of `i++` is the current value of i; after this value is obtained, 1 is added to i.

The expressions `--i` and `i--` are called *auto-decrement* expressions. They work like the auto-increment expressions except that they subtract 1 from i instead of adding.

The expression `A?B:C` is called a *conditional* expression. The value of the expression is the value of B if A is nonzero, and the value of C if A is zero.

When an expression contains more than one operation, the operations are evaluated according to an *order of precedence*. The order of evaluation can be changed by using parentheses.

The `getchar` library function reads a single character and returns it as an **int** value. The special value EOF is returned to indicate end-of-file.

The **switch** statement is a shorthand way of writing a series of **if** statements. The **break** statement jumps out of an enclosing loop or **switch** statement. The **continue** statement jumps out of one cycle of an enclosing loop, but does not stop the looping.

A variable may have *block scope* or *file scope*. It has block scope if it is declared inside a function, or if it is a function parameter. It has file scope if it is declared outside any function.

A file scope variable is "visible" from its declaration to the end of the file in which it is declared. A block scope variable is "visible" from its declaration to the end of the block in which it is declared. The declaration of a block scope variable "hides" any other variables of the same name until the end of the block.

Variables may be *initialized* when they are declared, as in

```
int a = 1;
```

A block scope initialization is performed every time the block begins execution. A file scope initialization only happens once, before the program begins execution.

The **typedef** statement can be used to associate names with types. Using named types makes source code easier to read, and can simplify program changes.

Enumerated types are **int** data types with names representing **int** values. An enumerated type is defined with

```
enum tag {
  name, name, ...
};
```

The first name in the list is associated with the **int** 0. Later names are numbered consecutively. Once an enumerated type has been defined, enumerated variables may be declared with

      enum *tag variable_name* ;

Enumerated values may be passed as arguments to functions and returned as function results.

chapter 6   Arrays

An **array** is a list of data objects that all have the same type. For example, an integer array is a list of **int** values. The individual items in the list are called the **members** of the array.

6.1 Declaring Arrays

An array is declared with a declaration of the following form:

type name[*size*];

The *type* tells the type of each member in the array. The *name* is the name of the array. The *size* is the number of members in the array. For example,

```
float farr[4];
```

declares an array named farr, containing four **float** values.

A single declaration can declare both normal variables and arrays. For example,

```
int i, ia[40], j, ia2[30];
```

declares two **int** variables (i and j) and two arrays with **int** members (ia and ia2).

The *size* in an array declaration must be a constant or constant expression. For example, it is valid to declare

```
char list[5*10];
```

but you cannot declare

```
char list[x];
```

where x is a variable in your program.

Arrays can have block scope or file scope, just like ordinary variables. The use of large block scope arrays can be inefficient for a variety of reasons (for example, the array must be created and possibly initialized every time the block begins execution). For this reason, we recommend that you think twice about using large block scope arrays. (It is hard to put an exact figure on how large is too large. We would say that an array with more than 20 members is a big one, but you should not take this as a firm limit.)

Individual members of an array are numbered, beginning at zero. To refer to a particular member of an array, give the name of the array, followed by an integral value in square brackets. For example, the members of `farr` declared above are

```
farr[0], farr[1], farr[2], farr[3]
```

(pronounced "farr-sub-zero", "farr-sub-one", and so on). The numbers in the square brackets are known as **subscripts**.

☞ Because the subscripts of an array begin at 0, the maximum subscript is one less than the size of the array.

The subscript operation belongs to the same precedence class as function calls.

IMPORTANT NOTE: Most implementations of C have no facilities for determining if a specified subscript is greater than the declared maximum. This means that you will not be given an error message if you use too large a subscript. However, a program that uses too large a subscript will be accessing computer storage past the end of the memory allocated for the array. The same sort of problem happens if you use a negative subscript (trying to access storage before the beginning of the array).

In some cases, you might get away with such an error (if the memory isn't being used for any other purpose). In the majority of cases, however, the error will cause mysterious bugs, because you are using memory that is actually allocated to other data objects (or even executable code). For this reason, you should always make sure that your program's subscripts do not go "out of bounds."

Each member of an array is like a separate variable. The member can be assigned a value, as in

```
farr[0] = 1.0;
```

used in expressions, as in

```
i = ia[4] + ia2[5] + j;
```

or used in function calls, as in

```
printf("%g\n",farr[0]);
```

Subscripts can be expressions as well as constants. For example,

```
for (i = 0; i < 4; i++)
    printf("%g\n",farr[i]);
```

prints out the current contents of each of the members of `farr`.

```
farr[i+2] = farr[i] + farr[i+1];
```

adds two consecutive members of `farr` and assigns the result to the next member.

Functions may not return arrays as their results. An entire array cannot be passed as an argument to a function, but C has a feature that makes the entire contents of an array available to a function. This is done using a "pointer", so we will not discuss it until Section 7.

Here is a simple program that uses arrays. It calculates how many ways there are to roll two six-sided dice and get a certain result.

```
#include <stdio.h>
#include <stdlib.h>
int rolls[13];
int main(void)
{
    int d1, d2, i;
    for (i = 0 ; i <= 12; i++)
        rolls[i] = 0;
    for (d1 = 1; d1 <= 6; d1++)
        for (d2 = 1; d2 <= 6; d2++)
            rolls[d1+d2] += 1;
    for (i = 2 ; i <= 12; i++)
        printf("There are %d ways to roll %d\n",
            rolls[i],i);
    return EXIT_SUCCESS;
}
```

The subscripts for `rolls` run from 0 to 12. The program begins by setting all of these to zero. The d1 and d2 loops then simulate dice rolls and use the members of `rolls` to count how often the various values occur. The final **for** loop prints the results; since there is no way to get 0 or 1 rolling two dice, the loop begins at 2.

The **typedef** statement may be used to make user-defined array types.

```
typedef int LIST[20];
```

says that the LIST type refers to an array of 20 integers. Once LIST has been declared, you can make declarations like

```
LIST ia;
```

This is equivalent to

```
int ia[20];
```

You can also create arrays whose members have a user-defined type. For example,

```
typedef float MONEY;
MONEY budget[30];
```

declares budget to be an array of 30 MONEY members.

6.1.1 Exercises

1. What does the following print out?

```
#include <stdio.h>
#include <stdlib.h>
int main(void)
{
    int i, j, ia[8];
    for (i = 1; i <= 7; i++)
        ia[i] = 0;
    ia[0] = 1;
    for (i = 1; i <= 7; i++)
        for (j = 0; j < i; j++)
            ia[i] += ia[j];
    for (i = 0; i <= 7; i++)
        printf("%d ",ia[i]);
    printf("\n");
    return EXIT_SUCCESS;
}
```

2. What does the following print out?

```
#include <stdio.h>
#include <stdlib.h>
typedef long VEC[10];
int main(void)
{
    int i;
    VEC xx;
    for (i = 0; i < 10; i++)
        xx[i] = (i / 3) * i;
    for (i = 0; i < 10; i++)
        printf("%d\n",(int) xx[i]);
    return EXIT_SUCCESS;
}
```

3. In the previous question, what would the program print out if we changed the **typedef** declaration to

```
typedef float VEC[10];
```

4. Write a program that uses `scanf` to read in 20 integers from the standard input, stores these integers in an array, then writes them out in reverse order.

5. Write a program that reads from the standard input unit and keeps track of how often each letter appears in the input. Nonalphabetic characters are ignored. Input characters may be in upper- or lowercase. However, the program will lump both upper- and lowercase characters together (so that the input line Aa has two occurrences of the letter "A"). When the program reaches EOF, it will print output lines of the form

```
The letter A appeared 14 times.
The letter B appeared 6 times.
      /* and so on */
```

6. CONCORDANCE QUESTION: Write a program that reads in a single word (length less than 20 characters) and stores it in an array. The program should then read through input text and count how many times the original word appears in the text.

6.2 Multidimensional Arrays

The arrays we have been discussing so far have only required one subscript when referring to a member. These are called **one-dimensional arrays** or **vectors**. C also lets you create arrays that require several subscripts to refer to an individual member. These are called **multidimensional arrays**.

```
char strarr[20][10];
```

defines a two-dimensional array whose members are characters. To refer to a particular character, you must specify two subscripts, as in strarr[0][0]. The maximum value of the first subscript is 19 (one less than the size given in the declaration) and the maximum value of the second subscript is 9.

A two-dimensional array can be used to represent a table (or *matrix*) of data. The array member a[m][n] could represent the table entry in the mth row in the nth column.

Multidimensional arrays can be made with arrays of arrays. For example, you might have

```
typedef double VEC[20];
VEC table[10];
```

Effectively, table is a two-dimensional array that is equivalent to

```
double table[10][20];
```

A single multidimensional array can occupy a lot of memory. For example,

```
int mult_arr[10][10][10];
```

may not seem big at first sight, but multiplying the dimension sizes, you see that it actually requires enough memory space to store a thousand integers. For this reason, you should think twice about using large multidimensional arrays; if there is another way to approach the problem, it may be wise to choose it.

6.2.1 Exercises

1. What does the following print out?

```
#include <stdio.h>
#include <stdlib.h>
int main(void)
{
    char graph[10][5];
    int x, y;
    for (x = 0; x <= 9; x++)
        for (y = 0; y <= 4; y++)
            graph[x][y] = ' ';
    for (x = 0; x <= 9; x++)
        graph[x][x%5] = '*';
    for (y = 4; y >= 0; y--) {
        for (x = 0; x <= 9; x++)
            printf("%c",graph[x][y]);
        printf("\n");
    }
    return EXIT_SUCCESS;
}
```

2. Suppose we declare a file scope array

```
char picture[15][30];
```

that represents a picture or graph made with 15 rows of 30 characters. Write a function

```
void draw(void);
```

that prints out this picture, character by character.

3. Write a program that uses the `picture` function of Exercise 2 to draw a graph of the mathematical function y=x/2 between x=0 and x=29.

6.3 Memory Allocation of Arrays

In the computer's memory, an array is stored in one block of contiguous storage. With one-dimensional arrays, members are stored in subscript order. Thus `arr[0]` is immediately followed by `arr[1]` which is immediately followed by `arr[2]` and so on.

With multidimensional arrays, members are stored in "row-major order." As an illustration of this order, let us declare

```
long int la[10][10];
```

The members of `la` are stored one after another in the following order:

```
la[0][0]
la[0][1]
la[0][2]
   ...
la[0][9]
la[1][0]
la[1][1]
   ...
```

C goes through all possible values of the right subscript, then increments the left subscript by one and goes through all possible values of the right subscript again. **This process is easy to remember, because it works just like the digits in ordinary counting:**

```
00 01 02 ... 09 10 11 12 ...
```

The pattern repeats itself for arrays of higher dimensions. The rightmost subscript increases quickly; subscripts to the left increase more slowly, with the leftmost subscript the slowest.

6.3.1 Initializing Arrays

An array declaration may include an initializer that specifies values for one or more array members. An array initializer uses a list of values separated by commas and enclosed in brace brackets. For example,

```
char digits[10] = {
    '0','1','2','3','4','5','6','7','8','9'
};
```

declares an array and initializes its members to the digit characters. Notice that an equal sign must appear before the initialization list and that a semicolon is still needed to mark the end of the declaration. (This is one difference between declarations and executable statements. When a block of code ends in a ' } ', a semicolon is not needed; however, a semicolon *is* needed in declarations.)

The initialization rules for variables apply to file scope and block scope arrays too.

☞ Array members can only be initialized with constants or constant expressions.

An initializer does not have to initialize all the members of an array. For example,

```
long fib[100] = {
    1L, 1L
};
```

only initializes the first two members of `fib`. Any members that are not initialized explicitly will be initialized as if they were assigned the value zero. This is true for all partly-initialized arrays, whether they have file or block scope. If none of the members in a block scope array are initialized, the program must explicitly assign values to members; members cannot be assumed to have any particular value.

If a one-dimensional array declaration has an initialization list, the size may be omitted from the declaration, as in

```
int ia[] = {
    5,10,15,20
};
```

In this case, the number of members in the array is the number of values in the initialization list. In our example, `ia` will have four members, with a maximum subscript of 3.

Multidimensional arrays can also be initialized. The values in the initialization are grouped with brace brackets. For example,

```
int iarr[3][5] = {
    {00, 01, 02, 03, 04},
    {10, 11, 12, 13, 14},
    {20, 21, 22, 23, 24}
};
```

initializes `iarr[0][3]` to `03`, `iarr[2][4]` to `24`, and so on. As another example,

```
float farr[3][2] = {
    { 0.1, 0.2 },
    { 1.1, 1.2 },
    { 2.1, 2.2 }
};
```

initializes `farr[2][1]` to `2.1` and so on.

As with one-dimensional declarations, an initializer for a multidimensional array does not have to initialize all the members. For example,

```
unsigned uarr[3][10] = {
    { 1U },
    { 1U },
    { 1U }
};
```

initializes `uarr[0][0]`, `uarr[1][0]`, and `uarr[2][0]` to 1U. Uninitialized members are initialized as if they are assigned a zero value.

If a multidimensional array has an initializer, the size of the leftmost dimension may be omitted. For example,

```
double d[][5] = {
    {0.0, 0.1, 0.2, 0.3, 0.4},
    {1.0, 1.1, 1.2, 1.3, 1.4},
    {2.0, 2.1, 2.2, 2.3, 2.4},
    {3.0, 3.1, 3.2, 3.3, 3.4}
};
```

declares an array whose leftmost dimension has a size of 4, maximum subscript 3. In this case, internal braces are important in determining the size of the dimension. For example,

```
char ca1[][4] = {
    {'a', 'b', 'c', 'd'}
};
```

is a one-by-four array, while

```
char ca2[][4] = {
    { 'a' },
    { 'b' },
    { 'c' },
    { 'd' }
};
```

is a four-by-four array, with only the first member in each row initialized.

6.3.2 Strings in Initializations

Strings can be used to initialize one-dimensional character arrays. Like the format string for `printf`, such strings are enclosed in double quotes. For example,

```
char str[10] = "hello" ;
```

declares and initializes a character array named `str`. (Note that brace brackets are not necessary with this kind of initialization.) The first member of `str` gets the first character of the string, and so on. Thus we have

```
str[0] == 'h'
str[1] == 'e'
str[2] == 'l'
str[3] == 'l'
str[4] == 'o'
```

To mark the end of the string, a NUL character ' \0' is assigned to the member following the one that gets the last letter. (The NUL character is represented with a backslash followed by a zero. We mentioned NUL in Section 3.2.2 when we talked about escape sequences.) This means that

```
str[5] == '\0'
```

The remaining members will be assigned 0.

The NUL character is only added if the array has room. For example, in

```
char str2[3] = "abc" ;
```

the ' \0' will not be added because str2 only has space to contain the three characters specified.

If a character vector is initialized with a string, the size of the vector may be omitted, as in

```
char str3[] = "abcd";
```

The vector will be big enough to hold all the characters in the string plus a terminating ' \0'. In the above example, str3 will have five members (four letters, plus the ' \0').

6.3.3 Exercises

1. Write a declaration for a vector named alpha whose members are all the lowercase letters.

2. Write a declaration for a two-dimensional array named ULalpha, whose first "row" is all the uppercase letters and whose second row is all the lowercase letters.

3. What does the following print out?

```
#include <stdio.h>
#include <stdlib.h>

int vect[10] = {
    100, 200, 300
};

int main(void)
{
    int i;
    for (i = 0; i < 10; i++)
        printf("%d\n",vect[i]);
    return EXIT_SUCCESS;
}
```

Box 6.1: The sizeof Operator

The **sizeof** operation calculates the number of bytes of memory required to hold an object or type. To find the size of an object, use

> **sizeof** *name*

where *name* is the name of the object. For example, with

```
int arr[] = {
    1, 2, 3, 4
};
```

the result of the expression

```
sizeof arr ;
```

is the number of bytes required to hold the entire array.

```
(sizeof arr) / (sizeof arr[0])
```

is the size of the array, divided by the size of one member of the array. This gives the number of members in the array. This is a handy trick to use if you need to calculate the number of members in an array.

The **sizeof** operator can also be applied to arbitrary types. The name of the type must be put in parentheses. For example,

```
sizeof (double)
```

gives the number of bytes required to hold a **double** value.

```
sizeof (MONEY)
```

gives the number of bytes required to hold a value of the MONEY type (created with a **typedef** declaration in Section 5.5).

The result of **sizeof** has a type called size_t, a standard name like EXIT_SUCCESS. It is created with a **typedef** statement in the standard header <stdlib.h> (and in several other standard headers). The size_t type is one of the **unsigned** integer types; whether it is **long**, **short**, or **int** is implementation-defined.

6.4 The #define Directive

    As we noted in Section 1.2, computer programs are often modified after they have been written. For example, suppose we have an array

```
MONEY income[20];
```

which contains the annual income from each of 20 restaurants in a fast-food franchise. If more restaurants are added to the chain, the size of the array must increase and the program must be changed. One small change like this may force a number of changes throughout the program, anywhere the size of the array is used. The person modifying the program may have to look through the entire program to find all the places that changes must be made.

    When you first write a program, you can allow for later changes by using the **#define** directive.

#define *name value*

indicates that the given *name* should be replaced by the *value* wherever it appears in the program code. For example,

```
#define SIZE 20
```

says that SIZE should be replaced with 20 wherever it appears in the program. This replacement takes place as the program is being *translated*. For example,

```
int arr[SIZE];
```

turns into the code

```
int arr[20];
```

and program translation continues on from there. In other words, the replacement is *textual*: one piece of text (the name) is replaced by another (the associated value). A name that has been given a value in this way is called a **manifest**.

    Here is an example of a program that uses a manifest:

```
#include <stdio.h>
#include <stdlib.h>
#define SIZE 20

int main(void)
{
    int arr[SIZE];
    int i,j;
    arr[0] = 1;
```

```
        for (i = 1; i < SIZE; i++)
            arr[i] = 0;
        for (i = 1; i < SIZE; i++)
            for (j = 0; j < i; j++)
                arr[i] += arr[j];
        for (i = 0; i < SIZE; i++)
            printf("%d\n",arr[i]);
        return EXIT_SUCCESS;
    }
```

This uses SIZE to represent the number of members in the arr array. In the array that is printed out, each member is the sum of all the previous members.

Because we have always referred to the size of the array using the SIZE manifest, we can easily change the program just by changing the **#define** directive. For example, if we changed the directive to

```
#define SIZE 30
```

the program would print out 30 numbers instead of 20. Changing this one directive is a lot less work than making changes throughout the program. It is also safer: if you have to change many things in a program, there is always the chance you will miss one and the program will stop working.

You might be wondering why we couldn't say something like

```
int size = 20;
int arr[size];
```

In other words, why do we need to **#define** a manifest? The answer is that the size of an array needs to be known at the time the program is *translated*. The size variable above only has a value when the program is *executing*. Thus we cannot use a variable to specify an array size. A manifest is acceptable because it is given its value at translation time.

The **#define** directive always takes up a single line by itself. Unlike other instructions in C programs, it normally cannot be split over several lines and cannot be preceded or followed by other material on the line.

The **#define** directive is actually more versatile than the examples we have shown so far. The text associated with a manifest name can be an expression instead of a single value. For example, we could have

```
#define PI_BY_2   (3.14159 / 2.0)
```

This also shows that blanks are allowed in manifest definitions. The text associated with the manifest name begins at the space immediately following the name and goes to the end of the source code line.

☞   Most programmers use manifest names that are all uppercase letters. This helps distinguish these names from other kinds of names in your program.

Manifests are **not** replaced if they appear in character or string constants. For example, the above manifest definition would not affect

```
printf("Do not replace PI_BY_2.\n");
```

6.4.1 The C Preprocessor

The **#define** construct is an example of C's **preprocessing** facilities. Preprocessing is the first operation performed on source code when it is read in.

The C preprocessor works on the *text* of your source code, before the *meaning* of the code is determined. For example, if the preprocessor finds the **#define** statement given at the end of the previous section, it will begin replacing PI_BY_2 with the associated text wherever it appears in your program (except in character or string constants). The meaning of your program is only interpreted after the replacement occurs.

The other preprocessing directive we have seen is **#include**. When the preprocessor sees an **#include** directive, it obtains source code from the associated standard header and inserts the code in your program in place of the **#include** directive.

C has a number of other preprocessing directives, but **#include** and **#define** are probably the most widely used. Other directives are described in the Reference Manual.

6.4.2 Macros

The **#define** directive can also be used to define **macros**. A macro is an advanced kind of manifest that takes arguments like a function. However, its result is still *textual*: it changes your program code as the code is being translated. Here is a simple macro definition:

```
#define OUTINT(N) printf("%d\n",N)
```

The name of the macro is OUTINT. It takes one argument, represented in the definition by the parameter N. In a program, OUTINT is used with the same form as a function call, as in

```
OUTINT(5);
```

This reference to OUTINT is replaced by the text associated with the macro. Everywhere the parameter N appears in this text, it is replaced by the argument 5. This means that the above macro call turns into

```
printf("%d\n",5);
```

Macros serve several purposes. Like manifests, they can make your program simpler to change. For example, suppose we define

```
#define PRINTMONEY(X) printf("$%8.2g\n",X)
```

as a macro that is always used to print money values. If we decide that we need more digits to print our money values (the company did well last year!), we can change every output operation in the program just by changing the macro definition to

```
#define PRINTMONEY(X) printf("$%10.2g\n",X)
```

Macros can also make your program easier to read. A single name like PRINTMONEY is easier to understand at a glance than the corresponding printf instruction. To understand what the printf prints, you have to look at the format string or know that the argument represents a money value. With PRINTMONEY, the name says it all.

Macros may be used to represent any action your program will perform frequently. For example, the following macro can assign the same value to all the members of an integer array:

```
#define ASSIGN(A,SIZE,V) for (i=0;i<SIZE;) A[i++]=V
```

To use this macro, we might say

```
int arr[40];
ASSIGN(arr,40,5);
```

This sets every member of arr to 5.

Manifests can be passed as arguments in macro calls. For example, we can use the ASSIGN macro we just defined, with

```
#define ARRSIZE 40;
int arr[ARRSIZE];
ASSIGN(arr,ARRSIZE,5);
```

The ARRSIZE manifest is replaced with the value 40 and the ASSIGN macro uses this in the **for** loop.

6.4.3 Pitfalls

Suppose you define a manifest with

```
#define A 1+1
```

When using a manifest like this, you should bear in mind that the manifest name is blindly replaced by the associated text wherever it appears in your program (except in string and character constants). For example, you might think that the manifest A has the value 2 so that

```
A*A
```

would have the value 4. This is not true. In fact, each A is replaced with the text 1+1 to get

```
1+1*1+1
```

Because multiplication is performed before addition, this has the value 3.
You can avoid this kind of problem.

☞ When you define a manifest, enclose the value in parentheses.

For example, if you define

```
#define A (1+1)
```

the value of A*A will be 4 as expected.
Similarly, suppose you define

```
#define MULT(A,B) (A*B)
```

If you make the macro call

```
MULT(1+1,1+1)
```

you again get the expression

```
1+1*1+1
```

and get 3 instead of 4.

☞ To avoid problems, parenthesize the names of macro parameters wherever they
appear in the macro definition.

For example, you might write

```
#define MULT(A,B) ((A)*(B))
```

☞ When using macros, try to avoid arguments that have "side-effects."

For example, suppose you define a macro named SQUARE which obtains the value of a
number times itself. If your program contains

```
SQUARE(i++)
```

it looks like i is only being incremented once. However, if the macro is defined with

```
#define SQUARE(A) (A*A)
```

the macro expands to

```
(i++ * i++)
```

and i is actually incremented *twice*. This confusing situation can be avoided if the arguments for the macro are not expressions that change values in memory.

As a rule of thumb, avoid macros that contain the semicolon character. To see what might happen, consider:

```
#define PRINTINT(I) printf("%d",I);
         ...
if (value != 0) PRINTINT (value);
else printf("Value is zero.\n");
```

This expands to

```
if (value != 0) printf("%d",value);;
else printf("Value is zero.\n");
```

An **else** statement must immediately follow the associated **if**. In the above code, however, there is a null statement (just a semicolon) immediately after the **if**. Therefore the **else** is not properly associated with the **if** and the program has a syntax error. This kind of error is subtle; it might take you a lot of time to figure out what went wrong. To prevent such problems, watch out for semicolons in macro definitions and avoid them whenever possible.

6.4.4 Exercises

1. Rewrite all the programs and functions you have written in the exercises for this chapter so that manifests are used in all references to array size.

2. What does the following print out?

```
#include <stdio.h>
#include <stdlib.h>

#define DIAG(A,B) { {A,0},{0,B} }
#define DIM1 2
#define DIM2 2

int iarr[DIM1][DIM2] = DIAG(1,1);
int zarr[DIM1][DIM2] = DIAG(0,0);
int xarr[DIM1][DIM2] = DIAG(3,4);
```

```
int main(void)
{
    int i,j;
    for (i = 0; i < DIM1; i++) {
        for (j = 0; j < DIM2; j++) {
            printf("%d",iarr[i][j]);
            printf(" %d",zarr[i][j]);
            printf(" %d\n",xarr[i][j]);
        }
    }
    return EXIT_SUCCESS;
}
```

3. Write a macro named OUTC that prints a single character (supplied as an argument to the macro).

6.5 *Enumerated Values vs. Manifests*

In Section 5.6, we showed how to create enumerated types using a simple list of names, as in

```
enum days {
    Sunday, Monday, Tuesday, Wednesday,
    Thursday, Friday, Saturday
};
```

In this kind of enumerated type, the first name in the list has the **int** value 0, the second has the **int** value 1, and so on.

There is a second way of setting up an enumerated type. Consider:

```
enum coins {
    penny = 1,
    cent = 1,
    nickel = 5,
    quarter = 25,
    dime = 10,
};
```

Once again, we have names standing for **int** values. However, in this form of the declaration, we *assign* the values we want. Notice that we can assign the same value to both penny and cent. Notice also that we didn't have to state the values in any sort of order: the definition for quarter came before dime, even though quarter has the larger value.

Each name in the enumeration list is an **int** constant, with the value given. These constants can be used anywhere **int** constants are valid.

Since an enumerated value is a constant, we can use it as the size in an array declaration. For example, we could have

```
enum tag {
    SIZE = 20;
};
int arr[SIZE];
```

This is perfectly valid. This version of `SIZE` could be used in the same way as the `SIZE` manifest that we discussed in previous sections. In addition, using a `SIZE` enumerated constant isn't subject to most of the pitfalls of using a similar manifest. An enumerated constant is an ordinary constant expression; it isn't a *textual* entity like a manifest.

In the above example, the `tag` after **enum** is not useful or meaningful. It can be omitted, as in

```
enum { SIZE = 20; };
```

Enumerated constants are always **int** values. Therefore they can't be used as substitutes for floating point manifests like

```
#define PI_BY_2   (3.14159 / 2.0)
```

However, they are perfectly good substitutes for integer manifests, and superior in some ways.

Enumerated constants are relatively recent additions to the C language. The majority of C programs and C programmers still tend to use manifests for everything, which is why we introduced them first in this book. However, we believe that the use of enumerated constants can avoid some of the problems associated with manifests; new programmers may find them the best solutions to many problems.

6.6 Review

An *array* is a list of data objects that all have the same type. Array declarations have the form

type name[*number*];

where *number* is the number of members in the array. Named array types can be created with the **typedef** statement. Subscripts are used to refer to members of an array, as in

```
array[4]
```

Subscripts run from 0 to one less than the total number of members in the array.

Multidimensional arrays use more than one subscript to refer to an individual member, as in

```
multi_array[1][2][3]
```

Declarations for multidimensional arrays have a similar form.

Arrays may be initialized by specifying a list of initialization values enclosed in brace brackets. Multidimensional initializations use nested braces. Character arrays may be initialized with strings.

The **sizeof** operator calculates the number of bytes that make up an object or type. The result of **sizeof** has an unsigned integral type named size_t, which is declared in <stdlib.h> and several other standard headers.

The **#define** directive associates a string of text with a name; **#define** can create manifests and macros. A manifest is usually used like a constant. A macro is used in a form similar to a function call.

Enumerated constants can be used in place of manifests in many instances. Enumerated constants may be created with definitions of the form

> **enum** *tag* {
>   *name = value*,
>   *name = value*,
>   ...
> };

chapter 7   Pointers

A **pointer** is a piece of data that refers to another data object. To contrast pointers and normal variables, a variable is a *name* used in C source code to refer to a location in memory; a pointer is a *data object* that refers to a location in memory. Thus a pointer is a piece of data that can be used by the program during execution; a variable name is just a convenient identifier that is forgotten once the program is translated.

In most implementations, a pointer holds the "memory address" of an object. However, it is possible that a C pointer may not be exactly the same as a normal address on the machine you are using. (To speak technically for a moment, C must be able to refer to individual characters in the machine. On systems where standard addresses can only refer to machine words, C pointers must contain more information than just the word address.)

Every pointer points to a particular type of information. For example, a program may have pointers to **char**, pointers to **int**, pointers to **float**, and so on.

A **pointer variable** holds a pointer value. Pointer variables are created with declarations of the form

    type *name;

as in

```
char *cp;
```

The *type* indicates the type of value to which the pointer refers. The *name* is the name of the pointer variable. In our example, cp is a pointer variable whose value will point to a character.

It is possible that different types of pointers may have different sizes. For example, some implementations find it necessary for **char** pointers to be bigger than **int** pointers. Operations that mix different pointer types require a good deal of attention, so for the moment we will only look at operations where all the pointer values have the same type.

User-defined pointer types may be created with **typedef** statements. For example,

```
typedef char *STRING;
```

associates the name STRING with the **char** pointer type. The declaration

```
STRING cp;
```

is equivalent to

```
char *cp;
```

You can also create pointers to named types. For example,

```
typedef float MONEY;
MONEY *mp;
```

declares mp to be a pointer to a MONEY value.

7.1 Pointer Operators

There are two operators that are exclusively used in connection with pointers. The **address operator** is a single ampersand & (often pronounced "amper").

☞ The address operator creates a pointer value that points to a particular data object.

For example,

```
int i, *ip;
```

declares two variables: i can hold an integer; ip can hold a pointer to an integer.

```
ip = &i;
```

obtains a pointer to i and assigns this pointer value to ip.

The **indirection operator** is the asterisk * (pronounced "star").

☞ If P is a pointer, *P is the object to which P points.

For example, if the value of ip points to i,

```
*ip = 2;
```

has the same effect as

```
i = 2;
```

In general, if

```
P == &X
```

(the value of a pointer P is the address of object X)

```
*P == X
```

(the value P points to is the value of X).

Here are some more examples of the use of &, *, and pointers:

```
int i, j, *ip, *jp;
ip = &i;
jp = &j;
i = 2;
*jp = 3;
printf("%d %d\n",*ip,j);
```

This will print out 2 and 3—ip points to i, so *ip is the value of i; jp points to j, so assigning a value to *jp assigns the value to j. Now consider:

```
jp = ip;
printf("%d\n",*jp);
```

This will print out 2. Why?

```
jp = ip;
```

assigns the pointer value in ip to the pointer variable jp. This means that jp now points to i, so *jp is the value of i.

The indirection operator ' * ' must be applied to an object with a pointer type. The address operator ' & ' can only be used to obtain pointers to functions or to data objects that may be assigned values (for example, variables or array members). The indirection and address operators have the same precedence as the logical negation operator ' ! '.

7.1.1 Exercises

1. What does the following print out?

```
#include <stdio.h>
#include <stdlib.h>
int main(void)
{
    float *xp, x;
    xp = &x;
    *xp = 1;
    printf("%g\n",x);
    return EXIT_SUCCESS;
}
```

2. What does the following print out?

```
#include <stdio.h>
#include <stdlib.h>
#define SIZE 20
```

```
char str[SIZE] = "gobbledygook";
char *cp;

int main(void)
{
    int i = 0;
    cp = &str[3];
    *cp = 'X';
    while (str[i] != '\0')
        printf("%c",str[i++]);
    printf("\n");
    return EXIT_SUCCESS;
}
```

7.2 Using Pointers

In this section, we will discuss some general principles for using pointers.

7.2.1 Initializing Pointer Variables

The declaration of a pointer variable may include an initializer. The initialization value will usually be an expression using & to obtain the address of an object. For example,

```
double d, *dp = &d;
```

declares a **double** variable d and a pointer dp which is initialized to point at d.

The initialization value for a pointer variable may also be the name of an array. In this case, the variable will be initialized with a pointer to the first member in the array. For example,

```
short sa[30], *sp = sa;
```

initializes sp to point at sa[0].

This same operation may be expressed in an assignment operation. For example,

```
long la[10], *lp;
lp = la;
```

assigns lp a pointer to la[0].

7.2.2 Pointer Arithmetic

When a pointer points at an array member, C lets you add integer values to the pointer to point at different array members. For example, suppose we have

```
double d[40], *dp;
dp = &d[0];
```

If we now add 1 to dp, the pointer value in dp will be changed so that it points to the next member of d (d[1]). (From a technical standpoint, this may not be the same as adding 1 to the actual machine address of d[0]; C makes adjustments for the size and alignment of the array members.) This kind of addition works for any pointer into any array, provided that the type of the pointer is the same as the type of the array members. For example, here is a simple loop that writes out the contents of a string:

```
char *cp, ca[20] = "hello there!";
for (cp = &ca[0]; (*cp) != '\0'; cp += 1)
    printf("%c\n",*cp);
```

The **for** statement initializes cp to point to the first member of ca. It then loops, printing out a character and adding 1 to cp until cp points to a NUL ('\0') character. C uses a NUL to mark the end of the string, as we discussed in Section 6.3.2.

The ++ operator may be applied to pointer variables in order to increment their value. For example, the loop above could have been written

```
for (cp = &ca[0]; (*cp) != '\0'; cp++)
    printf("%c\n",*cp);
```

Just as adding positive integers to a pointer moves forwards through an array, subtracting positive integers moves backwards. For example, if cp points to ca[5], then cp-2 points to ca[3]. For example,

```
cp = &ca[5];
*(cp - 1) = 'X';
```

begins by pointing cp towards ca[5]. This means that cp-1 is a pointer value referring to ca[4]. Thus

```
*(cp - 1) = 'X';
```

has the same effect as

```
ca[4] = 'X';
```

The -- operator may be applied to pointer values. For example, the following code prints out the members of an array in reverse order:

```
int *ip, ia[10] = {
    0,1,2,3,4,5,6,7,8,9
};
for (ip = &ia[9] ; ; ip--) {
    printf("%d\n",*ip);
```

```
if (ip == &ia[0])
    break;
}
```

The above example used the comparison

```
ip == &ia[0]
```

to determine when to break out of the loop. This compares the pointer value in ip with a pointer to the beginning of the array. If the two are equal, the **break** statement is executed.

You might be wondering why we didn't just say

```
for (ip = &ia[9]; ip != &ia[0]; ip--)
    printf("%d\n",*ip);
```

This loop would not print out ia[0]; it stops first. If you tried to fix this by writing

```
for (ip = &ia[9]; ip >= &ia[0]; ip--)
    printf("%d\n",*ip);
```

you run into another problem. This loop doesn't stop until ip is less than &ia[0], which means it points to a memory location before the beginning of ia. ANSI C won't let you do this: ip points into the ia array, and it's an error to aim the pointer at some location before the beginning of the array. (For technical reasons, **ANSI** C does let you aim a pointer at the location immediately after the last member in an array. There are situations in which this ability is useful.)

Any two pointers of the same type may be compared for equality or inequality. This determines whether they point to the same location in memory. If two pointers point into the same array, you can also use the relational operators

```
>    >=    <    <=
```

☞ One pointer p1 is less than another pointer p2 if the array member that p1 points to comes before the member that p2 points to.

For example, in

```
long lp[30], *lp1, *lp2;
lp1 = &lp[4];
lp2 = &lp[10];
```

lp1 will be less than lp2.

If two pointers of the same type point into the same array, one pointer can be subtracted from the other. The result will be the difference between the subscripts of the array members to which the pointers point. In the above example,

```
lp2 - lp1 == 6
```

since lp2 points to la[10] and lp1 points to la[4].

☞ Subtraction of pointers and greater than/less than comparisons are only meaningful operations when the pointers point into the same array. Comparing for equality or inequality is always meaningful, provided the two pointers have the same type.

Operations involving pointers of different types will be discussed in Section 9.

7.2.3 Exercises

1. What does the following program print out?

```
#include <stdio.h>
#include <stdlib.h>
#define SIZE 10

int ia[SIZE] = {
    0,1,2,3,4,5,6,7,8,9
};

int main(void)
{
    int i, *ip = &i;
    for (*ip = 0; i < SIZE; i++ )
        printf("%d\n",ia[*ip]);
    for (ip = &ia[SIZE-1]; ip > &ia[1]; ip -= 2)
        *ip *= 2;
    for (ip = &ia[0]; ip < &ia[SIZE-1]; ip++)
        printf("%d\n",*ip);
    return EXIT_SUCCESS;
}
```

2. What does the following print out?

```
#include <stdio.h>
#include <stdlib.h>
#define SIZE 10

typedef long NUMBERS;
NUMBERS list[SIZE];

int main(void)
{
    NUMBERS *np;
    int i;
```

```
              for (i = 0; i < SIZE; i++)
                  list[i] = i * ( (NUMBERS)i / 3 );
              for (np = &list[0]; np <= &list[SIZE-1]; np++)
                  printf("%d\n", (int) *np);
              return EXIT_SUCCESS;
          }
```

3. What does the program in the last question print out if we change the **typedef** statement to

```
       typedef float NUMBERS;
```

4. What does the following program print out?

```
       #include <stdio.h>
       #include <stdlib.h>

       char str[] = "abcdefg";

       int main(void)
       {
           char *cp1 = &str[0], *cp2 = cp1;
           while ( *cp2 != '\0')
               cp2++;
           for (--cp2 ; cp2 != cp1; cp2--)
               printf("%c%c",*cp2,*(cp2-1));
           printf("\n");
           return EXIT_SUCCESS;
       }
```

5. A program has defined the two file scope arrays

```
       char strl[] = "abcdefghijklmnopqrstuvwxyz";
       char stru[26];
```

Write a function that uses **char** pointers to copy the contents of strl into stru, converting characters into uppercase as it goes.

7.3 Passing Pointers as Function Arguments _____

Pointer values can be passed as arguments to functions. For example,

```
       void printit(int *ip)
       {
           printf("%d\n",*ip);
```

```
        return;
    }
```

receives one argument which is a pointer to an integer. The function prints the integer pointed to, then returns.

If a function is passed a pointer to a value, the function can use the pointer to change that value. For example,

```
char upperp(char *cp)
{
    *cp = *cp - 'a' + 'A';
    return *cp;
}
```

uses the passed pointer to change whatever the pointer points to. For example,

```
char ch = 'm';
upperp(&ch);
printf("%c\n",ch);
```

will print out an uppercase M; upperp has used the pointer to ch to change ch's value.

This is perhaps the most important reason for using pointers. A C function always works with a *copy* of the arguments that are passed. If a function call gives a variable as an argument, the called function only gets a copy of the variable's value so it cannot affect the variable. However, if a function call contains a *pointer* to a variable as an argument, the called function receives a copy of the pointer. This pointer can then be used to refer to the original variable, and possibly change its value. When the function returns, the variable will have its changed value.

Pointers allow a called function to affect the caller. For example, here is a function that switches the values of two integer variables:

```
void switcher(int *a, int *b)
{
    int temp;
    temp = *a;
    *a = *b;
    *b = temp;
}
```

The switcher function saves the value of the integer that a points to, assigns the value pointed to by b to the memory location indicated by a, then assigns the saved value to the memory location indicated by b. We could call this function with

```
int x = 2, y = 3;
switcher(&x,&y);
```

and at the end, x would have the value of y and vice versa. If we had written the function as

```
void fakeswitch(int a,int b)
{
    int temp;
    temp = a;
    a = b;
    b = temp;
}
```

we would not get the same result. The `fakeswitch` function switches its copies of the arguments, but this has no effect on values in the caller; the function is only working with copies.

In an external prototype declaration for a function that takes a pointer parameter, the name of the parameter can be omitted. For example, we could say

```
extern void switch(int *,int *);
```

to show that `switch` takes two integer pointers and does not return a value. (Parameter names may also be omitted for other types of parameters.)

7.3.1 More about Scanf

By now, you may have realized that `scanf` is a function that is passed pointer arguments. The function call

```
scanf("%d",&i);
```

passes `scanf` a pointer to the variable `i`; `scanf` can use this pointer to assign an input value to `i`. Now that we understand what sort of values are being passed to `scanf`, it makes sense to discuss the function in more detail.

The placeholders in a `scanf` format string represent values that should be read and assigned to the data objects indicated by corresponding pointer arguments. If the format string contains other characters besides placeholders, `scanf` checks to see if these characters are present in the input. For example, in

```
scanf("A = %g\n",&x);
```

`scanf` will check to see if the input contains "A = " followed by a floating point number, followed by a new-line. If the input that is read does not match what the format string says, `scanf` will stop reading as soon as it finds something that is out of place. For example, if your program contains

```
char name;
int value;
int Number_in;
Number_in = scanf("%c = %d",&name,&value);
```

and the corresponding input is

```
X + 5
```

the `'X'` will be read and stored in the variable name. However, `scanf` finds a `'+'` where it expects a `'='`, so it stops reading at that point. The next time `scanf` (or `getchar`) is asked to read, it will begin with the `'+'` character.

In the above example, `Number_in` is assigned 1 because only one input value is read successfully. If both input values were read successfully, `scanf` would return 2.

If `scanf` reaches end-of-file before it can read and assign any values, it returns EOF. The EOF integer is negative, so it can be distinguished from other possible return values.

EOF is also returned by `scanf` if an error occurs while reading data. Read errors occur for a variety of reasons, often because of hardware problems. For example, you may get a read error if you try to read a floppy disk that has been damaged in some way.

A space character in a `scanf` format string stands for any number of space characters, tabs, and new-lines in the input. Thus if you write

```
scanf("%d %d",&a,&b);
```

the input values for a and b may be separated by any number of spaces and/or tabs, and can even be on different input lines.

For `%d`, `%e`, `%g`, `%o`, and `%x` placeholders, `scanf` will skip over any leading blanks, tabs, or new-lines and look for a digit or sign. If it finds some other character, it will stop reading. The next call to `scanf` will begin reading at the character that stopped the previous call. For example, if `scanf` stops looking for a number because it finds the character `'A'`, the next call to `scanf` will begin reading at the `'A'`.

If `scanf` finds a digit or a sign, it starts to gather a number from the input. It keeps on reading characters until it comes to a character that cannot be part of the sort of number it is reading. As an example, suppose the input is

```
18.93
```

If the corresponding placeholder is `%g`, `scanf` will read the entire number `18.93`. If the corresponding placeholder is `%d`, `scanf` will stop at the period and just get the integer `18` (the next call to `scanf` will begin reading at the period). If the corresponding placeholder is `%o`, `scanf` will stop at the `'8'`, because this digit cannot be part of an octal number. In this case, `scanf` obtains the value `1`, and the next call to `scanf` will begin at the `'8'`.

A width value may be specified after the `%` of a placeholder to indicate a specific number of characters to be read. For example, suppose the input is

```
12345
```

and your program makes the call

```
scanf("%3d%2d",&i,&j);
```

This will assign the integer 123 to i and 45 to j. When a width is specified, scanf does not skip over leading blanks in search of the number.

Table 7.1 summarizes possible placeholders in scanf format strings, the type of pointer that should correspond to the placeholder, and the type of value read.

Table 7.1
Placeholders for scanf

%c	char *	single character
%d	int *	decimal integer
%e	float *	floating point
%f	float *	floating point
%g	float *	floating point
%i	int *	integer (decimal, octal, hex)
%o	int *	octal integer
%s	char *	char array (see below)
%u	unsigned int *	unsigned integer
%x	int *	hexadecimal integer
%hd	short *	decimal integer
%hi	short *	integer (any format)
%ho	short *	octal integer
%hu	unsigned short *	unsigned integer
%hx	short *	hexadecimal integer
%ld	long *	decimal integer
%le	double *	floating point
%lf	double *	floating point
%lg	double *	floating point
%li	long *	integer (any format)
%lo	long *	octal integer
%lu	unsigned long *	unsigned integer
%lx	long *	hexadecimal integer
%Le	long double *	floating point
%Lf	long double *	floating point
%Lg	long double *	floating point

The %s placeholder is associated with a **char** pointer that points to a member in a **char** array. scanf will place input characters into the array until a whitespace character is read. In place of the whitespace character, scanf will put a '\0' into the array. For example,

```
char *cp, line[80];
cp = &line[0];
scanf("%s",cp);
```

reads characters into the `line` character array. (The `cp` variable is a pointer value that points to the beginning of the array.) If the input line is

```
abc
```

you will have

```
line[0] == 'a'
line[1] == 'b'
line[2] == 'c'
line[3] == '\0'
```

We could also have said

```
cp = &line[25];
scanf("%s",cp);
```

This reads a string into `line` beginning at member 25. There is no reason why `cp` has to point to the beginning of the array.

Note: `printf` accepts a `%s` placeholder too. The argument corresponding to the placeholder should be a **char** pointer that points into an array; `printf` will write out characters from the array until it finds a `'\0'`. With our above example,

```
printf("%s\n",cp);
```

would print out

```
abc
```

and start a new line.

7.3.2 Exercises

1. What does the following program print out?

```
#include <stdio.h>
#include <stdlib.h>
#define SIZE 15
extern void initit(int *,int);

int main(void)
{
    int i, x[SIZE];
    initit(&x[0],SIZE);
    for (i = 0; i < SIZE; i++)
        printf("%d ",x[i]);
```

```
        printf("\n");
        return EXIT_SUCCESS;
    }

    void initit(int *array,int length)
    {
        for ( ; length > 0; length--) {
            *array = length;
            array++;
        }
    }
```

2. Write a function with the prototype

    ```
    void initarr(float *array,int length,float value)
    ```

   where `array` is assumed to point to the first member of a **float** array, `length` is the number of members in the array, and `value` is a value that the function will assign to every member of the array.

3. Using `scanf`, read in a line of input, then write out the line with each input word on a separate line.

4. Using `scanf`, read in a line of input, then write it out with all the letters in uppercase.

7.4 Pointers and Arrays

In several of our examples, we have seen functions that receive a pointer to the first member of an array, then use this pointer to work with all the members of the array. This is the usual method for passing an array as a function argument: pass a pointer to the first member of the array, and let the function use this pointer to access other members of the array.

One problem with using pointers to refer to array members is that the code becomes less readable. When you see

    ```
    a[10]
    ```

it is clear that you are referring to a member in an array. When you see

    ```
    *p   or   *(p + 5)
    ```

it's less clear. To make things easier, C lets you use subscripts with pointers:

    ```
    p[5]
    ```

is precisely equivalent to

```
*(p + 5)
```

but it is much easier to understand. As an example of how this can be used, here is the initarr function from the last set of exercises, written to use subscripts with the pointers.

```
void initarr(float *array,int length,float value)
{
    while (--length >= 0)
        array[length] = value;
}
```

We had to decrement length before using it as a subscript because the length of a vector is one more than the maximum subscript.

Notice that the above version of initarr runs *backwards* through the array. This is a typical C "idiom", a programming trick that is often used in C but cannot be used in some other languages. A more conventional way of writing the function might be

```
void initarr(float *array,int length,float value)
{
    int i;
    for (i=0; i < length; i++)
        array[i] = value;
}
```

This runs through the array in a forward direction.

Since a pointer can be used as an array name, C also lets you use an array name as a pointer.

☞ If the name of an array is used without a subscript, it represents a pointer to the first member of the array. The type of this pointer is a pointer to the type of the members in the array.

We have already noted that if we declare

```
short sa[30], *sp;
```

then the following statements are equivalent

```
sp = &sa[0];
sp = sa;
```

In the same way, we can use the name of the array in function calls when the function expects a pointer.

```
float f[30];
initarr(f,30,1.0);
```

uses the initarr function to set all the members of f to 1.0.

A function that receives a pointer to an array as an argument can declare this argument to be a pointer, as in

```
char f(char *s)
```

or as an array name, as in

```
char f(char s[])
```

There is no difference between the two. In both of our above examples, s can be used as a pointer or it can be subscripted like an array name. Notice that no size was specified inside the brace brackets for the array parameter. The size is irrelevant, because the value that is really passed is a pointer.

You should be certain you understand the difference between passing an array *member*, as in

```
f1(a[3])
```

and the array itself, as in

```
f2(a)
```

When you pass an array member, the function receives a copy of the value that is stored in the member. When the function call contains the name of the array itself, the called function receives a pointer to the first member in the array.

You might think that the entire array has been passed to the called function, but this is still not true. For example, the called function has no way to determine how big the array is; all it has is a pointer to the first member.

In an external prototype declaration that contains an array parameter, the name of the parameter may be omitted, as in

```
extern double f(double []);
```

This says that f takes a pointer to a **double** array and returns a **double** result. We would recommend, however, that you use the prototype

```
extern double f(double *);
```

to emphasize that the function receives a pointer as an argument.

Box 7.1: Arrays, Pointers, and sizeof

In the last chapter, we showed how the expression

```
sizeof arr
```

calculated the number of bytes in the array arr. The **sizeof** operator can be applied to pointer objects and types, to calculate the size of the pointer. It is important to be careful about how this is used. For example, suppose that the copystr function with the prototype

```
void copystr(char *destination,char *source)
```

applies the **sizeof** operator to the source argument.

```
sizeof source
```

calculates the size of the source pointer. Now, we have noted that the above prototype could also be written

```
void copystr(char destination[],char source[]);
```

If we wrote the prototype like this, you might think that

```
sizeof source
```

calculates the size of the array associated with source. **It doesn't.** The prototype may make source look like an array, but it is passed as a pointer and **sizeof** will only calculate the size of the pointer. This is why we have suggested that all array arguments be written as pointers in function prototypes; it emphasizes that C is only passing a pointer, not the whole array.

7.4.1 String Assignments

A **string literal** is a sequence of characters enclosed in double quotes. We have used these a number of times already—as format strings for printf and scanf, and as initialization values for **char** arrays.

String literals can also be used in assignments to **char** pointers. For example, you might say

```
char *cp;
cp = "Hello there!";
```

To carry out this kind of assignment, C first creates a character array containing the characters in the string literal: 'H', 'e', 'l', and so on. This array will have a NUL

('\0') after the last character to mark the end of the string. Once this array has been created, C creates a pointer to the first character of the array and assigns this pointer value to cp. A program should not attempt to change the characters inside a string literal.

As we have seen with printf and scanf, string literals can also be passed as arguments in function calls. The process is the same as the one used in assignments. A character array is created containing the appropriate string, then the function is passed a pointer to that array. For example,

```
void copystr(char *destination,char *source)
{
    while (*source != '\0') {
        *destination = *source;
        source++;
        destination++;
    }
    *destination = '\0';
}
```

is a function that copies one character array (indicated by source) into a second character array (indicated by destination). If we call

```
char *carr[40];
copystr("Good morning",carr);
```

the contents of the string literal will be copied into carr. You could not change the characters in the string literal, but you can change the contents of carr. This is another way to use the contents of a string literal to initialize a character array.

While we're discussing the copystr function, we might as well point out a more compact way to write it:

```
void copystr(char *destination,char *source)
{
    while (*destination++ = *source++)
        /* nothing */ ;
}
```

does the entire job. This loop copies one character from source to destination until the value of the assignment is zero (the NUL byte). The **while** loop doesn't even need a body.

Anywhere we have used a string literal in the preceding chapters, we could also use a pointer to a character array. For example,

```
char fs[30] = "%d\n";
printf(fs,10);
```

uses the contents of the fs array as a format string for printf. The only requirement is that the character array must contain a NUL character to mark the end of the string.

7.4.2 Exercises

1. Write a function that has the prototype

```
int findint(long *a,int length,long value)
```

The a argument is an array whose size is given by length. The function will look through a in search of a member that has the given value. If it finds the value, it returns the subscript of the member that has that value. If it has not found the value by the time it reaches the end of a, it will return -1.

2. Write a function with the prototype

```
void copyN(char *destination,char *source,int N)
```

The function copies the first N characters from the source array into destination. If you find a terminating NUL in source before you have copied N characters, fill out the destination array with blanks. Put a terminating '\0' on the end of destination.

3. What does the following print out?

```
#include <stdio.h>
#include <stdlib.h>

char sample[30] = "%s\nhello";

int main(void)
{
    printf(sample,sample);
    return EXIT_SUCCESS;
}
```

4. Write a function with the prototype

```
void strip(char *string)
```

that strips all the blank characters from the end of the string array. It does this by putting a NUL character after the last nonblank character in the array. The string stored in the array is presumed to end in a NUL character already, but there may be a number of blanks before the NUL.

5. Write a function with the prototype

```
int compare(char *s1,char *s2);
```

that compares two strings for equality. The function should return a zero if the two strings are the same. If the strings are different, the return value should depend on the comparison of the first character position where the two differ. If the character in s1 is greater than the character in s2, the function should return +1. Otherwise, it should return -1.

6. CONCORDANCE QUESTION: Write a program that reads in up to 100 words (maximum length 20 characters) and stores them in an array declared with

```
char words[100][20];
```

Convert all the characters to lowercase and print the words out in reverse order. The program should also print out the length of the longest word and the total number of words read.

7. CONCORDANCE QUESTION: Modify the program you wrote in the previous exercise so that it reads up to 100 words, then eliminates all the duplicates. (For example, if the word "the" appears several times in the original input, the first occurrence would be left in the words array and all subsequent occurrences would be written over with blanks.) After duplicates have been eliminated, the program prints out the remaining words.

8. CONCORDANCE QUESTION: Modify the program you wrote in the previous exercise so that it prints out the number of times each word appeared in the input text. For example, if the input is

```
The dog bit the boy, and the boy cried.
```

the output might be

```
the:    3 occurrences
dog:    1 occurrence
bit:    1 occurrence
boy:    2 occurrences
and:    1 occurrence
cried:  1 occurrence
```

9. CONCORDANCE QUESTION: Modify the program you wrote in the previous exercise so that it prints out the words in alphabetical order.

7.5 Returning Pointer Values

Functions cannot return values that are arrays. However, they can return pointer values that point into arrays. For example, here is a function that reads through a **char** array in search of a specified character and returns a pointer to the character:

```
char *csearch(char *str,char c)
{
    while ( (*str != '\0') && (*str != c) )
        str++;
    return str;
}
```

Notice that the prototype for the function indicates that the function returns a character pointer by putting **char *** in front of the function name. The **while** loop moves through the characters in the array until the function finds the required character or a NUL character marking the end of the string. The function returns a pointer to the first occurrence of the desired character or to the terminating '\0'.

7.5.1 Null Pointers

If the csearch function above cannot find the desired character, it returns a pointer to the NUL on the end of the characters in the array. We can do this when we are searching through character arrays because of the convention that puts a NUL on the end of every character string. However, suppose we want to search through an **int** array for a particular value. Our function might have the prototype

```
int *isearch(int *iarr,int length,int value)
```

The array indicated by iarr has the given length. The function is supposed to return a pointer to the first member that has the given value.

If no member of the array has the given value, how do we indicate the situation? An **int** array doesn't end with a NUL, so things aren't as easy as they are with character arrays. It wouldn't make sense to return a pointer to an array member that doesn't have the right value; nor would it make sense to return a pointer to some arbitrary location outside the array. For this reason, C lets you create a special kind of pointer value called a **null pointer**.

☞ A null pointer is a valid pointer value that does not point at anything.

This is not the same as an uninitialized pointer. An uninitialized pointer is one that has not been assigned a particular value, so it could contain anything, including a valid pointer to a location in memory. A null pointer is guaranteed *not* to point to a usable memory location.

Every null pointer has a type. For example, you may create a null **int** pointer or a null **char** pointer. Null pointers of different types need not be numerically equal. Since different types of pointers may even have different sizes, you should not assume that different types of null pointers are related in any way.

You create a null pointer by assigning 0 to a pointer variable.

```
char *cp;
cp = 0;
```

stores a null pointer value in cp. (From a technical point of view, a null pointer value need not be a memory address that is equal to zero; using 0 in this way is just a convention.) We could use this to write the isearch function described above.

```
int *isearch(int *iarr,int length,int value)
{
    int i, *result;
    result = 0; /* null pointer */
    for (i = 0; i <= length; i++) {
        if (iarr[i] == value) {
            result = &iarr[i];
            break;
        }
    }
    return result;
}
```

The function begins by setting result to a null pointer value. If a matching value is found in the array, result is changed to point to the appropriate array member. If a match is not found, result will still be a null pointer when its value is returned.

The following main routine shows how isearch can be used:

```
#include <stdio.h>
#include <stdlib.h>

#define SIZE 100
int a[SIZE];

extern int *isearch(int *,int,int);

int main(void)
{
    int i, n, *ip, value;
    scanf("%d",&value);
    for (i = 0; i < SIZE; i++) {
        n = scanf("%d",&a[i]);
        if (n != 1)
            break;
        /* stop if EOF or non-numeric */
    }
    ip = isearch(a,SIZE,value);
    if (ip == 0) /*null pointer*/
        printf("Value not found\n");
    else
        printf("Value found\n");
    return EXIT_SUCCESS;
}
```

This reads a value that you want to find, then a list of other numbers. Up to 100 numbers can be read; the loop reading the numbers stops as soon as scanf fails to find a number (either because the input contains a character that cannot belong to an integer or because end-of-file has been reached). The isearch function is then called to find the given value. The program prints the message Value not found if isearch returns a null pointer.

7.5.2 The NULL Symbol

When you are reading a program and see the statement

```
x = 0;
```

you must look at the declaration for x before you can tell if this is a normal numeric assignment or if x is a pointer being assigned a null pointer value. To make null pointers more obvious, a standard header named <stddef.h> defines a symbol named NULL.

NULL is a "generic" null pointer. It stands out more clearly in your code, and it doesn't have to be cast into the right type in most cases. For example, we could rewrite isearch as

```
int *isearch(int *iarr,int length,int value)
{
    int i, *result;
    result = NULL;
    for (i = 0; i <= length; i++) {
        if (iarr[i] == value) {
            result = &iarr[i];
            break;
        }
    }
    return result;
}
```

When you want to refer to a null pointer, use NULL instead of zero—it makes code easier to read. Since NULL is defined in the standard header <stddef.h>, you should have

```
#include <stddef.h>
```

in any source code that uses NULL.

7.5.3 Exercises

1. Write a function with the prototype

```
char *concat(char *str1,char *str2,char *str3)
```

The function should add the contents of the character arrays `str2` and `str3` to the end of `str1`. For example,

```
char a[20] = "abc",
     b[20] = "def",
     c[20] = "ghi";
concat(a,b,c);
```

should assign a the string `"abcdefghi"`. The function should be able to cope with either `str2` or `str3` being a null pointer. The result of `concat` should be a pointer to the `'\0'` that marks the end of the concatenated string contained in `str1`.

2. The **binary search method** locates a desired value in a *sorted* array by following these instructions:

(a)   Look at the middle member of the array.

(b)   If the desired value is equal to this member's value, return a pointer to the member.

(c)   If the desired value is greater than the member's value, restrict your attention to the last half of the array.

(d)   If the desired value is less than the member's value, restrict your attention to the first half of the array.

(e)   Look at the middle member of the remaining part of the array.

(f)   Repeat steps (b) to (e) until a match is found or you are reduced to a single member whose value does not match. Return a null pointer if there is no matching member.

The binary search method only works when the values in an array are sorted in increasing order. With a large sorted array, a binary search is much faster than a search that starts at the beginning of the array and searches linearly. Write a function with the prototype

```
long *bin(long *la,int length,long value)
```

that uses the binary search method to search for `value` in the array `la` with the given `length`.

7.6 Void * Pointers

Programmers have found a number of situations where it is useful to have "generic" pointers—pointers that are not associated with any particular type of data. In C, such pointers are declared to be **void ***, as in

```
void *generic_ptr;
```

This is just a notational convention, saying that the pointer does not point to a specific type of data; it does not mean that the pointer points to a **void** object (a concept more suited to Zen than C).

A **void *** pointer is compatible with any other pointer type. Any type of pointer value may be assigned to a **void *** pointer, as in

```
int *ip;
void *generic;
    . . .
generic = ip;
```

Similarly, a **void *** pointer value may be assigned to any other pointer type. However, you have to remember where the **void *** pointer value originated. Consider:

```
char *cp;
int *ip;
void *generic;
    . . .
generic = cp;
ip = generic;
```

A **char** pointer value is assigned to the **void *** generic, and then this value is assigned to the integer pointer ip. The problem is that the original **char** pointer may not have been properly *aligned* to serve as an **int** pointer. An **int** pointer must point to the beginning of a machine word, while a **char** pointer can point to any byte inside a word. If cp points to a character in the middle of a machine word, the value that is eventually assigned to ip also points to the middle of the word. As a result, ip ends up pointing to a memory location that is not properly *aligned* for integer values. Errors will likely arise because of this.

The moral is that your programs should be careful when assigning a **void *** pointer to a typed pointer. The *alignment* of the **void *** should be suitable for the type of data indicated by the typed pointer. Alignment is an implementation-dependent concept that we will not discuss further.

7.6.1 Void * Arithmetic

C will not let you perform pointer arithmetic with **void *** values. This makes sense if you think about it. For example,

```
int *ip;
  ...
ip++;
```

Incrementing `ip` makes it point towards the next integer. C knows how to adjust the address in `ip` because C knows how big an integer is. However, a **void *** pointer doesn't point to any particular type of object. If you try to add 1 to a **void ***, there is no obvious way to make the pointer point to the "next" object. Void pointer subtraction is invalid for the same reason.

Note that you can convert a **void *** value to a typed pointer, perform some arithmetic operation, then convert back, as in

```
char *cp;
void *generic;
  ...
cp = generic;
generic = cp+1;
```

After this operation, the `generic` pointer will point to the next character in memory. Similarly, with

```
int *ip;
void *generic;
  ...
ip = generic;
generic = ip+1;
```

`generic` will point to the next integer in memory.

7.6.2 Arguments and Return Values

Functions can accept **void *** values as arguments and can return them as results. For example, the library function `memcpy` can be declared with the prototype

```
void *memcpy(void *dest,const void *src,size_t N);
```

The `memcpy` function copies N bytes of data from the location indicated by the pointer `src` to the location indicated by the pointer `dest`. The value returned by `memcpy` is a pointer equal to `dest`. (The keyword **const** will be discussed in Section 8.3.1.)

If a pointer argument corresponds to a **void *** parameter in a function prototype, the argument value is automatically converted to **void *** in the function call. For example, in

```
int list1[SIZE], list2[SIZE], *ip;
       ...
ip = memcpy(list2, list1, sizeof(list1));
```

the contents of list1 are copied into list2. The number of bytes in list1 is obtained using **sizeof**. A **void *** pointer to list2 is returned and assigned to ip.

We could also write

```
ip = memcpy(list2, list1, SIZE*sizeof(int));
```

In this call, we calculated the number of bytes to copy by multiplying the number of bytes in a single integer by the total number of array members.

Since memcpy accepts generic **void *** pointers, we can use it to copy many different types of arrays.

```
float fa1[SIZEF], fa2[SIZEF], *fp;
double da1[SIZED], da2[SIZED], *dp;
char ca1[SIZEC], ca2[SIZEC], *cp;
        . . .
fp = memcpy(fa1, fa2, SIZEF*sizeof(float));
dp = memcpy(da1, da2, SIZED*sizeof(double));
cp = memcpy(ca1, ca2, SIZEC);
```

Generic pointers make it possible to have generic functions like memcpy. (Note: if you use memcpy in a program, you should specify

```
#include <string.h>
```

to obtain the prototype declaration for memcpy.)

7.6.3 Exercises

1. Write your own version of the memcpy function (call it mycopy or something similar).

7.7 *Review*

A *pointer* refers to the memory location of a data object or function. A pointer declaration has the following form:

    type *name;

A **typedef** statement may be used to create named pointer types.

The expression *P refers to the memory location that P points to. The value of &A is a pointer value pointing to A. It can be used to initialize pointer variables.

When a pointer of the appropriate type points to an array member, adding 1 will point to the next array member and subtracting 1 will point to the previous member.

Pointers can be passed as arguments to functions. The functions can then use these pointer values to change the objects that the pointers point to. In particular, pointers are passed to the `scanf` library function so that data may be read into data objects.

When an array is passed as an argument to a function, C actually passes a pointer to the first member of the array. Through this pointer, the function may change the value of any member in the array.

A *null pointer* is a pointer that purposely does not point anywhere. Null pointers can be represented by the integer 0, but the preferred method is to use the symbol NULL defined in `<stddef.h>`.

A pointer with the **void *** type is a generic pointer that may point to any type of data. You may not perform arithmetic with **void *** pointers.

chapter 8   Library Functions

Because we have been concentrating on the C language itself, we have said little about the library of functions that come with every implementation of C. This may have given you the impression that library functions are not used very often; however, nothing could be further from the truth.

☞   The C library is used *extensively* in almost every C program.

There are programs that call library functions on almost every line of code. As a result, learning about the standard library is an important part of learning C.

Each of the major sections in this chapter describes a set of related functions: functions for mathematical operations, memory allocation, string manipulation, and input/output. In addition, each section begins with a discussion of an important concept related to library function use.

Note that this chapter covers a fraction of the functions that are available in the **ANSI** standard C library; and since implementations almost always provide specialized library functions in addition to the standard ones, this chapter should only be regarded as a "taste" of what C really has to offer.

8.1 Mathematical Functions _____

The C library supports a number of basic mathematical functions. The majority of these take **double** arguments and return **double** values. Below, we list prototypes for the functions and explain what each does:

```
double sqrt(double x);
```
    returns the square root of x.

```
double sin(double x);
double cos(double x);
double tan(double x);
```
    return the sine, cosine, and tangent of x. The argument x is assumed to be given in radians.

```
double asin(double x);
double acos(double x);
double atan(double x);
```
return the arcsine, arccosine, and arctangent of x. For asin and acos, the value of x must be in the range −1.0 through 1.0. The result of asin and atan is in the range -π/2 through π/2. The result of acos is in the range 0.0 through π.

```
double atan2(double y,double x);
```
returns the value of the arctangent of y/x, using the sign of both arguments to determine the quadrant of the return value; x and y cannot both be zero.

```
double sinh(double x);
double cosh(double x);
double tanh(double x);
```
return the hyperbolic sine, cosine, and tangent of x.

```
double exp(double x);
```
returns the value of e (2.71828...) to the power of x.

```
double log(double x);
```
returns the natural logarithm of x.

```
double log10(double x);
```
returns the base 10 logarithm of x.

```
double pow(double x,double y);
```
returns x raised to the power y.

```
double fabs(double x);
```
returns the absolute value of x.

```
double ceil(double x);
```
returns the **double** representation of the smallest integer not less than x. For example,

```
        ceil(4.5)   == 5.0
        ceil(4.0)   == 4.0
        ceil(-4.5)  == -4.0
```

```
double floor(double x);
```
returns the **double** representation of the largest integer not greater than x. For example,

```
        floor(4.5)   == 4.0
        floor(4.0)   == 4.0
        floor(-4.5)  == -5.0
```

Box 8.1: Round-Off Error

Suppose we wrote a loop with

```
for (x = 0.0; x != 3.141592; x += 0.3141592)
```

so that the loop stops when x *equals* π. Floating point arithmetic on any computer is subject to a small amount of **round-off error**. Although it *looks* as if we could add 0.3141592 ten times to get 3.141592 exactly, a tiny error would likely creep in. The result is that x would *never* equal 3.141592 exactly (though it would be close) and the **for** statement would never stop looping.

Because of round-off error, you should think twice about comparing floating point values for equality or inequality. It is often better to use operations like < or > because these are much less affected by round-off error. You can also compare two values to see if they are very close, as in

```
if ( fabs(x-y) < 1.0E-6 )
    printf("x and y are very close\n");
```

The only time you can safely test for equality is if there is some statement that directly assigns an appropriate value to the data object being tested, as in

```
x = 0.0;
    ...
if (x == 0.0) ...
```

In order to use any of the mathematical functions, you should put

```
#include <math.h>
```

in your program before the functions are called; <math.h> includes prototypes for all the functions listed above, so you do not need to declare the prototypes explicitly.

Here is a simple program that uses some of these functions.

```
#include <stdio.h>
#include <stdlib.h>
#include <math.h>

double pi = 3.141592;

int main(void)
{
    double incr = pi / 10.0;
    double x;
```

```
        for (x = 0.0; x <= pi; x += incr) {
            printf("%9.6f %9.6f %9.6f\n",x,sin(x),cos(x));
        }
        return EXIT_SUCCESS;
    }
```

This prints out a table of sines and cosines for a number of angles from 0 to π radians (180°).

8.1.1 Error Reporting

The mathematical functions described in the previous section do not necessarily work for all possible argument values. For example, it is an error to pass sqrt a negative value, because negative numbers do not have real square roots. This means that the sqrt function must have some way to report when it has been passed a negative number.

C library functions report errors in two different ways. First, the value that they return may indicate that an error has occurred. Second, the function may assign a special **int** value to a symbol called errno.

The errno symbol behaves like an **int** variable defined by the C library. You do not have to declare errno; that is done by including the header <errno.h>.

When your program begins execution, errno will have the value 0. If, however, a function like sqrt encounters an error, it will assign errno a value that indicates what the error was.

All values for errno have names defined in <errno.h>. Implementations may have many different values for errno, but the ANSI standard only requires two: EDOM and ERANGE.

☞   A library function assigns EDOM to errno to indicate an invalid argument value. This is called a **domain error**.

For example, sqrt assigns EDOM to errno if the argument to sqrt is negative.

☞   A library function assigns ERANGE to errno when the result of a function cannot be calculated. This is called a **range error**.

For example, exp assigns ERANGE to errno if the result of the exponential operation would be too big to represent as a **double** value.

After any mathematical operation, you can test the value of errno to see whether an error resulted. For example, the following program reads in a series of numbers and prints out their square roots. If any of the input numbers are negative, it prints an error message.

```
        #include <errno.h>
        #include <math.h>
        #include <stdio.h>
        #include <stdlib.h>
```

```
int main(void)
{
    double x, y;
    int n;
    n = scanf("%g",&x);
    while ( n == 1 ) {
        errno = 0;
        y = sqrt(x);
        if (errno == EDOM)
            printf("ERROR: Negative number\n");
        else
            printf("Square root is %g\n",y);
        n = scanf("%g",&x);
    }
    return EXIT_SUCCESS;
}
```

This program keeps looping until it finds end-of-file or an input character that cannot be part of a floating point number.

We set `errno` to zero before the call to `sqrt`. If `errno` is equal to EDOM after the call, we know that the argument `x` was invalid. Thus we print out the error message. (Of course, in this simple program, we could have tested `x` before the call to `sqrt`. This example just shows how `errno` is used.)

Our program has to set `errno` to zero explicitly. If we don't set `errno` to zero before the call to `sqrt`, we do not know if the call to `sqrt` or if some other function set `errno` (for example, the call to `scanf`). Library functions *never* set `errno` to zero to indicate success; they only use `errno` to report errors. It is up to your program to set `errno` to zero when you want to use it.

Part IV of this book indicates which functions set `errno` to an error value and the conditions under which this happens; `errno` is used by many functions that want to indicate error conditions, not just the mathematical functions.

8.1.2 Exercises

1. Write a program that prints the squares and square roots of the integers from 1 to 20.

2. How does the following differ from `sqrt`?

```
#include <math.h>
double sqroot(double x)
{
    return sqrt(fabs(x)) ;
}
```

3. What is the relationship between

```
floor(x)
ceil(floor(x))
```

4. Write a program that reads pairs of numbers into variables x and y, then prints out x to the power y. If the result is too large to be represented as a **double** value, print out the error message Result too large. Stop looping when you reach end-of-file or do not successfully read a pair of numbers.

5. Trigonometry says that the square of the sine of an angle plus the square of the cosine should equal 1. To see how round-off error works, run the following program:

```
#include <math.h>
#include <stdio.h>
#include <stdlib.h>

int main(void)
{
    double x;
    double s, c;
    for (x = 0.0; x <= 1.0; x += 0.05) {
        s = sin(x);
        c = cos(x);
        printf("%e\n",s*s + c*c - 1.0);
    }
    return EXIT_SUCCESS;
}
```

For what values is the result exact? Is there a trend in the answers? What will the results be for large values of x?

8.2 *Memory Allocation*

Memory allocation is a process for obtaining memory without an explicit declaration. For example, suppose a program is going to read in a list of numbers and store them in an array, but the size of the list will be different each time you run the program. If your program declares the array to be a fixed size, the size will have to be big enough to hold the longest possible list. This leads to inefficiency. For example, you might find out that the input list is long once in a while, but most of the time it is short. If you reserve space for a large array every time you run the program, you will be wasting memory when the input list is actually small.

In such situations, it is more efficient to find out how big your list is going to be first, and *then* obtain memory for the array. For example, every time you run the program, the first number read in could be the number of items in the input list this time. Using this number and the memory allocation functions, you could obtain exactly the right amount of memory to hold the array.

The memory allocation functions take one or more arguments indicating how much memory you want to obtain. They return a pointer to a block of memory that is at least as big as the size requested. Locations in this block of memory can be referred to using the pointer and subscripts.

In order to use any memory allocation function, you must **#include** the standard header <stdlib.h>.

8.2.1 Memory Allocation Prototypes

The simplest memory allocation function has the prototype

```
void *malloc(size_t size)
```

The malloc function obtains the number of bytes specified by the size argument and returns a generic **void *** pointer to the memory obtained. (Remember that size_t is the name of the type returned by the **sizeof** operator.) For example,

```
char *cp;
cp = malloc(100);
```

uses malloc to obtain space for 100 characters. Several automatic conversions take place in the assignment statement. The 100 is automatically converted to the size_t type and the **void *** result of malloc is automatically cast to **char ***. From this point onward, cp points to the block of memory. This will probably be treated as an array containing 100 characters. We can read material into this array with

```
scanf("%s",cp);
```

We can also refer to individual members by adding subscripts to cp: cp[0], cp[1], and so on.

As another example of malloc, the following allocates enough space to hold a **double** array with 20 members.

```
double *dp;
dp = malloc( 20*sizeof(double) );
```

The **sizeof** operator calculates the size of one **double** value; multiplying by 20 gives the size of 20.

The calloc function is similar to malloc, but is more obviously geared towards obtaining space for arrays. It has the prototype

```
void *calloc(size_t Nmem,size_t memsize)
```

The Nmem argument is the number of members in the array you want to allocate; the memsize argument is the size of each member. For example,

```
long *lp;
lp = calloc( 30, sizeof(long) );
```

obtains space for an array of 30 **long** values. The array members can be referenced as `lp[0]` through `lp[29]`.

To show how `calloc` can be used, here is a function that in some sense makes an array twice as long as it already is. The arguments for the function are a pointer to an existing **int** array and a value giving the length of the array. The result of the function is a pointer to a new array that is twice as long. The first half of the new array equals the contents of the old array, while the members in the second half are all set to zero.

```
int *growiarr(int *old,size_t size)
{
    int i, *new;
    new = calloc( 2*size, sizeof(int) );
    for (i = 0; i < size; i++)
        new[i] = old[i];
    for (i = size; i < 2*size; i++)
        new[i] = 0;
    return new;
}
```

As the name of this function suggests, `growiarr` can be used to "grow" an existing array. For example, suppose `ip` is a pointer to an array of 20 members. The statement

```
ip = growiarr( ip, 20 );
```

makes `ip` point to an array of 40 members whose first 20 members match the old array. Effectively, the array indicated by `ip` is now twice as large. (NOTE: If the pointer `ip` was the only way to find the old array, the old array is now lost: it is out in memory somewhere, but you don't know where. Shortly, we will discuss the `free` function, which lets you avoid filling up memory with old arrays you can no longer find.)

Notice that in `growiarr`, the `new` pointer is a block scope variable and therefore disappears at the end of the function. However, the space obtained by `calloc` stays allocated, which means that functions calling `growiarr` can use the space that `growiarr` obtains.

The memory obtained by `malloc` and `calloc` can be freed for other purposes when you are finished using it. To do this, use the `free` function. The function has the prototype

```
void free(void *ptr)
```

(which is automatically provided for you when you **#include** `<stdlib.h>`). The `ptr` argument is a generic **void** `*` pointer that points to memory obtained by `malloc` or `calloc`. For example,

```
free(lp);
```

would free the **long** array we obtained with `calloc`. Once the memory has been marked as "free", the program is able to use it for other purposes. For example, the next time your program calls `malloc` or `calloc`, it may be given a pointer to memory that was just freed.

8.2.2 Exercises

1. Write a function with the prototype

```
char *grow(char *ptr,size_t Nold,size_t Nnew)
```

The `ptr` argument points to an existing **char** array with `Nold` members. The function should return a pointer to a newly allocated array with `Nnew` members. `Nnew` may be larger or smaller than `Nold`. The members of the old and new arrays should be equal, up to the end of the smaller array. (Note: this function is similar to a library function named `realloc`.)

2. Write a function with the prototype

```
char *newupper(char *lc)
```

The `lc` argument points to a string ending in the usual `'\0'`. The function returns a pointer to a new string that has the same contents as the old one, except that lowercase letters have been converted to uppercase. The contents of the old string are not changed.

3. A class of 30 students wrote a test that was marked on a scale of 0 to 20. The marks were stored in no particular order in an **int** array. Write a function with the prototype

```
int stats(int *marks)
```

to analyze the marks in the array. The function should return the average mark. It should also print out lines of information in the following format:

```
 3 students had marks in the range 0-5.
 8 students had marks in the range 6-10.
13 students had marks in the range 11-15.
 6 students had marks in the range 16-20.
The most common mark was 13.
```

(SUGGESTION: use `calloc` to allocate a 21-member array and record how many students got each mark between 0 and 20. The statistics are easy to obtain from this array. Free the array when you are finished with it.)

4. CONCORDANCE QUESTION: In the exercises of Section 7.4, we stored input words in an array declared with

```
char words[100][20];
```

Rewrite those exercises so that they start out with the array

```
char words[20][20];
```

If the input has not reached end-of-file by the time 20 words have been read, the program calls the `grow` function (written in Exercise 1 above) to grow the `words` array to obtain space for another 20 words. The program will continue to grow the array in 20-word chunks until end-of-file is reached.

5. CONCORDANCE QUESTION: Modify the programs of the previous exercise so that they work with an array that is declared as

```
char *word_ptr[20];
```

(an array of 20 character pointers). As the programs read in words, they dynamically allocate space for each word and store a pointer to the allocated space in the `word_ptr` array. Using the `grow` function of Exercise 1, the program should increase the size of the `word_ptr` array as needed. (NOTE: This exercise removes the 20-character limit on the size of words, since the amount of space needed to hold each word is dynamically allocated.)

6. CONCORDANCE QUESTION: Write a "clean" version of the Concordance program using all the techniques we have discussed so far. It should use dynamic memory allocation for each word and for the array of pointers that point to those words. It should eliminate duplicates from the list. Once duplicates have been eliminated, the `word_ptr` array should be *compressed* to fill in the gaps left when duplicates were eliminated. Finally, call `grow` to shrink `word_ptr` down to the minimum size needed. Once all this has been done, the program should print counts of number of characters, words, and lines that were read, and the number of occurrences of each word.

8.3 String Manipulation Functions

Text strings are often stored in **char** arrays. The library has many functions that work with such strings; all of these functions assume that the strings end in a `'\0'` character.

Many of the string manipulation functions make use of the **const** keyword in their prototypes. For this reason, we will discuss **const** before we talk about the functions themselves.

8.3.1 The Const Type Qualifier

When a function is passed a pointer to a variable or an array, the function can normally use that pointer to change the value of the variable or array members. There are times, however, when using the pointer in this way is undesirable.

For example, suppose you pass a string literal to a function. The literal is passed as a pointer to a **char** array whose contents are the characters in the string, so the function receives a **char** pointer. However, you do not want the function to use this pointer to change the contents of the literal, since the members of a string literal should not be changed.

The **const** keyword is used in function prototypes to assure the caller that the function will not use a pointer argument to change values. For example, here is a function that counts how many characters are contained in a standard string:

```
size_t length(const char *s)
{
    size_t i;
    for (i = 0; *s != '\0'; i++)
        s++;
    return i;
}
```

The `length` function does not change any of the characters in the string to which s points. Therefore it uses the **const** keyword to show that it does not make any changes. In fact, once a function has declared an object **const**, the function is not allowed to change the object's value through the pointer.

You may be asking yourself, if a **const** object can't be changed, how does it get a value in the first place? There are two possibilities:

(a) The declaration of a **const** object may contain an initialization value. You can *initialize* a **const** object, even though you can't assign it a new value using a normal assignment operation. For example, you might say

```
const double pi = 3.14159;
```

The initialization sets the variable `pi` to the given value. Once this has happened, the value of the variable cannot be changed.

(b) A function parameter that is declared **const** may not be changed by the function itself. However, the parameter receives argument values when the function is called. As a result, it is the *caller* that gives the **const** object its value. For example, in 10.3 we show that `printf` declares its format string argument to be **const**. This indicates that `printf` does not (and cannot) change the value of the format string. However, different calls to `printf` may use different format strings. (Note that this use of **const** does not mean that the corresponding argument must be "constant." The function that receives the argument cannot use the argument to change anything; but the argument itself can be a variable, an array member, an expression, and so on.)

Box 8.2: The Position of const

The position of the **const** keyword in the declaration is important. The declaration

```
const char *s
```

makes sense if you read it from right to left: `*s` says that `s` is a pointer. What does it point to? Going left, we see it points to a **char**. What kind of **char**? Going left again, we see that the **char** is **const**. This shows that the character `s` points to cannot be changed; however, `s` itself can be changed, and the `length` function above does so.

The declaration

```
char * const p
```

shows a different position for the keyword **const**. If we read this right to left, we see that `p` is a different sort of object. The **const** in front of `p` says `p` is constant. The **char *** before this shows that `p` is a character pointer. In this case, it is the pointer itself that cannot be changed; the value to which the pointer points *can* be changed.

8.3.2 String Function Prototypes

Below we list the prototypes for some library functions that manipulate strings. Your program must have the line

```
#include <string.h>
```

before it calls any of these functions. The information in the `<string.h>` header includes prototypes for all these functions, so you do not have to write out the prototypes explicitly.

In the explanations that follow, we will sometimes use a declaration like

```
char *s;
```

and speak of the string `s`. By this, we always mean that **char** array to which `s` points.

```
char *strcpy(char *dest,const char *src)
```
(Commonly pronounced "ster-copy.") Copies the contents of string `src` into a **char** array pointed to by `dest`. The `dest` array must be big enough to hold the contents of `src`. The **const** keyword in the declaration of `src` shows that the contents of the string `src` are just copied, not changed. The function returns a pointer that is equal to the pointer `dest`. For example,

```
char s[20];
strcpy(s,"abc");
```

copies the string `"abc"` into the `s` array.

```
char *strncpy(char *dest,const char *src,size_t N)
```
(Commonly pronounced "stern-copy.") Is similar to `strcpy` but only copies the first N characters of the string `src`. For example,

```
char s[5];
strncpy(s,"hello there",5);
```

copies `"hello"` into the `s` array. If the `src` string is shorter than the length N, `strncpy` puts in extra `'\0'` characters to pad out `dest` to the required length.

```
char *strcat(char *orig,const char *add)
```
(Commonly pronounced "ster-cat".) Adds or concatenates the contents of the string `add` to the end of the string `orig`. It returns a pointer that is equal to the pointer `orig`. For example,

```
char s[40] = "abc";
strcat(s,"def");
```

changes the contents of `s` into `"abcdef"`.

```
char *strncat(char *orig,const char *add,size_t N)
```
(Commonly pronounced "stern-cat.") Is similar to `strcat` but only adds the first N characters of the string `add` to the end of the string `orig`.

```
int strcmp(const char *str1,const char *str2)
```
(Commonly pronounced "ster-comp.") Compares string `str1` to `str2`. If the strings are equal, it returns a 0. If string `str1` is greater than string `str2`, it returns a positive number. If string `str1` is less than string `str2`, it returns a negative number. To determine which string is "greater," `strcmp` compares them on a character-by-character basis. If `strcmp` comes to a spot where the two strings differ, the string with the numerically higher character is the greater of the two. For example, `"abd"` is greater than `"abc"`.

```
int strncmp(const char *str1,const char *str2,size_t N)
```
(Commonly pronounced "stern-comp.") Is similar to `strcmp`, but only compares the first N characters of the strings.

```
char *strchr(const char *s,int c)
```
(Commonly pronounced "ster-cher.") Searches for the character `c` in the string `s` and returns a pointer to the first occurrence of that character. The character is passed in an **int** value for historical reasons. If the character cannot be found in the string, `strchr` returns a null character pointer (`(char *) NULL`).

Box 8.3: Complex Declarations

The declarations we have used in our programs have become more and more complex over recent chapters. In fact, C data types can be even more complicated than we have shown so far, but the declarations can be understood if you read them carefully from right to left.

If a declaration contains material *after* the variable name as well as before, the declaration is still easy enough to figure out. Read everything *after* the variable name from left to right, then read everything *before* the variable name from right to left. In other words, start at the middle and work out. For example, to understand

```
char *x[20];
```

read everything after the variable name first. Therefore x is an array with 20 members. Now read the things before the name, from right to left. What kind of members does x contain? The * indicates that the members are pointers. What do they point to? They point to **char** objects. Therefore, x is an array of 20 **char** pointers. Since **char** pointers usually represent strings, you can think of x as an array of 20 strings.

Parentheses can be used to group things together in different ways. For example, consider:

```
char (*x2)[20];
```

In this declaration, you handle the parenthesized part first. The *x2 says that x2 is a pointer. Now, outside the parentheses, we go right then left. On the right is [20], so the pointer x2 points to an array with 20 members. On the left is **char**, so each member is a **char**. This means that x2 is a pointer to an array of 20 characters. The array itself is *x2, so the members of the array are

```
(*x2)[0], (*x2)[1], ..., (*x2)[19]
```

---

char *strrchr(const char *s,int c)
> (Commonly pronounced "ster-are-cher.") Searches through the string s for the character c and returns a pointer to the *last* occurrence of that character. If the character cannot be found in the string, strrchr returns a null character pointer.

char *strstr(const char *str,const char *substr)
> (Commonly pronounced "ster-ster.") Searches through the string str for the string substr. If the string is found, strstr returns a pointer to its first occurrence. If the string substr is not found, strstr returns a null character pointer.

size_t strlen(const char *s)
> (Commonly pronounced "ster-len.") Returns the number of characters in the string s (not counting the '\0' that marks the end of the string).

8.3.3 Exercises

1. Write a program that reads in a string, then reads in lines of input until it finds a line that contains the desired string.

2. Write a program that reads in a string, then reads in lines of input until it reaches end-of-file. The program writes out how many times the given string appeared in the input text.

3. Write a function that joins one string to the end of another and returns a `size_t` value giving the number of characters in the resulting string.

4. Write a function that takes a string argument and returns an **int** value indicating how many blank characters appear in the string.

5. Write a function that takes a string argument and returns a pointer to a second string. The second string is like the first string except that the second has four blank characters everywhere that the first has a tab character. (Remember that the escape sequence `'\t'` represents a tab character.)

6. CONCORDANCE QUESTIONS: Rewrite your Concordance program to make use of the standard string manipulation functions (for example, `strcmp`).

8.4 I/O Functions

Standard **ANSI** I/O functions treat input and output as a continuous "stream" of bytes. In a **text stream**, these bytes represent characters in the machine's character set, and the I/O is broken into "lines" of text. In a **binary stream**, these bytes represent arbitrary information that usually has nothing to do with printable text.

A file that contains data written as a binary stream is called a **binary file**. A file that contains data written as a text stream is called a **text file**. I/O to and from a terminal is almost always performed using text streams, so a terminal is often considered a special sort of text file.

Text I/O is sometimes changed slightly during I/O operations to put it into a standard "text format." For example, if you write lines of text to a file but do not put a new-line character on the last line, the C I/O software may add a new-line for you because the standard text format requires that every line end in a new-line. If another program reads this file later on, it does not read exactly what the first program wrote; it finds the added new-line character. Additional small changes are also possible, with the result that you can write one set of characters and read back a slightly different set.

With binary streams, one C program reads *exactly* what the previous C program wrote. A C implementation is allowed to change the form of binary output to suit the characteristics of the machine being used, but the data must be changed back as it is read in by another program so that there is no difference between what was written and what is read.

In order to use functions that read and write I/O streams, the line

```
#include <stdio.h>
```

must appear before any I/O function calls. This provides prototypes for the I/O functions (for example, `printf`, `scanf`, `getchar`). You do not have to specify the prototypes explicitly. It also defines several symbols that are important in I/O operations, such as `EOF`.

8.4.1 Opening a Stream

Before reading or writing information, your program must "open" an I/O stream. This operation does several things.

(a)   It indicates whether you want a text stream or a binary stream.

(b)   It tells whether you will be writing a stream or reading one.

(c)   It associates the stream with an appropriate file or I/O device. For example, if the opening process associates the stream with a particular disk file, reading the stream reads the contents of the file and writing to the stream writes data to the file.

(d)   It builds up a block of information needed by the I/O software when reading or writing to the stream. This block of information is an object of the type `FILE`; the `FILE` type is defined with a **typedef** statement in `<stdio.h>` and the exact nature of the `FILE` type is irrelevant to most programmers.

The library function that opens a file is called `fopen`. It has the following prototype:

```
FILE *fopen(const char *filename,
            const char *desc)
```

The function takes two arguments: a filename string giving the name of the file you want to open, and a description string that tells how you will use the file. We will say more about both of these in a moment.

The return value of `fopen` is a pointer to the block of information that the open operation creates. If the open operation failed for some reason (for example, you tried to open a file for reading but the file did not exist), `fopen` returns a null pointer:

```
(FILE *) NULL
```

The format of the `filename` string varies from system to system. To find out what file names look like on your computer, you will have to read the system documentation or ask someone who is familiar with the machine. The examples in this tutorial will use short simple names that consist only of lowercase characters. Such names are acceptable to most implementations of C, but some systems may require different formats.

The description string indicates whether the file should be opened for reading or writing, and whether it should be treated as a text stream or a binary stream. Possible values for the description string are:

"r"   Open file for reading a text stream.

"w"   Open file for writing a text stream. If the file doesn't already exist, it will be created. If it does exist, the current contents of the file will be discarded.

"a"   Open file for text stream appending. If the file doesn't already exist, it will be created. If it does exist, its current contents will be retained; new output written to the file will be added onto the end of the existing contents.

"rb"   Open file for reading a binary stream.

"wb"   Open file for writing a binary stream (similar to "w").

"ab"   Open file for appending to a binary stream (similar to "a").

For example,

```
FILE *fp;
fp = fopen("myfile","r");
```

opens a file named "myfile" for text stream reading. The fopen routine returns a pointer to the block of information about the stream that has just been opened.

8.4.2 Reading and Writing Text Streams

Once a stream has been opened, you may perform I/O operations on it. The most common functions for reading from a text stream are fgetc and fscanf.

We have already seen that getchar is a function that gets a single character from the standard input stream. The fgetc function is like getchar, except that fgetc gets a single character from some other stream. The fgetc function takes a single argument: a FILE pointer that points to the information block associated with the stream you want to read. The result of fgetc is an **int** value that is either a single character read from the stream or the EOF value indicating end-of-file.

```
int i;
FILE *fp;
fp = fopen("myfile","r");
i = fgetc(fp);
while (i != EOF) {
    printf("%c",i);
    i = fgetc(fp);
}
```

opens a file named "myfile", then reads in one character after another and writes out the characters on the standard output stream. This is a simple way to print out the contents of a text file.

The fscanf function is similar to scanf. The first argument of fscanf is a FILE pointer argument pointing to the information block of the stream you want to read. Subsequent arguments are exactly like arguments for scanf. For example,

```
int i, j;
FILE *fp;
fp = fopen("myfile","r");
fscanf(fp,"%d %d",&i,&j);
```

reads two integers from "myfile" and stores their values in i and j.

The most common function for writing to a text stream is fprintf. This is like printf, but it takes a FILE pointer argument pointing to the information block associated with the output stream. For example,

```
FILE *fp;
int i;
fp = fopen("out","w");
for (i = 1; i <= 20; i++)
    fprintf(fp,"This is line %d\n",i);
```

writes several (trite) lines to a file called "out." Bear in mind that this output is in the form of *text*: in particular, the numbers are written as one or more digit characters, not as actual binary numbers.

8.4.3 Reading and Writing Binary Streams

Text streams are streams of characters. Binary streams are streams of any kind of data. For example, a binary stream may consist of a list of integers in normal **int** format, or a list of **double** values, or an alternating list of **double** values followed by **int** values, or any other possibility.

The fwrite function is the simplest routine for writing to a binary stream. It writes an array of values to a binary stream that has been opened for writing. The function has the prototype

```
size_t fwrite(const void *arr,size_t size,size_t N,FILE *fp)
```

The arr argument points to the array whose contents you want to write; size gives the size of a single member in this array; N is the number of members to write out; and fp points to the information block associated with the output stream. The value returned by the function is the number of members successfully written. This will be equal to N, unless some error happens during the writing process. As an example,

```
#define SIZE 30
double x[SIZE];
```

```
FILE *fin, *fout;
size_t i;

fin = fopen("infile","r");
for (i = 0; i < SIZE; i++)
    fscanf("%g",&x[i]);
fout = fopen("outfil","wb");
i = fwrite(x,sizeof(double),SIZE,fout);
if (i != SIZE)
    printf("Writing problem!");
```

reads in 30 floating point numbers from a text file named "infile" and writes the values in **double** format to a binary file named "outfil." Notice that we used the name of the array x as a pointer in the call to fwrite.

The fread function reads from a binary stream. Its format is similar to fwrite.

```
size_t fread(void *arr,size_t size,size_t N,FILE *fp)
```

The arr argument points to an array of N members, each with the given size. These are read from the stream associated with the information block indicated by fp. The value returned by fread is the number of members successfully read. As an example,

```
#define SIZE 30
FILE *fin;
long la[SIZE];
size_t i;

fin = fopen("infile","rb");
i = fread(la,sizeof(long),SIZE,fin);
```

reads 30 **long** numbers from "infile" into the la array.

The result of fread could be less than N if an error occurs during the reading operation or if end-of-file is reached before N members are read. To determine whether end-of-file has been reached, use the feof function.

```
int feof(FILE *fp)
```

returns a nonzero value if the stream indicated by fp is at end-of-file; otherwise, it returns zero. Similarly,

```
int ferror(FILE *fp)
```

returns a nonzero value if an error has occurred while reading or writing the stream indicated by fp; otherwise, it returns zero. Using feof and ferror, you can determine when fread has reached end-of-file or has encountered some sort of error. Continuing our previous example, we might write:

```
i = fread(la,sizeof(long),SIZE,fin);
if (i < SIZE) {
    if (feof(fin))
        printf("End of file\n");
    if (ferror(fin))
        printf("Read error\n");
}
```

8.4.4 Closing a File

When you are finished with a file, you should "close" it. This gets rid of the information block associated with the stream and performs a variety of "clean-up" operations. For example, when you close an output file, the program does whatever is necessary to mark end-of-file after the last data written to the file.

The function that closes a file has the prototype

```
int fclose(FILE *fp);
```

The argument indicates the stream you want to close. The function returns an **int** 0 if the stream was successfully closed; it returns a nonzero value if the stream was already closed or some other error occurred. For example, we might write:

```
FILE *fp;
int i;
fp = fopen("file","r");
    ...
i = fclose(fp);
if (i)
    printf("Some kind of error\n");
```

Files that are still open when the program finishes execution will automatically be closed.

8.4.5 Standard Streams

At the time that your program begins execution, three streams have already been opened. These are

```
FILE *stdin, *stdout, *stderr;
```

all declared in <stdio.h>.

The stdin stream is the standard input stream. This is the stream that getchar and scanf always read. Thus the following statements have the same effect:

```
i = getchar();
i = fgetc(stdin);
```

The `stdout` stream is the standard output stream. This is the stream to which `printf` writes. Thus the following statements have the same effect:

```
printf("%d",i);
fprintf(stdout,"%d",i);
```

The files or devices associated with `stdin` and `stdout` vary from one implementation of C to another. For example, many implementations of C say that `stdin` and `stdout` refer to an interactive terminal used by the person who executes a C program. On the other hand, some implementations can run C programs that are not attached to a terminal in any way. It is also common for C implementations to provide ways to change what `stdin` and `stdout` mean, every time a program is executed; for example, a user could say, "This time I want `stdin` to refer to my terminal" or "This time I want `stdin` to refer to a particular file."

The `stderr` stream is the standard "error" stream. Like `stdout`, this is a text stream opened for writing. Historically, `stderr` was always associated with the program user's terminal so that a program could print out error messages by writing them to the `stderr` stream. These days, C programs are not always executed by someone using a terminal, but `stderr` is still set up so that error messages will be written to some sensible place.

8.4.6 Exercises

1. Write a function with the prototype

   ```
   FILE *readopen(const char *filename)
   ```

   which opens the named file for reading as a text stream and returns a pointer to the stream information block.

2. Write a function with the prototype

   ```
   int text_to_bin(FILE *in,FILE *out)
   ```

   which reads an **int** value from the text stream indicated by `in` and writes this value to the binary stream indicated by `out`. The function returns the **int** value that was read.

3. Write a function with the prototype

   ```
   void errorout(const char *msg)
   ```

   which writes the given `msg` string to `stderr`.

4. Suppose a binary file named "in" contains a list of **double** values. Write a program that reads in the values of "in" one by one. Negative values should be displayed on the standard output unit. Positive and zero values should be written to a binary file named "out."

5. Suppose there are two binary files named "inone" and "intwo" that both contain integers sorted in ascending order. Write a program that *merges* the contents of the files into a single binary file named "out." The contents of "out" should be the contents of "inone" plus "intwo", again sorted in ascending order.

6. CONCORDANCE QUESTIONS: Rewrite your current Concordance program to write output to a file instead of the standard output stream.

8.5 *Miscellaneous Functions*

This section briefly covers several functions that perform a variety of operations.

8.5.1 The Exit Function

The `exit` function terminates your program prematurely. It can be called anywhere in the program. For example,

```
if (ferror(fp)) exit(1);
```

stops program execution if there is an error on the stream indicated by `fp`.

Notice that `exit` takes a single **int** argument. This argument serves the same purpose as the return value of `main`, and can take the same values.

```
exit(EXIT_SUCCESS);
```

indicates successful program termination.

```
exit(EXIT_FAILURE);
```

indicates program failure.

8.5.2 Reading and Writing from Strings

The `sprintf` function is similar to `fprintf`. However, instead of writing information to a text file, `sprintf` copies information into a string. For example,

```
char s[100];
sprintf(s,"%d\n",12);
```

stores the string "12\n" in the s character array; sprintf puts the usual ' \0' character after the last character written to the array.

    The sscanf function is the counterpart of sprintf. It obtains information from a string in the same way that fscanf obtains information from text input. For example,

```
int i;
char s[100] = "123 456 789";
sscanf(s,"%d",&i);
```

obtains an integer value from the string s and stores that value in the variable i.

8.5.3 Sorting and Searching

    The qsort function sorts an array of data. Its prototype (found in <stdlib.h>) can be written:

```
void qsort(void *array,size_t N,size_t size,int (*compar)());
```

where

array	points to the first member of the array you want to sort.
N	is the number of members in that array.
size	is the size of each member in the array.

The final argument, compar, is a function, which a program passes as an argument to qsort. This function is used when qsort has to compare two array members to see which is larger. When necessary, qsort will call this function with

```
compar(&member1,&member2)
```

where member1 and member2 are two array members that qsort wants to compare. The function should take two **void *** pointers as arguments and return an integer: a negative value if the first member is less than the second, a positive value if the first member is greater than the second, and zero if they are identical.

    An example should make this clearer. Here is a function that reads ten integers into an array, calls qsort to sort the values, then writes out the sorted array:

```
#include <stdlib.h>
#include <stdio.h>

enum { SIZE = 10 };

extern int intcompar(void *a,void *b);
```

```
int main()
{
    int number_list[SIZE];
    int i;
    for (i = 0; i < SIZE; i++)
        scanf("%d",&number_list[i];
    qsort(number_list,SIZE,sizeof(int),intcompar);
    for (i = 0; i < SIZE; i++)
        printf("%d\n",number_list[i]);
    return EXIT_SUCCESS;
}

int intcompar(void *a,void *b)
{
    int *ia = a;
    int *ib = b;
    return (*ia) - (*ib);
}
```

The main function just reads in the numbers, calls qsort to sort them, then prints out the numbers again. For the compar argument of qsort, it passes the name of the function that qsort should use in its comparisons. This function is intcompar.

The intcompar function is supposed to take two **void *** pointers to array members. It is supposed to return a negative value if the first member is less than the second, a positive value if the first member is greater than the first, and zero otherwise. To do this, our intcompar just converts the **void *** pointers to integer pointers (because the pointers point to the **int** members of number_list) and then subtracts the second integer from the first. This will return the proper kind of value.

If we wanted to modify the above program to sort a **double** array, we would have to write a function that compared two **double** values in the same way that intcompar compares two integers.

As a final example, suppose we have

```
char *word_list[SIZE];
```

where word_list is an array of character pointers that point to strings. We could write a comparison function with

```
int word_compare(void *a,void *b)
{
    return strcmp(*a,*b);
}
```

When it needs to compare two words, qsort will call word_compare, passing pointers to two of the members in word_list. Thus word_compare will receive pointers to character pointers. Our word_compare function then compares the associated character strings by passing the character pointers themselves to `strcmp`. This trick will be useful in the following exercise.

8.5.4 Exercise

1. Write a program that reads in lines of text from a file named "in", sorts them according to the order of the standard character set, then writes them to a file named "out."

2. Change the program written for the previous exercise so that it sorts lines, ignoring the case of letters. (In the ASCII character set, for example, all lowercase letters are "greater" than uppercase letters, so all the lines beginning with uppercase letters will appear before the lines beginning with lowercase letters. The program should be changed so that the two types of lines are intertwined.)

8.6 Review

Implementations of C provide a wide variety of library functions that can be called by C programs. Below we list prototypes of the functions discussed in this chapter. For further information on any of these, see Part IV.

```
#include <math.h>
/* All results and arguments are double */
acos(x)       ⇒ arc cos
asin(x)       ⇒ arc sin
atan(x)       ⇒ arc tan
atan2(y,x)    ⇒ arc tan (y/x)
ceil(x)       ⇒ ceiling
cos(x)        ⇒ cos (radians)
cosh(x)       ⇒ hyperbolic cos
exp(x)        ⇒ exponential
fabs(x)       ⇒ absolute value
floor(x)      ⇒ floor
log(x)        ⇒ natural logarithm
log10(x)      ⇒ base 10 logarithm
pow(x,y)      ⇒ x to the power y
sin(x)        ⇒ sin (radians)
sinh(x)       ⇒ hyperbolic sin
sqrt(x)       ⇒ square root
tan(x)        ⇒ tan (radians)
tanh(x)       ⇒ hyperbolic tan
```

```
#include <stdlib.h>
void *calloc(size_t Nmem,size_t memsize);
    /* allocate array, with "Nmem" members *
     * of size "memsize"                    */

void exit(int status);
    /* terminate program      */

void free(void *ptr);
    /* free allocated space  */

void *malloc(size_t size);
    /* allocate "size" bytes */
```

```
#include <string.h>
char *strcat(char *orig,const char *add);
    /* append "add" to "orig" */

char *strchr(const char *s,int c);
    /* find first "c" in "s"  */

int strcmp(const char *s1,const char *s2);
    /* compare "s1" to "s2"   */

char *strcpy(char *dest,const char *src);
    /* copy "src" into "dest" */

size_t strlen(const char *s);
    /* find length of "s"     */

char *strncat(char *orig,
           const char *add,size_t N);
    /* append N characters from "add" to "orig" */

int strncmp(const char *s1,
        const char *s2,size_t N);
    /* compare N characters from "s1" to "s2"   */

char *strncpy(char *dest,
           const char *src,size_t N);
    /* copy N characters from "src" into "dest" */

char *strrchr(const char *s,int c);
    /* find last "c" in "s" */
```

```
char *strstr(const char *str,
          const char *substr);
     /* find "substr" in "s" */
```

#include <stdio.h>
```
int fclose(FILE *stream);
     /* close a stream */

int fgetc(FILE *stream);
     /* read character from stream */

FILE *fopen(const char *filename,
          const char *desc);
     /* open stream */

int fprintf(FILE *stream,const char *format, ...);
     /* formatted write to stream  */

size_t fread(void *arr,size_t size,
          size_t N,FILE *fp);
     /* read array from stream */

int fscanf(FILE *stream,const char *format, ...);
     /* formatted read from stream */

size_t fwrite(const void *arr,
          size_t size,size_t N,FILE *fp);
     /* write array to stream */

int sprintf(char *s,
          const char *format, ...);
     /* write to string  */

int sscanf(const char *s,
          const char *format, ...);
     /* read from string */
```

The `errno` symbol behaves like a variable that library functions assign values when they want to indicate an error has occurred; `errno` should be checked after any library function returns to make sure that an error did not occur.

A function declares a pointer argument to be **const** when it does not intend to use the pointer to change the value of the objected pointed to. Many library functions declare pointer arguments to be **const**.

All of C's I/O is performed on *streams*. A *text stream* consists of lines of text; what you write out may be modified slightly to conform with the system's idea of what a text file should look like. A *binary stream* is not modified: if you write to a binary stream and then read the data back, you will read *exactly* what you wrote.

Streams must usually be opened before performing I/O on them. However, there are three streams that are opened automatically: the standard input stream stdin, the standard output stream stdout, and the standard error stream stderr.

chapter 9   Advanced Data Types

An array is a collection of objects (members) that all have the same type. The data types we will discuss in this chapter are collections of objects that may have *different* types.

9.1 Structures

A structure groups several different pieces of data into a single object. Here is a typical structure declaration:

```
struct {
    int I_D_Number;
    char name[30];
    float salary;
} George;
```

The declaration begins with the keyword **struct**, indicating a structure. The members or **elements** of the structure are then listed inside brace brackets. Each element of the structure is described with a declaration in the usual form. After the closing brace, we have given the name of a variable that will have this structure type.

To refer to an element of a structure variable, give the name of the variable, followed by a period (also called "dot"), followed by the element name. For example,

```
George.I_D_Number = 1234;
strcpy(George.name,"George Peabody");
George.salary = 30000.00;
```

assigns values to elements of the George structure variable. Notice that we had to use strcpy to copy a string into the name array. If we just said

```
George.name = "George Peabody";
```

it would be a syntax error. The name element is an array. You can make assignments to array *members*, but you can't make assignments to arrays as a whole. (One of the problems, of course, is that C initializations like

```
char s[20] = "abc";
```

make it look as if you *can* assign strings to arrays. However, an initialization just *looks* like an assignment because the notation is similar.)

The dot operator belongs to the same precedence class as subscripting. Operations in this class are carried out from left to right. Thus

```
George.name[0]
```

refers to the initial character of the `name` element inside the `George` structure.

The **sizeof** operator may be applied to structures, as in

```
sizeof George
```

☞ The size of a structure is the number of bytes between the start of the structure and the next memory location where a similar structure could start. This may be larger than the space actually taken up by the elements of the structure.

For example, suppose we have:

```
struct {
    double x;
    char c;
} svar;
```

On some machines, **double** values must be stored at memory locations with a particular *alignment* (for example, their memory address might have to be an even multiple of two or four). Since this structure starts with a **double** element, the structure must start at a point with **double** alignment. This means that the **sizeof** the structure `svar` will be

```
sizeof(double) + sizeof(char)
```

plus however many additional bytes are needed to get to the next **double** alignment boundary. The size of the whole may indeed be greater than the size of its parts.

No two elements of the same structure may have the same name. However, element names may be the same as names outside the structure. For example, we could have:

```
int x;
struct {
    double x;
    char c;
} svar;
```

There is no conflict between the **int** x outside the structure and the **double** x inside. The x inside the structure is always referenced using expressions like

```
svar.x
```

and C has no difficulty distinguishing between this kind of reference and a reference to just plain x.

9.1.1 Structure Tags

A structure declaration may contain a structure **tag**, a sort of user-defined type name similar to ones defined by **typedef**. The structure tag comes immediately after the keyword **struct**, as in

```
struct PERSONNEL {
    int I_D_Number;
    char name[30];
    float salary;
};
```

This declaration says that the tag PERSONNEL will be associated with a structure that contains the given elements. Once we have declared what a PERSONNEL structure contains, we can use the tag in declarations *without* listing the elements again. For example,

```
struct PERSONNEL George;
```

says that George is a structure of the type associated with the tag PERSONNEL. We do not list the contents of the structure again; that is only done in the first declaration that refers to the structure.

Notice that a structure tag is not quite the same as a type defined with **typedef**. **The keyword struct must always appear before the structure tag.** A type name defined with **typedef** can stand on its own, as in

```
typedef int TEMPERATURE;
TEMPERATURE fahrenheit;
```

Structure types may be given their own typedef names. For example,

```
typedef struct {
    double re, im;
} COMPLEX;
```

associates the type name COMPLEX with the given structure type. This can then be used in declarations like

```
COMPLEX z1, z2;
```

Because COMPLEX is a **typedef**-defined name, the **struct** keyword is not used.

Structure tags may be used in **sizeof** expressions, as in

```
sizeof (struct PERSONNEL)
```

This gives the size of a PERSONNEL structure.

9.1.2 Structure Operations

A structure value can be assigned to a structure variable of the same type. For example, suppose we have

```
COMPLEX z1, z2;
```

where COMPLEX is the structure type defined in the previous section. We can say:

```
z1.re = 0.0;
z1.im = 0.0;
z2 = z1;
```

The last assignment assigns the values of each element in z1 to the corresponding elements in z2. Note that this kind of structure assignment is only valid when the two structures have the same type. You must also make sure that every element in the structure on the right hand side of the assignment has been assigned a value; none of these elements may be undefined.

Structures may be passed as arguments to functions and may be returned as function results. For example, the following function takes a PERSONNEL record as an argument and returns a version of the record that has the salary raised by 5 percent.

```
struct PERSONNEL raise_salary(struct PERSONNEL person)
{
    person.salary *= 1.05;
    return person;
}
```

This just multiplies the salary element by an appropriate amount and returns the adjusted structure. An assignment like

```
George = raise_salary(George);
```

raises George's existing salary and stores the resulting information back in the George structure.

A structure type may contain elements that are also structures. For example, we might define:

```
struct DATE {
    unsigned short year;
    unsigned short month;   /* 1 to 12 */
    unsigned short day;     /* 1 to 31 */
}
```

This kind of structure may be contained inside another structure. For example, here is a structure that might be used to keep track of cases of grocery items:

```
struct GROCERY {
     int Product_Number;
     int Case_Number;
     char Product_Name[40];
     struct DATE delivered;
     struct DATE expiry;
}
```

The two DATE structures tell when the case was delivered and when it should be removed from the shelves. As an example,

```
struct GROCERY milk;
milk.Product_Number = 1234;
milk.Case_Number = 5678;
strcpy(milk.Product_Name,"Homogenized Milk");
milk.delivered.year = 1990;
milk.delivered.month = 12;
milk.delivered.day = 31;
milk.expiry.year = 1991;
milk.expiry.month = 1;
milk.expiry.day = 10;
```

assigns values to all the elements of the milk variable, including the elements of the DATE structures. The milk was delivered December 31, 1990, and expires January 10, 1991.

9.1.3 Structure Arrays

C lets you declare arrays of structures. For example,

```
struct PERSONNEL dept[15];
```

declares an array of 15 structures.

```
for (i = 0; i < 15; i++)
     printf("%s\n",dept[i].name);
```

prints the name fields of all the structures in the array. (A note to people who have used the Cobol programming language: while Cobol accepts either

```
dept[i].name
dept.name[i]
```

C will only accept the first form.)

As another example of a structure array declaration,

```
#define SLEN 40
struct BOOK {
    char title[SLEN];
    char author[SLEN];
    int Year_Published;
};
struct BOOK booklist[100];
```

combines the array declaration with a description of the contents of a BOOK structure.

9.1.4 Structure Pointers

Programs create pointers to structures in the same way that they create other pointers.

```
struct BOOK *bkptr;
```

creates a variable named bkptr which points to a structure with the BOOK tag.

```
bkptr = &booklist[0];
```

gives bkptr a pointer value pointing to the first element of the booklist array.

```
printf("%s\n",(*bkptr).title);
```

prints out the title element of the structure to which bkptr points.

Referring to a structure element using a pointer to the structure is so common that C has a separate operator for the operation.

```
bkptr -> title
```

is equivalent to

```
(*bkptr).title
```

Both refer to the title element in the BOOK structure to which bkptr points.

The -> operator is made up of a minus sign followed by a "greater-than" character. If the left operand points to a structure type, the right operand must be the name of an element of that type of structure. The -> operator has the same precedence as the dot operator.

As an example of how -> can be used, here is a function that fills in the elements of a BOOK structure:

```
void getbook(struct BOOK *ptr)
{
    printf("Please enter title of book: ");
    scanf("%40s",ptr -> title);
    printf("Name of author: ");
```

```
        scanf("%40s",ptr -> author);
        printf("Year published: ");
        scanf("%d",&(ptr -> Year_Published));
    }
```

The calling function passes a pointer to a structure of the type with the BOOK tag. This pointer can then be used by getbook to refer to elements of the structure. Notice that we had to use the & operator to obtain the address of the Year_Published element because scanf requires pointer arguments. We did not need the & operator for the other two elements because the use of an array name without subscripts is automatically treated as a pointer to the first member of the array.

Arithmetic with structure pointers works the same as arithmetic with pointers to simpler kinds of data. For example, if a structure pointer points into an array of structures, adding one to the pointer points to the next structure in the array. For example,

```
    bkptr = &booklist[0];
    while (bkptr <= &booklist[99]) {
        if ( (bkptr -> Year_Published) == 1955 ) {
            printf("%s ",bkptr -> title);
            printf("by %s\n",bkptr -> author);
        }
        bkptr++;
    }
```

prints the titles and authors of all the books in the list that were published in 1955. The ++ operation increments the bkptr pointer at the end of each loop.

9.1.5 Exercises

1. A zoo keeps track of its animals using a C program. Each species is represented by a structure declared with

```
    #define SLEN 40
    typedef float MONEY;
    struct SPECIES {
        char common_name[SLEN];
        char latin_name[SLEN];
        int females; /* number of females */
        int males;   /* number of males */
        int babies;  /* number < one year old */
        MONEY food;  /* cost of one month's food */
        MONEY insurance;
            /* amount animals are insured for */
        int enclosure;
            /* number indicating where animals kept */
    };
```

Write a function with the prototype

```
void enter_species(struct SPECIES *ptr)
```

which takes a pointer to a `SPECIES` structure and prompts a user for values to fill into each element of the structure.

2. The species description structures are held in a file scope array declared with

```
struct SPECIES collection[100];
```

Write a function with the prototype

```
MONEY food_bill(int where)
```

which takes an argument indicating the number of an enclosure and prints out the common names of all the species in that enclosure. The value returned by the function is the total cost of feeding every species in the enclosure for a month.

3. CONCORDANCE QUESTION: Create the definition of a structure that will be able to store information about the occurrences of a word in text. One element of the structure should be a **char** pointer pointing to a dynamically allocated string containing the word itself. The structure should also contain a pointer to a dynamically allocated array of integers that will record the line number of each occurrence of the word in input text. Write a program that

— creates an array of such structures;

— reads in input text and sets up a structure for each distinct word in the input;

— calls `qsort` to sort the resulting array of structures (if necessary);

— displays all the accumulated information in a readable way.

9.2 Using Structures

This section describes common operations involving structures.

9.2.1 Initializing Structures

A structure declaration can initialize some or all of the elements of the structure. The format of a structure initializer is similar to that of an array initializer: a list of values enclosed in brace brackets. Initialization values are assigned to structure elements in the order they appear. For example,

```
struct SPECIES wolf = {
    "Wolf", "Canis Lupus", 5, 4, 2,
    50.00, 800.00, 6
};
```

initializes the elements of a SPECIES structure. If there are fewer initialization values in the list than elements in the structure, the first elements of the structure will be initialized and the remainder will not be.

An array of structures is initialized in a similar way. For example,

```
struct SPECIES primate[4] = {
    { "Gibbon" },
    { "Gorilla" },
    { "Orangutan" },
    { "Spider Monkey" }
};
```

initializes the first element of each structure in the array.

9.2.2 Reading and Writing Structures

Structure values may be read from and written to binary streams. For example, the following main function uses the enter_species function from the last set of exercises to create a collection array, then writes the contents of that array to a file named zoo:

```
int main(void)
{
    int i;
    FILE *fp;
    for (i = 0; i < 100; i++)
        enter_species(&collection[i]);
    fp = fopen("zoo","wb");
    fwrite(collection,sizeof(struct SPECIES),100,fp);
    fclose(fp);
    return 0;
}
```

Once this zoo file has been created, it can be read and used in other programs. For example, the following main function calculates the total insured cost of the zoo's collection:

```
int main(void)
{
    MONEY total = (MONEY) 0;
    FILE *fp;
    int i;
    fp = fopen("zoo","rb");
```

```
            fread(collection,sizeof(struct SPECIES),100,fp);
            for (i = 0; i < 100; i++)
                total += collection[i].insurance;
            printf("Total value is $%12.2f",total);
            return EXIT_SUCCESS;
        }
```

(As an exercise, write a `main` routine that does the same calculation, this time by reading in one structure at a time rather than everything all at once.)

9.2.3 Dynamic Allocation of Structures

In our zoo examples, we have been using a fixed-length array named `collection` to hold our `SPECIES` structures. Since the number of species that a zoo actually has will change with time, it makes more sense to use an array allocated with `malloc` or `calloc`. For example, here is a modified version of the `main` routine from the previous section, calculating the total insurance value of the zoo collection. The number of species in the collection is read from the standard input unit.

```
        int main(void)
        {
            MONEY total = 0;
            FILE *fp;
            int i, n;
            struct SPECIES *zoolist;
            printf("Please enter number of species: ");
            scanf("%d",&n);
            zoolist = calloc(n,sizeof(struct SPECIES *));
            fp = fopen("zoo","rb");
            fread(zoolist,sizeof(struct SPECIES),n,fp);
            for (i = 0; i < n; i++)
                total += zoolist[i].insurance;
            printf("Total value is $%12.2f",total);
            return EXIT_SUCCESS;
        }
```

Notice that the program subscripts the pointer `zoolist` as if it were an array.

9.2.4 Linked Lists

The example in the preceding section needs someone to enter the number of `SPECIES` structures that are currently stored in the "zoo" file. This means extra work for the person using the program, because he or she has to keep track of how many species are currently on file. It would be much simpler for the program user if the program didn't need to be given this information. We can make this improvement by introducing the concept of **linked lists**.

A linked list is made up of a collection of structures. Each of these structures contains normal information (for example, data about a particular animal species). In addition, each structure contains an element that points to another structure in the list. This pointer is the **link** between the two structures.

A linked list may be pictured as a railway train. Each structure is a railway car containing normal information. Just as each railway car is linked to the next car by a coupling, each structure in the list is linked to the next by a pointer.

In our zoo program, we can use `malloc` to obtain space for one structure after another until we reach end-of-file. As each structure is read in, it is linked into the list. The ·end of the list can be indicated by a null pointer (just as the last car in a·train is not followed by anything).

Here is a function that reads `SPECIES` structures stored in the "zoo" file and stores them in a linked list. It returns a pointer to the first element of this list.

```
#include <stddef.h>
#include <stdio.h>
#include <stdlib.h>

#define SLEN 40
typedef float MONEY;

struct SPECIES {
    char common_name[SLEN];
    char latin_name[SLEN];
    int females;
    int males;
    int babies;
    MONEY food;
    MONEY insurance;
    int enclosure;
};

struct LIST_ITEM {
    struct SPECIES desc;
    struct LIST_ITEM *link;
};

typedef struct LIST_ITEM *LPTR;
/* pointer to LIST_ITEM, defined for convenience */

LPTR makelist(void)
{
    LPTR top, end;
    FILE *fp;
    fp = fopen("zoo","rb");
    top = end = make_item(fp);
```

```
        while ( (end -> link) = make_item(fp) )
            end = end -> link;
        fclose(*fp);
        return top;
}

LPTR make_item(FILE  fp)
{
    LPTR new;
    if ( feof(fp) )
        return NULL;
    new = malloc( sizeof(*new) );
    fread( new->desc, sizeof(struct SPECIES), 1, fp);
    return new;
}
```

The key to `makelist` is the way that it uses the secondary function `make_item`, which checks to see if the file is at end-of-file. If it is, it returns a null pointer (which you will remember is represented by the symbol NULL). If the file is not at end-of-file, `make_item` allocates space for a new SPECIES structure, uses `fread` to read in such a structure, and returns a pointer to the new structure.

Now observe how `makelist` uses `make_item`. The `makelist` function starts by opening the zoo file for reading. It then sets `top` (the beginning of the zoo list) and `end` (the end of the new list) to the first list item set up by `make_item`. Next comes the **while** loop:

```
        while ( (end -> link) = make_item(fp) )
            end = end -> link;
```

In the **while** expression, `make_item` is evaluated first. If a SPECIES structure is read successfully, `make_item` returns a pointer to an appropriate list element. This pointer is assigned to `end->link` (to link it into the list), and then the body of the loop changes `end` to point to the new item on the end of the list.

If a SPECIES structure is *not* read successfully, `make_item` returns a null pointer. This is assigned to `end->link` (marking the end of the list) Also, the value of the **while** expression is zero (the null pointer), so the loop stops looping. The pointer `end` will be left pointing at the last item in the list. The file is then closed and `makelist` returns the pointer to the top of the list.

We should point out that `makelist` and `make_item` skip some steps that may turn out to be important. For example, they do not do any error-checking, even though errors are possible: `fopen` may fail to open the file, `malloc` may fail to obtain appropriate space for new list items, `fread` may have an error while reading, and so on. In a more carefully written program, we would have to take all these possibilities into consideration.

Once the list has been created, it can be used in much the same way that you use an array. For example, the following function determines the number of species in the list:

```
int count_species(struct LIST_ITEM *list)
{
    int i = 0;
    while (list != NULL) {
        i++;
        list = list -> link;
    }
    return i;
}
```

This starts at the beginning of the list and uses the links to move from one item to the next until it finds a null pointer. It returns the number of items found in the list.

9.2.5 Exercises

1. Write a function with the prototype

   ```
   void names(LPTR list)
   ```

   which prints the common names of all the species in the list.

2. Write a function with the prototype

   ```
   MONEY food_bill2(LPTR list,int encl)
   ```

   which goes through the list species by species and calculates the amount of money required to feed all the species in the given enclosure for a month. This MONEY value is returned as the result.

3. The zoo decides to increase its insurance coverage, and raises the insured price of every species by 10 percent. Write a program that reads in the contents of the "zoo" file, closes it, opens it again, then writes out the SPECIES structures with the insurance elements showing the new amounts.

4. In our BOOK structure (defined in Section 9.1.3), the title and author elements were strings with fixed lengths. It is often better to use variable length strings, in order to accommodate long titles. Redefine the structure as

   ```
   struct NEWBOOK {
       char *title;
       char *author;
       int Year_Published;
   };
   ```

   where title and author point to strings stored in memory obtained with malloc. Write a function with the prototype

```
void get_newbook(struct NEWBOOK *ptr);
```

which creates a NEWBOOK structure in the same way that getbook (in Section 9.1.4) creates a BOOK structure.

5. Write a function with the prototype

```
void outbook(FILE *stream,struct NEWBOOK *ptr)
```

which writes out a NEWBOOK structure to the given binary stream. After the structure has been written out, also write out the title and author strings indicated by the title and author pointers in the NEWBOOK structure.

6. Write a function with the prototype

```
struct NEWBOOK inbook(FILE *stream)
```

which is the reverse of outbook from the previous exercise. It reads in a NEWBOOK structure from stream, plus the title and author strings that follow the structure in the stream. The result of inbook is a NEWBOOK structure. The title and author pointers in this structure point to strings in memory obtained with malloc.

7. CONCORDANCE QUESTION: Modify your previous Concordance program so that it dynamically allocates the structure array instead of declaring an array of fixed size.

9.3 Using Linked Lists

Linked lists are used extensively in many C programs, so it is worthwhile to spend more time on the subject. In this section, we will look at some of the operations that can be performed on linked lists and how they can be used in programs.

9.3.1 Deleting a List Item

To delete a list item, just adjust the linking pointers to point around the item. For example, the following function searches for a given species in the zoo list and deletes it from the list. It returns a pointer to the changed list.

```
LPTR del_item(LPTR list,char *name)
{
    LPTR cur, prev;
    /*
     *   Run through list until match is found or
     *   the end is reached.
     */
```

```
        for (prev=cur=list;cur == NULL;cur = prev -> link) {
            if ( !strcmp( (cur->desc).common_name, name ) ) {
                /*
                 *   Match has been found.
                 */
                if (cur == list) /* match is first in list */
                    list = list -> link;
                prev -> link = cur -> link;
                free(cur);
                return list;
            }
            prev = cur;
        }
        return list;
    }
```

The heart of this routine is the **for** loop consisting of

```
        for (prev=cur=list;cur == NULL;cur = prev -> link) {
            ...
            prev = cur;
        }
```

This loops from one list item to the next. Within the loop, `cur` points to the item currently being examined; `prev` points to the item previously examined.

```
        cur = prev -> link;
```

points `cur` towards the next item in the linked list. The loop stops if `cur` is found to be the null pointer (which will happen when `cur` gets to the end of the list). Notice that if the `list` argument starts out as NULL, the **for** loop does nothing because the condition is met immediately. In this case, the **return** statement just returns `list` (which is NULL). The same **return** statement is used if no match is found.

The **if** statement inside the **for** loop tests to see if the name in the current list item matches the name being sought. If so, the following statements are executed:

```
        if (cur == list) list = list -> link;
        prev -> link = cur -> link;
        free(cur);
        return list;
```

The **if** statement tests to see if cur equals `list`. This will only happen if the first item in the list is the matching item. If it is true, the `list` argument is changed so that the new list begins at what was the second element. Next, we take the link in the previous record (`prev->link`) and give it the value of `cur->link` (the link to the record after cur). This removes the cur item from the list. We can then free the space occupied by the cur item and return the `list` pointer.

Note that `del_item` works correctly even under several unusual conditions: when there are no items in the list; when the first item in the list is the one you want to delete; and when the given name matches none of the species in the list.

☞ Try to foresee all the unusual conditions that might happen when your program is being used, and make sure that the program can handle those situations appropriately.

9.3.2 Adding Items to a List

There are several ways to add items to an existing list. The way that usually comes to mind first is to add new items to the *end* of the list. This means that you have to start at the top of the list, walk all the way through the list items until you come to the null pointer at the end of the list, then change this null pointer to point to the new item.

If you think for a moment, this is clearly inefficient. When you don't care about the order of the items in the list, it is easier to add new items to the *start* of the list. For example, suppose `new` points to a list item you want to add and `list` points to the existing list.

```
new -> link = list;
list = new;
```

puts `new` in front of whatever is currently at the start of the list, then changes the `list` pointer to point to `new`. This is obviously easier than running through the entire list to find where it ends.

When the order of the list matters, new items must be "spliced" into the proper positions in the middle of the list. As an example, let's take a simplified list that uses the definitions

```
struct ILIST {
    int i;
    struct ILIST *link;
};
typedef struct ILIST *IP;
```

Suppose we have a list that has been sorted with the integer elements in ascending order and also suppose we have a new `ILIST` structure that should be inserted into the list in the proper place. Below, we give a function that does this insertion. The `list` argument points to the first item in the existing list; the `new` argument points to the structure that should be inserted; and the result of the function is a pointer to the first item in the modified list.

```
IP insert(IP list, IP new)
{
    IP prev, next;
    /*
     *  "new" could be null pointer.
     */
    if (new == NULL) return list;
```

```
/*
 *  Otherwise, "new" should be real item.
 */
prev = NULL;
next = list;
/*
 *  Loop to find place to insert item.
 */
while ( (next != NULL) && (new->i > next->i) ) {
    prev = next;
    next = prev -> link;
}
/*
 *  Set up links in "new" and surrounding items.
 */
new -> link = next;
if (prev != NULL) {
    prev -> link = new;
    return list;
}
else
    return new;
}
```

As an example of how to use this function, here is a `main` function that reads a list of integers from a text file named "in" and prints them out in ascending order:

```
int main(void)
{
    IP ptr, list;
    FILE *fp;
    list = NULL;
    fp = fopen("in","r");
    while ( !feof(fp) ) {
        ptr = malloc(sizeof(struct ILIST));
        fscanf(fp,"%i",&(ptr->i));
        list = insert(list,ptr);
    }
    fclose(fp);
    ptr = list;
    while ( ptr != NULL) {
        printf("%d\n",ptr->i);
        ptr = ptr -> link;
    }
    return EXIT_SUCCESS;
}
```

With repeated calls to `insert`, we create a list of numbers which are sorted into ascending order as they are read. This sorting technique is not particularly efficient, but it's simple.

9.3.3 Exercises

1. Referring to the zoo programs, write a function with the prototype

   ```
   LPTR del_encl(LPTR list,int encl)
   ```

   that deletes all list items for species found in the given enclosure.

2. Write a function with the prototype

   ```
   IP join(IP list1,IP list2)
   ```

   which creates a single list by joining the two argument lists. Order of the list elements is not important. The function returns a pointer to the resulting list.

3. Write a function with the prototype

   ```
   IP arr_to_list(int *arr,size_t length)
   ```

   which takes an array with the given length (number of members) and changes it into a linked list.

4. Write a function `list_to_arr` with the prototype

   ```
   int *list_to_arr(IP list,size_t *length);
   ```

   which is the converse of `arr_to_list` (written in the previous exercise). The result of `list_to_arr` is a pointer to an array of integers, containing the integers in the list indicated by `list`. Your function should store the length of this array in the object that the `length` argument points to. (HINT: use the `realloc` library function.)

5. CONCORDANCE QUESTION: Modify your Concordance program so that it stores information in a linked list of structures instead of an array. This will require redefining the original structure so that it contains linking fields. As items are added to the list, they should be inserted in alphabetical order so that the list doesn't have to be sorted afterwards. When the program reaches end-of-file, it should print out the list showing each word and all the lines on which the word occurs.

6. CONCORDANCE QUESTION: Most Concordances do not record occurrences of very common words like "the", "in", "a", and so on. Create a file named "ignore" which contains a set of such common words that your Concordance program should ignore. Modify your Concordance program so that it reads "ignore" and does not print out occurrences of the words that appear in "ignore."

9.4 Unions

A union is a single data object that can be interpreted in a number of different ways. For example, you could create a union that would sometimes be considered a **float** value and sometimes an **int**.

The format of a union declaration is similar to a structure declaration. For example,

```
union IF {
     int i;
     float f;
} ifvar;
```

declares a variable `ifvar` that has a union type. The `IF` that appears after the keyword **union** is known as the **union tag**.

The declarations inside the brace brackets list the possible interpretations of the union. To refer to a particular interpretation, you use the same notation as a reference to a structure element. For example,

```
ifvar.i = 2;
```

says that you want to treat `ifvar` as an **int** and that you want to assign it the value 2. You could also say

```
ifvar.f = 4.0;
```

The different interpretations of a union all begin at the same memory location, which means they overlap. For example, assigning a value to `ifvar.i` automatically changes the value of `ifvar.f` because the two overlap in memory. In general, the new value of `ifvar.f` will not be meaningful; the bit representation of the integer value is not directly related to the floating point value. With one exception that we will discuss in Section 9.4.1, the ANSI standard does not let you assign to one interpretation, then use the value of another.

The size of a union is the maximum of the sizes of all the interpretations. For example,

```
sizeof (union IF)
```

is the larger of

```
sizeof (int)
sizeof (float)
```

Union arrays and pointers are declared in much the same way as structure arrays and pointers. The `->` operator may be used to refer to a particular interpretation of a union indicated by a pointer. For example, if you have

```
union IF ifvar, *ifp;
ifp = &ifvar;
ifp -> i = 2;
```

assigns 2 to the **int** interpretation of ifvar.

Functions may take union arguments and return union values. Note the difference between a function call like

```
f1(ifvar)
```

where the argument is a union and

```
f2(ifvar.i)
```

where the argument is an *interpretation* of a union. These two functions might have prototypes of the form

```
void f1(union IF arg)
void f2(int arg)
```

It is not valid to pass a union type to a function that expects a different type. For example,

```
f2(ifvar)
```

is incorrect because f2 expects an **int** argument. It doesn't matter that ifvar can be interpreted as an **int**; if you want the **int** interpretation, you must ask for it explicitly.

Declarations of union variables may include initialization values. The first interpretation of the union is always the one that is used in an initialization. Therefore,

```
union IF ifvar = 1;
```

stores an **int** 1 in ifvar (because the first interpretation is **int**). If we declared

```
union FI {
    float x;
    int i;
} fivar = 1;
```

a **float** 1.0 would be stored in fivar, since the 1 will be cast automatically to **float**.

9.4.1 Structures and Unions

Unions are often used inside structures and vice versa. For example, suppose a school has a C program that uses structures to keep track of student marks. It might look something like this:

```
struct STUDENT {
    char name[40];
    int grade;
    union {
        struct {
            int read;
            int print;
            int spell;
            int arith;
        } grade1;
        struct {
            int read;
            int spell;
            int arith;
            int hist;
            int geog;
        } grade2;
        /* and so on */
    } subj;
}
```

The first two elements in the structure are always the same. The last element is a union type named subj. This union has several different interpretations, each of which is a structure. Each of these structures corresponds to the set of subjects that are taken in a particular grade. To determine which interpretation is appropriate, a program would look at the grade element that is found in every STUDENT structure. For example, here is a function that prints a student's marks:

```
void printmark(struct STUDENT s)
{
    printf("Name: %s\n",s.name);
    printf("Grade %d\n",s.grade);
    if (s.grade == 1) {
        printf("Reading: %d\n",s.subj.grade1.read);
        printf("Printing: %d\n",s.subj.grade1.print);
        printf("Spelling: %d\n",s.subj.grade1.spell);
        printf("Arithmetic: %d\n",s.subj.grade1.arith);
    }
    if (s.grade == 2) {
        printf("Reading: %d\n",s.subj.grade2.read);
        printf("Spelling: %d\n",s.subj.grade2.spell);
        printf("Arithmetic: %d\n",s.subj.grade2.arith);
        printf("History: %d\n",s.subj.grade2.hist);
        printf("Geography: %d\n",s.subj.grade2.geog);
    }
    /* and so on */
}
```

In an expression like

```
s.subj.grade2.read
```

s is the name of a structure, subj is the name of a union element in the structure, grade2 is the name of an interpretation of the union, and read is an element inside this (structure) interpretation.

The declaration of a STUDENT structure looks large, but a given structure will not take up as much memory as it seems. Each structure only contains the marks that are appropriate to the student's grade, even though the structure declaration lists the possibilities for *every* grade. In this way, the union actually conserves memory space.

The declaration of the STUDENT data type could be written in a different way:

```
union STUDENT2 {
    struct {
        int grade;
        char name[40];
        int read, print, spell, arith;
    } grade1;
    struct {
        int grade;
        char name[40];
        int read, spell, arith, hist, geog;
    } grade2;
    /* and so on */
};
```

This is a union type where each possible interpretation is a structure. The first element of each structure is an **int** value named grade. *All these elements occupy the same space in memory* because they are at the beginning of the union. If u is a variable of the STUDENT2 type, we can always be certain that the expressions

```
u.grade1.grade
u.grade2.grade
```

have exactly the same value. They are the names used by different interpretations for the same memory location. The same holds for the name fields in each structure. This is the one exception to the rule that says you shouldn't assign a value to one interpretation, then use the value of a different interpretation. Thus we could rewrite the printmark function as

```
void printmark(union STUDENT2 u)
{
    printf("Name: %s\n",u.grade1.name);
    printf("Grade %d\n",u.grade1.grade);
```

```
        if (u.grade1.grade == 1) {
            printf("Reading: %d\n",u.grade1.read);
            printf("Printing: %d\n",u.grade1.print);
            printf("Spelling: %d\n",u.grade1.spell);
            printf("Arithmetic: %d\n",u.grade1.arith);
        }
        /* and so on */
    }
```

9.4.2 Exercises

1. A store uses a C program to keep track of its credit accounts. Some accounts belong to individuals, while others belong to companies. Individuals are given account numbers in the range 1 to 1000; companies are given account numbers greater than 1000. The store often gives companies two discount rates: one rate on stationery and a different rate on other office supplies. Individuals usually are assigned a spending limit. Each account is represented by a structure declared with

```
struct ACCT {
    int id;             /* account number */
    char name[40];
    MONEY balance;      /* current account balance */
    union {
        MONEY limit; /* individual spending limit */
        struct {
            float st_disc; /* stationery discount */
            float other_disc; /* other discount */
        } comp;
    } type;
};
```

Write a function with the prototype

```
int newacct(struct ACCT *ap)
```

that prompts the program user to enter values to fill into the elements of the ACCT structure pointed to by ap. The value returned by newacct is the account number.

2. Write a program that uses newacct to get information for a number of ACCT structures and writes these structures into a file named "acctfile."

3. Write a program that reads "acctfile" and calculates the total of all the account balances.

4. Write a program that reads the structures in "acctfile", stores them all in a linked list sorted by account number, then writes the result back to "acctfile."

9.5 Review

A *structure* is a collection of objects, each of which may have a different type. Elements in a structure are referred to with expressions of the form

```
structure . element
```

or

```
pointer -> element
```

Structure types may be named with **typedef** declarations or by using a *structure tag*. Structure variables are initialized in much the same way as arrays.

Linked lists are made out of structures. Each structure in the list has an element that points to the next structure in the list. This element is called the *link*. Elements can be added and deleted in linked lists with relative ease.

A *union* is an object that can have several *interpretations*. Unions are often found inside structures, so that the structure can have several different forms. Unions can also have several different structure interpretations.

chapter 10   Large Programs

The programs that we have dealt with so far have usually been less than a page of code. These are useful for illustrating aspects of the C language, but they are not typical programs. Most C programs are much larger, stretching to dozens or even hundreds of functions. In this chapter, we will discuss some of the principles of writing large programs.

10.1 Multiple Source Files

The most important principle when writing large programs is that the code for the program should be broken up into a number of reasonably small files. Commonly, each function or group of related functions will be stored in a separate file. There are several reasons for splitting up your program.

(a)   Small files are easier to work with than large ones. If you want to change a line of code, it is easier to find the line in a small file than a big one.

(b)   A program is easier to understand when it is divided into "bite-sized chunks." For example, it is easier to write a function that solves a small part of a problem than to write a function that does a large number of things. **The philosophy of programming in C is to break up a problem into small manageable parts instead of trying to do everything at once.**

(c)   Debugging is easier when your program is broken into small pieces. Usually, you work on one piece until it is correct, then move to another piece. Errors are often localized—you only have to look at one part of the program instead of slogging through *all* the code.

(d)   C lets you translate pieces of your program separately, then "link" the pieces into an executable whole. If you are modifying or debugging one of the parts, you only have to translate that part after making a change, then link it with the other translated parts. You do not have to translate the whole program every time you make a small change.

For all these reasons, it makes sense to divide large programs into several different files. These files are called the **source files** of your program. Each source file should only contain a few functions; most programmers prefer to have one function per file unless there is a very good reason to put in more.

10.1.1 Shared Information

Some information should be made available to every function in every source file. For example, it will be useful for every source file to have an external prototype declaration for every function in the program, so that any function can call any other function. Similarly, functions often need access to manifests and macros set up with the **#define** directive. Lastly, **typedef** definitions and declarations for structure and union types often need to be available to a number of functions.

You could enter this information explicitly at the beginning of each file, but this is not recommended. Not only is this a lot of work, but there is a great possibility of typing errors (so that definitions and declarations that should be the same in each file are not). Also, if a declaration changes, you will have to edit every file that uses the declaration.

☞   The easier approach to sharing information is to create a single file that contains all the declarations and definitions that need to be shared.

Source files that want to use this information can obtain it by using an appropriate **#include** directive.

> **#include** *"filename"*

obtains all the C code stored in the given file and inserts it into the source file that contains the **#include** directive. For example,

```
#include "defs"
```

gets all the information stored in the file called "defs." This includes declarations, definitions using **#define**, and anything else the file holds. It is as if the **#include** line is replaced by the entire contents of the "defs" file.

Notice that the name of the file is given inside double quotes. This helps to differentiate between **#include** directives that obtain user definition files and ones that obtain <headers> supplied as part of the implementation package.

Traditionally, programmers put ".h" on the end of the name of any file that is intended to be included in this way. This is to emphasize the similarity between such files and the standard headers (<stdio.h>, <math.h>, and so on). In this book, we will not use names that end in ".h" because some implementations may not be able to support ".h" names.

A file that is included in this way can have **#include** directives of its own, including standard headers like <stdio.h> or other user files. This means that we could put all the prototypes in one file (say "proto"), all the **#define** statements in another (say "defines"), all the type declarations in a third (say "types"), and have a file with the contents

```
#include "proto"
#include "defs"
#include "types"
```

to obtain all the shared declarations and definitions.

10.1.2 External Variables

In the small programs discussed in earlier chapters, file scope variables could be used by all the functions in the file. When a program is broken into several source files, the situation becomes more complex. Sometimes you want to have variables that can be used by all the functions in the program, while at other times a variable should only be available to the functions in a single source file.

In order to have a file scope variable that is only available to the functions in a single source file, put the keyword `static` in front of the declaration of the variable. For example, if

```
static int i;
```

appears in a file (outside of any functions), it declares a file scope variable that will only be available to functions following the declaration, in the same source file that contains the declaration. As another example,

```
static struct {
    double x;
    int i;
} s[100];
```

declares a static array of structures.

In order to make a file scope variable available to all the functions in all the source files in the program, have *one* of the source files contain a normal file scope variable declaration, as in

```
int varname;
```

This is called the variable **definition**. All the other source files that refer to this variable should contain a declaration of the form

```
extern int varname;
```

In other words, they should have a declaration that looks like the original variable definition preceded by the keyword **extern**. This fully describes the variable, but the **extern** indicates that the actual variable definition is found in some other file. A variable that is available to all source files in the program is called an **external variable**.

If you want to initialize an external variable, the initializer must be given with the *definition* of the variable, not with any of the **extern** declarations.

A function may contain **extern** declarations for variables declared outside the function. These variables may be defined in the same source file or a different source file.

10.1.3 Static Functions

Just as a **static** variable can be accessed by all the functions in a file but not all the functions in a program, a **static** function can only be called by functions in the *same* source file.

A static function is defined by putting the keyword **static** in front of a normal function definition. For example,

```
static void switch(int *a,int *b)
{
    int temp;
    temp = *a;
    *a = *b;
    *b = temp;
}
```

is a function that can only be called by other functions in the same source file.

10.1.4 Exercises

1. CONCORDANCE QUESTION: Split your Concordance program so that each function is contained in a separate source file. There should also be a separate source file containing all external variable definitions.

10.2 Program Arguments

Just as a function may be passed arguments when it is called, a program may be passed arguments when it is invoked. Generally, these arguments are specified on the **command line** that invokes the program, but some systems have other ways to specify program arguments. Read your documentation or ask someone to find out how arguments are passed to programs on your machine.

Program arguments are generally used to specify **options** for the program. For example, recall the zoo programs we discussed in Section 9. Suppose we had a program that would print information from the "zoo" file in any one of a number of orders (by alphabetical order of common or Latin name, by enclosure number, by insurance value, and so on). The user could specify an option indicating which order was desired.

10.2.1 Arguments to the main Function

Regardless of how an implementation asks users to specify program arguments, a C program always *receives* the arguments in the same way. They are received as normal arguments to the main function of the program.

Box 10.1: Program Arguments

With **C2C**, program arguments are just specified, in order on the command line, as in

```
prog arg1 arg2 arg3 ...
```

Arguments may be separated with one or more spaces and/or horizontal tab characters.

Redirection symbols like <*filename* are removed *before* command line arguments are passed to your program. Therefore, the program will never see redirection symbols that may have appeared on the command line.

Up until now, we have been using the prototype

```
int main(void)
```

When a program accepts program arguments, the prototype for main is

```
int main(int argc,char *argv[])
```

or equivalently

```
int main(int argc,char **argv)
```

☞ The argc argument tells how many program arguments have been specified by the program user (argc stands for "ARGument Count"). The argv argument is an array of strings (represented as **char** pointers) and each string is an argument specified for the program (argv stands for "ARGument Vector").

The parameters need not be called argc and argv, but these names are almost universally used.

A program may use either of the two given prototypes for main. If the first (**void**) prototype is used, the program will ignore any program arguments specified by the user. If the second (argc, argv) prototype is used, the program arguments will be prepared for use by the program. (The program can still ignore the arguments, just as a function can ignore arguments it receives. However, it doesn't make much sense for a program to behave this way.)

10.2.2 Properties of Argc and Argv

When they are used, the argc and argv parameters always have the special properties described in this section.

There is always at least one member in the argv array: argv[0] is a string representing the program's name (as that is defined on the system running the program). If the program name cannot be obtained for the C program, *argv[0] will just be the NUL character (an empty string).

Because there is always at least one member in `argv`, the value of `argc` is always at least 1. If the user did not specify any program arguments, `argc` will be exactly 1.

The strings `argv[1]` to `argv[argc-1]` contain the program arguments, represented as normal strings terminated by `'\0'` characters. These strings can be modified by the program once it begins execution. In general, programs should expect that alphabetic characters in the argument strings may be either upper- or lowercase, although some systems automatically convert program arguments to a single case before passing the strings to the C program.

The memory location `argv[argc]` always contains a null **char** pointer. This helps to mark the end of the `argv` array.

10.2.3 Analyzing Options

As an example of how the `argc` and `argv` arguments can be used to control a program, let's consider a simple application. We will write a program based on our work of Section 9. The user will specify one or more enclosure numbers; the program will read the "zoo" file and print the common names of all the species that are found in that set of enclosures.

We begin by creating our shared information file. We will call this file "defs" and give it the following contents:

```
#include <stddef.h>
#include <stdio.h>
#include <stdlib.h>
#include <string.h>
#define SLEN 40

        /* TYPE DEFINITIONS */

typedef float MONEY;

struct SPECIES {
    char common_name[SLEN];
    char latin_name[SLEN];
    int females;
    int males;
    int babies;
    MONEY food;
    MONEY insurance;
    int enclosure;
};

struct LIST_ITEM {
    struct SPECIES desc;
    struct LIST_ITEM *link;
};
```

```
struct ILIST {
    int i;
    struct ILIST *link;
};

typedef struct LIST_ITEM *LPTR;
typedef struct ILIST *IP;

    /* FUNCTION PROTOTYPES */

extern LPTR makelist(void);
extern IP insert(IP,IP);
extern void printspecies(LPTR,int);
```

The makelist and insert functions were given in Section 9. We will assume that they are contained in a separate source file from main. The printspecies function is defined in the same source file as main (shown below).

Now, here is the source file containing the main function:

```
#include "defs"
#define IPSIZE (sizeof(struct ILIST))

int main(int argc,char **argv)
{
    IP ptr, enclist;
    LPTR speclist, sptr;
    int j;
    enclist = NULL;

    /* Get list of enclosures, in order */

    for (j = 1; j < argc; j++) {
        ptr = malloc(IPSIZE);
        sscanf(argv[j],"%d",&(ptr->i));
        enclist = insert(enclist,ptr);
    }

    /* Now get list of species */
    speclist = makelist();

    ptr = enclist;
    while (ptr != NULL) {
        printspecies(speclist,ptr->i);
        ptr = ptr -> link;
    }
    return EXIT_SUCCESS;
}
```

```
void printspecies(LPTR list,int encl)
{
    LPTR sp;
    if (list == NULL)
        /* Nothing in list */
        return;
    printf("\nSpecies in enclosure %d:\n",encl);
    sp = list;
    while (sp != NULL) {
        if (sp -> desc -> enclosure == encl)
            printf("    %s\n",sp->desc->common_name);
        sp = sp ->link;
    }
}
```

The part of this program that examines the program arguments is the loop:

```
for (j = 1; j < argc; j++) {
    ptr = malloc(IPSIZE);
    sscanf(argv[j],"%i",&(ptr->i));
    enclist = insert(enclist,ptr);
}
```

This uses the `sscanf` function to read integers from the strings in the `argv` array. One integer is read from each member in the array. These integers are sorted as they are read from the array because the `insert` function automatically sorts its integer list. In this way, the species will be printed in order of enclosure number.

The `printspecies` function runs through the items in the SPECIES list looking for all the species in a particular enclosure. This means that the program reads through the whole list for every enclosure. This is not the most efficient way to get the computer to do this work, but it is the easiest for a beginning programmer to write.

10.2.4 Exercises

1. Consider ways to make the program of the last section more efficient. How could you reduce the number of times the program had to go through the species list? How could you reduce the size of the list?

2. Change the program to take program arguments in different formats. Let M and N represent integers. If the user enters M,N as a program argument, the program will print out the species in all enclosures whose numbers are in the range M through N (inclusive).

3. CONCORDANCE QUESTION: Modify your Concordance program so that it accepts a command line argument that states a "pagelength." For example, the argument might state that a page is 60 lines long (so that input line 61 begins page 2 of the input text). If no such command line argument is specified, the program should choose a reasonable default. The Concordance program should print out both the page number and line number (on the page) of each occurrence of each word.

10.3 *Functions with a Variable Number of Arguments* _____

The `printf` and `scanf` functions do not always take the same number of arguments. For example,

```
printf("Hello.\n");
printf("%d",i);
printf("%d %8.2f\n",i,x);
```

illustrate calls to `printf` that take one, two, and three arguments. You may have thought that these functions could behave in this way because they were library functions. The actual reason is that they are declared in a special way that indicates their number of arguments can vary.

The prototype for `printf` takes the form

```
int printf(const char *format, ...)
```

The **int** value returned by `printf` indicates how many characters were printed out; we have been ignoring this value in all our programs, and can continue to ignore it.

The important part of the prototype is the ellipsis (. . .). This special notation in a prototype stands for an indefinite number of possible arguments (zero or more). The prototype for `printf` thus shows that every function call must specify a `format` string, and may also have additional arguments.

As further examples, here are prototypes for the other "variable argument" functions that we have discussed so far:

```
int fprintf(FILE *fp,const char *format, ...)
int fscanf(FILE *fp,const char *format, ...)
int scanf(const char *format, ...)
int sprintf(char *s,const char *format, ...)
int sscanf(const char *s,const char *format, ...)
```

The ellipsis always appears at the end of the parameter list. The other items in each list must be given in any function call.

10.3.1 Writing Variable Argument Functions

To demonstrate how to write a function that takes a variable number of arguments, we will write a function that can take an arbitrary number of integer arguments and return the value of the largest integer in the list. This function will have the prototype:

```
int imax(int count, ...)
```

The count parameter gives the number of integers in the list that follows. For example, in

```
imax(3,i,j,k)
```

the 3 indicates that three integers follow. The result of imax is the value of the largest of these integers.

10.3.2 Referring to Items in the Variable List

A function that takes a variable argument list obtains the values of arguments in the variable part of the list using special macros. You obtain the definitions for these macros with the line:

```
#include <stdarg.h>
```

The actual definitions for the macros will vary from system to system and are not important to most programmers. The important thing is how to use the macros.

All the macros refer to a variable of the type va_list. This is a special type defined with a **typedef** statement in <stdarg.h>. Every function that takes a variable number of arguments must declare a variable of this type, as in

```
va_list ap;
```

This variable will be used to refer to the arguments in the variable part of the argument list. To initialize the variable, you use a macro named va_start. The first argument of va_start is your va_list variable and the second is the name of the parameter that immediately precedes the ellipsis in the function prototype. For example, imax would use the macro call

```
va_start(ap,count);
```

to initialize the ap variable.

To refer to individual arguments in the variable part of the argument list, use a macro named va_arg. The first argument of the macro is the va_list variable. The second argument is the *type* of the value that you want to obtain from the argument list. The va_arg macro expands to an expression whose result is the appropriate argument value from the list. For example,

```
i = va_arg(ap,int);
```

obtains an **int** value from the variable part of the argument list and assigns it to the variable i.

Each call to va_arg obtains the next value from the argument list. For example, if you were writing your own version of printf, you would make repeated calls to va_arg to obtain values to print. The placeholders in the format string would tell you what types to specify in your calls to va_arg. If you found a %d placeholder, you would ask va_arg to obtain an **int**; if you found a %f placeholder, you would ask va_arg to obtain a **double**; and so on.

When you have finished obtaining values from the variable part of the argument list, you must call a routine named va_end, which performs any clean-up operations that may be necessary after moving through the list. The argument of va_end is the va_list variable.

Putting all these things together, here is a version of the imax function:

```
#include <stdarg.h>
int imax(int count, ...)
{
    int max, i;
    va_list ap;
    if (count <= 0) {
        printf("No arguments for imax.\n");
        return 0;
    }
    va_start(ap,count);
    max = va_arg(ap,int);
    for (count--; count > 0; count--) {
        i = va_arg(ap,int);
        if (i > max)
            max = i;
    }
    va_end(ap);
    return max;
}
```

The function returns a 0 if the value of count is negative or zero.

10.3.3 Argument Types in Variable Argument Lists

When a normal function is called, C converts all arguments to the types specified in the function's prototype. This cannot be done with a variable argument function, because the function's prototype does not indicate the types of arguments in the variable part of the list. For this reason, C performs the following **default argument conversions** for arguments in the variable part of the list:

(a)   **float** values are converted to **double**

(b)   **double** and **long double** values are passed without conversion

(c)   signed and unsigned **short** and **char** values undergo the integral promotions (to **int** or **unsigned**)

(d)   signed and unsigned **int** and **long** values are passed without conversion

As an example of the effect this has, suppose you want to write a function which takes a number of character arguments and returns a string that consists of the characters concatenated together. The last argument in the list will always be ′\0′. For example,

```
char cha = 'a';
char chb = 'b';
char chc = 'c';
s = concat(cha,chb,chc,'\0');
```

concatenates the arguments into the string "abc". We might write this function as

```
#include <stdarg.h>
#include <stdlib.h>
char *concat(char first, ...)
{
    va_list ap;
    char *string;
    int i, c;
    va_start(ap,first);
    /* First count number of args */
    for (i = 0; va_arg(ap,int) != '\0'; ++i)
        /* don't need body */ ;
    va_end(ap);
    /* Now start over at beginning */
    va_start(ap,first);
    string = malloc(i+1);
    for (i=0; (c=va_arg(ap,int)) != '\0'; ++i)
        string[i] = c;
    string[i] = '\0';
    va_end(ap);
    return string;
}
```

The calls to va_arg have to obtain an **int** value from the variable part of the list, not a **char**. In a variable argument function call, all **char** values are converted to **int**, so the va_arg macro call must specify the **int** type. The same principle applies to **float** values (which turn into **double**).

10.3.4 Exercises

1. Write a function with the prototype:

```
int strtot(int count, ...)
```

The function determines the total number of characters in one or more strings. The `count` argument tells how many strings are found in the variable part of the argument list. For example,

```
i = strtot(3,"abc","def","ghi");
```

would assign the value 9 to `i`.

2. Write a function with the prototype:

```
double *makearray(int count, ...)
```

Again, the `count` argument tells how many values are found in the variable part of the argument list. All of these are **double** values. The function should return a pointer to a **double** array whose members are the values given in the variable part of the argument list.

3. Write a function with the prototype:

```
float average(float first, ...)
```

This function's caller will pass one or more **float** values, and `average` will return the numeric average of all these values. The end of the list is indicated by the value `0.0` which is not included in calculating the average.

10.4 Review

Large programs should always be split over a number of small source files. Shared information should be contained in files obtained with **#include**. External variables should be defined in one or more external definition files.

A program's `main` function may have the prototype:

```
int main(int argc,char **argv);
```

The `argc` value is the number of *program arguments* passed to the program. The `argv` value points to the first element of an array of strings containing the program arguments.

Functions may be defined to take a *variable argument list*. This is represented by an ellipsis (`...`) in the function's prototype. The routines `va_list`, `va_arg`, and `va_end` help functions work with variable argument lists.

PART II
ANSI C: Programming Strategies

Learning about C doesn't stop when you have mastered the structure of a **for** loop and the rules of data conversion. In any sport, there is a great difference between knowing the game's *rules* and understanding the game's *strategy*. The same principle applies to programming.

Until now, we have been concentrating on the rules of C. In Part II, we will discuss strategies for using C productively in the "real world."

Much of this section deals with issues of programming *style*. It is easy for a programmer to underestimate the role of style in programming; one can say, "If the program works, who cares if it's pretty?" But experience teaches many lessons:

(a)   A well-organized program is easier to debug—and by now, you know that debugging takes much longer than writing the first draft of the program. By spending a little extra time on a clean first draft, you can save a lot of time in the debugging process.

(b)   Large programs are often written by programming teams. Each member of the team has to be able to read and understand what the others have written.

(c)   The vast majority of programs need to be changed after they have been in production for a while. Often the changes must be made by someone other than the original programmer. Good style is more than just making a program easier to understand; it's making the program easier to change.

(d)   A successful program will often be transferred (*ported*) from its original system to other systems so that it can be made available to new groups of users. Programs with good style are much easier to port.

For all these reasons, we think it is important to discuss style and how C programming works in practice—the strategy of C.

We should point out that there are always areas of disagreement about strategy. In football, for example, everybody (or almost everybody) agrees that a team should punt on the last down unless they're very close to making the required yardage; but there is strong disagreement over such questions as who should be the starting quarterback for next week's game.

In the same way, there will always be areas of agreement and disagreement in programming. For example, UNIX programmers have one set of biases, MS-DOS programmers have another set, and so on. Programmers who have experience with C may already have strong opinions about the way programs should be written, and may disagree with what we say here. To them, we reply that **ANSI** C is a different "playing field," and that some old strategies are no longer appropriate. We ask that all readers *think* about every suggestion we will make, and only make a decision after weighing all the alternatives.

chapter 1   The Seven Ages of a Program

Before we start talking about the contents of programs, it is useful to look at the programming process in general—how programs start, how they are carried through to completion, and how they are used, revised, and moved about. There is much more to programming than just writing code, and the good programmer pays attention to each aspect of the job.

For the purposes of this chapter, we have broken the programming process into the following stages:

> Design
> Coding
> Translation
> Linking
> Execution and Use
> Debugging
> Maintenance and Modification

As we will show, a great deal of time can be saved in the later stages by making a little extra effort in the earlier stages. In this chapter, we will discuss each of the stages briefly, in order to prepare you for some of the points we will make in the chapters to come.

1.1 Design

The process of designing a program has two major aspects:

(a) The first is producing a description of a program or set of programs that will solve a given problem or provide a required service, and that will do so in a way that human users will find satisfactory. This aspect of design is called **specification**.

(b) The second is developing a general outline or breakdown of how to write the program, bearing in mind any restrictions that might be imposed by the execution environment or the requirements of the job. In other words, you must decide on a practical approach towards meeting the specifications with the resources you have available. We will call this aspect of design **planning the implementation**.

It is common to have some conflict between these two aspects. An ambitious design that gives users everything they could possibly ask for may be impractical or impossible to implement. A design that is easy to implement may turn out to be too cumbersome to use. A compromise between the two aspects is frequently required. Nevertheless, every design must deal with these two factors: you have to decide what you want to do, and how you're going to do it.

Obviously, the design stage has an extensive effect on the other stages of programming. The design stage is the time to look for possible flaws in the way you will approach the program. It is better to avoid troubles right from the start than to look for a way to fix problems when you're halfway through the project.

All software designs operate under some restrictions: the abilities of the hardware that will be used; limits on time and money available for the implementation; and stipulations imposed by other people (for example, customers or corporate managers). Within these restrictions, programmers should design with a number of aims in mind. These aims are outlined in the sections that follow.

1.1.1 Defining the Real Task

The key to solving a problem is understanding the problem. In our context, the key to writing a program is understanding what the program is supposed to do—what it is *really* supposed to do, not necessarily what someone else has told you it is supposed to do.

Most programmers do not write programs on their own initiative; they write programs when someone asks them to do so. Student programmers are given assignments by their teachers; professional programmers are given assignments by their managers or their customers. This means that the programmer may not have firsthand experience of the task that the program will perform.

If an assignment comes through an intermediary in this way, it is important for the programmer to learn more before beginning the design. To put it bluntly, intermediaries may not be reliable; at the very least, they are usually biased.

For example, suppose a company has a task that can be handled by a computer. A company representative looks at the task and decides that it can be handled by a program that behaves in a certain way. That person may then approach a programmer and ask the programmer to write a program that behaves in the chosen way.

At this point, the programmer should take some time to investigate the original task. The company representative may well be wrong; there may be a better way to deal with the task. A professional programmer has experience using computers; a company representative may not. Program designers should understand the program's *job*, not someone else's idea of how the program should work.

Of course, there are many factors that limit a programmer's freedom to question a programming assignment. It can be inadvisable to imply that your boss or customers don't know what they're talking about. In the long run, however, you will serve everybody's interest better if you make sure that what people ask for is really what they want. Here are some points to check:

(a)   Who will be using the program? The "flavor" required by a program aimed at computing professionals is often different from the flavor of a program for inexperienced users. For example, computing professionals frequently demand that programs minimize the amount of keyboard typing that the user has to do. Trained secretaries, on the other hand, are usually skilled typists; they often find it easier to type a few extra letters on the main part of the keyboard than to take their hands off the keyboard to reach for a mouse or a special-purpose key.

(b)   What will people want to be able to do with the program? For example, suppose you are going to write a program that reads accounting information from a file and prints out bills to be sent to customers at the end of the month. Consider everything that users might want this program to do. It should be able to print out bills for all customers; but it should also be able to print out a duplicate bill for any given customer (in case someone spills coffee on the original). Maybe it should produce a report giving such useful statistics as the total amount owed by all customers, the average size of the bills printed, how many customers owe more than a specified amount, and so on. Try to foresee what the users will want to do, and give them the ability to do it.

(c)   What program features will be used most often? These are the ones that should be most efficient. They should also be the quickest and easiest to use. Bear in mind that users (even those with no computer experience) will soon memorize how to use the most common features. Such features do not need automatic memory aids like menus. Indeed, menus can be counterproductive if the user has to wade through a number of menu selections before being able to perform a simple operation.

(d)   What are people used to doing? If you write a program that is similar in style to existing programs in use on the same system, users will find it familiar and easier to learn. Consistency with other software should be a strong influencing factor, even if you think the other software is not as good as it should be. Unless you have a revolutionary approach whose superiority clearly outweights its unfamiliarity, aim for consistency with software that the users already know—it will let your users get results faster. (On the other hand, if you *do* have a revolutionary idea, don't let user inertia hold you back.)

(e)   What else could people want from this kind of program? The best programs give users what they want and a little bit more. For example, as a programmer you know that users are going to change their minds, even if the users themselves don't know it. Thus if a user asks for a program that prints out a report in a particular format, you should bear in mind that the user will inevitably want a different format sooner or later. Make it easy for users to tailor the report format when they change their minds.

1.1.2 Learning from Existing Programs

"Don't try to reinvent the wheel" is a popular saying among programmers. When you are writing a program, don't start from scratch; look at similar programs and learn from them. We aren't suggesting that you should copy or plagiarize, nor are we suggesting that you should avoid innovation. All we are saying is that you shouldn't write programs in a vacuum.

Whatever kind of program you are going to write, there is bound to be something similar that is already on the market. Have a look at the competition. Ask questions such as:

—   What are the good points of the programs?

— What are the bad points (and how can they be avoided)?

— Who actually uses the programs?

— Which features do they use most often, and which do they seldom use?

— What do users like and dislike about the programs? (A number of publications review programs currently on the market. Computer magazines also review new products.)

— Is there some way to write a program that would be more appealing to these users?

— Is there some way to write a program that would appeal to a different set of users (opening up a new market segment)?

In companies whose business is writing software, these questions are usually the direct concern of marketing personnel rather than programmers. Nevertheless, programmers need to know the answers just as much as salespeople do. A little research can avoid a lot of mistakes.

1.1.3 Planning for the Future

We have heard people argue that some programs are "one-shots." Supposedly, the programs will only be used once and then discarded, so it doesn't matter how carefully written they are, as long as they work.

☞ In our experience, there is no such thing as a one-shot program.

If it is useful to do some job once, circumstances will probably make it useful to do a similar job later on. For this reason, you should always work on the assumption that any program you write will be used again, possibly in a modified form and possibly by someone other than the original programmer. Every program has a future.

In the design stage, you should plan for the program's future. In particular, you should do your best to guess how the program may have to be changed and to make it as easy as possible for those changes to be made. Two major directions of change are:

Expansion
Expanding a program gives the program new abilities. Programs should be designed so that new abilities are easy to add. For example, you should avoid designs that require tables of information to have a fixed length. Later on, it may become necessary to add new information to such tables. Perhaps structure types should contain extra space to allow for future expansion.

Predict where it may be necessary to add new data, and make it possible to add that data. Similarly, predict where it may be necessary to add new functionality, and make it possible to add that functionality. Foresee situations where the program should print additional output (for example, more detailed reports) or less output (for example, reports that do not show some kinds of information, in the interests of secrecy). You should also expect that report formats may change from time to time.

In many cases, a design may allow for more functionality than will be implemented to begin with. The first version of a program doesn't have to do everything; however, there should be nothing in the program that prevents the addition of desirable features later on.

Porting

The second major direction of change is "porting"—transferring the program to a different machine and/or operating system. Computing equipment improves every year. You must design and write programs in such a way that they are easy to port to new systems. If you cannot port your programs, your users will be stuck using equipment that becomes more and more obsolete as time goes on.

The **ANSI** standard makes it possible to write portable code, but you have to be careful. For example, you should never use the / operator when dividing one integer by another if it is possible for either integer to be negative. The behavior of / is system-dependent. You must use the `div` library function instead (`div` is described in Section IV.4).

Much of the material in this Strategy section is aimed at making code portable. Follow these guidelines; otherwise, you may encounter serious difficulties if you want to bring up your programs on a new machine.

1.2 Coding

At first glance, writing the source code for a program may appear to be the most important step in the programming process. In a programming textbook (like this one), most of the pages are devoted to writing source code.

In practice, however, writing source code occupies less of a programmer's time than many other programming stages. Debugging is far more time-consuming; it is common for a programmer to spend an hour looking for a bug that can be corrected in seconds. The preliminary design stage often takes longer than actually writing the code, and testing can also be a lengthy process.

☞ Studies suggest that, on the average, professional programmers write less than ten lines of code a day; the rest of their time is spent on other stages of the programming process.

Thus if you want to improve your productivity and get your programs finished faster, speeding up the coding stage is not going to have as much of an effect as speeding up debugging or testing or maintenance. There is no point in "cutting corners" while coding, especially if it makes debugging or maintenance more difficult. In fact, taking extra care while coding may make for a lot less trouble later on. For this reason, most of Part II describes things you can do while coding that will simplify other aspects of programming.

1.3 Translation

Once source code has been written, it must be translated into machine code. Two basic approaches to the translation stage are:

Interpretation
   Interpretation works one statement at a time. The first statement is analyzed and executed, the next is analyzed and executed, and so on.

Compilation
   With compilation, the entire program is translated into machine code. Once this has been done, the translated code may be executed.

The difference is that interpretation performs translation and execution simultaneously, while compilation separates them into different stages.

With C programs, compilation is much more common than interpretation. Furthermore, C programs are usually written so that the source code is divided into a number of source modules, each of which can be compiled separately. It is much easier to work with a number of small files than one big one. For example, if you make a change in one source module, you only have to recompile that one module; you do not have to recompile everything.

1.4 Linking

When a source module of a program is compiled, the result is called an **object module**. The **linking** stage combines all the separate object modules (from the separate source modules) into a single program. The program that does this work is called the **linker** or **link editor**.

The linker's job is to resolve references. For example, suppose a module contains a call to a function defined in a different module. The linker must search through all the object modules to find the one that contains the desired function. Then the linker must adjust the object code in the original module so that it contains a complete reference to the given function. The details of this reference could not be figured out at the time the source code was translated, because only one source module is translated at a time. External references must be resolved later on.

On many systems, the linker is a very primitive piece of software; for some reason, linkers don't tend to be improved as quickly as other software. Because these linkers are not sophisticated, they can affect the way C programs must be written.

For example, many linkers truncate the names of functions and other symbols. Such linkers may only look at the first six or eight characters of the symbol's name. As a result, the linker might not be able to distinguish between names like `function1` and `function2` (where the names differ in the ninth character).

On systems that use such linkers, functions and objects with external linkage must be given names that differ in the first six or eight characters. Otherwise, the linker will not be able to distinguish one symbol from another. To assure portability, every function and every object with external linkage in *every* program should use names that are unique in the first six characters.

On some systems, the linker also ignores the case of letters in symbol names. For example, such a linker would believe that `NAME` and `name` referred to the same object. This means that your program should never rely on case distinction to differentiate external names.

The linking stage does more than link your separate object modules together. It also links in other software with your program. Specifically, it links in object code for all the library functions that your program calls. This library object code is stored in object files just like your translated object files, or else in a special **object library** which is essentially a number of object files gathered into a single file.

In order to simplify the linking process, you should attempt to minimize the number of ways in which separate modules interface with one another. The ways in which they interact should be made as obvious as possible. For example, the function call process is nicely unambiguous: a collection of arguments are passed explicitly, and a result is returned.

Using external variables for communication is much more obscure. For example, you should avoid having function A assign a value to an external variable which in turn affects the behavior of function B. This kind of coding is much more difficult to keep straight.

Programmers should pay special attention to the interfaces between modules. It is easy to make incorrect assumptions. For example, a programmer may believe that a function in a different module returns `0` for success and `-1` for failure, when the function actually returns `1` for success and `0` for failure. This is especially common when you have more than one person working on the same program, each person writing separate modules.

1.5 Execution and Use

Once the object modules of a program have been linked, the program is ready for execution. On most systems, you do this by invoking a program called a **loader**. Often the loader is invisible in some respects: you may think that you just type the name of the program and the program is executed. What actually happens in this case is that the loader is invoked automatically whenever you type in a command, and the loader loads the program you requested.

Programs are executed during the testing stage to see whether they work properly. Later on, they are executed by real users in order to perform jobs. In the section on design, we discussed some of the principles that govern interactions between programs and users, so we will not go into this matter any further.

1.6 Debugging

The debugging stage has several aspects. The simplest of these is getting rid of translation errors. Since the translator will provide error messages describing your translation errors (almost always typing mistakes), these bugs are not difficult to find and correct. Detection of these errors can be helped by using a good indentation style and by keeping source modules short (usually less than a page).

Execution errors are generally more difficult to handle. Implementations of C usually print out diagnostic messages for execution errors; but the mistake that caused the error may be some distance away from the place where the error actually occurred. For example, suppose your program aborts because the expression A/(*P) is division by zero. Obviously, *P has been assigned the value zero somewhere in the program; but finding where the assignment was made may be difficult. The assignment might be in another module. Particularly nasty bugs can occur when subscripts go out of bounds, as in

```
int array[20];
   ...
array[20] = 0;
```

Since the size of the array is 20, the maximum subscript of the array is 19. However, few implementations of C will detect that the given assignment is invalid. The assignment will still set some memory location to zero, but it won't be inside the array. This sort of mistake can change the value of a data object that is entirely unrelated to array. It can be a baffling error.

Logic errors are usually the hardest to locate. Your program runs without aborting, but the results are incorrect. In Section 5.10, we give a few hints that may help you find and correct your bugs more easily.

Testing is part of the debugging stage. It is not enough to correct all the bugs that immediately present themselves. You must design a set of tests that will detect more subtle bugs. For example, you must test the program on many different kinds of erroneous input, to make sure that the program can handle user mistakes. You certainly don't want a simple typo irrevocably destroying important information.

The testing stage should also test the documentation for the program. Does the documentation tell beginning users everything they need to know about the program? It is pointless to have a wonderful program that outsiders don't know how to use. As part of the testing, you should give both the program and the documentation to a typical user and see whether it is enough for that person to start doing useful work.

1.7 Maintenance and Modification

Someone once said that programming is the only job where adding another lane to a bridge is considered maintenance. Indeed, program "maintenance" is a misnomer. To maintain a program, you make whatever modifications become necessary as time goes on—either to correct bugs, to make improvements, or to adapt to changes in the way the program is used. Maintenance can involve a substantial amount of reprogramming, even if the end result seems to be a minor change.

Maintenance requires all the other steps of programming: designing, coding, compiling, and so on. A maintenance job may indeed take just as much work as you spent writing the original version of the program.

You can make the maintenance process easier for yourself if you accept that every program you write *will* have to be changed. Many of the suggestions we make in the chapters to come discuss ways in which you can write code to make change an easier task.

chapter 2   Code Lay-Out

A program should be written for maximum readability. This makes it easier for everyone (including yourself) to understand the program's logic. It can also make it easier to locate bugs while you are working on the program. In this chapter, we will discuss some ways in which code can be written to improve clarity.

2.1 Indentation

Experienced C programmers often have strong opinions on the "best" way to indent source code, place brace brackets, and so on; there have been many heated arguments on the topic. It would therefore be absurd for us to claim that the way we write source code is the *only* good way. Different people have different preferences, and we should not lay down our own style as if it were "religious dogma."

Nevertheless, beginners have to start somewhere, and even experienced programmers may find that a style which was well suited to older versions of C may not be as appropriate for the new **ANSI** C. Therefore, in this chapter we will give some general models for various source code constructs. These may be regarded as good starting points for developing a personal style of your own. Modify the models as you see fit, but always remember that the primary goal is to make source code easy to read and understand.

2.2 Line Length

C source code is commonly displayed either on paper or on a CRT (TV) display screen. The most common CRT screens show 80 characters per line. Paper printouts usually have longer lines—120 characters or more, depending on the type of printer being used.

If a source code line is longer than 80 characters, the line must be **folded** when it is displayed on a CRT screen. This means that the source code line must be split over more than one line on the screen. Folding makes the line harder to read and easier to misunderstand, so you should restrict source code lines to 79 characters or less.

Of course, complicated expressions may be longer than 79 characters, especially if the expressions have been indented several times. In such cases, split the expression over several lines yourself, breaking it at logical points. For example, you might write

```
if (    (c != ' ')
    && (c != '\t')
    && (c != '\n')
    && (c != '\f') ) {
    /* body of if */
```

This example breaks the condition of the **if** statement into several lines, making the split at a logical point in the expression. Also, by breaking up the **if** condition into its component parts, the statement is easier to read and to change (if necessary).

2.3 Comments

Comments at the beginning of a source file or preceding a function definition should not be indented. Comments inside a function should be indented to the same extent as the code surrounding them.

There should be a blank line before and after every large comment. The usual format of a comment should be

```
/*
 * This is a major comment
 * extending over several lines.
 */
```

In other words, the beginning /* and ending */ should be on separate lines, and lines inside the comment should begin with a *.

Minor comments (one or two words) can appear on a single line or at the end of a line. They should not appear in the middle of a line except in certain special cases that we will discuss in Section 2.5.2.

Every source file should begin with a comment describing the contents of the file. If the file contains several functions, it is often a good idea to put a comment in front of each function, explaining what the function does. In general, a function's parameter names should be sufficient to explain what each argument value means. Where there is doubt, however, the comment at the beginning of the function should explain how arguments and parameters are used.

Comments should be inserted into source code at any point where it is necessary to explain the intention of the code or to point out subtleties that may not be apparent. When writing a comment, take time to make its meaning as clear as possible—a comment that is misunderstood is worse than no comment at all.

In general, a comment should explain what a piece of code is intended to do, instead of going into long detail about how the job is done. The best description of the details of a job is the code itself; but the code may be incomprehensible without a description of what it is doing and why.

Most comments do not have to be long. A lengthy comment may do more to obscure than to clarify the program. If you find that a comment is growing too long, consider reducing the comment's job. For example, if a comment describing thirty lines of code is too long, you might consider using three comments that each describe ten lines of code. Short comments placed at appropriate points in a program are often more helpful than a single large comment at the beginning of the code.

If a comment *is* long, don't be stingy with white space inside it. When a comment looks like a single large block of text, readers will be inclined to skip it. If a long comment is broken into sections of three or four lines, each separated by blank lines, people will be more likely to read what you have written, and will find it easier to do so.

Comments should be kept up to date. Whenever code is changed, check all the nearby comments to make sure that they are still correct and relevant.

You can make it easier to keep comments up to date by putting them in the right place. For example, when a comment describes a data structure, make sure the comment appears in the actual file that defines that structure. If you put the comment in another file (for example, one that `#include`s the actual structure definition), it is quite likely that you may change the structure at a later date, but forget to change the comment.

2.3.1 White Space

It is often helpful to separate sections of your program with blank lines. For example, put a blank line after the comment at the beginning of a program. If a source file has a number of `#include` directives, put a blank line after the last one to separate the directives from the rest of the program. If a file contains more than one function, use blank lines to separate functions (or even put in a formfeed character so that a new function starts on a new page). Blank lines are also appropriate to separate a function's declarations from the function's statements and to separate the statements of a function into logical sections.

Indentation at the beginning of a line is crucial in illustrating the logical structure of a program. The most straightforward "unit" of indentation is the horizontal tab character, so that each level of indentation is represented by a single tab. In this book, we assume tab stops are set every four spaces along the line, but settings of five or eight spaces are also common.

2.4 Declarations

All declarations should specify a type for the function or object being declared. It is true that a default type of **int** is used when no type is explicitly declared, but your program will be much easier to understand if **int** data is explicitly declared as **int**.

The **auto** storage class specifier is never needed; it should be omitted. Other storage class specifiers are discussed in later sections. When a storage class specifier is present in a declaration, it should always precede the type specifier.

When several variables are declared in the same declaration, they should be directly related. For example, you could say

```
int upperbound, lowerbound;
```

when the two variables act as bounds on some value. Declaring these two variables in the same declaration *shows* that they are related. However, when variables are closely related in this way, they should be declared separately, as in the following routine which reads ten integers from the standard input and returns the average value.

```
int average(void)
{
    int input;      /* input number */
    int sum = 0;    /* sum of numbers */
    int i;          /* loop counter */
    for (i = 1; i <= 10; i++) {
        if (1 != scanf("%i",&input)) {
            fprintf(stderr,"\aExpected integer\n");
            exit(EXIT_FAILURE);
        }
        sum += input;
    }
    return sum/10;
}
```

The `average` function above is simple enough that we didn't really need to put comments on each variable declaration. In a larger piece of code, however, it is often helpful to add a comment to each declaration, in order to explain how the declared symbol will be used.

Never declare more than one variable in a single declaration if the variables have different types or if they have a derived type. For example, you will find

```
char *a, *b, *c;
```

to be difficult to change if you want to use a defined name, as in

```
typedef char *STRING;
STRING a, b, c;
```

Also, statements like

```
char *  a, b, c;
```

can be misleading. At first glance, you may think the three variables all have the **char *** type. In fact, only a will be **char *** and the others will just be **char**.

2.4.1 Symbol Names

Symbol names should be meaningful. Abstract names are occasionally acceptable (for example, using i for a counter in a **for** loop, or ch for an input character), but only in short pieces of code that are easily understood as a whole. In general, a symbol's name should suggest the symbol's use.

In general, you should not depend upon the case of letters to distinguish different names that have the same scope. For example, your program should not have variables named var and VAR in the same scope. It is too easy to confuse the two when you are entering or reading the program.

Underscore characters are useful in long names. For example,

```
struct LP_ALBUM {
      int    order_number;
      char   *artist_name;
      char   *company_name;
      MONEY  wholesale_price;
      MONEY  retail_price;
      int    year_published;
};
```

shows a structure declaration that makes extensive use of the underscore in names that are each made up of several words. (Note that we indented the structure member names to line them up; this improves readability somewhat.)

By convention, manifest names should always have their letters entirely in uppercase. Putting such names in uppercase makes them stand out more clearly in source code, so you can distinguish them from normal variables.

Usually, you should avoid macros that have side effects; use real functions instead, to avoid confusion. If there is some compelling reason to create a macro that might have side effects, give the macro a name that is entirely in uppercase, to remind you to be careful.

Other macros may be put in lowercase or mixed case; since they have no side effects and are used like functions, there is no reason to differentiate them from functions in a visible way. (Remember that the C library can implement routines as either macros or functions.)

Type names defined in **typedef** statements should usually be put into uppercase or mixed case. Again, the point is to distinguish them from ordinary names and make them stand out.

Other symbols should be written in lowercase or mixed case. While some programmers find mixed case appealing, others prefer to use lowercase exclusively, because this eliminates the need to remember which letters are in which case. We regard this as a matter of personal preference.

Remember that you should avoid names beginning with the underscore character, since these may be used for the internal workings of C. You should also avoid names that begin with any of the sequences

```
is    mem    str    to    E    SIG
```

because future versions of the standard may use such names for special purposes.

2.4.2 Global Symbols

In any program that is broken into several source files, there will be some symbols that are used by more than one file. These include

(a)   defined types that are used in more than one file (structures, unions, **typedef**, and **enum** types);

(b)   variables with external linkage;

(c)   manifests of various kinds;

(d)   names of functions that are not declared **static**.

We call such symbols **global** symbols.

When the source files for a program are translated, it is important that they all use the same definitions for these global symbols. For example, errors are almost sure to occur if two source files have substantially different declarations for the same structure.

The best way to ensure that global symbols are uniformly defined or declared in all source files is to create one or more **global declaration files**. Such files serve the same purpose as standard header files like <stdio.h>; they group together a number of declarations or definitions for global symbols.

Source files that use a particular global symbol should **#include** the global declaration file that declares that symbol. Individual source files should *not* contain their own declarations for the symbol. There are several advantages to this practice.

(a)   It saves typing. You do not have to type in a symbol's declaration for every source file that uses that symbol. Not only does this save time, but it also avoids errors due to mistyping.

(b)   It makes source files smaller and therefore more readable. There is a single **#include** directive instead of a large number of declarations.

(c)   It simplifies changes. For example, suppose you want to add another element to a particular structure type. All you have to do is change the structure definition in the appropriate global declaration file, and all the source files that **#include** the file will automatically "inherit" the change. Without a global declaration file, you would have to change the declaration in every source file that referred to the structure.

(d)   It gathers many global declarations in a single place. To obtain information about global symbols, you just have to look at the appropriate declaration file; you do not have to look through a large number of source files in search of a declaration.

The global declaration files of a program should contain the following:

(a)   A declaration for every data object with external linkage. Each declaration should use the **extern** storage specifier and should not contain an initializer.

(b)   An external prototype declaration for every user-written function that is not declared as **static**.

(c)   All **typedef** declarations in the program (except for ones local to a single function).

(d)   A definition for each **struct**, **union**, and **enum** type not local to a single function. Each of these definitions should have a tag and list all the type's members. Other source files should *not* attempt to redeclare the members of such types.

(e)   A definition for each macro and manifest that is pertinent to more than one function.

Global declaration files should *only* contain declarations and definitions; they should not contain executable code or initializations.

For some programs, it may be simplest to put all global declarations into a single file. In large programs, it is usually better to have several global declaration files, each containing a group of related symbols. This is similar to the way that <stdio.h> deals with symbols related to I/O, <math.h> deals with mathematical symbols, and so on.

2.4.3 External Variables

As noted in III.5.3.4, data objects that have external linkage may have any number of *declarations* but can only have one *definition*. A definition of such an object is a declaration that does not contain the **extern** keyword or one that has an initializer.

Experience shows that it is useful to create a small number of files containing definitions for all external data objects. We call such files **external definition files**. These files keep all the definitions together, instead of scattering them through other source files where they may be overlooked amidst executable code.

The definitions in an external definition file are declarations without the keyword **extern**. Any initializers should also be given in this file. The file should contain nothing but object declarations; it should not contain any function definitions.

The external definition file should **#include** all global declaration files. This may be necessary to obtain necessary type and manifest definitions. It is also useful to ensure that the declarations in the global declaration file coincide with the object definitions in the external definition file. If, for example, the global declaration file declares a variable x to be **int** but the external definition file defines it as **long**, you will find out about the problem when you translate the definition file (because the translation phase will generate an appropriate error message).

Notice that the declarations of external objects in the global declaration file should all have the keyword **extern** and not contain initializers. This makes them declarations, not definitions. The only definition for an external object is the one in the external definition file. All other source files use the simple declaration from the global declaration file.

2.4.4 Array Declarations

Array declarations should use manifests or **enum** values to represent the array dimensions. For example, use constructs like

```
#define SIZE1 (20)
enum { SIZE2 = 30 };
int iarr[SIZE1];
float farr[SIZE2];
```

instead of

```
int iarr[20];
float farr[30];
```

NOTE: The above examples are not as good as they could be. Ideally, the names of manifests or **enum** values chosen should be *descriptive*, not generic like SIZE1 and SIZE2. In the context of a real program, it should be possible to use names that indicate why a particular size value was chosen.

Different arrays should usually have different size manifests or **enum** values unless the arrays are directly linked in some way. Don't use the same symbol for two array sizes if the sizes just happen to be the same.

2.4.5 Structure and Union Declarations

There are two models for structure declarations.

> **struct** *tag* {
>   *type name*;
>   *type name*;
>   ...
> };

declares the contents of a structure. This will appear in a global declaration file, unless the structure type is local to a single function.

> **struct** *tag identifier*;

declares an object with a structure type. Union types and objects are declared similarly.

Do not combine a declaration of the members of a structure or union type with a declaration of an object of the type. Use two separate declarations. For example,

```
struct TAG {
    /* elements */
};
struct TAG variable;
```

is better than

```
struct TAG {
    /* elements */
} variable;
```

The second example tries to do too much; it is more compact, but harder to read.

Declarations of members within structures or unions should follow the usual rules for declarations. For example, a separate declaration should be given for each member. It is often helpful to provide comments explaining how each element is used.

Many programmers like to put structure and union tags in uppercase so that they stand out clearly in source code. This is not as necessary as putting manifests in uppercase, since tags can only appear after appropriate keywords (**struct** or **union**).

It is usually a good idea to declare structures using a **typedef** statement, as in

```
typedef struct {
            /* fields */
} NAME;
```

Once you have done this, you should use NAME instead of normal structure declarations. Often, you don't need to add a structure tag to this kind of structure, because the **typedef** name is the only identifier you need. A structure tag is only required if the structure contains embedded pointers to structures of the same type.

2.4.6 Enumerated Types

Enumerated types follow many of the same rules as structures and unions. The declaration that lists the values of the type should be separate from declarations for objects of the type. In general, the declaration that lists the values of the type should be given in a global declaration file, unless the type is local to a single function.

In order to make enumerated values stand out more clearly in source code, many programmers always write them in uppercase (like manifest names).

2.4.7 Initializations

As much as the language allows, an initialization value should have the same type as the object being initialized. For example, you should say

```
double x = 1.0;
```

instead of

```
double x = 1;
```

The second version is valid, but the first emphasizes that x is a floating point number.

If an initialization value is the result of an expression, show the expression. For example, the expression in

```
const double pi_by_2 = 3.1415926536 / 2.0;
```

more clearly conveys the meaning of the symbol than the single number 1.5707963. (With floating point numbers like this, it is also a good idea to make sure you have written the value with as much precision as your machine allows.)

Initializers for multidimensional arrays should *always* use internal braces to group together initialization values. For example, you should say

```
int arr[3][4] = {
    { 1, 2, 3, 4 },
    { 5, 6, 7, 8 },
    { 9, 10, 11, 12 }
};
```

instead of

```
int arr[3][4] = {
    1,2,3,4,5,6,7,8,9,10,11,12
};
```

even though the two have the same effect. The same holds for structure initializations.

All initializations should be explicit. It is true that external objects are initialized to zero by default, but you should not make use of this feature. If you want an object initialized, specify an explicit initializer in the object's definition, even if the initialization value is zero.

```
int x = 0;
```

shows that you really want x to have an initial value of zero. In this way, the initializer becomes a kind of comment to the reader. If an object has no initializer, you indicate that it will be set explicitly before it is used; if it has an initializer, you indicate that it will (probably) be used immediately, without being set.

2.4.8 Function Prototypes

Function declarations should always use the prototype form. Ideally, every prototype should list both the types and names of the function's parameters. Specifying parameter names makes it clearer how each argument will be used, and also makes it easier to understand complicated types. For example, it is easier to understand

```
extern double f( double (*func)() );
```

than

```
extern double f( double (*)() );
```

The presence of the name helps determine how to interpret a parameter declaration.

Never declare a parameter to be an array; instead, declare it to be a pointer of the appropriate type. Our reasoning is that the parameter is going to *be* a pointer, and declaring it to be an array will only be confusing. As an example of confusion, consider the following:

```
int f(int a[])
{
    int b[20];
    ...
}
```

If the function takes the **sizeof** b, it will obtain the total number of bytes in the array. However, if the function takes the **sizeof** a, it will obtain the size of an **int** pointer. Such oddities can be avoided if a is declared an **int** pointer to begin with.

Many programmers like to begin function definitions with prototypes written as

> *type*
> *name*(*arguments*)

as in

> ```
> double
> f(double x)
> ```

This format puts the name of the function at the beginning of a source code line, often making it easier for text editor programs to find the start of the function. Human readers sometimes find the format more convenient too.

Long lists of parameters should be split over several lines. For example, the prototype for the bsearch library function might be written

```
void *
bsearch(
    const void *key,
    const void *table,
    size_t N,
    size_t keysize,
    int (*compar)(const void *,const void *)
);
```

2.5 Statements

In this section, we provide models for common statement types.

2.5.1 Expression Statements

Any expression may serve as a C statement, but the only ones that serve a purpose are expressions that perform assignments, function calls, or increment/decrement operations.

Assignment statements have the form

> *expr* = *expr* ;

If an assignment is too long to fit on a single source code line, one natural place to break up the statement is after the ′=′ sign, as in

```
struc1.struc2.element =
    (a[i+j] + a[j+k] + a[k+i]) * 5;
```

A statement should only perform a single assignment, except in very simple cases like

```
x = y = z = 0.0;
```

where all the variables have the same type and are related in some way. This rules out expressions like

```
a = 9 + (b=2) ;
```

Do not cast the right-hand side of the assignment to the type of the left-hand side. To understand why we make this recommendation, consider

```
float *fp;
    . . .
fp = f();
```

If f is not a function that returns a **float** pointer, the assignment will cause an error, telling you that something has gone wrong. However, if you wrote

```
fp = (float *) f();
```

the statement would be valid no matter what kind of value f returns. Without an error message, this assignment would be an "invisible" trouble spot, possibly yielding execution errors or invalid results. We believe programmers should write programs in such a way that the C translator *warns* you of potential difficulties. This approach is much better than writing code that avoids translation errors but may result in harder to trace errors later on.

In general, comma expressions should be avoided. This is especially true in function arguments, where comma expressions may easily be misread. For example,

```
f((a,b))
```

is a function call with a single comma expression argument; however, it would be very easy to mistake for a function taking two arguments. Argument values should *not* be explicitly cast into the type expected by the function. In a program that has been properly written using prototype declarations for every function called, arguments are automatically cast to the expected type.

If you are passing the value of an object as argument to a function, make sure that the object has been explicitly assigned a value, either with an initializer or an assignment statement. Errors may occur if you attempt to pass the value of an object that has not been initialized, even if the function that is being called does not try to use the value. The procedure that passes the argument values may produce an error if an invalid value is passed.

2.5.2 Loops

The model for a **while** loop is

```
while (condition) {
    statements
}
```

The model for a **do-while** loop is

```
do {
    statements
} while (condition);
```

The model for a **for** loop is

```
for (init; cond; incr) {
    statements
}
```

Brace brackets may be omitted if the body of a loop is a single statement. If there are no statements in the body of a loop, put in a comment to point this out, as in

```
while ( s[++i] != '\0' )
    /* nothing */;
```

This makes the statement easier to recognize as a loop with no body.

The three expressions at the beginning of a **for** loop should be as simple as program logic permits. For example,

```
for (i=0; i<=10; printf("%d",++i))
    /* nothing */;
```

is valid, but it is hard to read.

```
for (i=0; i<=10; ++i)
    printf("%d",i);
```

is much more understandable. (NOTE: Some programmers may think that the hard-to-read example can be justified on the grounds that it is "more efficient." With most modern implementations, this is simply not true; the translation software is competent enough to use the same code for both.)

2.5.3 If Statements

The model for an **if** statement is

```
if (condition) {
    statements
}
```

The model for an **if-else** is

```
if (condition) {
    statements
}
else {
    statements
}
```

If there are several sequential **else**-**if** combinations, they should all be at the same level of indentation, as in

```
if (condition) {
    statements
}
else if (condition) {
    statements
}
else if (condition) {
    statements
}
else {
    statements
}
```

In **if-else** constructions, the condition should be chosen so that the **if** clause is shorter than the **else** clause (if the two are of unequal length). For example, if you have

```
if (x == 1) {
    /* Many statements */
}
else {
    /* Few statements */
}
```

you should rewrite the code as

```
if (x != 1) {
    /* Few statements */
}
else {
    /* Many statements */
}
```

By starting with the shorter clause, the **if** and **else** lines are relatively close together in the source code and the reader will have an easier time associating them with each other.

Whenever possible, avoid code of the form

```
if (condition) ...
    if (condition) ...
    else ...
else ...
```

If there is a lot of code in the **if** and **else** clauses, the second **else** ends up too far from the original **if** and the program is harder to understand. It is usually better to rewrite the code (possibly changing the condition expressions) to get the form

```
if (condition) ...
else if (condition) ...
else ...
```

In this form, each **else** is more closely associated with its **if**.

Use a **switch** statement instead of constructs of the form

```
if (x == 1) ...
else if (x == 2) ...
    ...
```

2.5.4 Switch Statements

The model of a **switch** statement is

```
switch (expression) {
case const-expr:
    statements
case const-expr:
    statements
case const-expr:
    statements
    ...
default:
    statements
}
```

In this case, indentation is only two spaces, half the usual indentation. Through experience, we have found that you get too much indentation if you use full indentation for every case (especially when you have **switch** statements inside **switch** statements). The constant expressions in the **case** labels should be as simple as possible. The **default** label should be the last in the block.

If the statements for one case fall through into the next case, put in a comment to indicate this, as in

```
case '-':
  sign = -1;
  /*FALLTHROUGH*/
case '+':
  n = (n*10) + (c-'0');
```

Without this kind of comment, a reader may not notice that the code for one case continues into the next.

If a statement has a large number of **case** labels, they may be put on the same line, as in

```
case '0': case '1': case '2': case '3': /* etc */
```

Otherwise, each **case** label should appear on a separate line.

2.6 Mixing Styles

If you are asked to modify an existing program, you may find that the program is written in a style that is different from yours. In this case, your new code should use the style of old code, even if the style is not to your tastes—unless you are willing to rewrite the entire program. Consistency is more important than niceties of form.

chapter 3   Construction of Functions

We know that a program is made up of functions. Conceptually, however, it is often useful to think of a program as a separate entity that calls upon functions to perform various tasks. From this point of view, a function is a *tool* that a program uses to do work.

To be a good tool, a function must be easy to use and easy to control. It should do its job, and *only* its job. For example, a well-written function does not have unexpected side effects; it only performs actions that are relevant to its work.

In this chapter, we will suggest many ways to write functions that are useful and easy to understand. While a particular program may require a function that violates one of these rules, we believe that such exceptions are actually quite rare. In programming, as in many other pursuits, letting yourself get sloppy will eventually come back to haunt you.

3.1 Function Size

The source code for a typical C function should be less than a page in length. If it is any longer, the function is probably trying to do too much. Take suboperations of the function and put them into separate functions.

The only kinds of functions that may be substantially longer than a page are ones that contain large **switch** statements. If a **switch** has many possible cases, it can grow quite large, even if there are only a few lines of code for each case. Some effort should be made to keep the code for each case relatively small. For example, each case might call a separate function to perform the appropriate work.

It is most convenient to keep each function in its own separate file. With this scheme, the name of the file can reflect the name of the function it contains, making it easy to find a function in a set of source files. If you keep more than one function in a file, it is often difficult to figure out which source file contains which functions.

3.2 Isolating Functionality

If a particular operation is performed at many points during program execution, create a function to perform that operation. This makes sure that the operation is always performed the same way.

For example, suppose your program can issue error messages at several different points in execution. You could have the program write these messages directly with printf, but it is better to write a separate function that every other function in the program calls when an error message has to be written out. Such a function might have the same sort of prototype as printf, as in

```
int error_message(const char *format, ...)
```

so the function is used in the same way as `printf`. For example,

```
error_message("Invalid number '%d'",value);
```

specifies a format string and value to fill into the string's placeholder.

Why should you use a special function instead of `printf`? Writing a distinct `error_message` function has several advantages.

(a) A call to `error_message` can be distinguished from calls to `printf`. When a function makes a call to `error_message`, you immediately know an error message is being printed. If the source code just contains a call to `printf`, you have to do more reading before you figure out if the call prints out an error message or something else.

(b) Calls to `error_message` stand out in source code. If you want to determine which functions issue error messages, or get a list of all error message issued by the program, just look for calls to `error_message`.

(c) The `error_message` function can do additional processing before the error message is written. For example, `error_message` may add the name of the program to the text of the error message or format the message in some other way (for example, splitting long messages into more than one line of output). This additional processing is done in a uniform way, which means that the format of error messages is always consistent.

(d) Changes are easier to make. For example, suppose you decide that error messages sent to interactive terminals should cause the terminal to "beep" or issue some other special signal to attract the user's attention. If you have an `error_message` function to print all error messages, all you have to do is modify `error_message` to arrange for the beep. If you just use `printf` directly, you have to go through your program and modify every `printf` command that issues an error message.

(e) Bugs are often easier to track down. If an error message is not printed out properly, the obvious place to start looking for the bug is the `error_message` routine.

Using a specialized error message routine instead of the more general `printf` is called **isolating functionality**. This means that a particular operation (writing error messages) is performed in only one place in your program (the `error_message` routine) instead of in several places throughout the program.

Isolating functionality makes your program easier to read, to analyze, to modify, and to debug. It can also lead to programs that are more attractive to users. For example, suppose that a particular type of terminal can print output in a variety of colors. You would like to print error messages in red on this kind of terminal, but on other terminals, the messages will have to be printed as normal text. If your program uses `error_message`, the function can be modified to determine which type of terminal is being used and to do whatever extra processing is needed to print red on color terminals.

But what would happen if your program just used direct calls to `printf`? In order to get colored error messages, you would have to add extra code to every function that writes an error message. That might need a lot of extra code and a lot of extra work. Many functions would become bigger, and your program would take up more room in the computer's memory. You might decide the change is more trouble than it's worth.

The contrast is clear: a program which isolates a particular functionality can be given special features more easily than a program which does not. The technique makes it easier to write more versatile programs. Naturally, this is of great importance in commercial programs, but even if you're just writing programs for personal use, you'll find the flexibility worthwhile.

3.3 Cover Functions

The `error_message` routine discussed in the last section is an example of a **cover function**. It acts as an intermediary between the user-written functions of your program and a particular library function (in this case, `printf`).

Using such intermediary functions is particularly helpful when you want a particular program to be able to run on several different computer systems. The reason is that library functions often vary from system to system. In addition, a library function found on one system may not be available on a different system. If your program calls a particular library function directly in several different places, you will run into trouble if you try to move the program to a system where the function isn't available. You will also have trouble if the function is available but is slightly different on the new system.

Such problems can be avoided if all calls to the library function go through the intermediary of a cover function. The library function is *only* called by the cover function. If the library function is not available or behaves differently on a new system, the *only* thing that needs to be changed is the cover function. The other functions in the program need no adjustment; they just call the cover function and let it handle any problems that arise.

As we saw with `error_message`, cover functions offer more than just adaptability; they also let you improve on functionality. You can enhance a cover function so that it does more than just call a particular library function. The cover function may perform error-checking that the library function does not, or additional processing that is useful in some situations.

For example, suppose a program always calls `malloc` through a cover function. The cover function can always check that `malloc` does not return the `NULL` pointer (indicating a failure to obtain appropriate space). Checking for this possibility requires a lot of extra coding if you call `malloc` directly in several parts of your program; however, you can put it into a single cover function without trouble.

Many programmers find it useful to have cover functions for every major library routine. The one exception is `setjmp` which cannot have a cover function for technical reasons; as noted in Part IV, `setjmp` is useless once the function that contains the function call has returned. Thus there is no point in putting `setjmp` in a cover function that is called and then immediately returns. One way around this problem is to create a "cover macro" that calls `setjmp` in a standard way. This serves the same purpose as a cover function but does not involve an actual function call.

3.3.1 Function Arguments

In general, a function should check its arguments to make sure that the values are valid. This is particularly true of high-level functions in a program. Low-level ones (performing very simple jobs and used frequently) may be permitted to assume that their arguments are correct, so that they can do their job quickly. However, never forget that detecting problems before they happen is easier than recovering from errors after they happen.

Cover functions should be particularly careful about checking argument values. In many implementations, library functions do little error-checking; therefore, the cover function must check the arguments first.

The order of function arguments should follow some consistent scheme. Most library functions specify arguments serving as output before ones serving as input. For example, the `strcpy` function has the prototype

```
char *strcpy(char *dest, const char *source)
```

The `source` string is copied into the `dest` string, so the `dest` argument is specified first.

Another useful convention is to put the most-important arguments first and less-important arguments afterwards. For example, if you have a function `add_item` which adds an item to a linked list, you might use the prototype

```
LIST add_item(LIST l, LIST_ITEM i)
```

The `LIST` argument precedes the `LIST_ITEM` argument, because the entire list is more important than a single item.

If you have this kind of consistent plan for ordering the arguments to user-written functions, you won't get confused and write arguments in the wrong order. Avoiding such problems is important because they are often difficult to detect when reading code.

3.4 Return Values

Never return a pointer to a variable with block scope. When the function returns, the space that is used for block scope variables is freed for use by other functions. Therefore the value stored in a block scope variable may be overwritten by other function calls. You can use the pointer to look at what is stored in the variable's old location, but there is no assurance that the value stored in this location is correct.

If a function has to return a pointer to something that the function creates, use `malloc`, `calloc`, or `realloc` to obtain space for the object being created. Space allocated through these library routines is *not* freed when the function returns, and therefore it retains its value.

3.5 *Coalescing Functions*

In the stepwise refinement approach to programming, you break a program up into smaller operations, break up those operations into suboperations, and so on. When the code for the program is written, you have the `main` function calling a number of secondary functions, each secondary function calling smaller functions, and so on. Each major function leads to a number of minor (low-level) functions.

As a program is being written, it is a good idea to keep an eye on the low-level functions that it uses. You will often find that you have several low-level functions that perform the same operation (or closely related operations). This happens because the stepwise refinement process "separates" operations into smaller operations.

Of course, having several functions that duplicate each other's work is inefficient. Therefore you should occasionally check your program and get rid of this sort of duplication. We call this process "coalescing" a group of duplicate functions into a single function.

Several functions may be coalesced into one even if the original functions are not exactly identical. As an example, consider the `qsort` library function (described in the Reference Manual). This is a general purpose function for sorting arrays of data, regardless of the type of the array. By using this one routine, you can avoid writing different routines for sorting integer arrays, character arrays, structure arrays, and so on. You can create your own general purpose functions in similar ways and avoid having a number of different functions that do almost the same thing.

This leads us to the concept of a **user library**. A user library is a collection of functions that serve the same purpose as the library functions supplied as part of the C implementation. They are general purpose functions that are applicable to a number of different programs.

As a C programmer, you begin building your own library of functions—routines that may be used in many different programs. There are several reasons why different programs can use the same routine.

(a)   The routine has a sufficiently general nature (like the ones in the standard C library).

(b)   The programs all handle the same sort of work. For example, a programmer in the accounting department of a large company may be required to write several different accounting programs, but the programs can often use many of the same functions.

(c)   Even when programs are unrelated, a programmer's personal way of looking at problems may lead to similarities in coding. For example, a programmer is likely to prefer a particular method of reading and analyzing user input, even though there are many possible approaches. By building up a collection of routines that reflect your personal programming preferences, you can simplify the amount of work you do in writing any one program.

The arguments in favor of creating your personal function library are the same as those in favor of cover functions. If many programs use the same function, you can improve all those programs by improving the one routine (either by making the routine more efficient or by giving the routine new functionality). You also reduce the effort of writing a particular program: instead of writing code from scratch, you can make use of your existing routines. Since an existing routine has already been debugged, you save time in both the coding and the debugging stages.

3.6 Black Boxes

In many disciplines, the term **black box** is used for a machine whose internal workings are invisible to the user. The user only knows that if you feed a certain type of input into the black box, a certain effect occurs. For example, a car's braking system is a black box to many people: all they know is that when they step on the brake pedal, the car will stop. Even if you know how brakes work, you treat them as a black box when you're driving; if you have to make an emergency stop, you don't take time out to contemplate the mechanisms involved, you just stamp on the pedal. No manufacturer would build a car with brakes that could only be used by a driver with expert mechanical knowledge.

The black box way of thinking is central to good programming. Functions should be written so that they can be used as black boxes.

☞   You should not have to know how a function works to be able to use that function.

As an example of a function that works as a black box, consider `printf`, which must read through the format string, convert each of the output argument values into the required form, and then set in motion the complicated electronic and mechanical processes that will eventually display characters on a terminal or printer. As a user, you don't have to understand how `printf` does all this; you just have to know that it will do what you ask it to do.

As an example of a function that doesn't work as a black box, picture a function whose behavior is determined by the values of several external variables. Such a function is much harder to use; you may have to look at the function's code to figure out all the interdependencies.

If the functions of a program behave as black boxes, the program is usually easier to modify. When function X calls function Y, X doesn't care *how* Y gets its result; the result is the only important thing. This means that you can entirely rewrite Y without affecting X in the least, provided that Y still gives the same result with a given set of arguments.

If your functions aren't written as black boxes, a change in function Y may force you to change all the functions that call Y . . . and all the functions that call those functions, and so on in a domino effect. The black box approach to designing software eliminates this domino effect: functions don't depend on the inner workings of other functions, so you can change those inner workings without upsetting the whole program.

chapter 4   Error Handling

Dealing with errors is one of the most difficult aspects of writing a program. When we say this, we are not talking about debugging. We are talking about writing programs that can handle errors that occur while the program is running. Errors can arise from a variety of sources.

Typing Mistakes

Typing mistakes account for a great variety of error conditions: incorrect data of all kinds; files that can't be found because their names were spelled wrong; incorrect actions resulting from mistyped instructions.

Other Human Errors

Typing mistakes are the most common of human errors, but there are many others as well. For example, if a user doesn't adequately understand how to use a particular program, (s)he may make mistakes. In such cases, the program should do its best to explain the user's error and suggest ways to correct the problem.

Hardware Errors

Modern computing equipment is quite reliable, but in the course of billions of complicated operations, mistakes do happen. Hardware errors most frequently occur in I/O operations, since I/O devices commonly undergo more wear and tear than other parts of a computer system.

In this chapter, we will examine how programs can be written to cope with errors. Our emphasis will be on internal features (for example, how one function can tell another that an error has occurred). In Section 5.11, we will discuss external features (for example, how a program can inform a user that an error has occurred).

4.1 Standard Error Handling

Upon encountering an error, most programs should simply issue an error message and terminate execution. Once an error occurs, the odds are good that a program will not be able to finish its job properly. If the program continues in a "business as usual" state, it just runs the risk of getting into worse trouble.

Of course, there are many exceptions to the principle we have just stated; otherwise, dealing with errors would be much easier. Still, we shouldn't forget that the most desirable way to handle errors is usually to issue a message and quit.

4.2 Independent Actions

When a program consists of a sequence of operations that are independent of each other, an error in one operation need not cause the whole program to terminate.

As an example, suppose a program is designed to print out the contents of each file in a specified list of files. If one of the files in the given list cannot be found (for example, because its name was misspelled), there is usually no reason to abort the entire job. The program can simply issue a message saying that the particular file could not be found, and then go on to the next file in the list.

In some ways, this is just a modification of standard error handling. Instead of terminating the entire program when the error occurs, you terminate one "stage" of the program and go on to the next stage. This is a useful approach when a program's job can be divided into independent stages.

4.3 Library Routines

The routines in the C library do not use the standard approach of aborting the program when an error occurs. This is because the library routines must be general enough to be used in programs that want to perform sophisticated error handling.

When a library routine encounters an error, the usual practice is to return to the caller, with a special value that indicates some kind of error has occurred. For example, getchar returns the special integer EOF upon reaching the end of a file, and EOF can be distinguished from all other values getchar would normally return.

Programs should always test the results of such functions to see if they are returning a value indicating an error. For example, every time you call fopen, you should test the return value to make sure that it is not the null pointer (indicating that the open operation failed). If you do not test for this, you will run into trouble if an error ever occurs; moreover, you may have difficulty determining what caused the trouble, since the problem may not become noticeable until long after the actual error occurred.

As noted in Section 3.2, cover functions provide the best solution to this situation. A good cover function will always test the return value, making it unnecessary for the rest of the program to do the test.

4.3.1 Cover Function Behavior

What should a cover function do if a library function returns an error indication? The most desirable reaction to an error is usually to issue an error message and quit.

However, there are exceptions to this. Take the example we gave a few sections ago: the program that prints out the contents of each file in a list of files. If the name of one of the files is misspelled, what part of the program will discover the problem? The cover function that calls fopen. The fopen function will not be able to open the file using the misspelled name, so it will return the null pointer. Under normal circumstances, the cover function would abort the program when this happens. How do we stop it?

There are several approaches to making the cover function more versatile. For example, suppose we define the cover function in this way:

```
enum abort_code {ABORT,NO_ABORT};
FILE *cover_fopen(const char *name,
                  const char mode,
                  enum abort_code code)
{
    FILE *fp;
    fp = fopen(name,mode);
    if ( (code == ABORT) && (fp == NULL) ) {
        fprintf(stderr,"Cannot open file %s\n",name);
        abort();
    }
    return fp;
}
```

If code equals ABORT and fopen fails (returns a null pointer), the cover function still issues a message and aborts. However, if code is NO_ABORT, the cover function returns the result of fopen, whether or not that result is a null pointer. This cover function could be called using code like this:

```
FILE *f;
f = cover_fopen("name","r",NO_ABORT);
if (f == NULL) ...
```

By specifying NO_ABORT, the program tells the cover function not to abort if the open fails. The program itself has to deal with the possibility of the file pointer being null.

You might be wondering why we call the cover function at all if we are going to use NO_ABORT to prevent the cover function's error checking. The cover function is still valuable for several reasons.

(a)   The cover function may be rewritten to do more than it currently does (for example, additional error-checking or the production of debugging information). At this point, calling the cover function definitely will be better than calling fopen directly.

(b)   The purpose of having a cover function is defeated if it is not used uniformly throughout the program. Every call to fopen should go through the cover function so that fopen is always used in the same way.

This is not the only way we could have written the cover function to deal with possible failure to open a file. For example, here's a different approach:

```
FILE *cover_fopen(const char *name,
                  const char mode,
                  int *status)
{
    FILE *fp;
    errno = 0;
```

```
    fp = fopen(name,mode);
    if ( (status == NULL) && (fp == NULL) ) {
        fprintf(stderr,"Cannot open file %s\n",name);
        abort();
    }
    else {
        *status = (fp != NULL) ? 0 : errno;
    }
    return fp;
}
```

In this case, the cover function is called with an integer pointer called status. If this is null and the open fails, the cover function aborts the program. If status is not a null pointer, the cover function sets *status to 0 if the open succeeds and the value of errno if the open fails; the FILE * pointer is returned regardless. This means that a call like

```
    cover_fopen("name","r",NULL)
```

will abort if the file can't be opened, while

```
    cover_fopen("name","r",&i)
```

will not.

This second cover function has another advantage that is not shown in this simple example. A more advanced cover function could do additional work to determine why a particular open operation failed, and return different statuses for different causes of failure. The main program could take different steps, depending on the status value returned by the cover function.

As a final example, here is a very simple version of the same cover function:

```
    FILE *cover_fopen(const char *name,
                      const char mode};
    {
        FILE *fp;
        fp = fopen(name,mode);
        if (fp == NULL)
            fprintf(stderr,"Cannot open file %s\n",name);
        return fp;
    }
```

This version is very much like the real fopen; it has the same set of arguments and returns whatever fopen returns. The one difference is that this function prints out an error message if the fopen operation fails. This added feature may be the only addition that a program needs. Cover functions do not have to be ambitious; even simple additions are useful.

4.3.2 Personal Library Functions

As noted in Section 3.5, you should begin to develop your own personal library of functions to supplement the library routines that come with the implementation. These functions should start out with the standard error handling behavior: issuing an error message and aborting the program. The functions can be modified later to incorporate whatever additional error handling becomes necessary. For these modifications, you have the same options that are available with normal library routines and cover functions:

(a)   The function will abort the program on an error unless an external variable or passed argument is set to some value.

(b)   An argument indicates that the function should return a status rather than aborting.

(c)   The function never aborts; it just returns a status that must always be checked (just as a library routine does).

Which solution is most appropriate will depend on the application.

There is an alternative approach that is occasionally useful. This approach will be easier to understand if we start with an example. Suppose you want to be able to handle errors that happen in I/O on a particular stream. When you open that stream, you pass your cover function an option that says you want to allow errors on that stream. The cover function records this option in some way.

When you perform I/O on any stream, you call appropriate cover functions. The cover functions always check to see if the I/O operations are successful. If an I/O operation fails, the cover functions will detect the failure. If the stream was not opened with the special option that allows error handling, the cover functions will issue a message and abort the program. However, if the option was specified, the user is prepared to handle errors and the cover functions return. In this way, errors are only allowed on streams that were opened with the appropriate option.

This approach associates error recovery with a particular stream. In this way, it is more specific than having functions that can perform error recovery on any stream. This allows more control over error handling. On the other hand, it does mean that all your I/O cover functions must be aware that errors are allowed on some streams. Thus more care is required in using this approach to error handling.

Below we give a simple example of this kind of cover function.

```
FILE *okaylist[LENGTH];
size_t cover_fread(void *ptr,
                   size_t size,
                   size_t N,
                   FILE *stream)
{
    size_t Nread;
    int i;
    int okay = 0;
    Nread = fread(ptr,size,N,stream);
```

```
        if ( (Nread < N) && !feof(stream) ) {
            for (i=0; i < LENGTH; i++)
                if (okaylist[i] == stream) okay = 1;
            if (!okay) {
                fprintf(stderr,"Read error on stream\n);
                abort();
            }
        }
        return Nread;
}
```

This function assumes that the array `okaylist` contains a list of `FILE` pointers. If there is a read error on a stream, and the stream is not in the list, the cover function will print an error message and abort. Otherwise, the cover function will just return the value returned by `fread`.

No doubt you can suggest improvements to the above function. For example, the error message is not very informative. It would be useful to be able to figure out the name of the file associated with the erroneous stream, so that the error message could provide that information as well. One way to do this would be to change your cover function for `fopen` so that it created a linked list that recorded the file name associated with each `FILE` pointer.

4.4 Popping Back From Errors

Suppose you have a program that reads commands from a user and performs actions based on those commands. As the program reads a command, there is always the possibility that it will discover some kind of error (for example, through a typing mistake). One of the most common ways to deal with such a situation is to issue an error message and then prompt the user to type in a new command. No action is taken for the command that contained the error.

Dealing with an error in this way presents (at least) one important difficulty. There are usually several routines involved in reading and processing an input command:

(a)   A function that says, "Start reading a new command."
(b)   A function that determines what kind of command this is.
(c)   A function that reads command arguments.
(d)   A function that actually performs the action associated with the command.

Of course, all these functions will probably call other functions while processing the command (for example, I/O functions to read the input).

The error in the command may be detected by any of these functions. Once the error is detected, the program will want to print out an error message, then go back to the function mentioned in (a) above, the one that says, "Start reading a new command."

One easy way to go back to the function mentioned in (a) is to use the `longjmp` function (described in Part IV). Before processing a command, the function in (a) uses the `setjmp` function to prepare for a possible `longjmp`. If and when an error is encountered, you can call an error handling routine to print an error message and longjmp back to the appropriate location. The program can then start gathering a new input command. This approach is easier than having functions return error statuses up the line until getting back to the beginning.

Sometimes as a command is being processed, a program like the one we have been describing will use malloc or calloc to allocate storage for temporary data objects. Normally, the space for these objects will be freed (with free) when the command is successfully executed. If, however, an error is discovered, a problem arises. The program would like to longjmp back to a high-level function to begin processing a new command line. Before this can happen, however, the space that has been allocated with malloc and calloc must be freed; otherwise, the space will remain allocated for the rest of program execution—a waste of memory.

One way to avoid this problem is to maintain a linked list that keeps track of all memory allocated by the program. Each list item holds a pointer to one chunk of memory allocated with malloc, calloc, or realloc. This list is created and maintained by the cover function(s) that the program uses to call malloc and its associated routines.

When allocated space has to be freed, the program can have a routine that goes through all or part of the list and releases all the chunks of memory recorded there. It will also release the space taken up by the list items. If an error is encountered, this routine can be called to free up allocated space before the program uses longjmp to go back to the "read a command" function. The same routine can be called to free allocated space when a command is successfully completed and the space is no longer needed.

As an example, here is a routine that allocates space and keeps a linked list that records the space:

```
struct Malloc_list {
    void *              space;
    struct Malloc_list *next;
};
struct Malloc_list *root = NULL;

void *get_space(size_t size,
                struct Malloc_list **listptr)
{
    void *obtained;
    struct Malloc_list *new;
    obtained = cover_malloc(size);
    new = cover_calloc(1,sizeof(struct Malloc_list));
    new -> space = obtained;
    new -> next = *listptr;
    *listptr = new;
    return obtained;
}
```

The first argument of get_space is the amount of space you want to allocate. The second is a *pointer* to a pointer to the first item in the current linked list. For example, you might call the function with

```
    ptr = get_space(100,&root);
```

to obtain 100 bytes of space. The `get_space` function allocates the space using the `malloc` cover function, then calls the `calloc` cover function to obtain space for a `Malloc_list` item. A pointer to the newly obtained space is saved in the item, and then the `next` field is given the address of what used to be the first item in the list. The new item then becomes the first element on the list (we assign the address of the new item to the pointer that used to point to the beginning of the list).

To free all the space that is recorded in the list, we can use the following function:

```
void free_list(struct Malloc_list *list)
{
    if ( (list -> next) != NULL)
        free_list(list->next);
    cover_free(list->space);
    cover_free(list);
}
```

This function works recursively. When it is passed a pointer to the first item of the list, it calls itself to free everything after the first item; then it calls the `free` cover function to free the space that is recorded in the first list item and the first list item itself. The call

```
free_list(root);
```

would free the entire list that begins at `root`. Notice that this set-up lets us have several separate lists, each with its own root.

chapter 5 Miscellaneous Points

This chapter will cover a potpourri of stylistic points.

5.1 Constants

As much as possible, you should avoid the use of constants in source code. The reason is simple: constants aren't as constant as you might think. As time goes on and the requirements of the program change, the values of certain constants may need to be changed as well.

Instead of using explicit constants, use manifests or enumerated types. Enumerated types are preferred for integer values. For example, you might use

```
enum { SIZE=20 };
    . . .
int arr[SIZE];
```

This kind of **enum** value has the advantages of a manifest, but not the pitfalls. This is because the **enum** value behaves like a normal integer data object, while a manifest is purely textual. Using an **enum** value doesn't have odd side effects.

When a program uses an enumerated value in a declaration, it should use the same value throughout the program. For example,

```
enum { SIZE=20 };
int arr[SIZE];
    . . .
for (i=0; i <= SIZE-1; ++i)
    arr[i] = 0;
```

uses the expression SIZE-1 for the value of the maximum subscript of the array. It would be pointless to define the SIZE value, then write

```
for (i=0; i <= 19; ++i) ...
```

For nonintegral constants, you must use manifests. For example, you might define

```
#define PI (3.141592653589793)
```

An expression that refers to PI is more concise and easier to understand than one using the full form of the number.

Never use a constant to represent the size of an object. The **sizeof** operator gives the number of bytes that the object occupies. If you need to know the number of bits, the header <limits.h> defines a manifest named CHAR_BIT that gives the number of bits in a byte on a particular machine. For more information about such manifests, see Appendix D.

Whenever constants *are* used in source code (including **#define** directives), you should use a constant of the type that is appropriate to the way the constant is being used. For example, it is valid to say

```
double x;
     ...
x = 2;
```

because the **int** 2 will be converted to floating point automatically. However,

```
x = 2.0;
```

is better style because the form of the statement reinforces the fact that x is **double**.

Variables which are intended to remain contants should be marked with the **const** qualifier, as in

```
const double e = 2.7182818284;
```

The **const** makes sure you don't accidentally change the value and also serves as a kind of comment, indicating the intended behavior of the variable.

5.1.1 Lists of Constants

Many programs need to define a series of symbols that are each associated with an integer. As an interesting example, consider a computer adventure game in which the player can pick up various objects: a sword, a magic scroll, a bird's egg, and so on. In the source code, each object should be represented by a name: SWORD, SCROLL, EGG, and so on.

Each of these names will be associated with an integer. The integers can then be used for various purposes, such as the subscripts for an array. The program could have various arrays of information describing the objects; for example, it might have an array called value indicating the value of each object (so that value[SWORD] is the value of the sword) or an array called weight indicating the weight of each object (so that weight[EGG] is the weight of the egg).

In such situations, the best method for associating a name with an integer is to create an enumerated type. For example, you might declare

```
enum OBJECTS = {
     SWORD, SCROLL, EGG, /* and so on */ END_OBJECTS
};
```

This associates integers with the object names in the order they are given in the declaration. Notice that we put something called END_OBJECTS as the last value (after the last real object). Since `END_OBJECTS` is one more than the total number of objects, we can use it in array declarations, such as

```
int object_array[END_OBJECTS];
```

This creates an array that has a member corresponding to each object.

There are other methods of associating integers with object names. You could, for example, create a series of manifests, as in

```
#define SWORD 0
#define SCROLL 1
#define EGG 2
    . . .
```

The problem with this approach is that it requires more typing, providing more chance for error. It also means that you have to number every symbol by hand; if you use the enumerated type approach, the computer does the numbering for you. If you decide to change the order of the symbols for some reason, it takes a lot of work when you use manifests; it's much easier if you are using the enumerated type.

5.2 Simple Variables

Usually, there is no point in creating simple **char** variables. All **char** items are immediately converted to **int** when they appear in expressions, so working with **char** values just adds the extra work of converting back and forth from **int**. The same applies to **short** values. Usually, **char** and **short** are best suited for arrays or as members of dynamically allocated structures.

Unsigned arithmetic can be confusing. For example, suppose i is a **signed int** and u is **unsigned int**. The comparison

```
i < u
```

is performed with **unsigned** numbers because of the usual arithmetic conversion rules. If i is a negative number, the conversion rules turn it into a large positive **unsigned** number, with the result that a negative **int** may turn out to be *larger* than a positive **unsigned**. Because of surprising results like this, you should avoid using any unsigned types unless they are clearly required.

NOTE: On some machines, the **char** type will be **signed** while on others it will be **unsigned**. If you are going to be using **char** values for significant arithmetic, you should make sure you specify **signed char** or **unsigned char** instead of just **char**. This will make sure that your program works if it is ported from a signed **char** machine to an unsigned one.

5.3 Gotos

Programs that contain **goto** statements are almost always hard to read. Without **goto** statements, code can simply be read from top to bottom; **goto**s force you to jump back and forth to understand what's going on.

Use of **goto** statements also causes the "come-from" problem. For example, suppose you find a statement label in the middle of a function. Since statement labels are only used in **goto** operations, you can be fairly sure that there is a **goto** statement that jumps to the label. The question is, where *is* the **goto** statement? You have to search through the code to find it. Since several **goto** statements may jump to the same label, you cannot stop searching once you have found one appropriate **goto**; you must find *all* appropriate **goto**s.

All this difficulty is unnecessary, because **goto** statements can almost always be avoided. The other structures of C (loops, **if-else**, and so on) can handle any piece of program logic, so **goto** statements are not needed. Any time you are tempted to use a **goto**, reconsider; a better way almost certainly exists. The **goto** statement is only justified if the use of other constructs would distort your code more than a **goto** would. (This is sometimes the case when you are trying to cope with an error condition inside code that is already heavily nested.)

5.4 Embedded File Names

An embedded file name is a file name that is given implicitly in source code, as in

```
fp = fopen("myfile","r");
```

In general, these should be avoided; changing circumstances often make it necessary to use a different file. At the top of the code, define a manifest, as in

```
#define INFILE "myfile"
      ...
fp = fopen(INFILE,"r");
```

Better still, use a construct like

```
#define INFILE "myfile"
const char filename[] = INFILE;
      ...
fp = fopen(filename,"r");
```

and put the **#define** statement and the **const** declaration in a global definition file. That way, you only have to retranslate the global definition file if you want to change the name of the file. If every source file that refers to the input file uses the manifest, you would have to retranslate every such source file.

5.5 *Flags*

A flag is a data object whose purpose is to indicate that a particular condition exists. For example, a program might have a variable whose value is zero while a file is not at end-of-file but whose value is set to one upon reaching end-of-file.

Avoid the use of flags that change the behavior of a function. Ideally, a function should always return the same value for a given set of arguments. This is not always possible, of course, but a function whose return value depends on an external flag can be confusing to use. If a function's behavior must depend on a flag value, pass this value as one of the function's arguments.

When a flag must be used, it should *not* be given a name like `flag`. Instead, it should be given a name that indicates its meaning or its effect when the flag is set. For example, the code fragment

```
if (eof_reached) ...
```

is easy to understand because the flag `eof_reached` has a name that makes its meaning clear.

Flags can often be replaced by **query functions**. A query function is a function that investigates the "status" of some part of the program. For example, the library function `feof` (described in Part IV) is a query function that determines whether a particular I/O stream is at end-of-file.

Query functions are more versatile than simple flags because they can provide more functionality (for example, in error-checking). They also make your program easier to change. If a particular test must be changed, you just have to change the query function that makes the test; you do not have to change all the functions that want to make the query.

Query functions do not have to be actual functions. For reasons of efficiency, they may be defined as macros. On the other hand, they can be redefined as actual functions if changes in the program make this necessary.

5.6 *The scanf Function*

The `scanf` function and its relatives (`sscanf`, `fscanf`) should only be used to obtain one input item at a time. This makes it simpler to cope with erroneous input. In addition, you should always check to make sure that an input item is read correctly, as in

```
int i;
    ...
if ( 1 != scanf("%i",&i) ) {
    /* handle error */
}
```

5.7 Fixed Memory Requirements

Avoid the use of arrays with fixed sizes. Whenever possible, allocate memory for every array using `malloc`. If the initial allocation is too small, provide more memory with `realloc`. This allows greater flexibility in programming and reduces the amount of memory that your program wastes.

5.8 Portability Warnings

The **#error** directive should be used liberally throughout programs, to mark any construct that may not be portable to other systems. For example, suppose that on System X the function f is system-dependent. We might write

```
#if !defined(SYSTEM_X)
#error The function "f" is system-dependent
#endif
/* Definition of "f" */
```

When the program is translated for System X, put the statement

```
#define SYSTEM_X 1
```

in the global definition files. This will mean that the **#error** statements are not executed. On other systems, however, leave the SYSTEM_X symbol undefined so that the **#error** warnings are printed. This will quickly tell you which routines contain system dependencies. By making **#error** messages more explicit than the one given above, the messages printed by the translation process will tell you everything you have to look at when the program is ported to another system.

Many versions of C come with predefined symbols to name the translation and/or execution environment. In this case, you do not need your own **#define** statement. Just use the predefined symbol supported by your particular implementation of C.

5.9 Inappropriate Efficiencies

A lot of hard-to-read code is written in the name of efficiency. People often believe that compressing source code and making it as terse as possible results in the most efficient programs. However, this isn't necessarily so. Rewriting a line of code here and there has little impact on program performance; the most significant gains in program efficiency are achieved through improvements to basic algorithms.

As an example, let's assume that we have an array of structures declared with

```
enum { LENGTH = 1000 };
typedef struct {
    int key;
    /* other elements */
} S;
S Sarray[LENGTH];
```

Let us also assume that the members of Sarray have been sorted in increasing order of their key elements. The following function searches through the array and locates the first member whose key element matches a given argument. The function returns a pointer to this array member. If a matching member is not found, the function returns a null pointer.

```
S *search(int wanted_key)
{
    extern S Sarray[];
    int i;
    for (i = 0; i < LENGTH; i++) {
        if (wanted_key == Sarray[i].key)
            return &(Sarray[i]);
    }
    return NULL;
}
```

Now how can we make this more efficient? Well, we can make it more *compact* by writing it as follows.

```
S *search(int wanted_key)
{
    extern S Sarray[];
    int i = LENGTH;
    while (i-- && (wanted_key != Sarray[i].key));
    return (i>=0) ? &(Sarray[i].key) : NULL;
}
```

The code looks shorter, but is it really an improvement? The answer is that it is probably no more efficient than the first version, and it is certainly harder to understand. In the first version of the function, it was clear that i started at 0 and was incremented until it reached LENGTH. The second version works its way backwards through the array, and we expect that you will have to study the code for quite a while before you can figure out exactly what the value of i does in each part of each statement.

Instead of making the code hard to read, we could *really* improve the function by changing the way in which it searches the array. Since it starts at the beginning of the array and reads forward one member at a time, the function looks at an average of 500 members before finding the desired key.

A better approach would be to use a *binary search*. This was described in Exercise 2 of Section I.7.5.3. The binary search algorithm is much faster than the **linear search** with which we began. It turns out that this binary search will always find the required array member within ten steps (if the array member is there). This is obviously more efficient than the first search algorithm. We can write the new `search` routine as

```
S *search(int wanted_key)
{
    extern S Sarray[];
    int first = 0;
    int last = LENGTH - 1;
    int middle;

    while (last > first) {
        middle = (last + first) / 2;
        if (wanted_key > Sarray[middle].key)
            first = middle + 1;
        else
            last = middle;
    }
    if (last == first)
        return &(Sarray[last]);
    else
        return NULL;
}
```

This function is longer than the previous versions, and yet it finds the desired member much faster. With larger arrays, the difference in speeds is even more dramatic.

Does this mean that we should always choose the last version of `search` over the other two? Not necessarily. For example, space is at a premium on some microcomputers. On these machines, it may be more important to have a short simple function than to find the desired member quickly. In this case, using the "linear" version of `search` may be better, even if it is much slower. The linear search is also more efficient with short arrays (say, ten members or less). The complications built into the binary search make it slower when there are only a few items to search.

Now suppose our program is running on a large computer with plenty of memory, and also suppose that the requirements of the job make it crucial that this search be performed very quickly. Should we automatically choose the binary search function? Again, not necessarily. For example, suppose that we know all the keys will be in the range 0 through 1000. The most efficient search might be to declare an array

```
S *(Sptr[1001]);
```

that is, an array of pointers to **struct** objects. We initialize the members of Sptr so that member N is a pointer to the member of Sarray whose key element is equal to N. If there is no Sarray member whose key is equal to N, Sptr[N] is a null pointer. With this set-up, the search function is just

```
S *search(int wanted_key)
{
    return Sptr[wanted_key];
}
```

This function just obtains the appropriate pointer from the table. No searching is done, so the function is much faster than a binary search. For that matter, we could create a macro

```
#define search(X) (Sptr[X])
```

so that when the program says

```
search(N)
```

it is immediately replaced with

```
(Sptr[N])
```

Using a macro this way is even faster than defining a function, because the program doesn't have to do the work associated with performing a function call.

Is this the most efficient approach? It's certainly the fastest ... but its memory requirements are much greater. You need memory space for the 1001 members of the Sptr array. You also need to do the extra work of setting up the Sptr array before search can be used. In some cases, the extra space and extra work are justified by the gain in speed; in others, the extra speed just isn't worth the trouble.

In order to determine the approach that is optimal for a given program, you must think about the job that the program will do and the machine environment in which the program will run. Different situations will require different solutions. Sometimes it is a good idea to try several approaches to see what actually works out best.

How does all this relate to programming style?

☞   A good programming style lets you *understand* what your program is doing, making it easier to analyze algorithms and design improvements. It also makes it easier to add changes to see whether program performance is improved.

For example, even though our search routine went through several versions, it always had the prototype

```
struct S *search(int wanted_key)
```

We might change the internal form of search, and we might even make it into a macro instead of a function, but the program always calls the routine in exactly the same way. This makes it easy for us to experiment to see which version of the routine is most suitable. By isolating the search operation, we can easily change the routine without having to change the rest of the program.

This suggests a general principle of program optimization. Optimization efforts are often more effective *after* a version of the program has been written. Once you have a working version of the program, you can experiment with various approaches to some problems. You can also examine program execution to find out where the program spends most of its time, so that you know where optimization will have the greatest effect. If a program uses routine A very frequently and does not use B very much at all, a small improvement in A may improve program performance more than a large improvement in B.

We are not suggesting that you should throw programs together haphazardly and then set about improving them. If a program starts out sloppily, it will be very hard to improve. On the other hand, it is often difficult to foresee how a program will behave and how it will be used, until the program is actually written. Once you have something concrete to work with, the time you spend in optimization will be more productive.

5.9.1 Outsmarting the Implementation

Programmers have prejudices about what implementations can and can't do well. Some of these prejudices are correct; most are not.

For example, some programmers believe that **switch** statements handle some situations inefficiently, and it is true that some C packages implement **switch** statements in ways that are sometimes inefficient. However, this is not a good reason for avoiding **switch** statements.

(a)   Implementations of C tend to improve faster than code written in C. The current implementation may handle a construct like **switch** somewhat inefficiently; however, the next version will probably be better. Software companies are always at work to improve their implementations.

On the other hand, if you use **if** statements in your programs where you should be using **switch** statements, you probably will *not* go back and rewrite your programs if the performance of **switch** is improved. You will be stuck with a less-efficient program.

(b)   You may port your program to a different system, where **switch** and **if** work differently. On the new system, **switch** may be much more efficient than the equivalent **if** statements; but once again, you probably won't change your code, and you will be stuck with a program that is less efficient than it could be.

(c)   A **switch** statement is easier to read than the equivalent **if** statements. We have already pointed out that a readable program is easier to optimize and more likely to *be* optimized. Therefore, the use of **switch** increases the probability that you can and will be able to make your program perform better.

The same principle applies to a number of other ways in which programmers avoid features of the implementation, in the interests of efficiency. For example, suppose you have to copy N bytes of data from one memory location to another. You could do this with

```
char *p1, *p2;
    ...
for (i=0; i<N; i++) *(p1++) = *(p2++);
```

or you could do it by calling the library function

```
memcpy(p1,p2,N)
```

Some programmers would choose the first approach, saying that it is more efficient. After all, they argue, the memcpy function has to do the same work; why not write the code directly and save the expense of making a function call?

There are two reasons to prefer memcpy. First, it is easier to read and understand. Second, it may be more efficient. Instead of being written in C, the implementation's version of memcpy may be written in assembler, using a special machine instruction that can copy a large chunk of memory in one lump. Using this single instruction will usually be more efficient than the many machine instructions required by a **for** statement.

Many library routines are implemented in the same way, using special machine code that is more efficient than code produced for normal C statements. This means that it is often *more* efficient to call a library routine than to write equivalent C code, even though there is a certain amount of expense involved in setting up a function call. (Of course, you don't even have this expense if the library routine is actually implemented as a macro, or if the implementation recognizes the name of the library routine and handles the call in some special way.)

5.10 Debugging Hints

Debugging is an art and craft that requires as much practice as writing code. Unfortunately, it is difficult to teach; because there are so many ways in which bugs may occur, there is no easy prescription for finding and correcting such errors.

On the other hand, you can write your programs using simple techniques to facilitate the debugging process. In this section, we will discuss some of these techniques.

5.10.1 Version Numbers

Most useful programs are subject to change. Because of this, you will find it helpful to put version numbers in source code, translated code, and most data files.

For example, suppose an error occurs while a program is executing. One of the first things you want to determine is whether the program with the problem is the most up-to-date version there is. If it is not the most-recent version, the problem may have already been corrected in later versions. If it *is* the most-recent version, comparison of this version of the program with earlier versions can tell you whether the problem was introduced in the latest round of changes; this often makes it easier to locate the source of the problem.

If, however, you cannot determine which version of the program is being used, you are in for a lot of frustration. Which version of the source code should you look at? Has the problem already been fixed? Is the difficulty caused by running one version of a program but using data files created by a different version? All of these difficulties add an extra layer of complication to the usual problems of locating and correcting a bug.

It is useful to note that many software companies today have to deal with complaints and bug reports over the telephone. In this situation, it is crucial for the program to have an identifying version number that is easy for the user to find. Otherwise, the user and the person dealing with the complaint will find it difficult to make sure that they are talking about the same thing.

For source code, specify the version number in a comment at the beginning of each source file. To put a version number into translated code, you might create an appropriate external or static string variable, as in

```
char *version = "2.3";
```

This is easy enough to find with common debugging tools (for example, with a symbolic debugger or in a program dump). In many cases, it is convenient for the program to write out the version number when it begins execution. This immediately tells you which version is being used.

When a data file is created by a program, the program should usually write its version number somewhere in the data file (often at the beginning). If and when the data file is read, this lets the reader determine which version of the program created the file. The program version number often affects how a file is read, since different versions may use different data formats. Note that a version number is not needed if a data file is shortlived (for example, if it is a temporary work file that will be discarded when the program finishes execution).

5.10.2 Data File Dumps

Many programs and systems make use of binary (nontext) data files. You can make the debugging process significantly easier by writing a program to "dump" such a file, that is, to read the file and translate its data into a human-readable format. Even if such a program is not necessitated by the requirements of the system, the time invested in writing the program will be more than repaid by the time saved in debugging.

In some sense, a data file dump program is also documentation for the format of the file. The output of the dump program tells what the file should contain. The source code of the dump program tells what format is expected. By keeping the dump program up-to-date, you also provide up-to-date documentation for the file format.

As a simple example, suppose a set of programs will be used to manipulate a file providing information on a company's personnel. In preparing these programs, one of the first steps should be to write a program that will print out the file in a readable form. Let's suppose, for example, that the file consists of the following information for each employee:

(a)   A string of characters giving the employee's name. This does not have a fixed length, but the string is always terminated by a ' \0 ' character.

(b)   A code letter indicating area of employment. For example, 'A' might stand for Administration, 'S' for Secretarial staff, 'C' for Custodial staff, 'R' for Research staff, 'M' for Manufacturing, and so on.

(c)   Two **short** integers indicating the month and year when the employee began working for the company. Months are numbered from 1 to 12.

(d)   A **float** number indicating the employee's monthly pay.

We can easily write a program that reads in records from such a file and prints a readable translation on the standard output.

```c
#include <stdio.h>
#include <stdlib.h>
#define EMPFILE "filename"
    /* name of personnel file */

char *month_array[] = {
    "",   /* No month numbered 0 */
    "Jan", "Feb", "Mar", "Apr", "May", "Jun",
    "Jul", "Aug", "Sep", "Oct", "Nov", "Dec"
};

extern void do_emp(FILE *fp);
extern void early_eof(const char *location);

int main(void)
{
    FILE *emp_file;
    emp_file = fopen(EMPFILE,"rb");
    if (emp_file == NULL) {
        fprintf(stderr,"Cannot open %s\n",EMPFILE);
        exit(EXIT_FAILURE);
    }
    while ( ! feof(emp_file) )
        do_emp(emp_file);
    return EXIT_SUCCESS;
}

/*
 * "early_eof" prints error message and terminates
 * program if end-of-file found anywhere but the
 * end of a record.
 */

void early_eof(const char *location)
{
    fprintf(stderr,
        "Premature EOF while reading %s\n",location);
    exit(EXIT_FAILURE);
}
```

```
/*
 *  "do_emp" prints an employee record.  It returns
 *  1 if record is printed successfully, 0 if end
 *  of file is reached.
 */

int do_emp(FILE *fp)
{
    int c;
    short month, year;
    float pay;

    /* First print out name */
    while ( (c = fgetc(fp)) && (c != EOF) )
        putchar(c);
    putchar('\n');
    if (c == EOF)
        early_eof("employee name");

    /* Print out area of employment */
    c = fgetc(fp);
    switch (c) {
      case EOF:
          early_eof("employment area");
      case 'A':
          printf("\tAdministration\n");
          break;
      case 'C':
          printf("\tCustodial\n");
          break;
      case 'M':
          printf("\tManufacturing\n");
          break;
      case 'R':
          printf("\tResearch\n");
          break;
      case 'S':
          printf("\tSecretarial\n");
          break;
      default:
          printf("\t***Unknown Employment Code:");
          printf(" %c (octal %o)\n",c,c);
    }
```

```
/* Next, month and year */
if ( 1 != fread(&month,sizeof(short),1,fp) )
    early_eof("beginning month");
if ( (month > 12) || (month < 1) )
    printf("\t***Invalid month: %d\n",month);
else
    printf("\t%s ",month_array[month]);
if ( 1 != fread(&year,sizeof(short),1,fp) ) {
    printf("\n");
    early_eof("beginning year");
}
printf("%d\n",year);

/* Next, monthly pay */
if ( 1 != fread(&pay,sizeof(float),1,fp) )
    early_eof("pay");
printf("\t$%10.2f\n\n",pay);
}
```

The output from this program might look like

```
John Smith
    Manufacturing
    Jun 1970
    $    1000.00

Mary Jones
    Administration
    Dec 1982
    $   11200.00

    /* and so on */
```

This output is not particularly pretty; a different format might be required for a report that would be passed on to an official user. Nevertheless, the given format is good enough for the programmer who is trying to debug programs that use the file. It shows the information that is in the file, in a readable format. This is sufficient for the programmer's needs (for example, to check up on the program that creates the file in the first place).

Dump programs of this sort also have the effect of documenting the format of the data file; by looking at what the program prints out, you can get a feel for the kind of information that the file contains. It is usually easier to understand dump output than the source code that creates the data file in the first place.

Finally, dump programs can serve to *verify* the contents of a data file. As the program reads through the file, it can check the contents of the file to make sure that they are reasonable. For example, if file entries contain dates, the program can check that the dates are in the correct format and that the dates fall within a range that is reasonable in the given context. In this way, you can use the dump program to discover whether a data file has been created and manipulated correctly.

5.10.3 Data Structure Dumps

In the same way that you should create a program to dump data files, you should create functions for preserving and dumping data structures. For example, if your program creates a linked list or a binary tree, you should create functions that can write the structure to a file and/or print the contents of the structure in some suitable format. Again, this should be done very early in the programming process, even if it is not a necessary component of the final system. The investment of time will be more than compensated by the time you save in the debugging process.

5.10.4 Debugging Statements

During the debugging process, it is often helpful to add extra statements to a program. For example, many programmers put in extra `printf` statements that print out values at important points of the program, to make sure that the program is working with correct data. It is also common to put in calls to routines to dump data structures (discussed in the previous section) to make sure that such structures are set up properly.

When you have finished debugging a program, you no longer want these extra statements to be executed. However, it would be a lot of work to go through the program deleting such statements, and of course, there is always the possibility you will delete the wrong statement. In addition, bugs may show up later on, in which case you may have to add debugging statements again.

To avoid such problems, we recommend using

```
#ifdef DEBUG
/* Debugging statements */
#endif
```

whenever you add debugging statements to a program. This immediately labels the enclosed statements as debugging statements, so they will be easy to identify in source code. It also makes the statements easy to add or subtract. The definition

```
#define DEBUG 1
```

at the beginning of a source file or in a suitable global declaration file "turns on" all the debugging statements in your program. Omitting this definition deletes all the debugging statements. However, the statements are easy to put back, just by putting back the **#define** statement.

NOTE: Some programmers prefer to "comment out" debugging statements. This is done by enclosing the statements in /* and */, as in

```
/* printf("This statement is commented out"); */
```

There are several reasons why we disapprove of this practice.

(a)   It is harder to notice in source code. The enclosing /* and */ constructs are easy to miss.

(b)   It takes more work to add or subtract the statements; you have to go through the program by hand and find each debugging statement.

(c)   Errors will occur if the commented-out code contains comments. Remember that C does not let you nest comments.

For all these reasons, we recommend that you use **#ifdef** instead of commenting out debugging statements.

5.11 User Interface

A program's **user interface** is made up of the aspects of the program that a normal user sees: diagnostic messages, requests for input, command format, and so on. The user interface of any program should be designed to minimize user annoyance and maximize user productivity. In the sections that follow, we will discuss some aspects of good user interfaces.

5.11.1 Diagnostic Messages

Diagnostic messages tell the user about errors that have occurred and warn about possible troubles. Remember that these messages will always be issued *from* the computer *to* a human being. For this reason, the wording of a diagnostic message should never heap blame on the user—people don't want to be scolded by a machine. A good message has the general tone of "I'm sorry, I didn't understand that," not "You just made a mistake!" Therefore a message that starts

```
Unexpected input character
```

is preferable to

```
Illegal input
```

Both messages may mean that the user left out something in a line of input, but the first message is less accusing. The difference is small and often subtle; however, unsympathetic diagnostic messages can have a cumulative effect leading to significant (and unnecessary) user dissatisfaction.

At the same time, a diagnostic message should explain a problem as precisely as possible, giving any information that will help the user figure out what has gone wrong. For example, the message

```
Unexpected input character
```

does not provide enough useful information. The message should tell what the character was, and where it appeared in the input, as in

```
Unexpected input character 'X' in word "helloX"
     at line 10 in file MYFILE
```

This tells you the character, and the word, line, and file in which it appeared. Of course, there's a chance that the unexpected character is not printable. In this case, you should give the octal or hexadecimal equivalent of the character, as in

```
Unexpected input character, octal 016,
     after "hello" at line 10 in file MYFILE
```

If possible, the error message should try to indicate the sort of character that *was* expected.

In a similar vein, diagnostic messages are often issued when an input value falls outside a prescribed range. In this case, print out the invalid value, the range of valid values, and what the values are used for, as in

```
Given number for month is 30; should be in range 1 to 12
```

(Of course, it is usually friendlier to accept the name of the month as well as the number, but that depends on the context.)

Often, it is a good idea for diagnostic messages to give the name of the program issuing the message. This is because programs are sometimes executed from "command files," a file containing a series of commands executed one after another. By adding the name of the program to a diagnostic message, you make it easier for users to determine which command in a command file encountered the error.

5.11.2 Dialogue With Users

Users are often expected to enter input to a program. The program should allow the maximum amount of freedom in this process. For example, if the user is asked to type in a line of input, allow for blank space at the beginning, extra blanks in the middle of the line, and so on. Do not expect a particular piece of input to begin at a fixed column location (unless the program itself moves the cursor to that column first). If a floating point number is expected, the program should still be prepared to accept an integer (or to issue a diagnostic message indicating why an integer cannot be accepted).

Programs should be prepared to tell the user what sort of input is expected. This does not necessarily mean that the program should precede every request for input with a description of what kind of input is desired; users do not need such crutches once they have become familiar with the program, and soon resent this unnecessary prompting. However, if a user types an incorrect input, the program should be able to indicate what kind of input is desired, and then give the user a second chance.

Ask reasonable questions and expect reasonable answers. For example, if you need information from a user, asking yes/no questions is a good approach. When you ask such a question, accept the answers y and n as well as yes or no. Don't require special codes; for example, don't ask the user to type in a one for "yes" and zero for "no."

When modifying a program, remain consistent, even if the current user interface is poor. For example, if an existing program currently asks the user to enter 1 for "yes" and 0 for "no," don't add a new question that requires ′y′ or ′n′; you'll just confuse the users. However, it might be a good idea to change the program to accept any of

```
1   y   yes
0   n   no
```

as synonyms for each other.

5.11.3 Input Verification

Always verify that input is correct, or at least reasonable. For example, if the user is asked to type in a date, the program should catch obvious errors such as February 30.

Many programs ask the question

```
Do you really want to do this?
```

when the user enters a command that will get rid of data. This sort of question is useful if it is something the user rarely sees; it will catch the users' attention and emphasize that they should think twice about the operation. However, do not use it in operations users will perform frequently. The users will just get in the habit of answering "yes" to the question, without thinking, and the question loses any value it might have as a safeguard.

For "destructive" operations that are performed frequently, it is better to give users the ability to undo the effects of the operation. For example, many text editors do not discard text that the user has just deleted. Instead, the text is simply moved to a temporary holding area. If the user wants to undo the deletion, the text can be retrieved from the holding area.

As another example, suppose a user invokes a program that may write over the current contents of a file. Instead of asking the user whether it is all right to overwrite the file, the program might save the old file under a different name and then write out the new one. In this way, users who decide that they want to hold onto the old contents can still find the old file under the changed name.

5.11.4 Menus

A menu is a list of possible actions presented to a program user. To give instructions to the program, the user selects actions from the given list. Sometimes menu items are selected using a special device like a mouse or a trackball; sometimes menu items are labelled and the user selects an item by typing in the label.

In our experience, menus are good for actions that are performed infrequently but not for actions that are performed often. With infrequently used operations, users may need to be told what their options are, and menus can be helpful. With frequently used operations, however, the process of repetition lets users quickly memorize how to perform common actions.

In this way, most menus become unnecessary after the first day or two. From this point on, the menus are an unnecessary hindrance: the space they take up on the display screen would be better used for real information, and the time it takes to draw up the menu and choose an item would be better spent doing real work directly.

In our opinion then, the majority of menus are only helpful for a short time, while the user is becoming familiar with the software. Beyond this point, menus are annoying, except for operations that are performed very infrequently.

☞   If the only way to perform an action is through a menu, users will never be able to perform that action faster than they do at the end of their first day using the program.

Bearing this principle in mind, it is usually a poor idea to force users to rely on menus. Give them alternate methods of requesting actions (for example, special key sequences) so that they can improve their speed once they know what they're doing.

PART III
ANSI C: User's Guide

There is only one true description of **ANSI** standard C, and that is the official **ANSI** standard document. Other descriptions of the language (like this manual) cannot be regarded as "official" because **ANSI** C is *exactly* what is described in the standard; nothing more and nothing less. As soon as we begin interpreting what the standard says, we can no longer claim to be presenting "the letter of the law."

Nevertheless, an interpretation of the standard is important if we want to understand just what **ANSI** C is. The standard describes the language as tersely as possible; it does not attempt to list all the consequences of these requirements. **ANSI** C has many subtleties and side effects that would be lost if we simply copied out the official standard verbatim.

For these reasons, an **ANSI** C reference manual is something of a contradiction. If it is anything but a word-for-word copy of the standard, it is not truly authoritative. If it *is* merely a word-for-word copy of the standard, it leaves too much unsaid.

Our solution to this dilemma is to state that the problem exists, then ignore it. We will be paraphrasing and expanding on the descriptions in the standard, so we must acknowledge that we are not presenting the official standard in all its precision. On the other hand, we have taken pains to be accurate and to illuminate everything that the standard *means* as well as what it says. In the long run, this should give a better picture of what **ANSI** C really is.

We should also note that Parts III and IV of this book are intended for those who will be *using* implementations of **ANSI** C, not those who will be *creating* them. The **ANSI** standard puts many constraints on implementations, but we will only make note of those that affect the way programs should be written. For example, to make sure that existing programs continue to work, implementations are required to accept some outdated code constructs. We will avoid mentioning these, because new programs should not use such constructs.

In a small number of cases, we have overstated some restrictions in the interests of "safety." For example, we state that programmers should not use names that begin with the underscore character because such names are reserved for internal use. In fact, there are some contexts in which you can use some names that begin with an underscore, but the rules are complicated and mistakes are easy to make. If you do make such a mistake, your program may still work on some machines but may fail mysteriously on others. We therefore state the safe and simple rule "no leading underscores;" the standard gives you a little more freedom than this, but we don't think the price is worth it.

chapter 1   Fundamental Concepts and Terminology

This chapter explains words and concepts that we will be using in the rest of the manual. Some of these are shared by other programming languages; others are unique to C or have special meanings when used in connection with C.

1.1 Behavior Classes

The **ANSI** standard lets implementations choose how they will handle certain specified features of C. This means that some program constructs will behave differently under different implementations. Program constructs are therefore divided into the following classes:

Constructs with Fully Defined Behavior
Such constructs are correct C code and behave the same under every implementation conforming to the standard.

Constructs with Implementation-Defined Behavior
Such constructs are correct C code, but their behavior depends on the individual implementation. The implementation must provide documentation explaining how such constructs behave. For example, if a variable name or other identifier is longer than 31 characters, the implementation is free to ignore the extra characters, or pay attention to all characters in the name, or pay attention to some number of characters greater than 31, and so on. However, the documentation for the package must state what the implementation chooses to do.

Constructs with Unspecified Behavior
Such constructs are correct C code, but the standard does not fully define how they should behave. For example, in evaluating the expression

```
(A+B)  *  (C+D)
```

the standard allows the implementation to choose whether it will evaluate (A+B) or (C+D) first. No documentation is required, and indeed, the implementation is free to behave differently at different points in the same program. Effectively, the implementation may do whatever is most efficient or convenient at the time.

Constructs with Undefined Behavior

Such constructs are erroneous or nonportable (which means that a particular implementation may choose to accept or reject the code). For example, if an arithmetic operation produces a result that is too large to be stored in a particular data object (called an **overflow**), the implementation is free to take any action. It could ignore the problem, issue a warning message but continue execution, abort the program, or choose some other response. Undefined behavior need not be documented.

Program constructs are fully defined unless stated otherwise. Programmers who wish to write portable programs (programs that can be run under different implementations of C with little or no changes to their source code) should pay particular attention to constructs whose behavior is not fully defined, and should avoid such constructs wherever possible.

1.2 Computing Environments

A computing **environment** is a particular combination of hardware and support software. Often the support software is an operating system (for example, UNIX System V), but the **ANSI** standard also discusses environments that do not have operating systems. If an environment has an operating system, it is called a **hosted environment**. Otherwise, it is called a **freestanding environment**.

An implementation of C operates in two environments: a **translation environment** where the C source code is read and processed, and an **execution environment** where the resulting program runs. These two environments may or may not be the same. For example, a cross-compiler does its translation (compilation) on one machine, but the compiled program runs on another machine. With a more conventional compiler, the program is executed in the same environment that it is compiled.

The work that is done in the translation environment is called the **translation stage**. Actually running the program is called the **execution stage**. Conceptually, the two stages are very different. The standard accepts C interpreters that simultaneously translate and execute C programs, but only if the interpreters make it look as if translation and execution are distinct stages.

1.2.1 The Translation Stage

It is common (but not necessary) for programmers to break a program's source code up into parts called **source files** or **source modules**. Each part is translated separately, then the results are **linked** together into a complete executable program. The linking can take place in either the translation or execution environment (or in another environment entirely), and can be performed by the C implementation or by support software.

The process of translating a particular source file is broken into several **translation phases**. In Chapter 7, we will give a more precise description of what these phases are, but for now we will just give a rough outline.

Preprocessing

> Preprocessing modifies the source code that is found in the source file. This may include such operations as mapping some or all of the code to a new character set, obtaining additional code from other source files, discarding pieces of source code at the request of **preprocessing directives**, or replacing the original source code with other text (as in macro expansion). The code that you have after preprocessing is called the **translation unit**.

Parsing

> Once preprocessing has prepared the source code, the program may be "parsed." This means that the source code is broken down into pieces according to the syntax of the language. The smallest pieces (constants, symbol names, operators, keywords, punctuation characters) are called **tokens**. The parsing process makes sense of how the tokens go together to form expressions, statements, blocks, and so on. Most syntax errors are detected as the source file is parsed (although some syntax errors are detected in other translation phases).

Interpretation

> Once the source code has been broken down syntactically, the meaning of each construct may be interpreted in preparation for execution. In the case of a compiler, this means generating machine code that will perform the operations required by the source code. For an interpreter, this means doing any work that is necessary before actually executing the source code.

1.2.2 The Execution Stage

The execution stage takes place in the execution environment after the translations of all the source files have been linked together. Execution is also broken into phases.

Initialization

> A number of operations usually have to be performed before code written by the programmer can be executed. For example, variables that are supposed to start out with a particular value must be assigned that value. Some initialization operations may be performed in the linking process (or even in the translation stage); other initializations may be performed in system-dependent ways before a program is invoked; still other initializations may be performed after the program has been invoked but before user-written code begins execution.

Program Startup

> This is the point at which the execution environment begins running what the programmer has actually written.

Program Execution

> In this phase, the execution environment runs the code written by the programmer. The program may also call upon library functions provided as part of the C implementation package.

Program Termination

There are a number of things that may terminate a program: certain kinds of errors; an explicit `abort` or `exit` operation; a special event of some kind (for example, a terminal user pressing the BREAK key); or simple completion of the program's `main` routine. An implementation often performs "clean-up" operations after it has left user-written code but before terminating the program altogether. For example, an implementation may close any files that are still open after the user-written code is finished. In a hosted environment, control is then returned to the software that invoked the program in the first place. In this case, there are facilities that allow the program to return a status code to the caller.

1.3 Program Constructs

A C program consists of **functions** and **declarations**. The functions describe the actions that should be carried out when the program is executed. The declarations describe the data manipulated by the functions. Declarations also define symbols that are used for various purposes in the source code of the program.

Typically, a C program will have a separate function for each action the program performs. For example, there may be one function that handles input and another that handles output. To perform a desired action, the program *calls* the function that does that action. For example, to read input the program would call an appropriate input function.

Since the executable code of the program is entirely made up of functions, each function call will take place inside another function (or inside the same function—C functions can call themselves). The function that contains the function call is known as the **caller**. The function that is called is sometimes referred to as the **callee**.

When a function is called, the caller may pass information as "input" to the function. For example, when calling a function that prints output, the caller may pass values that should be printed out. The pieces of information passed by the caller are known as the **arguments** of the function call.

In the code for a function, symbols are needed to refer to the argument values passed by the caller. These symbols are known as the function's **parameters**. They stand for the values that will be received when the function is actually called. Parameters behave like variables that are initialized with the passed argument values; a parameter's first value is the one passed as the corresponding argument, but the parameter's value can be changed.

In addition to functions written by the programmer, a program may make use of **library functions**. These functions are supplied as part of the C implementation package. Some library functions perform work that user-written functions cannot do directly (for example, input/output or memory allocation), while others are just supplied to save programmers the trouble of writing the code themselves (for example, calculation of square roots). Library functions are used in exactly the same way as user-written ones—they do not have any "special" status.

The **ANSI** standard describes a large number of library functions that must be supplied in any hosted implementation of C. These are described in Part IV of this book. If a C implementation is **freestanding**, the only library functions that must be supplied are those in `<float.h>`, `<stdarg.h>`, `<stddef.h>`, and `<limits.h>` (described in

Part IV). Individual implementations of C almost always supply more library functions than the basic set required by the **ANSI** standard.

1.4 C Source Code

C source code is written for the *translation* environment but describes things that happen in the *execution* environment. It is important to remember that these two environments may be different. For example, they may not use the same character set. In this case, string and character constants appearing in the source code must be mapped from the source character set to the execution character set.

The **ANSI** standard does not demand that source code be written in a particular character set. However, it does state that the source and execution character sets should have both upper- and lowercase letters of the standard English alphabet, as well as the ten decimal digits and the special characters

```
!  "  '  #  %  ( )  +  -  *  /  .  ,  ;
:  < >  =  ?  \  [ ]  { }  ~  ^  _  |
```

plus the space character, and characters representing the horizontal tab, the vertical tab, and the formfeed. These characters make up the **minimum character set**.

The source character set must be able to indicate the end of each source line. This is treated as a single character called the **new-line** character, although there may actually be more than one character at the end of the line or there may be an entirely different way to mark the end of the line. Suitable character sets include seven-bit ASCII and EBCDIC.

The execution character set must have the minimum character set, and all of the characters represented by escape sequences (as described in Section 1.4.2).

1.4.1 Trigraphs

The standard recognizes that some widely-used character sets do not support all the characters that C code needs. To provide for this, the standard allows some characters in the source code to be represented by character sequences called **trigraphs**. Below we list the recognized trigraphs and the characters they represent:

```
??=     #
??(     [
??)     ]
??<     {
??>     }
??/     \
??!     |
??-     ~
??'     ^
```

These trigraphs make it possible to write source code using the ISO 646 character set.

A sequence of two question marks followed by another character is only special if the sequence is one of the trigraphs listed above. Other sequences beginning with two question marks are not treated specially.

1.4.2 Escape Sequences

Trigraphs represent characters that are pertinent in the *translation* stage. Special characters that will be pertinent in the *execution* stage can be represented with **escape sequences**. An escape sequence consists of a backslash (\) followed by one or more characters. The standard defines the following escape sequences. (Note that many of these descriptions refer to the **active position** of a display device. This is the position where a new output character would be displayed, for example, the cursor position on a terminal display screen.)

\a   The **alert** character. When this is sent to a display device, it produces an audible or visual signal. For example, it might make a terminal "beep." The active position does not change.

\b   The **backspace** character. When this is sent to a display device, the active position moves backwards one character position. If the active position is already at the beginning of a line, the behavior is undefined.

\f   The **formfeed** character. When this is sent to a display device, the active position moves to the start of the next logical page. A CRT terminal might clear the display screen; a hardcopy terminal might skip to the next paper page.

\n   The **new-line** character. When this is sent to a display device, the active position moves to the beginning of the next line.

\r   The **carriage return** character. When this is sent to a display device, the active position moves to the beginning of the current line.

\t   The **horizontal tab** character. When this is sent to a display device, the active position moves to the next horizontal tab position on the current line. The behavior is unspecified if the active position is already past the last horizontal tab position on the line.

\v   The **vertical tab** character. When this is sent to a display device, the active position moves to the beginning of the line at the next vertical tab position. The behavior is unspecified if the active position is already past the last vertical tab position.

\?   The question mark character. This escape sequence is only needed when you have two adjacent question marks (for example, in a character string). If you were to write ?? it would be taken as the start of a trigraph; writing ?\? avoids this problem.

\'   The single quote character. This is needed to represent single quote characters inside character constants (see Section 2.1.5).

\"   The double-quote character. This is needed to represent double-quote characters inside string literals (see Section 2.1.5).

\\   The backslash character itself. This escape sequence is needed because a single backslash would be taken as the start of an escape sequence.

\ddd   Consists of a backslash followed by one, two, or three octal digits. This represents the character from the execution character set whose value corresponds to the given octal integer. In particular, \0 stands for a special character called the **NUL** character. This is a character whose bits are all zeros. It is used to mark the end of string literals (described in Section 2.1.5).

\xddd   Consists of a backslash followed by an 'x' followed by one, two, or three hexadecimal digits. This represents the character from the execution character set whose value corresponds to the given hexadecimal integer.

The standard lets implementations define additional escape sequences, provided that the first character after the backslash is not a lowercase letter.

Escape sequences may only be used in character constants and string literals (described in Section 2.1.5). Trigraphs may be used in any source code construct.

1.4.3 Comments

A comment consists of the character sequence /*, followed by zero or more characters, followed by the character sequence */, as in

```
/* This is a comment. */
```

The comment ends at the first */ that is found. Thus comments do not nest.

```
/* This /* will result in */ an error */
```

The above comment stops at the first */. The rest of the line is not valid C code and results in an error.

Any character may appear in a comment, including the new-line character. This means that a single comment may be several lines long.

```
/* This comment
   is three lines
   long */
```

Comments may appear between any two source code tokens. They may not be put in the middle of a single token (for example, in the middle of a string literal). If a character constant or string literal contains /*, the sequence is *not* interpreted as the start of a comment.

1.4.4 White Space

Space characters, horizontal tabs, vertical tabs, new-lines, and comments are called **white space**. White space must be used to separate keywords, identifiers, and constants that would otherwise be adjacent. For example, in the code

```
extern int X;
```

there must be white space separating the first three tokens. There does not have to be white space separating the token X from the semicolon. However, white space may appear between any two tokens if desired. For example, all of the following are valid and equivalent.

```
A=B+C;
A = B+C;
A=B + C;
A = B + C;
A = B + C /* Comment is white space */;
/* And other combinations */
```

Because the new-line character is white space, you can break up source code constructs over several input lines, as in

```
A =
B + C ;
```

If white space is valid in a particular location, you can put in any amount of white space. For example, you can use indentation of input lines to reflect program structure, as in

```
if (A > B)
    if (A > C)
        printf("A is biggest");
    else
        printf("C is biggest");
else
    if (B > C)
        printf("B is biggest");
    else
        printf("C is biggest");
```

1.4.5 Keywords

The keywords of C have special meanings and may not be used for other purposes (for example, variable names). The **ANSI** C keywords are as follows:

```
auto        double      int         struct
break       else        long        switch
case        enum        register    typedef
char        extern      return      union
const       float       short       unsigned
continue    for         signed      void
default     goto        sizeof      volatile
do          if          static      while
```

All keywords must be written in lowercase.

1.4.6 Identifiers

Identifiers serve as names for functions, data objects, data types, and other features of the C language. An identifier is a sequence of characters that may be upper- or lowercase letters, digits, or the underscore (_). The first character may not be a digit. In addition, identifiers beginning with the underscore character are reserved for the use of the implementation itself and should not be created by the user.

Any identifier that is part of the standard library should be regarded as reserved, whether or not your program makes use of that library item. Appendices C, D, and E list the contents of the standard library.

C distinguishes between the case of letters in identifiers. In other words, an uppercase letter in an identifier is *not* equivalent to the corresponding lowercase letter. This means that the identifiers NAME, Name, and name all refer to *different* entities.

To conform to the **ANSI** standard, an implementation must pay attention to at least the first 31 characters of an identifier. If an implementation pays attention to additional characters, the number is implementation-defined.

The process of linking translated source files together may reduce the number of characters that are significant in some identifiers. In particular, some implementations may only pay attention to the first *six* characters of identifiers with "external linkage" (described in Section 5). In addition, some implementations may ignore the case of letters in identifiers with external linkage.

1.5 Locales

C originated in the United States, but it is intended to be an international language. For this reason, the **ANSI** C library has been designed to allow support for **locale-specific** conventions. For example, this book has used the North American convention of putting a period (dot) between the integer and fractional parts of a floating point number (as in 3.14159). However, in some parts of the world, a comma is used instead. In such places, functions like `scanf` (which reads floating point values) and `printf` (which prints them) should take the different conventions into account.

In order to allow for this kind of variation, **ANSI** C introduced the notion of **locales**. A locale is a set of conventions that C and the C library should observe. Each locale is identified by a string giving the name of the locale. The standard header `<locale.h>` declares manifests, types, and functions used in working with locale-specific concepts.

The default locale is named `"C"`. The conventions of the `"C"` locale are the ones that we have been describing up to this point in the book. All implementations must support the `"C"` locale.

Implementations may support other locales as well. The library function `setlocale` is used to change locales. As shown in the description of `setlocale` in Section IV.4, the function can change all or just some of the conventions currently being used. Since `setlocale` is a function, a program can change locales in the middle of execution. For example, an interactive program might ask users to choose their favorite locale, then call `setlocale` to set up conventions accordingly.

In the rest of this section, we will describe some of the conventions that can vary from locale to locale.

1.5.1 Characters

Many languages contain extensions to the basic English character set. For example, some have additional characters, especially punctuation characters; some can attach accents and other marks to certain letters; and some (like Chinese) have very large numbers of different characters. **ANSI** C has two different approaches to handling locale-specific characters: extended character sets and multibyte characters.

The **extended character set** approach uses the basic **char** type to represent characters beyond the minimum character set. For example, a letter with an accent would have a different **char** value than the same letter without the accent. Since the **char** type must have at least eight bits, it can represent at least 256 different values, and this is enough to handle the requirements of most locales. When a locale has extensions to the character set, various library functions must behave differently. Examples are given below:

`isalpha`
> This library function determines whether a character is alphabetic. In the `"C"` locale, `isalpha` only recognizes the 52 upper- and lowercase letters of English. In other locales, the function may have to recognize other **char** values as letters (for example, values representing accented letters). The same kind of change is required in the library functions `isalnum`, `iscntrl`, `isgraph`, `islower`, `isprint`, `ispunct`, `isupper`, `toupper`, and `tolower`.

`strcoll`
> The `strcoll` function compares two strings according to the **collating sequence** of the current locale. In the `"C"` locale, the collating sequence is just the numeric value of the **char** values, but in other locales, the collating sequence may be different. In particular, the collating sequence in a particular locale may be based on "alphabetical order" in that locale, and that will be affected by the alphabet, accents, and so on.

The other approach to different character sets is the use of **multibyte characters**. As the name suggests, this approach may use more than one byte to represent a single character. Different characters may use different numbers of bytes in the same locale.

A multibyte character scheme may use **shift dependencies**. This term arises from the way that a "shift lock" key works on a normal typewriter. Once you press "shift lock" all letters are typed in uppercase until you press "shift lock" again to take off the lock. In the same way, a multibyte character scheme may use a number of special "shift characters." When a shift character is encountered, all subsequent characters are interpreted in a particular way; after another shift character, the same characters may be interpreted in different ways. This means that the interpretation of any character depends on the shift character most recently seen.

All multibyte character strings are assumed to begin in an "initial shift state." From that point on, shift characters in the string may change into different shift states. The `mblen` function (described in Section IV.4) can be used to determine if the multibyte character scheme in the current locale uses shift dependencies.

All implementations must define an integral type named `wchar_t`. This is called the **wide character** type. For every possible multibyte character in any locale, there is a unique `wchar_t` (wide character) integer associated with the character. This mapping simplifies the program's job in working with multibyte characters, because it is easier to work with single integers than with multibyte characters of varying lengths. Several library functions map wide character integers to multibyte characters and vice versa: `mbtowc`, `wctomb`, `mbstowcs` and `wcstombs`.

In source code, extended characters and multibyte characters may only appear in comments, character constants, string literals, and header names. This means, for example, that you cannot have identifiers that use extended or multibyte characters. When a comment, character constant, string literal, or header name is a multibyte character sequence, it must begin and end in the initial shift state.

The minimum character set is part of every extended character set. The null character (a byte with all bits zero) is the null character in all extended character sets.

1.5.2 Numbers

Several locale-specific conventions affect numbers:

(a)   The character or character string that serves as a decimal point.

(b)   The character or character string that indicates when a number is negative (for example, the minus sign).

(c)   The character or character string used to separate groups of numbers to the left of the decimal point. For example, the North American convention is to use the comma, as in `1,000,000` but other locales may use other characters (for example, the space). In the `"C"` locale, no such separator is recognized.

(d)   The format of monetary values, including the currency symbol used to indicate monetary units (for example, the dollar sign `'$'`), the position of the currency symbol, the number of figures that should follow the decimal point (for example, two, as in $1.99), and so on.

Locale-specific functions that make use of the decimal point character are

atof	localeconv	fprintf	fscanf
printf	scanf	sprintf	sscanf
strtod	vfprintf	vprintf	vsprintf

The decimal point character is used in both input and output operations.

1.5.3 Date and Time

The `strftime` function creates a formatted date/time string. The function works much like `printf`: you give it a format string with placeholders representing various parts of the date and time. The placeholder `"%x"` stands for the current locale's "standard" date representation and `"%X"` stands for the current locale's standard time representation.

chapter 2   Data and Data Objects

This chapter describes the types of data that appear in C programs. These descriptions sometimes show declarations of data types in order to clarify certain points. Full rules for the construction and use of declarations are given in Section 5.

The fundamental unit of data storage in C is the **byte**. A byte is a unit of data storage capable of holding a single character in the execution environment's data set. This must be at least eight bits long. All data objects (except for bit fields, described in Section 2.6) are composed of contiguous sequences of bytes, with "no bits left over."

For example, if a machine has integers that are 36 bits long, its bytes could be 9, 12, 18, or 36 bits long. The bytes cannot be 8 bits long, because 36 is not an exact multiple of 8.

Many machines gather bytes into larger groupings called **words**. On such machines, memory is divided into equal length words and each word is subdivided into the same number of bytes. On the majority of systems, words are either two bytes long or four bytes long, but other lengths are possible. Words are sometimes grouped themselves into double word groups, four-word groups, and so on.

On many machines, some types of data objects must be suitably **aligned** when they are stored in memory. For example, the memory for a particular data object might have to start at the beginning of a word; the hardware would not accept the data object starting at some byte in the middle of a word. Other data objects may have to start at the beginning of a double-word, and so on.

In general, C makes sure that all data objects are stored with appropriate alignment. This has some side effects that we will discuss in later sections.

2.1 *Integers*

An integer is a number without a fractional part or exponent. C recognizes the following integer data types:

short int
> can represent integers in the range −32767 to 32767. It is possible that an implementation may have a **short int** type that can represent a much larger range of numbers, but only the above range is guaranteed for all implementations. The names **short**, **signed short**, or **signed short int** are all equivalent to **short int**.

unsigned short int
> can represent integers in the range 0 to 65535. Some implementations have **unsigned short int** types that can handle higher values, but **unsigned**

values are never negative. The name **unsigned short** is equivalent to **unsigned short int**.

int

can represent integers in the range -32767 to 32767. As with **short**, some implementations may be able to represent a much wider range of numbers with **int** values. The name **signed int** is equivalent to **int**.

unsigned int

can represent integers in the range 0 to 65535. Some implementations can represent greater values. The name **unsigned** is equivalent to **unsigned int**.

long int

can represent integers in the range -2147483647 to 2147483647. Some implementations can represent a wider range. The names **long**, **signed long**, and **signed long int** are equivalent to **long int**.

unsigned long int

can represent integers in the range 0 to 4294967295. Some implementations can represent greater values. The name **unsigned long** is equivalent to **unsigned long int**.

The ranges required for these data types ensure that **short** and **int** values must be at least 16 bits long, and **long** values must be at least 32 bits long. There is no requirement that these types should actually be different from the point of view of the hardware, and indeed, they may all be the same size.

2.1.1 Integer Constants

There are several ways to express integer constants: in decimal, octal, hexadecimal, and character format. An integer constant expressed in one of the first three formats is called a **numeric integer constant**.

The programmer can specify a particular type for an numeric integer constant by adding a *suffix* on the end of the constant. If a numeric integer constant is followed by U or u, its type is **unsigned int** (or **unsigned long int** if the value is outside the **unsigned int** range). If a numeric integer constant is followed by L or l, its type is **long int** (or **unsigned long int** if the value is outside the **long int** range). If a numeric integer constant is followed by both L or l and U or u, its type is **unsigned long int**. For example, we have

```
123u    /* unsigned int*/
123l    /* long int*/
123UL   /* unsigned long int*/
```

If there is no suffix, the type of a numeric integer constant is determined by its size and its representation, as described in the subsections that follow.

2.1.2 Decimal Integers

Decimal integer constants are written as ordinary integers with no leading zero, as in

```
2400    5    87    1340932
```

A decimal integer without a suffix has one of the following types: **int**, **long int**, **unsigned long int**. C uses the first of these types whose range contains the given constant value.

2.1.3 Octal Integers

Octal integer constants are written as integers formed with only the octal digits (from 0 to 7). To distinguish octal integers from decimal integers, octal constants must begin with at least one leading zero, as in

```
01    007    000400    0777
```

An octal integer without a suffix has one of the following types: **int**, **unsigned int**, **long int**, **unsigned long int**. Again, C uses the first type whose range contains the given constant value.

2.1.4 Hexadecimal Integers

Hexadecimal integer constants are written as a string of hexadecimal digits. These include the numeric digits ′0′ to ′9′, as well as the letters ′A′ through ′F′, standing for the values 10 through 15. The letters may be upper- or lowercase. To distinguish hexadecimal integers from other integer forms, hexadecimal constants must begin with 0x or 0X, as in

```
0x10    0XC0BB    0x12c    0XffFF
```

A hexadecimal integer without a suffix has one of the following types: **int**, **unsigned int**, **long int**, **unsigned long int**. C uses the first of these types whose range contains the given constant value.

2.1.5 Character Constants

A character constant is a single multibyte character enclosed in single quotes, as in

```
′a′    ′1′    ′\n′
```

As shown above, escape sequences may be used to represent characters. In particular, you must use an escape sequence if you want to have a single quote character inside a character constant, as in

```
'\''
```

Character constants have the **int** type. This means that they may be big enough to hold more than one multibyte character, as in `'ab'`. If a character constant contains more than one character, its handling is implementation-defined.

2.1.6 Wide Characters

A wide character constant consists of an uppercase `L` followed by a multibyte character enclosed in single quotes, as in

```
L'a'      L'1'       L'\n'
```

In a wide character constant of this form, the multibyte character is converted to the corresponding wide character integer. The type of a wide character constant is `wchar_t`, a signed or unsigned integral type defined in `<stddef.h>`.

A normal character constant will always be numerically equal to the wide character constant that contains the same character. For example,

```
'a'  ==  L'a'
```

Remember that `'a'` is an **int** constant, while the type of `L'a'` is `wchar_t`.

2.2 *Floating Point Types*

A floating point number has a decimal point or an exponent or both. C recognizes the following floating point data types.

float
can represent numbers between -10^{37} and 10^{37}. Some implementations support larger ranges. Most implementations use **float** to refer to "single precision" floating point numbers, but this is not required by the standard. Indeed, there may be good reasons to use the name **float** for "double precision" numbers.

double
can represent numbers between -10^{37} and 10^{37}. Some implementations support larger ranges. Most implementations use **double** to refer to "double precision" floating point numbers, but again this is not required, and it is possible that **double** values are actually single precision numbers.

long double
can represent numbers between -10^{37} and 10^{37}. Some implementations support larger ranges.

There is no requirement that these three types should actually be different sizes. However, a **long double** must be at least as big as a **double**, and a **double** must be at least as big as a **float**.

2.2.1 Floating Point Constants

Floating point constants must have a decimal point or an exponent (or both). They may be preceded by leading zeros if desired.

The exponential part consists of an e or E followed by a signed integer exponent. If the sign of the exponent is positive, the + may be omitted. The following are examples of valid floating point constants.

```
2.3   1.   3.E5   72.48e-4   0.34e2   .123
```

Floating point constants normally have the **double** type. If the programmer adds the suffix F or f, the constant has the **float** type. If the programmer adds the suffix L or l, the constant has the **long double** type. For example, we have

```
1.234    /* double*/
1.234L   /* long double*/
1.234f   /* float*/
```

2.3 Characters

A character data object can represent a single character in the execution environment's character set. There is a direct relationship between character data and integers: the set of possible character values is a subset of the set of possible integer values. For this reason, characters may be freely converted into integers and may also be used in arithmetic expressions.

The characters in the execution character set must correspond to integers in a range that includes the numbers 0 through 127. A character data object is actually able to hold a wider range of values, since its width is a byte and therefore at least eight bits. This means that it is possible for a character object to hold a value that does not correspond to an actual character in the execution character set.

C recognizes the following character data types:

char
    can hold integer values in the range 0 to 127.

signed char
    can hold integer values in the range −127 to 127.

unsigned char
    can hold integer values in the range 0 to 255.

In fact, the **char** type is equivalent to either **signed char** or **unsigned char**. The choice of **signed** or **unsigned** is implementation-defined. The plain **char** type is the type that the particular implementation can handle more efficiently.

Character constants are often assigned to character data objects. Remember, however, that character constants are actually **int** values; therefore the assignment process performs a data conversion. Remember also that character constants are made from multibyte characters converted to **int**, and therefore may not be representable as single **char** objects.

A multibyte character is a sequence of one or more single-byte characters, and is typically stored as a **char** array or converted to a wide character. In this book, the generic term *character* will always mean a single-byte character of one of the **char** types. When we want to discuss one of the other character types, we will explicitly refer to multibyte characters or wide characters.

2.3.1 String Literals

A string literal is a sequence of zero or more multibyte characters enclosed in double quotes, as in

```
"this is a string"
""
"the above is a null string"
"this is split\nover two lines"
```

Note that the ′\n′ in the final example will break the string into two separate lines if the string is printed. This example also illustrates that escape sequences may be used inside strings.

Using an appropriate escape sequence is the only way to put a new-line character into a string literal. A construct like

```
"This string
ends on another line."
```

is invalid. Double quote characters that appear inside a string literal must also be represented by an escape sequence, as in

```
"He said, \"Hello there.\"\n"
```

A string literal is stored as an array of **char** with static storage duration (defined in Section 5). The characters are stored in sequential bytes. On systems where a machine word is larger than a byte, there will be several characters per word. The last character specified in a string literal is always followed by a NUL character ′\0′. Thus the string "abc" is represented as a vector with the elements ′a′, ′b′, ′c′, and ′\0′. Programs can locate the end of a string by looking for the ′\0′.

String literals cannot be modified in **ANSI** C. Many older versions of C let programmers modify such strings. Another difference between **ANSI** C and some older implementations is that **ANSI** implementations may "re-use" string literals that appear in several places in the program. For example, if `"abc"` appears several times in a program, the executable code may use the same literal at the same memory location. Older implementations created a different copy of the string for each separate reference.

A string literal must begin and end in the initial shift state if multibyte characters have shift dependencies.

2.3.2 Wide String Literals

A wide string literal is written as an uppercase `L` followed by a sequence of zero or more multibyte characters enclosed in double quotes, as in

```
L"this is a wide character string"
```

Each multibyte character in the string literal will be converted to the corresponding wide character, and the string literal will be stored as an array of `wchar_t` integral values with static storage duration. Just as a `'\0'` character is used to mark the end of a normal string literal, a value of zero is used to mark the end of a wide character string literal.

The rules for using normal string literals apply to wide string literals. For example, an implementation is allowed to re-use a wide string literal if it appears in several places in the same program.

A wide string literal must begin and end in the initial shift state if multibyte characters have shift dependencies.

2.4 Pointers

A pointer value refers to a particular location in memory. The type of the pointer indicates what type of data is stored in this memory location. For example, you might have a pointer to **int**, a pointer to **char**, or a pointer to some more complex type (for example, a pointer to a pointer). We will often use the phrase *pointer to type* to refer to a pointer that points to an object of the given *type*.

Many older C programs assume that pointers are similar to integers. This is *not* true for **ANSI** C: pointers may not have the same size as integers, and one pointer type may not be the same size as another pointer type. However, all pointers can be converted to some integral type and back again without loss of information.

It is possible to declare and obtain a pointer to a function as well as a pointer to a data object. For example, you can declare a pointer to a function that takes an **int** argument and returns an **int** value. A pointer to a function that takes a different set of arguments or that returns a different type of value is a different pointer type.

Function pointers do not always follow the same rules as object pointers. In reading this manual, you should watch for places where we distinguish between pointers to objects and pointers to functions.

2.5 Arrays

An array is a collection of individual data objects, each having the same type. For example, a program might have an array of **int**, an array of pointers to **char**, and so on. The objects that make up an array are called the **members** or **elements** of the array.

An array has two major characteristics: the number of members it holds, and the type of each member. For example, the declaration

```
int k[20];
```

declares an array named k which can contain 20 integer members.

The members of an array are numbered, beginning at 0. These numbers are called the **subscripts** of array members. The 20 members of k would be referred to as

```
k[0], k[1], k[2], ..., k[19]
```

Note that the maximum subscript of the array is one less than the number of members in the array.

C lets you define arrays of arrays. For example,

```
float r[10][20];
```

declares an array with 10 members. Each member is an array that contains 20 **float** numbers. Two subscripts are needed to refer to one of these **float** numbers, as in r[0][0], r[3][5], r[9][12], and so on. Because it takes two subscripts to refer to members of such an array, the array is said to be **two-dimensional**. Arrays whose elements can be referred to with only one subscript (one-dimensional arrays) are often called **vectors**.

The **ANSI** standard requires every implementation to support arrays of up to six dimensions. Some implementations may support even higher dimensions. Multidimensional arrays are stored in "row-major order" in contiguous memory. For example, the elements of a two-dimensional array a are stored in the order

```
a[0][0],a[0][1],a[0][2],...,
a[1][0],a[1][1],a[1][2],...,
    ...
```

The last subscript varies the fastest.

2.6 Structures

A structure is a data object consisting of several named sub-objects. These sub-objects are known as the **members** of the structure. Each member may have any type. For example,

```
struct record {
    char name[30];
    int age;
};
```

defines a structure type named `record`. (The name `record` is called the **structure tag**.) The structure has two members: a character vector named `name` and an integer named `age`.

The members of a structure are stored in memory in the order they are listed in the structure declaration. The first member of the structure has an alignment suitable for *any* data type. Subsequent members are aligned in a manner appropriate to their type. For example, in

```
struct abc {
    char c;
    double x;
};
```

the **double** member `x` is aligned on whatever sort of boundary is appropriate for **double** data. On many machines, this may leave a "hole" of unused memory in the middle of the structure, since extra space must be added after `c` to reach the correct alignment boundary.

In addition to normal members, structures may also contain **bit fields**. In a declaration, a bit field is written as a signed or unsigned **int** declaration, followed by a colon (`:`), followed by a constant expression, as in

```
int h : 3;
```

The number after the colon indicates how many bits the field should occupy. In this case, `h` occupies three bits. This feature may be used to optimize memory use in a structure, since an implementation may be able to fit a bit field into a "hole" in the structure. It may also be used to give names to bits or groups of bits in data structures (for example, those used by an operating system). Note that the use of bit fields is almost always nonportable.

C also allows you to specify unnamed bit fields. For example,

```
struct example {
    int top_bit: 1;
    : 6;
    int bottom_bit: 1;
};
```

includes an unnamed bit field of six bits. This nonportable example might be used to give names to the top and bottom bits of an eight-bit byte. An unnamed bit field can have a length of zero.

If a named or unnamed bit field cannot be packed into the "hole" between two other members, the way the bit field is stored and aligned is implementation-defined.

2.7 Unions

A union is a single data object that may have a number of different **interpretations**. For example,

```
union multi {
    int fix;
    char c[4];
    float flt;
};
```

declares a union type with the tag `multi`. An object of this type may be interpreted as an integer, a character vector containing four members, or a floating point number. The different interpretations of a union are sometimes called the **members** of the union.

The interpretations of a union all refer to the same location in memory. If one interpretation is assigned a value, the value of all the other interpretations will change as a consequence. For example, assigning a new value to `c[0]` in the above union automatically changes a byte in both the integer and floating point interpretations. The change that occurs in other interpretations is system-dependent.

The length allocated for a union object in memory is sufficient to hold the largest interpretation of the union. The alignment of a union object is chosen to be appropriate for all possible interpretations of the object.

2.8 Enumerated Types

Enumerated types are data types created by the programmer. The values of an enumerated type are represented by identifiers. An enumerated type is created by listing all the possible values, as in

```
enum wday {
    sun, mon, tue, wed, thu, fri, sat
};
```

The tag `wday` is used to identify the enumerated type itself. Listed inside the braces are the values that objects of this data type may have.

The values stated in the enumeration list are regarded as **int** constants and may be used wherever **int** constants are valid. Normally, the identifier that appears first in the enumeration list has the value 0, the next has the value 1, and so on. In the above example, `mon+3` is the integer 4, which is equivalent to `thu`.

You can specify different integer values for enumerated identifiers, as in

```
enum coins {
    cent=1, nickel=5,
    dime=10, quarter=25
};
```

In this example, cent is equivalent to the **int** constant 1, nickel is equivalent to 5, and so on.

Some of the values in the enumeration list may be given explicit integer equivalents while others are not. In this case, the ones with = enumerators will be given the specified values and the ones without will be assigned values by beginning at the specified values and adding one for each new item in the list. For example,

```
enum roman {
    I=1, II, III, IV
};
```

gives I the value 1, II the value 2, and so on.

It is possible to have several enumerated identifiers with the same integer value, as in

```
enum coins {
    cent=1, penny=1, nickel=5,
    dime=10, quarter=25
};
```

2.9 Functions

Even though functions are bodies of executable code, C lets you calculate pointers to functions and pass these pointers as arguments to other functions.

The *type* of a function is the type of value that the function returns. We may speak of the types "function returning **int**", "function returning pointer to **char**", and so on. The types of arguments that a function takes are also important in determining how a function may be used as data, but this will be discussed in Section 6.

2.10 The void Type

The **void** type represents the absence of data. For example, a function that does not return a value has the type "function returning **void**." Similarly, the **void** type can be used in declarations of functions that take no arguments. Lastly, converting an expression to the **void** type effectively discards the expression's result.

The **void *** type is a "generic" pointer type. This kind of pointer does not point to any specific type of data; it can point to *any* type of object. Note that **void *** pointers may only be used to point to data objects; you may not assign a function pointer to a **void *** pointer.

2.11 Type Terminology

C uses special names for certain groups of related types, as follows:

Integral types
All the signed and unsigned **int** and **char** types, plus the **enum** types.

Floating types
float, **double**, and **long double**.

Arithmetic types
All integral and floating types.

Scalar types
All arithmetic and pointer types.

Aggregate types
All array and structure types.

Derived types
All aggregate, union, function, and pointer types.

An **incomplete** type is a type that is missing some information. For example, an array that has been declared without stating the array size is an incomplete type. Similarly, in

```
typedef struct X *XPTR;
struct X {
    int node_value;
    XPTR left;
    XPTR right;
}
```

the X structure is incomplete at the time the XPTR type is created, since the contents of X have not yet been specified. By convention, **void *** is always regarded as an incomplete type.

The **top type** of a derived type is the type that is the first type named when describing the type. For example, the top type of "pointer to **char**" is "pointer."

A type is called a **qualified type** if its top type has a type qualifier (**const**, **volatile**, or both). Type qualifiers are described in Section 5. The **unqualified version** of a qualified type is the same type, without the qualifiers.

Two types are **compatible** if they are the same. For example, **unsigned** and **unsigned int** are compatible. Note, however, that even the plain **char** type is the same as one of **unsigned char** or **signed char**, these three are regarded as three distinct and incompatible types.

Two structure, union, or enumerated types declared in separate translation units are compatible if they have the same number of members, the same member names, and compatible member types. For structures, the members must be in the same order. For enumerated types, the enumeration constants must have the same values.

A **composite type** is one constructed from two types that are compatible. It is compatible with both types and combines the information from both. The following rules apply:

(a)   If one type is an array of known size, the composite type is an array of that size.

(b)   If only one of the types is a function type declared with a prototype, the composite type is a function type with that prototype.

(c)   If both types are functions with prototypes, the composite type is one with a prototype consisting of all the information that can be combined from the two prototypes.

2.12 Conversions

The process of converting a value from one type to another may seem simple, but there can be subtle complications. In particular, different machines may represent data in different ways.

The designers of the **ANSI** standard also had to choose between dictating a particular conversion process (which might turn out to be slow on some machines) or leaving each implementation to choose its own approach (in which case, a simple program might behave differently on different systems). Usually, they chose the option that would be most efficient on the machines most commonly used to run C programs. For example, all the signed to unsigned integer conversions may have complicated descriptions, but on a machine that uses the "ones' complement" or "twos' complement" method of representing negative integers, the conversion rules reduce to "Take the unsigned value that has the same bit pattern as the signed value."

The general rule for all conversions is to preserve the original value whenever possible. If the new type cannot represent the original value, the conversion attempts to find a value that will go back to the original value (or its best approximation) if converted to the original type.

2.12.1 Fundamental Data Conversions

Several operations may cause implicit or explicit conversions from one data type to another.

Character to Integer

A **char** object (signed or unsigned) may be used wherever an **int** object is valid. The **char** object is converted to the integer equal to the character's numeric representation. If the **char** object is signed, the sign of the resulting integer is the same as the sign of the original character value. The type of the converted value is **int** if an **int** can represent all values of the given **char** type; otherwise, the type is **unsigned int**.

Integer to Unsigned Character

When an integer (signed or unsigned) is converted to **unsigned char**, the result is the remainder of the integer value, modulo the largest possible **unsigned char** value plus one. For example, if an **unsigned char** has eight bits, the largest possible value is 2^8-1, so the integer value is reduced modulo 2^8. In many machines, this just means discarding the high order bits of the integer, down to the size of an **unsigned char**.

Integer to Signed Character

Converting an integer (signed or unsigned) to **signed char** is only a fully defined operation if the value of the integer is able to fit in the range of **signed char** values. Otherwise, the result of the conversion is implementation-defined.

Signed Integer to Longer Signed Integer

The value is unchanged by the conversion.

Signed Integer to Shorter Signed Integer

If the shorter integer type is capable of representing the value of the longer integer, the value is unchanged by the conversion. If the shorter type cannot represent the longer value, the result is implementation-defined.

Integer to Shorter Unsigned Integer

When an integer (signed or unsigned) is converted to a shorter unsigned integer, the result is the remainder of the integer value, modulo the largest possible **unsigned** value of the shorter type plus one. This is similar to converting an integer to **unsigned char**.

Signed Integer to Equal Length Unsigned Integer

If the signed integer is non-negative, its value is unchanged by the conversion. If the signed integer is negative, the value is converted to unsigned by adding to it the largest number that can be represented in the unsigned integer type, plus one. Note: with one's and two's complement hardware, this operation results in the unsigned value having the same bit pattern as the original signed value.

Signed Integer to Longer Unsigned Integer

If the signed integer is non-negative, its value is unchanged by the conversion. If the signed integer is negative, it is first converted to a signed integer of the same length as the unsigned type; then this longer signed value is converted to an unsigned value of the same length, following the process described above.

Unsigned Integer to Longer Unsigned Integer

The value is unchanged by the conversion.

Bit Field to Integer

Bit fields in structures may be used anywhere an **int** may be used. Their values are always converted to **int** (even if the bit field is declared **unsigned int**). The one exception is when the bit field is the same size as an **int** and is declared **unsigned**. In this case, the bit field is converted to **unsigned int**. The value of the bit field is unchanged by the conversion.

Integer to Bit Field
This follows the rules for converting (signed or unsigned) integers to shorter (signed or unsigned) integers.

Integral Type to Floating Type
If the integer can be represented exactly in the floating type, the result of the conversion is the exactly floating point equivalent. If the integer falls in the range of values that the floating type can represent but cannot be represented exactly, the result of the conversion is the nearest higher or nearest lower value, chosen in an implementation-defined way.

Floating Type to Integral Type
The fractional part of the floating type is discarded (so that 4.7 becomes 4 and −2.6 becomes −2). If the resulting integer does not fit in the integral type, the behavior is undefined.

Floating Type to Longer Floating Type
The value is unchanged by the conversion.

Floating Type to Shorter Floating Type
If the original floating value is outside the range of the smaller type, the behavior is undefined. If the original value is in the appropriate range but cannot be represented exactly, the result is one of the two nearest values that *can* be represented. The choice of *which* value is implementation-defined (for example, round to nearest value, always choose lower of two values, always choose higher).

2.12.2 The Integral Promotion

Signed and unsigned **char**, **short**, and bit field values may be used in expressions anywhere **int** or **unsigned** values may be used. With each of these types, the value is converted to **int** if the **int** type can represent all values of the original type; otherwise, the value is converted to **unsigned int**. This automatic conversion process is called the **integral promotion**.

Note that the integral promotion may convert an unsigned type (for example, **unsigned char**) into a signed type (**int**).

2.12.3 Usual Arithmetic Conversions

Many binary operators convert their operands so that the operands (and therefore the result) will have a common type. These automatic conversions follow the rules described below, known as **usual arithmetic conversions**.

(1)   If either operand is **long double**, the other is converted to **long double**.

(2)   Otherwise, if either operand is **double**, the other is converted to **double**.

(3)   Otherwise, if either operand is **float**, the other is converted to **float**.

(4)   Otherwise, the integral promotions take place on both operands if necessary. Then:

    (a)   If either operand is **unsigned long**, the other is converted to **unsigned long**.

    (b)   Otherwise, if one operand is **long** and the other is **unsigned**, the **unsigned** is converted to **long** if the **long** type can represent the whole range of values that an **unsigned** might have. If there are some **unsigned** values that cannot be represented as a **long**, both operands are converted to **unsigned long**.

    (c)   Otherwise, if either operand is **long**, the other is converted to **long**.

    (d)   Otherwise, if either operand is **unsigned int**, the other is converted to **unsigned int**.

    (e)   Otherwise, both operands will have type **int**.

The type of the result of the operation will be the type chosen for the two operands.

2.12.4 Other Conversions

All expressions with the type "array of *type*" are converted to an expression with type "pointer to *type*" by producing a pointer that points to the initial member of the array. There are two exceptions to this rule: when the array is an operand that may or must be an Lvalue (defined in Section 3.1) and when a string literal is used to initialize an array of characters (described in Section 5.6.5). In these cases, the array type is *not* converted to a pointer.

An identifier with type "function returning *type*" is always converted to an expression with type "pointer to function returning *type*." There is one exception: when the identifier is used as an operand that may or must be a function locator (defined in Section 3.1). In this case, the function type is not converted to a pointer.

Pointers with the type **void *** may freely be converted to any other object pointer type, and all object pointer types may be converted to **void ***. If a pointer to one type is converted to **void *** and that is converted to a second pointer type, there is no guarantee that the second pointer indicates memory with the proper alignment. For example, if you use this technique to convert a character pointer to a **double** pointer, there is no guarantee that the **double** pointer points to a memory location that has the alignment required for **double** values.

On the other hand, if a pointer to some type is converted to **void ***, and this new pointer is then converted back to a pointer of the same type, the resulting pointer will be identical to the original pointer.

An integral constant expression that has the value 0 may be assigned or compared to any pointer type. When 0 is assigned to a pointer, the result is a pointer value of the appropriate type that is guaranteed not to point to any data object or function. This pointer value is often called the **null pointer** for that particular type. For example, if you assign 0 to an integer pointer, you get the "null integer pointer." The null pointer for a type compares equal to the integer constant 0, and no other pointer value of that type does.

Using 0 as a null pointer value is only a source code *convention*. There is no guarantee that a null pointer will have an internal representation that matches the representation of the integer 0. Indeed, there are machines where it is an error for a pointer to have the (integer) value 0.

chapter 3   Expressions

The expressions of C perform arithmetic, comparisons, bit manipulation, and other operations. The operations in an expression are evaluated according to a fixed order of precedence. For example, multiplications in an expression are normally evaluated before any additions (as in conventional arithmetic). This standard order of operation may be altered using parentheses in the usual manner.

Some operations share the same precedence (for example, addition and subtraction). A group of operations that have the same precedence make up a **precedence class**. When the time comes for operations of this class to be performed, they may be evaluated from right to left or left to right, depending on the class. For example,

```
a - b - c
```

is evaluated from left to right, while

```
x = y = z
```

is evaluated from right to left.

The rules of operator precedence and right-left/left-right evaluation within a precedence class do not fully determine the order in which C evaluates an expression. For example, if A and B are expressions, A+B may be evaluated by calculating A first then B, or vice versa. In such situations, the order of evaluation is unspecified—the implementation is free to evaluate subexpressions in the most efficient or convenient way, even if the order of evaluation has side effects.

If an error occurs while an expression is being evaluated, the behavior is undefined. This means that the individual implementation must decide what to do about such things as division by zero, overflow and underflow, and so on.

The sections in this chapter describe the operators in each precedence class. These sections are arranged from highest precedence to lowest. Subsections within the sections describe individual operators. Before individual operator descriptions can be given, however, a few terms must be defined.

3.1 Expression Definitions

An **Lvalue** (pronounced "ell-value") is an expression that denotes an object (an actual memory location). The term Lvalue is used because this type of value was historically the only kind of expression that could appear on the *Left* of an assignment. This is no longer precisely true, but the principle is still useful to remember.

In some operations, an operand may or must be an Lvalue. If an Lvalue appears in any other context, it is replaced by the *value* of the memory location to which the Lvalue refers. For example, consider

```
A = 2;
B = A;
```

In the first assignment, A is on the left hand of an assignment, and this operand must be an Lvalue. Thus A is treated as a name for a particular memory location and the value 2 is stored in that memory location. In the second assignment, A is not in an Lvalue-only position. This means that the expression will use the *value* stored in the memory location to which A refers.

Array types receive special treatment in this respect. If an array type appears in an expression where it need not be treated as an Lvalue, it is converted to a pointer to the initial member of the array. For example, if `arr` is the name of an array,

```
p = arr;
```

obtains a pointer to the initial member of the array and assigns that pointer value to `p`. If an array is converted to a pointer in this way, it is no longer considered an Lvalue in this expression.

A **modifiable Lvalue** is an Lvalue that does not have an array type and does not have the **const** type qualifier (described in Section 5.4.1).

A **function locator** is an expression with function type. If a function locator is used in a context except as an operand that may or must be a function locator, it is converted to a pointer to a function, as described in Section 2. If a function locator is converted to a pointer in this way, it is no longer considered an Lvalue in this expression.

In the operation descriptions that follow, we will note when an operand is expected to be an Lvalue, a modifiable Lvalue, or a function locator.

3.2 Primary Expressions

A **primary expression** has one of the following forms:

> *identifier*
> *constant*
> *string-literal*
> (*expression*)

Primary expressions have the highest evaluation precedence.

3.2.1 Identifier Primary Expressions

An identifier is a primary expression, provided it has been suitably declared before it is used. Declarations are discussed in Section 5. The type of an identifier is given in its declaration.

3.2.2 Constant Primary Expressions

Constants and string literals were described in Section 2. A constant's type is determined by the constant's form and value. When we speak of string literals here, we mean both character and wide character string literals.

The appearance of a string literal in an expression creates an array of **char** or wchar_t containing the given characters plus a trailing `'\0'`. However, the value that is actually used in evaluating the expression is a pointer to the first character of this array. Thus when a string literal appears in an expression, the string is created but the value actually used in evaluating the expression is a pointer to **char** or pointer to wchar_t.

3.2.3 Parenthesized Expressions

Expressions enclosed in parentheses are regarded as primary expressions because the parentheses indicate high precedence of evaluation. The type and value of a parenthesized expression are the type and value of the expression inside the parentheses.

3.3 Postfix Expressions

A **postfix expression** has one of the following forms:

> *expression* [*expression*]
> *expression* (*expression-list*)
> *expression* . *identifier*
> *expression* **->** *identifier*
> *expression***++**
> *expression***--**

Postfix expressions group left to right, so that `arr[5]--` is equivalent to `(arr[5])--`.

3.3.1 Subscripted Expressions

An expression followed by an expression in square brackets denotes a subscripting operation. One of the expressions must have type "pointer to *type*" while the other must have an integral type. The result of the expression has type *type*.

A subscripted expression is used to refer to a single member of an array. Normally, the expression before the square brackets points to the array (remember that an array identifier is treated as a pointer to the initial member of the array), and the expression in the brackets gives the number of a particular array member. However, C lets you reverse the positions of the pointer and the integer if you wish. For example, if a is the name of an array and i is a suitable subscript integer, `a[i]` and `i[a]` are both valid and equivalent. (However, `i[a]` is generally considered poor style.)

More precisely, the expression `E1[E2]` is evaluated as if it were `(*(E1 + (E2)))`. This equivalence makes use of the properties of pointer addition and the indirection operator `*` (described in Section 3.4.3). As a result, the following are all equivalent.

```
a[0]    0[a]    *a
```

Multiple subscript operations are used to refer to elements in multidimensional arrays, as in `a[4][7]`.

3.3.2 Function Call Expressions

A function call is an expression followed by parentheses enclosing a list of argument expressions, as in

```
sin(x)     printf("%d",i+2)     f(x*x,y*y,z*z)
```

As shown, the argument expressions are separated by commas. An argument expression can be any kind of expression except a comma expression (described in Section 3.18). The type of an argument expression must not be **void**. The expression list may be empty, as in `getchar()`.

The expression before the parentheses must have the type "pointer to function returning *type*." (Remember that function locators are converted to such pointers automatically.) The result of the expression has type *type*. Functions may return any type of value except an array type.

To make a function call, the implementation first evaluates each argument expression. Arguments are always passed *by value*, which means that the function being invoked receives copies of the argument values, not the arguments themselves. For example, if a variable X is passed as an argument to a function, the function is given a copy of X's current value. The function works only with this copy; the function cannot affect the value of the real X. However, if a function call passes a pointer to a data object, the function may use its copy of this pointer to reach the original data object and change the object's value.

The order in which argument expressions are evaluated is unspecified. You should not write code where order of evaluation makes a difference. For example, suppose the integer variable i is 1.

```
f(i,i++)
```

results in `f(1,1)` if the first argument is evaluated first and `f(2,1)` if the second argument is evaluated first. (The ++ operation is explained in Section 3.3.4.) Different implementations may choose different orders of argument evaluation, and indeed, a single implementation may choose different orders at different times.

3.3.3 Structure and Union Member Expressions

The . and -> operators refer to members of a structure or interpretations of a union. The -> operator is made from a minus sign (-) followed by a "greater-than" character (>). In

> *expression . identifier*

the *expression* must have a structure or union type and the *identifier* must name a member of that type. The value is the named member of the given structure or union. This is an Lvalue unless the first expression is a value returned by a function call. In

> *expression -> identifier*

the *expression* must be a pointer to structure or union and the *identifier* must name a member of the type pointed to. The value is the named member in the structure or union to which the first expression points. The -> expression is an Lvalue.

If E is a structure or union and member is a member of E, the expressions

```
E.member
(&E) -> member
```

are equivalent (where & is the address operator described in Section 3.4.4).

If a value is assigned to one interpretation of a union and then the program uses the value of a *different* interpretation, the result is generally implementation-defined. However, if a union has two or more interpretations which are structures, and if each such structure begins with one or more members that have the same type as corresponding members in other structure interpretations, then you may assign a value to one of the shared members in one structure interpretation and use this value from the corresponding member in one of the other structure interpretations. For example, suppose we have

```
union example {
    struct s1 {
        float f1;
        int i1;
        char n1[30];
    } m1;
    struct s2 {
        float f2;
        int i2;
        double n2;
    } m2;
} u;
```

Both structure interpretations start with a **float** member followed by an **int** member. This means that we can assign a value to these members using one interpretation, as in

```
u.s1.i1 = 3;
```

and inspect its value using the other interpretation, as in

```
if (u.s2.i2 == 3) ...
```

The **ANSI** standard guarantees that this will work the way you expect.

3.3.4 Postfix Increment Expressions

In an expression of the form

operand++

the operand must be a modifiable Lvalue with a scalar type. The result of the expression is the value of the operand. Once this result has been obtained, the value of the Lvalue is incremented by 1 (1 is added to the Lvalue). Note that the result of the expression is the value of the operand *before* the operand is incremented.

3.3.5 Postfix Decrement Expressions

The postfix decrement expression

operand--

is exactly like the postfix increment expression, except that the value of the Lvalue operand is *decremented* by 1 (that is, 1 is subtracted from the Lvalue).

3.4 Unary Expressions

A **unary expression** has one of the following forms:

++expression
--expression
*expression
&expression
+expression
-expression
! expression
~expression
sizeof *expression*
sizeof (*type-name*)

Unary expressions are evaluated from right to left.

3.4.1 Prefix Increment Expressions

In an expression of the form

++*operand*

the operand must be a modifiable Lvalue with a scalar type. The Lvalue is incremented by one, and the result of the expression is the resulting value of the operand. Note that the result of the expression is the value of the operand *after* the operand is incremented.

3.4.2 Prefix Decrement Expressions

The prefix decrement expression

−−*operand*

is exactly like the prefix increment expression, except that the value of the Lvalue operand is *decremented* by one.

3.4.3 Indirection Expressions

In the expression

⋆*operand*

the operand must have a pointer type. If the operand is a pointer to a function, the result is a function locator. If the operand is a pointer to a data object, the result is an Lvalue referring to the object. If the type of the operand is "pointer to *type*", the type of the result is *type*.

If the value of the operand is invalid (for example, it is not aligned properly for the type of data to which it refers), the behavior is undefined.

3.4.4 Address Expressions

The operand of the unary & operator must be a function locator or an Lvalue referring to an object that is not a bit field and is not an object declared with the **register** storage class (described in Section 5.3.2). The result of the expression is a pointer to the memory location of the operand. If the operand's type is *type*, the result is "pointer to *type*."

If E is a function locator or Lvalue, ⋆&E is a function locator or Lvalue equal to E.

3.4.5 Unary Plus and Minus Expressions

The unary + and − operators require operands with an arithmetic type. The integral promotion is applied to the operand (if necessary).

The result of the unary plus has the same value as its operand. The result of the unary minus is the negative of the value of its operand. If it is applied to an unsigned value A, the result is the value that you get when you convert $(0-A)$ to an unsigned integer of the same size.

3.4.6 Logical Negation Expressions

The logical negation operator ! may be applied to any scalar type. The result is always **int**. If X has the value 0, !X has the value 1. If X is nonzero, !X is the integer 0.

If P is a pointer type, !P is 1 when P is a null pointer, and 0 when P is not null.

3.4.7 Bitwise Complement Expressions

The argument of the ~ (tilde) operator must have an integral type. The integral promotion is applied to the operand if necessary. The result of ~X is the **bitwise complement** of X. This is a value of the same length as X, but with a 0-bit everywhere X has a 1-bit, and a 1-bit everywhere X has a 0-bit.

If X is an **unsigned int**, ~X is equivalent to

```
UINT_MAX - X
```

where UINT_MAX is the largest **unsigned int** value. Similarly, if XL is **unsigned long**, ~XL is equivalent to

```
ULONG_MAX - XL
```

where ULONG_MAX is the largest **unsigned long** value. This is just another way of stating that 1-bits become 0-bits and vice versa. The symbols UINT_MAX and ULONG_MAX are defined in the header <limits.h> (see Appendix D for more details).

3.4.8 Sizeof Expressions

The operand of the **sizeof** operator is either an Lvalue that is not a bit field or incomplete type, or else the parenthesized name of a type that is not a bit field or incomplete type. The result of **sizeof** is the length (in bytes) of the given object or an object of the given type. For example, **sizeof(char)** is always 1, since a byte (by definition) is the amount of memory used to hold a **char** value.

If the operand of **sizeof** has an array type, the result is the total number of bytes in the array. As a result, if arr is an array,

```
(sizeof arr) / (sizeof arr[0])
```

is the number of members in the array: the total number of bytes in the array divided by the size of a single member.

Note that this will not work if the array was passed as an argument to the function that contains the **sizeof** expression. In this case, the argument is just a *pointer* to the array, and its size is the size of such a pointer.

If the operand is a structure or union type, **sizeof** returns the number of bytes that such an object would occupy if it were a member of an array of similar structures or unions. This means that the value returned is the number of bytes occupied by the structure plus any additional bytes needed to pad out to the next appropriate alignment boundary.

The operand of **sizeof** is *not* evaluated. For example,

```
sizeof i++
```

does not increment i; it merely returns the length of the result of the expression i++. This may not be the same as sizeof i. For example, if i is a **char**, its value will be converted to **int** during expression evaluation so the result of **sizeof** will be the size of an **int**.

In summary, there are four kinds of **sizeof** expressions:

(a) The size of a type gives the number of bytes in a data object of that type.

(b) The size of an array gives the total number of bytes in all the members of the array.

(c) The size of an Lvalue gives the number of bytes occupied by the corresponding data object.

(d) The size of an expression gives the size of the result of the expression.

Many implementations evaluate **sizeof** expressions at translation time. By execution time, only the value of the **sizeof** expression is known, not the original operand.

The type of the **sizeof** result is an unsigned integral type named size_t. The implementation may choose whether the length is **short**, **int**, or **long**. The name size_t is defined in the <stddef.h> header (described in Part IV.2).

3.5 Cast Expressions

A **cast expression** converts the result of another expression to a specified type. The result will not be an Lvalue. Cast expressions have the form

(*type-name*) *expression*

type-name may be any scalar type or **void**. If it is **void**, the operand may be any expression except one that already has the **void** type. If the *type-name* is not **void**, the operand must have a scalar type. As an example of a cast expression,

```
(int) (3.14 + a)
```

converts the floating type result of the addition into **int**.

A pointer may be cast to an integer, but the nature of the result and the length of integer required is implementation-defined. (The pointer must be able to fit into a **long** or **unsigned long** value, since these are the longest possible integer types.) Similarly, an integer may be cast to a pointer, but the result is implementation-defined.

A pointer to an object or incomplete type may be cast to a value of a different object or incomplete type, but the resulting pointer may not be aligned appropriately for the new type. In addition, the data pointed to may not be meaningful for the new type.

A pointer to one function type may be converted to a pointer to another function type. However, if the two types are not compatible, the result of using a converted pointer is undefined.

3.6 Multiplicative Expressions

A **multiplicative expression** has one of the following forms.

> *expression* * *expression*
> *expression* / *expression*
> *expression* % *expression*

Multiplicative expressions are evaluated from left to right.

3.6.1 Multiplication Expressions

The binary * operator denotes normal multiplication. Each of the operands must have an arithmetic type, and the usual arithmetic conversions are performed.

3.6.2 The Division Operator (/)

The binary / operator denotes normal division. Each of the operands must have an arithmetic type, and the usual arithmetic conversions are performed. A/B is the value of A divided by B. If the value of the second operand is zero, the behavior is undefined.

When one positive integer is divided by another, the result will be truncated towards zero if necessary. For example, 9/5 is 1.

When integers are divided and the division is inexact, and if at least one operand is negative, the implementation is allowed to decide whether the result is the integer immediately above or immediately below the exact answer. For example, (-9)/5 could be either -1 or -2, depending on the implementation.

3.6.3 Remainder Expressions

The binary % operator denotes the remainder or "modulo" operation. Each of the operands must have an integral type, and the usual arithmetic conversions are performed. If the value of the second operand is zero, the behavior is undefined.

If A and B are positive, A%B is A modulo B (the integer remainder obtained when A is divided by B). If at least one operand is negative, A%B is the number such that

```
(A/B)*B + A%B
```

is equal to A. This means that the value of A%B depends on the way the implementation performs integer division with negative numbers.

3.7 Additive Expressions

An **additive expression** has one of the following forms:

expression + expression
expression – expression

Additive expressions are evaluated from left to right.

3.7.1 Addition Expressions

The binary + operator denotes addition. If both operands have arithmetic types, the usual arithmetic conversions are performed and the result is the sum of the two numbers.

C also accepts additions with one pointer operand and one integral operand. If the pointer is a pointer to type T, it must point at an array member of type T. If we have

```
P  ==  &A[I]
```

then

```
P + J == &A[I+J]
```

For example, suppose p is a pointer to a particular type and it points to a member in an array of the same type; then p+1 points to the array member that follows *p; p+2 points to the member after that; and so on.

If the pointer operand in an addition expression does *not* point at an array member, the result of the addition is undefined. The same holds true if the addition adds an integer large enough to move too far beyond the end of the array. (In some contexts, you may refer to P_end+1 where P_end points beyond the end of the array. These are discussed below.)

3.7.2 Subtraction Expressions

The binary – operator denotes subtraction. If both operands have arithmetic types, the usual arithmetic conversions are performed and the result is the first operand minus the second.

C also accepts subtractions where the first operand is a pointer and the second is an integral type. In this case, the integral value is converted into an address offset by multiplying it by the length of the object to which the pointer points. The result is a pointer of the same type as the pointer operand. If p is a pointer to a particular type and points to a member of an array of the same type, p-1 is the member that precedes *p, p-2 is the member before that, and so on.

C also lets you subtract two pointers to the same type, provided that the pointers point at members of an array of that type. The result is an integral value that gives the difference between the subscripts of the two members. For example, if we have

```
p1 = &arr[3];
p2 = &arr[0];
```

then p1-p2 would have the value 3 and p2-p1 would have the value -3. (Note: you can only subtract pointers in this way; you cannot add them.)

The type of the result of subtracting two pointers is a signed integral type named ptrdiff_t. The implementation may choose whether the length is **int** or **long**. The name ptrdiff_t is defined in the <stddef.h> header (described in Part IV).

If you subtract two pointers that do not point into the same array object, the behavior is undefined. As a special consideration, however, if P_end points to the last member of an array,

```
(P_end+1) - p
```

is valid for any pointer p pointing at a member of the same array.

3.8 Bitwise Shift Expressions

A **bitwise shift expression** has one of the following forms:

expression << *expression*
expression >> *expression*

Bitwise shift expressions are evaluated from left to right.

3.8.1 Left Shift Expressions

The binary << operator shifts the bits of an integer to the left. Vacated bits are filled with zeros. The operands must both be integral, and the integral promotions are performed on each (if necessary). The result has the type of the (promoted) left operand.

The result of A<<B is the value obtained when the bits of A are shifted left B positions. For example, 007<<3 is 070.

If the right operand is negative, or greater than *or equal* to the number of bits in the left operand, the behavior is undefined.

3.8.2 Right Shift Expressions

The binary >> operator shifts the bits of an integer to the right. The operands must be integral, and the integral promotions are performed on each (if necessary). The result has the type of the (promoted) left operand.

The result of A>>B is the value obtained when the bits of A are shifted right B positions. For example, 070>>3 is 007.

If the left operand is unsigned, vacated bits are filled with zeros. If the left operand is signed, the implementation defines whether the vacated bits are filled with zeros or with a copy of the sign bit.

If the right operand is negative, or greater than *or equal* to the number of bits in the (promoted) left operand, the behavior is undefined.

3.9 Relational Expressions

A **relational expression** has one of the following forms:

> *expression < expression*
> *expression > expression*
> *expression <= expression*
> *expression >= expression*

Relational expressions are evaluated from left to right, but this is seldom useful.

The result of each relational expression is always **int**: 1 if the relation is true, and 0 if the relation is false. If A and B have arithmetic types, the usual arithmetic conversions are performed and

A<B	tests whether A is less than B;
A>B	tests whether A is greater than B;
A<=B	tests whether A is less than or equal to B;
A>=B	tests whether A is greater than or equal to B.

The operands of a relational expression may also be pointers of the same type pointing at members of the same array. A pointer A is greater than a pointer B if A-B is positive. If P_end points to the last member of an array, P_end+1 can be compared to pointers to any other members of the same array.

Expressions like A<B<C are seldom useful. The first relation A<B will be evaluated and a 1 or 0 obtained. This result will then be compared to C. Thus the expression does not determine if A is less than B and B is less than C.

You should be wary when comparing values of two different types, especially when one type is signed and another is unsigned. For example, suppose you are comparing an **unsigned int** with a **signed int**. The usual arithmetic conversions will convert the **signed int** to **unsigned**. If the **signed int** was negative, it will become a very large **unsigned** number. As a result, the negative number may be found to be greater than the (always positive) **unsigned** value. To avoid this situation, you may want to cast operands explicitly, as in

```
int i;
unsigned u;
if ( ((signed int) u) > i) ...
```

3.10 Equality Expressions

An **equality expression** has one of the following forms:

> *expression* == *expression*
> *expression* != *expression*

Equality expressions are evaluated from left to right, but this is seldom useful (for the same reasons given for relational expressions).

Like the relational operators, the equality operators return an **int** 1 if the specified relation is true and 0 if the relation is false. The == operator tests if its two operands are equal. The != operator tests if its two operands are not equal. If both operands are arithmetic types, the usual arithmetic conversions are performed before comparisons are made. It is also valid to compare pointers of the same type, a pointer of any object or incomplete type to a **void** * pointer, or a pointer value to an integer constant expression with the value 0.

One of the most common programming errors in C is to use the assignment operator = when the equality operator == is intended. You should watch for this problem when debugging.

3.11 Bitwise AND Expressions

A **bitwise AND expression** has the form

> *expression* & *expression*

Both operands must have integral type and the usual arithmetic conversions are performed. The result of the expression is the integral value that has 1-bits in positions where both operands have 1-bits and that has 0-bits everywhere else. For example,

```
0110 & 0101
```

gives the result 0100.

3.12 Bitwise Exclusive OR Expressions _____

A **bitwise exclusive OR expression** has the form

> *expression* ^ *expression*

Both operands must have integral type and the usual arithmetic conversions are performed. The result of the expression is the integral value that has a 1-bit in each position where exactly one of the operands has a 1-bit, and that has a 0-bit in each position where both operands have a 1-bit or both have a 0-bit. For example,

```
0110 ^ 0101
```

gives the result 0011.

3.13 Bitwise Inclusive OR Expressions _____

A **bitwise inclusive OR expression** has the form

> *expression* | *expression*

Both operands must have integral type and the usual arithmetic conversions are performed. The result of the expression is the integral value that has a 1-bit in each position that at least one of the operands has a 1-bit, and that has a 0-bit in each position where both operands have a 0-bit. For example,

```
0110 | 0101
```

gives the result 0111.

3.14 Logical AND Expressions _____

A **logical AND expression** has the form

> *expression* && *expression*

Both operands must have scalar type, but need not have the same type. The result is an **int** 1 if the two operands have nonzero values and **int** 0 if either or both are zero.

Unlike the bitwise &, && will always evaluate its operands from left to right. If the value of the first operand is 0, the second operand is *not* evaluated. For example, in

```
0 && i++
```

the value of i is *not* incremented.

3.15 Logical OR Expressions

A **logical OR expression** has the form

expression | | *expression*

Both operands must have a scalar type, but need not have the same type. The result of the operation is an **int** 1 if either of the two operands is nonzero and **int** 0 if both are zero.

Unlike the bitwise |, | | always evaluates its operands from left to right. If the value of the first operand is nonzero, the second operand is *not* evaluated.

3.16 Conditional Expressions

A **conditional expression** has the form

expression ? *expression* : *expression*

The first operand must have a scalar type. The other two operands must satisfy one of the following conditions:

(a)   Both have an arithmetic type. They will undergo the usual type conversions and the result will have the (converted) type of the operands.

(b)   Both have compatible structure or union types. The result will have the same type as the operands.

(c)   Both operands are pointers to qualified or unqualified versions of compatible types. The result has the compatible type with the qualifiers of the second operand plus the qualifiers of the third.

(d)   Both have the **void** type. The result will have the **void** type.

(e)   One is a pointer to an object or incomplete type and the other is a qualified or unqualified **void** *. The result will be the object or incomplete pointer type, plus the qualifiers of the **void** *.

(f)   One is a pointer type and the other is a null pointer constant. The result will have the pointer's type, plus any qualifiers associated with the null pointer constant.

The first step in evaluating a conditional expression is to evaluate the expression before the ?. If this expression is nonzero, the result of the entire conditional expression will be the value of the second operand (the one before the colon). If the value of the operand before the ? is zero, the result of the entire conditional expression will be the value of the last operand (the one after the colon). For example,

```
(a>b) ? a : b
```

returns the value of a if it is greater than b and otherwise returns the value of b. This means that the conditional expression returns the greater of a or b.

In any conditional expression, one of the operands after the ? is evaluated and the other is ignored.

3.17 Assignment Expressions

There is no specific "assignment statement" in C. Instead, there are a number of assignment operators which may be used in normal expressions. Assignments in an expression are executed from right to left. An **assignment expression** has one of the following forms:

> *Lvalue   = expression*
> *Lvalue += expression*
> *Lvalue -= expression*
> *Lvalue *= expression*
> *Lvalue /= expression*
> *Lvalue %= expression*
> *Lvalue >>= expression*
> *Lvalue <<= expression*
> *Lvalue &= expression*
> *Lvalue ^= expression*
> *Lvalue |= expression*

The Lvalue on the left of each assignment expression must be a modifiable Lvalue. In addition to assigning a value to the memory location indicated by the Lvalue, an assignment expression returns a value. The result of an assignment expression has the value of the Lvalue after the assignment, but it is not itself an Lvalue. For example,

```
a = 2 + (b=4);
```

would assign 4 to b and 6 to a. The type of the result of an assignment expression is the type of the left operand, without any qualifiers.

The **ANSI** standard does not specify the order of evaluation of the operands. Therefore in a statement like

```
arr[i++] = i;
```

the value assigned to the array member could be the value of i before or after it is incremented.

3.17.1 Simple Assignment Expressions

A **simple assignment** expression has the form

Lvalue = expression

One of the following must be true:

(a)   The *expression* has arithmetic type and the *Lvalue* has a qualified or unqualified arithmetic type.

(b)   The *Lvalue* has a qualified or unqualified structure or union type that is compatible with the *expression* type.

(c)   Both operands are pointers to qualified or unqualified versions of compatible types, and the type of *Lvalue* has all the qualifiers of the type of *expression*.

(d)   One operand is a pointer to an object or incomplete type and the other is a pointer to a qualified or unqualified version of **void ***; and the type of *Lvalue* has all the qualifiers of the type of *expression*.

(e)   *Lvalue* is a pointer and *expression* is a null pointer constant.

If both operands have arithmetic types, the right operand is converted to the type of the left operand before the value is stored.

If you attempt an assignment A=B and the storage for A partly overlaps the storage for B, the behavior is undefined. This can only happen when you are attempting to assign all or part of a union interpretation to another interpretation of the same union, or when you are making an assignment of the form

```
*p = *q;
```

3.17.2 Compound Assignment Expressions

A **compound assignment** expression has the form

Lvalue **op**= *expression*

where **op** is a suitable binary operator. This is equivalent to the expression

Lvalue = Lvalue **op** *expression*

except that the *Lvalue* is only evaluated once. For example,

```
A += 2
```

is equivalent to

```
A = A + 2
```

but

```
arr[i++] += 2
```

is *not* equivalent to

```
arr[i++] = arr[i++] + 2
```

since the first assignment only increments i once while the second does it twice.

The operands of a compound assignment must have arithmetic types consistent with the types allowed by the given binary operator. In addition, the left operand of += and -= may be a pointer type. In this case, pointer addition or subtraction takes place appropriately.

3.18 Comma Expressions

A **comma expression** has the following form:

expression , expression

The left operand is evaluated and then discarded (that is, its value is ignored). The right operand is then evaluated; the type and value of the result of the comma expression are the type and value of the right operand. For example, in evaluating

```
a = (pi = 3.14 , 2 * pi)
```

the variable pi is assigned 3.14 and then 2*pi is evaluated. The result of 2*pi is assigned to a.

In contexts where a comma has another meaning (for example, in a list of function arguments or in a list of variable initializations), comma expressions must be enclosed in parentheses. For example,

```
sin( (pi=3.14, 0.5*pi) )
```

has only one argument, namely 0.5*pi. On the other hand,

```
func( pi=3.14, 0.5*pi)
```

has two arguments: 3.14 (the result of the assignment) and 0.5*pi. Note that the first argument may or may not be evaluated before the second argument. Thus there is no guarantee about the value of pi that is used in evaluating the second argument.

Comma expressions group from left to right. Therefore the value of (X,Y,Z) is the value of Z.

3.19 Constant Expressions

A **constant expression** is effectively an expression that can be calculated at translation time instead of execution time.

An **integral constant expression** is an expression whose operands are only integer and character constants, enumerated value constants, **sizeof** expressions, and floating point values immediately cast to integral types. Any appropriate operators may be used. Operators like ++, --, assignment, or function calls may not appear. The operators

```
[]    .    ->    &
```

and unary * may only appear inside **sizeof** expressions. Thus

```
3 * sizeof( arr[0] )
```

is a valid integral constant expression, but

```
3 * arr[0]
```

is not.

An **arithmetic constant expression** follows the same rules as an integral constant expression, except that it may use floating point constants as operands. Cast operators may only convert arithmetic types to other arithmetic types, except as part of an operand to **sizeof**.

An **address constant expression** is a function locator or a pointer to an Lvalue with static storage duration. (Static storage duration is explained in Section 5.) Such an expression must be created explicitly using the & operator or implicitly using an expression with function or array type. Subscripting and operators for referencing structure members may be used, as well as &, *, and pointer casts; however, none of these should actually access the value of an object.

An **initialization constant expression** is an arithmetic constant expression or an address constant expression. An initialization constant expression can be used in declarations to initialize objects.

chapter 4   Statements

The statements of C control most of the actions performed by a program. Declarations may also perform actions; for example, they can assign initialization values to variables.

4.1 Expression Statements

An **expression statement** has the form

   expression ;

The *expression* may be any C expression. The most commonly used expression statements contain assignment operations or function calls, but any expression is valid. For example,

```
a + b;
```

is a valid expression statement, but it likely has no effect. Only expressions with side effects (for example, assignments or function calls) are useful as expression statements.

4.2 Compound Statements or Blocks

A **block** or **compound statement** may be used wherever a single statement is expected. Blocks consist of zero or more declarations followed by zero or more statements, all enclosed in braces. For example, a typical block might be

```
{
     int temp;
     temp = a;
     a = b;
     b = temp;
}
```

The variable temp declared in the block is local to the block (so it is only accessible within the block and will not be available to statements outside the block). The variables a and b used within the block must be declared somewhere in the source code that precedes the block.

4.3 The If Statement

The first form of the **if** statement is

> **if** (*expression*) *statement*

The given *expression* must have a scalar type. The expression is evaluated and if it is nonzero, the *statement* is executed. For example,

```
if (a) b=8;
```

executes the statement b=8; provided that a is nonzero.

The second form of the **if** statement is

> **if** (*expression*) *statement1* **else** *statement2*

Again, the *expression* must have a scalar type. If the value of the expression is nonzero, *statement1* is executed; otherwise, *statement2* is executed. For example,

```
if (A > B)
    printf("A is greater than B");
else
    printf("A is not greater than B");
```

the first printf call is executed if A is greater than B, and otherwise the second printf call is executed. Note that an **if-else** statement is a single statement even though it may contain several semicolons as shown above.

You may nest **if**s and **else**s. Each **else** is associated with the most recent **else**less **if**. Below we give two examples; **if-else** pairing is shown by indentation.

```
if (...)
    if (...) statement
    else statement
else statement

if (...) statement
else
    if (...) statement
    else statement
```

4.4 The While Statement

The **while** statement executes a statement or block repeatedly as long as a given condition holds. It has the form

while (*expression*) *statement*

If the *expression* is nonzero, the *statement* will be executed. The *expression* is evaluated again after the execution of the *statement* and if it is still nonzero, the *statement* will be executed again. This process is repeated until the *expression* evaluates to zero on some iteration.

Each time, the *expression* is tested **before** executing the *statement*. If the *expression* is zero to begin with, the *statement* will not be executed at all.

4.5 The Do-While Statement

The **do-while** statement also executes a statement or block repeatedly. It has the form

do *statement* **while** (*expression*) ;

The *statement* is executed and then the *expression* is evaluated. If the *expression* is nonzero, the *statement* will be executed again and so on.

Each time, the *expression* is tested **after** executing the *statement*. Thus the *statement* will be executed at least once, regardless of whether the *expression* is zero or nonzero.

4.6 The For Statement

The **for** statement has the form

for (*exp1* ; *exp2* ; *exp3*) *statement;*

where *exp1*, *exp2*, and *exp3* are valid expressions. Except for its behavior when a **continue** statement appears in the body of the loop, a **for** statement is equivalent to

```
exp1;
while ( exp2 ) {
    statement
    exp3;
}
```

The first expression performs initializations before the **while** loop. The second expression is the test used in the **while**. The third expression is executed at the end of each loop. The most common use of this third expression is to increment a variable that counts iterations, so the expression is often called the **increment expression**. For example,

```
for (i=0 ; i<10 ; ++i)
    a[i] = b[i];
```

initializes i to zero, then executes the given statement while i is less than 10. The ++i increments i by 1 at the end of each iteration. The result of the above **for** statement is to copy the first 10 members of b into a.

You may omit any or all of the expressions in the parentheses.

> **for** (*exp1* ; ; *exp3*) ...

is equivalent to

```
exp1;
while (1) {
    ...
    exp3;
}
```

while (1) will loop repeatedly because the expression (1) is never zero.

If either *exp1* or *exp3* is omitted, they are simply dropped from the **while** loop expansion.

4.7 The Break Statement

The statement

> **break** ;

is used to "break out" of the smallest enclosing **while, do-while, for**, or **switch** statement. Control passes to the statement immediately following the statement you break off. For example, consider

```
for (i=0 ; i<10 ; ++i) {
    if ( b[i] == -1) break;
    else a[i] = b[i];
};
```

This is much like the **for** loop in the last section that copies 10 members of b into a. However, if a b member is equal to -1, the **break** breaks out of the **for** loop and the remaining b members are not copied.

4.8 The Continue Statement

The statement

> **continue** ;

passes control to the "condition-testing" part of the smallest enclosing **while**, **do-while**, or **for**.

When **continue** is found in a **while**, control returns to the top of the loop to test the given expression and determine if another loop is required. For example,

```
while (++i<10) {
    if (a[i] <= -1.0) continue;
    b[i] = (a[i] + 2.0) / (a[i] + 1.0);
};
```

calculates b[i] unless a[i] is −1.0, in which case it drops out of the **while** loop and goes back to the condition of the **while** loop.

When **continue** appears in a **do-while** loop, it passes control to the condition-testing part at the end of the loop. When it appears in a **for** loop, it passes control to the increment expression, after which control passes to the condition-test at the start of the loop.

4.9 The Switch Statement

The **switch** statement evaluates an expression and passes control to one of a series of statements depending on the value of the expression. It has the form

> **switch** (*expression*) *case-list*

The *expression* must have an integral type. The *case-list* is allowed to be a single statement, but in practice it is almost always a compound statement made up of statements and blocks that have **case labels**. A case label has one of the following forms:

> **case** *constant-expression*:
> **default**:

The constant expression following the keyword **case** must be an integral constant expression. It is an error for two case labels in the same **switch** to have constant expressions with the same value (after any conversions that might take place).

A case of the form

> **case** *constant-expression*:

is said to be **satisfied** if the expression following the **switch** is equal to the *constant-expression* (after both have undergone the usual arithmetic conversions). If we have

> switch (i) ...

and the value of i is 3,

```
case 3:
case 1+2:
case 3L:
```

would all be satisfied cases. (These cases could not all appear in the same **switch** statement.)

The execution of a **switch** statement proceeds in the following manner:

(a)   The *expression* following the keyword **switch** is evaluated.

(b)   The first **case** label is examined. If this case is satisfied, execution will begin with the first statement following the **case** label.

(c)   If the first case is not satisfied, the second case will be examined and so on through all the cases until one is satisfied.

(d)   If no case in the list is satisfied, the **default** label will be sought. The *case-list* of each **switch** statement may contain at most one **default** label. If such a label is found, execution will begin with the first statement following the **default**.

(e)   If no case in the *case-list* is satisfied and there is no **default** label, execution will begin with the statement following the *case-list*. In other words, nothing inside the *case-list* will be executed.

If the code associated with one **case** is being executed and another **case** or **default** label is encountered, execution will continue on with the statements that follow the new label. C does *not* break out of the block of a **switch** statement when a new label is found. To break out of a **switch** statement before the end, you must use a **break** statement.

Below we give an example of a typical **switch** statement. The variable c has type **char**. If the value of c is ' + ', it is changed to a blank and the variable sign is set to 1. If the value is ' - ', it is left as is and sign is set to −1. If the value is anything else, sign is set to 0.

```
switch (c) {
  case '+':
    c = ' ';
    sign = 1;
    break;
  case '-':
    sign = -1;
    break;
  default:
    sign = 0;
}
```

A statement in a *case-list* may be preceded by several case labels, as in

```
switch (i%3) {
  case 0:
    printf("Divisible by 3");
    break;
  case 1:
  case -2:
    printf("Remainder is 1");
    break;
  case 2:
  case -1:
    printf("Remainder is 2");
}
```

(This shows one way to deal with the implementation-defined behavior of the remainder operation—if i is negative, some implementations will return a negative remainder while others will return a positive one.)

4.10 The Return Statement

The **return** statement lets a function return to its caller before reaching the last statement in the function. It also lets the function return a value to its caller.

The simplest form of the statement is

return **;**

When this statement is executed in a function, it will return to the function's caller. If the caller expected the function to return a value, the behavior is undefined.

The second form of the statement is

return *expression* **;**

This returns the value of the *expression* to the function's caller. For example,

```
return (a>b) ? a : b ;
```

returns the greater of a and b to the caller. If necessary, this return value is converted to the type declared for the function in which it appears. For example, if a function is declared "function returning **long**" and an ordinary **int** value is given in a **return** statement, the **int** value will be converted to **long** before it is returned to the caller.

4.11 Labels

Any statement may be preceded by one or more labels of the form

> *identifier* :

Such a label may be used as the target of a **goto**. Labels are local to the block in which they appear; however, any statement in a function may **goto** any label in the same function (even if the label is in a different block).

4.12 The Goto Statement

The statement

> **goto** *identifier* ;

transfers control unconditionally to a statement labelled by the given *identifier*. You may use **goto** to jump into blocks in the same function but not into different functions.

4.13 The Null Statement

The null statement is simply

It performs no action. It is useful for labels that require a statement (as in

```
label: ;
```

in which the null statement has the label `label`) and in looping constructs that do not need any body. For example,

```
for (i=0 ; i<10 ; a[i++] = 0 ) ;
```

assigns 0 to the first 10 members of a, and no body is needed.

chapter 5   Declarations

Declarations may appear at the beginning of any block, preceding the statements that describe the action of the block. Declarations may also appear outside blocks, either associated with a particular function (as in parameter declarations) or external to all functions.

A declaration tells how one or more identifiers are used. Identifiers may refer to types, functions, or data objects.

A **type declaration** describes a particular type. For example, one kind of type declaration describes the members of a structure or union. Another kind (known as a **typedef** declaration) gives a name to a particular type, after which the name can be used instead of the associated type. This is described in Section 5.3.5.

A **function declaration** indicates that a particular identifier refers to a function. The declaration may also indicate the type of value returned by the function, specify a "scope" for the function, and describe the "formal parameters" of the function.

A **variable declaration** indicates that a given identifier refers to a particular data object. In this case, the identifier is commonly called a **variable**. The declaration may also specify a type for the data object, a "storage class", and an initialization value.

Declarations provide information for the translation of the C program, but they may also result in activity at execution time. For example, some declarations must allocate memory for variables and assign initialization values to those variables.

5.1 Use of Identifiers

Before we describe the syntax of C declarations, we must first discuss some important concepts related to the use of identifiers.

5.1.1 Scope of Identifiers

The **scope** of an identifier is the region of source code in which the identifier may be used. There are four kinds of scope: function scope, file scope, block scope, and prototype scope.

The only kind of identifier that has **function scope** is a statement label. The label identifier is implicitly declared when it is used to label a statement. A label may only be used by **goto** statements that appear in the same function as the label. A **goto** statement referring to a particular label may appear before or after the statement that bears that label. All the label identifiers in a function must be unique; for example, you cannot have two different statements labelled A:.

If the declaration for an identifier appears outside all blocks, the identifier has **file scope**. The identifier will be recognized in all source code from the end of the declarator (where the identifier is declared) to the end of the translation unit.

If the declaration for an identifier appears inside a block or in the list of parameter declarations that begins a function, the identifier has **block scope**. The identifier will be recognized in all source code from the end of the declarator where the identifier is declared to the closing brace that ends the block that contains the declaration. If there is a declaration for the same identifier in some outer block or outside all blocks, the declaration in the inner block hides the outer declaration until the closing brace that ends the inner block. For example, in

```
int i;
func()
{
    float i;
    ...
};
```

`i` will refer to an integer outside the function `func` but will refer to an entirely separate floating point number inside the function.

If a declaration for an identifier appears in the list of parameters of a function prototype that does not start a function definition, the identifier has **prototype scope**. This extends from the end of the declaration of the parameter to the end of the function declarator. Function prototypes are discussed in Section 6.1.

5.1.2 Linkage of Identifiers

When the same identifier appears in different scopes of a program, the implementation must decide whether or not the different occurrences of the identifier refer to the same object or function. This means that the implementation must decide how different occurrences of the same identifier are *linked*.

An identifier may be linked in three different ways. If an identifier has **external linkage**, every occurrence of that identifier refers to the same function or data object, in every source file and in every library used to make up the complete program. If an identifier has **internal linkage**, every occurrence of that identifier in a particular source file refers to the same function or data object; however, if the identifier appears in another source file, it does not refer to the same item. If an identifier has **no linkage**, it is known within its particular scope but is not associated with any occurrences of the same identifier outside the scope.

The linkage of a particular identifier is determined by the form and position of the declaration that declares the identifier.

(a)   If an identifier does not refer to a data object or a function, it has no linkage. For example, a name given to a type in a **typedef** declaration is known within its scope, but is not associated with anything outside its scope.

(b)   An identifier declared as a function parameter has no linkage.

(c)   If the identifier of a function or object has file scope and contains the keyword **static**, it has internal linkage.

(d)   If a declaration of a function or object contains the keyword **extern**, the identifier has the same linkage as any previous declaration whose scope includes the **extern** declaration. If there is no such previous declaration, the identifier has external linkage. For example, if we have

```
static int i;
    ...
extern int i;
```

the identifier i has internal linkage—the first declaration contains the keyword **static** and rule (c) applies. However, in

```
int i;
    ...
extern int i;
```

the identifier i will have external linkage.

(e)   A function declared inside a block has external linkage unless the declaration contains the keyword **static** or a previous declaration of the function contained the keyword **static**. If there is such a **static** declaration, the identifier has internal linkage.

(f)   An identifier declared inside a block has no linkage unless the declaration contains the keyword **extern**. When an identifier has no linkage and block scope, there can only be one declaration for the identifier within its scope.

If a file scope object or function has some declarations that give it external linkage and some that give it internal linkage, the behavior is undefined. This means that declarations of the form

```
extern int i;
    ...
static int i;
```

do not conform to the **ANSI** standard: the **extern** declaration will try to give the variable external linkage (if it is not in the scope of a variable i) and the **static** declaration will try to give the variable internal linkage.

5.1.3 Name Space of Identifiers

C lets you use the same identifier for different purposes inside the same scope, provided that it is always possible to distinguish between the different uses of the identifier. For example, C lets you write a function that uses A both as a variable name and as a statement label. The two meanings of A can be distinguished easily: when the name appears in a **goto** statement, it is being used as a statement label; when the name appears in an expression, it is being used as a variable.

The ways in which identifiers may be used can be divided into separate categories. These categories are called **name spaces**. C has several kinds of name spaces.

(a)   Label names form one name space. They can be distinguished because they only appear in **goto** statements and as statement labels.

(b)   Each structure and union has a separate name space for its members. The name of a structure or union member can only appear in the declaration of the structure or union, and in expressions of the form

    expression . member
    expression -> member

By looking at the *expression* in front of the . or ->, C can tell which structure or union contains the member. Therefore structures A and B can have members with the same name, since it is easy to distinguish between

```
A . name
B . name
```

(c)   There is a separate name space for structure, union, and enumeration tags. While it is actually possible to distinguish between a name being used as a structure tag and the same name being used as a union tag, the **ANSI** standard requires that all tags in a given scope be unique. For this reason, you cannot have a structure and a union with the same tag in the same scope.

(d)   All other identifiers form a name space called the **ordinary identifiers**.

An identifier may be declared (implicitly or explicitly) with more than one meaning in a particular scope, provided that the meanings belong to different name spaces.

5.1.4 Storage Duration of Objects

If an object is declared inside a block without the **static** storage class specifier and it has no linkage, it has **automatic storage duration**. Each time execution enters the block that contains the declaration, a new instance of the object is created in memory. This happens whether the block is entered in the normal flow of execution or through a **goto** into the middle of the block. Automatic objects are discarded when execution leaves the block in any way (for example, by normal termination, by using **goto** to jump out of the block, or by executing a **break** or **return** statement).

The next time execution enters the same block, a new instance of the object is created. Usually, this new object is not stored in the same memory location as the previous object, and it is not likely to have the same value as it held when the block previously finished execution. If the block is called recursively, there will be several instances of the object in memory simultaneously.

All other objects have **static storage duration**. Such an object exists throughout the execution of the entire program and retains any value it is given until the program explicitly assigns a new value.

5.2 The Format of Declarations

A declaration consists of zero or more **specifiers**, followed by a **declarator list**, followed by a semicolon.

(a) Specifiers fall into three classes: **type specifiers**, which give a particular data type; **type qualifiers**, which may restrict the way that a program handles data; and **storage class specifiers**, which give information about how data objects should be stored and also deal with such matters as scope and linkage. Popular programming conventions put storage class specifiers before type specifiers and qualifiers, but the other order is also allowed. Specifiers may be omitted, in which case default specifications are used. However, every object declaration must have at least one specifier.

(b) The declarator list consists of zero or more declarators separated by commas. A declarator names the identifier being described by the declaration. It may also provide information about the identifier or give an initialization value.

As an example, consider the declaration

```
extern int i[12], j=10;
```

In this declaration, **extern** is a storage class specifier, **int** is a type specifier, and `i[12]` and `j=10` are declarators.

5.3 Storage Class Specifiers

Storage class specifiers control storage duration, scope, and linkage. A declaration may not have more than one storage class specifier. The recognized storage class specifiers are

```
auto
static
extern
register
typedef
```

If a declaration does not have a storage class specifier, a default storage class is assigned, based on where the declaration appears. When the declaration appears inside a function,

auto is assumed. When the declaration appears outside all functions, **extern** is assumed. (Omitting the keyword **extern** in such a declaration has a special meaning, described in Section 5.3.4.) If a function declaration has no storage class specifier, the function is assumed to be **extern** no matter where the declaration appears.

5.3.1 Automatic Declarations

Automatic or **auto** declarations may appear at the beginning of any block. An **auto** identifier has block scope, and the associated object has automatic storage duration.

When an **auto** declaration is encountered, memory will be allocated to the declared items. Initializations are also performed at this time (see Section 5.6.2).

Automatic variables are discarded upon completion of the block in which they are declared. The memory that was allocated to them is then made available for other purposes. If you attempt to access this memory location after the block has terminated (for example, using a pointer that points to the location), the behavior is undefined. In general, you cannot count on an automatic data object retaining its value once execution has left the block in which the variable was declared.

5.3.2 Register Declarations

The **register** storage class specifier may be used anywhere **auto** is allowed. A **register** identifier has block scope, and the associated object has automatic storage duration.

Historically, the **register** specifier was interpreted as a hint that the declared object would be used heavily and that efficiency could be improved if the object was stored in a hardware register instead of main memory. There was no guarantee that the object would actually be stored in a register, since the implementation might need such registers for other purposes. If the object couldn't be stored in a hardware register, it would be treated as if it were a normal **auto** object.

Recently, the **register** specifier has been used for more general optimization processes. Because the specifier once indicated that the object might be stored in a register, you may not use & to obtain the address of a **register** object. This guarantees that you will not be able to change the value of a **register** object through a pointer, and this knowledge can allow a C implementation to perform optimization operations, even if the object is not actually stored in a register.

5.3.3 Static Declarations

If an object is declared **static** and the declaration appears outside all blocks, the object will have static storage duration and internal linkage. If the declaration contains an initialization value, the object will have that value when the program begins execution. The identifier will have file scope.

If an object is declared **static** and the declaration appears inside a block, the object will still have static storage duration and no linkage. The storage used by a **static** object in a block is not discarded upon completion of the block. This means that you can still refer to the value of this object (indirectly through a pointer) even after the block has terminated.

The static object retains its value from one invocation of the block to the next. If the object has an initializer, it will only be initialized once (before program execution begins). Unlike other block scope objects, it will *not* be initialized each time the block begins execution.

5.3.4 Extern Declarations

A declaration with the **extern** specifier indicates that each item in the declarator list has an **external data definition** elsewhere in the collection of source files that make up the C program. An external data definition may have several forms.

(a) A function definition. If the function definition contains the **static** specifier, as in

```
static double f(double x)
```

the definition must be found in the same source file as the **extern** declaration; in this case, the function will have internal linkage. If the function definition does not contain the **static** specifier, as in

```
int g(int y)
```

the definition may appear in any source file and the function will have external linkage.

(b) A declaration of the identifier of an object that appears outside all functions and that has an initializer, as in

```
extern char alpha = 'a';
```

This can appear in any source file. The identifier will have external linkage.

(c) A declaration of the identifier of an object that appears outside all functions, that has no initializer, and that has no storage class specifier or the **static** storage class specifier, as in

```
float z;
```

If the same source file contains several declarations of the same object outside all functions, the first one that contains an initializer will be taken as the definition of the object. If none of these declarations has an initializer, the first declaration that does not contain a storage class specifier or that has the **static** storage class specifier will be taken as the definition of the object. If all of the declarations have the **extern** specifier, the definition of the object will be assumed to be found outside the source file. In this case, the object will have external linkage.

To give some examples, suppose a function contains the declaration

```
extern int y;
```

This says that y is defined somewhere outside of all functions in the program. The definition of y could appear in the same source file as the declaration or in a different source file. If the definition appears in the same source, it could have several forms.

```
static int y;
```

is a definition that says y has internal linkage and file scope. This must precede the **extern** declaration.

```
int y = 5;
```

has an initializer but not the keyword **static**. Therefore this definition would indicate that y has external linkage and file scope.

```
int y;
```

has no initializer. It will serve as a definition for y provided it is the first declaration of y that appears outside all functions in this source file and there is no other declaration of y that has an initializer.

If all the other declarations of y also have the form

```
extern int y;
```

the actual definition of y must appear in another source file. That definition will have an initializer, or else it will not have the keyword **extern**.

5.3.5 Typedef Declarations

Declarations with a storage class of **typedef** do not actually declare objects that can be stored in memory. Instead they define identifiers which can afterwards be used in place of type specifiers.

The form of a **typedef** declaration is

> **typedef** *type-specifier declarator*;

as in

```
typedef float TEMPERATURE;
typedef struct {
    float real, imag;
} complex;
```

This defines the identifier TEMPERATURE as synonymous with **float** and complex as synonymous with the given structure. One can then use declarations of the form

```
TEMPERATURE fahren, celsius;
complex u[10];
```

to declare two floating point variables `fahren` and `celsius`, and an array of ten members, each a structure consisting of two floating point fields named `real` and `imag`.

Defined types can also refer to derived data types. For example,

```
typedef char STRING[30];
STRING s;
```

declares s as a 30-element array of characters.

The **typedef** directive does not introduce new types—it merely provides a convenient way to define synonyms for existing types. Thus a variable of type TEMPERATURE has exactly the same type as any other **float** object.

5.4 Type Qualifiers

The type qualifiers **const** and **volatile** put limits on the way that data objects may be manipulated. The same type qualifier may not be used more than once in a list of specifiers.

If an array type is specified with qualifiers, the qualifiers apply to the array members, not the array itself. If a function type is specified with qualifiers, the behavior is undefined.

5.4.1 The Const Qualifier

The **const** qualifier indicates that an Lvalue is not *modifiable*; it hints that a particular data object may be stored in read-only memory. If you attempt to change such an Lvalue, you will normally receive an error.

The address of a **const** object cannot be assigned to a pointer to a type without the **const** attribute, unless you use an explicit cast operation. For example, suppose you have

```
int *p;
const int i;
```

Then the operation

```
p = &i;
```

would be invalid. The reasoning is that you might use p to change the contents of i, even though those contents are supposed to be "constant." If you really want to make this sort of assignment, you must use an explicit cast, as in

```
p = (int *) &i;
```

If you use p to try to change the value of i, the behavior is undefined.

If an aggregate object is declared **const**, every member of the aggregate is also considered **const**. For example, if a structure is declared to be **const**, each member of the structure is also regarded as **const**.

The **const** qualifier will often be found in pointer declarations, as in

```
const char *p;
```

This says that p is a pointer to a character and that character has the **const** attribute. The pointer p itself is not constant and can be changed to point to any character. However, the character to which p points is constant and the program will not be able to perform operations like

```
*p = 'x';
```

to try to change the character. Even if p is "aimed at" a nonconstant character, as in

```
char c;
p = &c;
```

you cannot use *p as a modifiable Lvalue.

The **const** qualifier is commonly used when declaring function parameters. For example, if a parameter is declared

```
const char *s;
```

the function may not use the s pointer to change the contents of the character or character string to which s points. In other words, this use of **const** says that the function can only *look* at the object pointed at by s; the function cannot change the object's value.

Since you cannot change the value of a **const** object, it must be given a value at the time it is created. This means the object must be a function parameter (which is given a value at the time the function is called), or the object must be initialized at the time it is declared.

5.4.2 The Volatile Qualifier

An object declared with the **volatile** qualifier may change without the program's knowledge or action. A good example of a **volatile** object is a system clock that is run by the hardware. Note that such a clock could also be regarded as **const** if the program was not allowed to change the time. This shows that a data object may be both **volatile** and **const**.

Declaring an object **volatile** tells the implementation to check the value of the object every time it is used. For example, an implementation is not allowed to store the value of the object in some temporary storage location in one statement and then use this stored value in a later statement, since the value of the original object might have changed in the meantime. The **volatile** specifier limits the number of "short-cuts" and optimizations that the implementation can perform with the object.

The address of a nonvolatile object may be assigned to a pointer that normally points to volatile objects. The address of a volatile object may not be assigned to a pointer to a nonvolatile type, except through an explicit cast. If you try to use such a pointer to refer to the object, the behavior is undefined.

5.5 Type Specifiers

A type specifier refers to a data type. The simple type specifiers are

```
char     long      float
short    signed    double
int      unsigned  void
```

The "derived" type specifiers refer to structure or union types, enumerated types, array types, or pointer types.

A declaration may have more than one type specifier. The arithmetic type specifiers may be combined with each other in the ways described in Section 2. Arithmetic type specifiers may not be combined with derived types.

If a declaration does not have a type specifier, a type of **int** is assumed. Thus

```
extern x;
extern int x;
```

are equivalent.

5.5.1 Structure Specifiers

A structure type specifier has one of the following forms:

> **struct** { *member-list* }
> **struct** *tag-identifier* { *member-list* }
> **struct** *tag-identifier*

A *member-list* consists of one or more declarations for the members of the structure. They will be stored in memory in the order they are listed. The optional *tag-identifier* is a name that can be used to refer to the structure type after it has been defined. For example, in

```
struct complex {
    double real, imag;
};
struct complex z1, z2;
```

the code defines a structure with the tag complex, then declares z1 and z2 to have the complex structure type.

Each structure specifier that has a *member-list* defines a new structure. Subsequent declarations of the structure in the same scope may use the *tag-identifier* but should not repeat the *member-list*.

An incomplete specifier of the form

struct *tag-identifier*

may be used before a *member-list* for the structure is given, provided that the size of the structure is not needed. For example, this kind of specifier can be used when declaring a **typedef** name as in

```
typedef struct xyz S;
```

even if the contents of the structure xyz have not yet been declared. It can also be used when declaring a pointer to a structure type. The classic example is a structure like

```
struct link_list {
    int value;
    struct link_list *next;
};
```

The member next can be declared as a pointer to a link_list structure even before the link_list structure has been fully defined. This sort of construction lets you make a list of structures in which each entry in the list has a pointer to the next entry in the list.

If a program uses an incomplete specifier of the above type, a complete specifier for the structure must eventually be declared in the same scope.

A special case occurs when you want to use an incomplete structure specifier in an inner scope and there is a structure with the same tag in an outer scope. For example, suppose you have

```
struct ll {
    /* file scope */
    int fvalue;
    struct ll *fnext;
};
void func(void)
{
    struct ll {
        /* block scope */
        float bvalue;
        struct ll *bnext;
    };
    /* and so on */
```

Since the block scope ll structure has not been fully declared when the bnext element is declared, bnext will be regarded as a pointer to a *file* scope ll structure. If you want bnext to point to the block scope structure, put a declaration of the form

```
struct ll;
```

inside the block, before the beginning of the full declaration of the block scope `ll`. This special declaration "masks" the outer scope `ll` so that incomplete structure specifiers will refer to the inner scope `ll`.

The scope of a structure begins at the end of its declaration. The scope of a structure member begins at the end of the member's declaration and extends to the end of the enclosing structure's scope.

5.5.2 Union Specifiers

A union type specifier has one of the following forms:

union { *member-list* }
union *tag-identifier* { *member-list* }
union *tag-identifier*

Union specifiers follow exactly the same rules as structure specifiers.

5.5.3 Enumeration Specifiers

An enumeration type specifier has one of the following forms:

enum { *enum-list* }
enum *tag-identifier* { *enum-list* }
enum *tag-identifier*

The elements in the *enum-list* have one of the following forms:

identifier
identifier = *constant-expression*

and elements in the list are separated by commas.

The rules for using **enum** tags are the same as those for structure and union tags.

5.6 Declarators

A declarator consists of an identifier and an indication of how the identifier will be used (for example, as a pointer, a function, or a normal variable). A declarator may also include an initializer for the identifier being declared. The possible declarator forms are

identifier
(*declarator*)
* *declarator*

> ** type-qualifier-list declarator*
> *declarator[constant-expression]*
> *declarator( )*
> *declarator(parameter-type-list)*
> *declarator(identifier-list)*
> *declarator = initializer*

The binding of the operators `*`, `()`, and `[]` are the same as for expressions.

When the declarator consists only of an identifier, the identifier will refer to a variable of the type and storage class given by the specifiers.

A declarator in parentheses has the same meaning as an unparenthesized declarator. Parentheses are merely used to alter the binding of operators associated with the declarator. Examples of the use of parentheses will be shown in later sections.

5.6.1 Pointer Declarators

A declarator of the form

> **declarator*

declares a pointer to an object of the type given by the declaration's specifiers. For example,

```
char *str;
```

indicates that `str` is a pointer to a **char** object.

In the form

> ** type-qualifier-list declarator*

type-qualifier-list can only contain the type specifiers **const** and/or **volatile** (separated by white space). For example, we might have

```
char * const const_ptr;
```

In Section 5.5.4, we will discuss the difference between this and

```
const char * ptr_to_const;
```

5.6.2 Array Declarators

A declarator of the form

> *declarator[constant-expression]*

declares an array whose members each have the type given by the type specifiers of the declaration. The number of members in the array is given by the constant expression in the square brackets. For example,

```
char j[30];
```

declares an array named j with space for 30 characters. Since the subscript of the initial member is 0, the maximum subscript for j is 29.

An array declaration may omit the size of the first dimension if the size can be determined by counting initialization values, or if the size is irrelevant (that is, when storage is not being allocated, as in a declaration that includes the word **extern**). For example, a function might contain the declaration

```
extern int arr[];
```

to say that arr is an array whose size is established in some external data definition.

5.6.3 Function Declarators

A declarator of the form

   declarator( )

declares a function that returns a value of the type given by the type specifiers of the declaration. For example,

```
double f();
```

indicates that the function f returns a **double** value. The form

   declarator(*identifier-list*)

is the historic way to begin the definition of a function. For example, you might see

```
double f(x,y,z)
double x,y,z;
{
     /* function definition */
};
```

at the start of a function definition. The identifiers in the parenthesized list after f name *all* the parameters of the function, in the order they will be passed by a caller. After this you see one or more declarations for the parameters, then the body of the function. If there are no identifiers in the *identifier-list* of a function definition, as in

```
unsigned rand()
{
    /* function definition */
};
```

the function takes no arguments.

The form

> *declarator*(*parameter-type-list*)

is called a **function prototype**. The elements of the *parameter-type-list* describe the arguments that the function accepts. Each element in the *parameter-type-list* is either a declaration of a function parameter, as in

```
double f(double x,double y)
char *strtrcpy(char *str1, const char *str2)
```

or a declaration that omits the parameter name, as in

```
double f(double,double)
char *strcpy(char *, const char *)
```

The only storage class specifier allowed in elements of a *parameter-type-list* is **register**. As a special case, the keyword **void** can be used in a function that takes no arguments, as in

```
unsigned rand(void);
```

Function prototypes may also use the notation "..." to indicate a "variable argument list", as described in Section 6.1.1.

Function prototypes may be used to begin a function definition or simply to describe the way a function is called. If a prototype begins a function definition, parameter names cannot be omitted from the *parameter-type-list*. The identifier names in the list will have function scope and will be used as parameters referring to the argument values passed by the function's caller.

If a prototype does not start a function definition, any identifier in the *parameter-type-list* has function prototype scope, which means that the scope of the identifier extends only to the end of the prototype.

Every prototype of a function must agree with the definition of the function in the number and types of the parameters, plus the use of the ellipsis "..." if there is a variable argument list. This includes agreement on the number of dimensions in arrays, and on the bounds of each dimension (including the first dimension if it is specified).

5.6.4 Reading Declarations

C declarations can be difficult to understand. Two declarations that look almost the same can lead to widely different data objects. You should therefore spend some time learning to read declarations.

The most important rule is to pull declarations apart piece by piece, starting at the identifier and going right as far as you can, then returning to the identifier and going left as far as you can. If the declaration contains parentheses, you may have to go right then left several times.

We will now give a few examples of declarations, emphasizing the format of items in the declarator list.

```
char c, ca[20], *cp;
```
The variable c contains a single character; ca is an array containing 20 characters, indexed from 0 to 19; cp is a pointer to a single character.

```
char *cpa[20];
```
We start by going right: cpa is an array with 20 members. What are the members? We go back to the identifier and go left. Each member is a pointer (because there is a * to the left of the identifier). What do the members point to? Keep going left. They point to characters. Therefore, cpa is an array of 20 character pointers.

```
float ff(), *fpf();
```
The first declarator declares a function ff that returns a **float** value. To understand fpf, we go right, then left: fpf is a function, it returns a pointer and the pointer points to a **float** value.

```
float (*ffp)();
```
The parentheses show that we look at (*ffp) first. Therefore, ffp is a pointer. Outside the parentheses, go right, then left. The thing that ffp points to is a function and the function returns a **float** value.

```
int (*ip[10])();
```
This declares ip to be an array of ten pointers to functions that return integers.

```
char stra[5][20];
```
This declares stra to be an array of five vectors with 20 characters each. It may be useful to think of this as an array of five strings, with each string 20 characters long: stra[0] refers to the first of these five strings, while stra[0][19] refers to the last character in the first string.

```
const char *ptr_to_const;
```
The variable ptr_to_const is a pointer that points to a character and the character cannot be modified (that is, it has the **const** attribute).

```
char * const const_ptr;
```
The variable `const_ptr` is not modifiable and it points to a character. Thus `const_ptr` is a "constant" pointer, while `ptr_to_const` points to a "constant" object.

```
long (*fxp)(void);
```
The variable `fxp` is a pointer to a function that takes no arguments. The function returns a **long** value.

```
double *diff(double x,int (*fp)(double));
```
This declares a function named `diff`. The parameters of `diff` are a **double** value named `x` and a function pointer named `fp`. The function that `fp` points to takes one **double** argument and returns an **int**; `diff` itself returns a pointer to a **double** value.

5.7 Initializers

Declarators may include initializers which assign values to the objects being declared. One exception to this is that declarations for the parameters of a function may not contain initializations.

5.7.1 Static Duration Objects

Objects with static storage duration (static or external objects) may only be initialized with initialization constant expressions (see Section 3.19). These constant expressions may include the & operator to obtain the address of a static duration object.

If a static duration object has no explicit initializer, the implementation initializes it as if the object (or each member of the object) is assigned the integer constant 0. This is not necessarily the same as setting all the bits of the object to 0. For example, if a **float** object is assigned the integer value 0, it becomes 0.0 and the bit pattern for 0.0 may not be all 0-bits.

5.7.2 Automatic Duration Objects

An object with automatic duration may be initialized with any expression involving constants, function calls, and assignments. The expression may also contain previously declared identifiers that have been assigned values. An automatic initialization behaves exactly like an assignment statement. Therefore,

```
        auto int i = 1;
        auto int j = i++;
```

not only initializes i and j, but also increments the value of i at the same time that j is being initialized.

Note that the scope of a local variable begins at the *end* of its declarator (after the initializer). This means that one can have code like

```
int i = 1;
float f()
{
    auto int i = i * 2;
        ...
```

Because the scope of the local i does not begin until the end of the declarator, the i in the initialization expression refers to the value of the external i. This sort of initialization leads to programs that are hard to understand, but it is valid.

If an automatic duration object is not initialized, its value is undefined until a value is assigned in some other way. Unlike static duration objects, automatic duration objects are not initialized in any default way.

5.7.3 Initializing Scalar Objects

An object with scalar type is initialized by putting an = after the declarator form, followed by a single expression. This expression may be enclosed in brace brackets if desired. For example,

```
int i = 7;
int i = {7};
```

are equivalent. The value of the expression after the = is the value used to initialize the object.

5.7.4 Initializing Array Objects

The initializer of an array object is a list of initialization expressions. These must be constant expressions, even if the array has automatic duration. The expressions are separated by commas and the entire list is enclosed in braces, as in

```
float x[3] = {
    3.1415, 2.0 * 3.1415, 3.0 * 3.1415
};
```

It is not necessary to initialize an array in its entirety. For example,

```
char alpha[26] = {
    'a','b','c'
};
```

initializes the first three members of the array and says nothing about the rest. In such cases, the remaining members are implicitly initialized to zero, whether the array has static or automatic storage duration.

To write a declaration for a multidimensional array, picture the object as an array of arrays. Each member of the array is itself an array which is initialized by a list of initialization expressions in brace brackets. Thus the initializer is a list of lists. For example,

```
int oct[4][4] = {
    { 000, 001, 002, 003 },
    { 010, 011, 012, 013 },
    { 020, 021, 022, 023 },
    { 030, 031, 032, 033 }
};
```

initializes `oct[1][2]` to `012`, `oct[3][1]` to `031`, and so on. The first level of nesting refers to the first subscript, the second to the second subscript, and so on.

Again, you do not have to initialize every member in a multidimensional array.

```
int lower_triangular[3][3] = {
    { 1 },
    { 1, 1 },
    { 1, 1, 1 }
};
```

only initializes some members in some "rows" of the array. Other members are implicitly initialized to zero.

Internal braces may be omitted when initializing multidimensional arrays, as in

```
int two_by_two[2][2] = {
    1, 2, 3, 4
};
```

In this case, initialization values are assigned to the array members in row major order (with the rightmost subscript varying fastest). In the above example, you would have

```
two_by_two[0][0] == 1
two_by_two[0][1] == 2
two_by_two[1][0] == 3
two_by_two[1][1] == 4
```

When an array declaration contains an initializer, the size of the leftmost dimension may be omitted. In this case, the size will be calculated from the number of initialization expressions provided. For example,

```
int vec[] = {
    0, 1, 2, 3
};
```

creates an array with four members because there are four initialization values.

```
int matrix[][3] = {
    { 0, 0, 0 },
    { 1, 1, 1 }
};
```

creates a 2 by 3 array, because the number of initialization values produces two "rows."

5.7.5 Initializing Char Arrays

In addition to the usual way of initializing arrays, you may initialize an array of **char** values with a string constant. For example,

```
char arr[10] = "abcd";
```

assigns `'a'` to `arr[0]`, `'b'` to `arr[1]`, and so on. A `'\0'` character is placed in the array member which follows the member that gets the last character shown in the string. In the above example, `a[3]` is assigned `'d'` and `a[4]` is assigned `'\0'`. If the size of the character array is exactly the number of characters in the string literal, the `'\0'` is not added.

Note the difference between the above declaration and

```
char *p = "abcd";
```

which creates a literal string and points `p` towards the first character. The values of the members of `arr` may be changed; the characters to which `p` points may not be changed because they belong to a string literal.

This sort of initialization may only be used for "plain" **char** arrays. It does not work for **unsigned char** or **signed char**.

5.7.6 Initializing Structure Objects

An automatic duration structure object may be initialized by a single expression whose value is the same type. For example,

```
auto struct X A = B;
```

is valid if `B` is a structure of type `X` and the members of `B` have already been assigned values (for example, in an outer scope).

Otherwise, a structure initializer is similar to an array initializer: a list of constant expressions separated by commas and enclosed in brace brackets. The values of the expressions are used to initialize the members of the structure in the order they are given. For example, you might have

```
struct person {
    char name[40];
    int age;
} john = {
    "John Smith", 30
};
```

If a structure contains another structure, nested brackets are used in the same way they are used to initialize multidimensional arrays. The same principle applies with arrays of structures.

```
struct person list[] = {
    {"John", 30},
    {"Mary", 36},
    {"George", 54}
};
```

This creates an array of three members, each of which is a `person` structure.

As with multidimensional arrays, brace brackets inside of brace brackets may be omitted to get one long list of initialization expressions. In this case, expressions will be taken from the list as needed. For example, the declaration above could have been written

```
struct person list[] = {
    "John", 30, "Mary", 36, "George", 54
};
```

It is not necessary to initialize all the members of a structure. For example,

```
struct person boss = {
    "Gwen"
};
```

initializes the `name` field of the structure but not the `age`.

5.7.7 Initializing Union Objects

When an initializer is specified for a **union** object, the first interpretation of the union is used. For example, in

```
union if {
    float x;
    int i;
} sample = 3;
```

the **float** interpretation will be used. Therefore the 3 will be converted to 3.0 before it is assigned.

5.8 Type Names

Type-names are used in cast operations, in function prototypes, and with the **sizeof** operator. Type-names are specified as declarations without object identifiers. They consist of a type specifier (for example, **int**) followed by an *abstract declarator*. Such declarators take the following forms:

> *null*
> (*abstract-declarator*)
> **abstract-declarator*
> *abstract-declarator*( )
> *abstract-declarator*[*constant-expression*]

null means that no declarator is specified. In order to avoid confusion, the declarator inside parentheses in *(abstract-declarator)* may not be null.

From these possibilities, one can construct type-names which reflect every data type that may be constructed in C. For example,

```
char          /* character */
char *        /* pointer to character */
char [10]     /* array of 10 characters */
char *()      /* function returning pointer to char */
char (*)()    /* pointer to function returning char */
char (*)[10]  /* pointer to array of 10 characters */
char *[10]    /* array of 10 pointers to character */
char * const  /* constant character pointer */
```

chapter 6   Program Structure

In this chapter, we will describe the layout of C programs. This will tie together the separate elements we have discussed in the preceding chapters.

A C program consists of a series of definitions. Some define objects, some define data types, and some define the functions that do the actual work of the program.

6.1 Function Definition

A function definition begins with a declaration of the function. This declaration should give the type of the function, its storage class, and the names of the function's parameters. If the type is omitted, **int** is assumed. If the storage class is omitted, **extern** is assumed.

The parameter names may be supplied in two ways. The preferred form uses a function prototype, in which case the prototype includes full declarations for all parameters, as in

```
int chkstr(char *s,char c)
```

With the second form, the first line of the function declaration just contains a list of the parameter names, in which case declarations of the parameters must immediately follow, as in

```
int chkstr(s,c)
char *s;
char c;
```

Note that the declarations of the parameters end in semicolons, but the function declaration itself does not. If this declaration form is used, no parameter can have the same name as a type named in a **typedef** statement.

The second approach is "deprecated" by the **ANSI** standard, which means it may not be supported in later updates. It is common in existing C programs, but new programs should all use functions defined with prototypes. We therefore use prototype declarations for all our function definitions.

The body of a function is enclosed in braces and follows the function prototype, or the declarations for the function arguments. Typically, the function body will begin with declarations for any automatic variables that will be used in the function. After the necessary declarations come the actual statements of the function.

As an example,

```
int chkstr(const char *s,char c)
{
    int i;
    for (i=0; *s != c ; ++i)
        if (*s++ == '\0') return -1;
    return i;
}
```

defines a function named chkstr. The parameters are named s and c. These represent a character pointer and a character that will be passed when chkstr is called by another function. The **const** in the declaration of s indicates that the function will not use s to change any data. The character pointer is assumed to point to a string whose end is marked with a NUL ('\0'). The chkstr function determines if the specified character represented by c appears in the string indicated by the character pointer. If the character is found, chkstr returns the offset of the character from the beginning of the string. Thus chkstr returns 0 if the character is the first character of the string, 1 if it is the next character, and so on. If chkstr reaches the '\0' at the end of the string and has not yet found the character, the function returns −1.

The parameters of a function may not be declared with any storage class except **register**. They have function scope. If they are declared without a type specifier, **int** is assumed.

If a function definition begins with a function declaration of the form

specifiers function-name( )

the function takes no arguments. This is equivalent to

specifiers function-name(**void**)

6.1.1 Variable Argument Lists

Most C functions are defined to take a fixed number of arguments. However, it is also possible to define a function whose number of arguments can vary from call to call. For example, you might define a function that determines the maximum value in a list of integer arguments. You could pass this function two integers, three integers, four integers, or more and it would work properly.

Many functions are designed to accept a fixed set of arguments plus a set of arguments whose number varies from call to call. For example, a function may require some arguments all the time, and may also accept some optional arguments as well. The best known example of this kind of function is printf, which always takes a format string and may take other arguments too.

If a function takes a variable number of arguments, its definition should begin with a prototype that has an ellipsis "..." on the end. For example, you might have

```
double f(double x, int count,...)
```

The function f takes two arguments that must always be present (x and count) and a variable number of arguments after that. The count argument could give the actual number of arguments that follow it in a particular function call. As another example, the prototype for printf is

```
int printf(const char *format, ...)
```

The set of arguments represented by the ellipsis is called a **variable argument list**. A function that takes a variable argument list is called a **variable argument function**. The set of arguments that must always be specified for a variable argument function are called the **fixed arguments**.

The precise method for accessing the arguments in a variable argument list is implementation-defined. However, **ANSI** C packages are required to supply library routines for accessing variable arguments. These are described in Part IV.

6.2 Argument Passing

As noted in Section 3.3.2, all arguments are passed by value. A function is passed *copies* of the argument values, not the actual arguments specified by the caller. If the function changes the value of one of its parameters, this change does not affect the caller's arguments. However, a function that is passed a pointer to an object can use this pointer to change the value of the object.

For compatibility between parameters and passed arguments, the argument value should have a type that can be assigned to the unqualified type of the parameter.

6.2.1 Argument Conversion Rules

When a function call is in the scope of a prototype of the function, all specified argument values are converted to the type given in the prototype. For example, in

```
void f(float x);
    ...
f(0);
```

the **int** constant 0 is automatically converted to a **float** 0.0 before being passed to the function. Similarly in

```
void g(int *p);
    ...
g(0);
```

the **int** 0 is converted to a null integer pointer.

If a function call is not in the scope of a prototype for the function, **argument conversion rules** are applied. When the caller passes a **float** value to a function, the value is automatically converted to **double**. Similarly, a **char**, **short int**, or bit field value undergoes the integral promotions, producing an **int** or **unsigned** value.

The argument conversion rules also apply when the function definition does not begin with a prototype. For example, consider

```
double f(x)
float x;
{
    /* function body */
};
```

Even though x is declared to be **float**, the corresponding argument value will be treated as if it were **double**, because it is expected that the argument value will undergo the automatic **float** to **double** conversion.

Finally, the argument conversion rules apply when a prototype contains ... to indicate a variable argument list. Since the prototype does not indicate types for arguments in the variable part of the list, those arguments are converted according to the argument conversion rules.

While the default argument conversions are sometimes unavoidable, consistent use of prototypes eliminates most of the confusion of automatic argument conversion.

6.2.2 Passing Derived Types

If a function call contains an argument which is the name of an array, the value passed to the function is a pointer to the first member of the array. Effectively, an argument value whose type is "array of *type*" is automatically converted to "pointer to *type*." For example, in

```
int a[10];
    ...
f(a);
```

f will be passed an **int** pointer to the first member of a. A function parameter declared as "array of *type*" is therefore treated as "pointer to *type*." For example, the prototypes

```
int f(char *s)
int f(char s[])
```

are equivalent. As shown, the first dimension of an array parameter need not be declared.

If a function call contains an argument which is the name of a function, the callee is passed a pointer to the named function. Thus an argument value whose type is "function returning *type*" is converted to "pointer to function returning *type*."

If a function expects to be passed a union value, the argument that is passed must be a union of compatible type. It is not enough to pass a value of a type that matches one of the interpretations of the union.

6.3 Return Values

If an expression appears in a **return** statement, the expression is automatically converted to the type that the function returns (specified in the function definition).

If a function call is within the scope of a declaration for the function, the result of the function is assumed to have the type given by the declaration. If a function call is not within the scope of a declaration, the result of the function is assumed to be **int**.

6.4 Flow of Control

When a function is called, execution begins at the start of the block that makes up the body of the function. Memory is allocated for any **auto** or **register** variables declared at the beginning of the function block. If any of the declarations have initializers, initializations are performed as if they were assignment statements appearing at the beginning of the block. After these initializations, execution proceeds to the first statement in the function block.

Execution of the function continues statement by statement until something passes control out of the block. This can happen in several ways.

(a)   The function executes a **return** statement. This returns control to the caller.

(b)   The function finishes execution of the last statement in the function block. Again, control returns to the function's caller.

(c)   The function calls a library function that passes control to some other part of the program or to support software. There are a number of library functions that work this way (described in Part IV of this book).

(d)   The function calls another function. The called function will then be executed until it returns or calls a library routine that passes control elsewhere. If the called function returns normally, execution of the caller will resume from where it left off, often continuing the evaluation of an expression that contained the call. Most library routines also return control to their callers instead of passing control elsewhere.

(e)   An error occurs, or another event interrupts normal execution (for example, the user presses BREAK to interrupt the program). Such events are dealt with by the *signal-handling* facilities of the program or implementation (described in Part IV).

Program execution consists of functions calling other functions. Obviously, there must be one function that is invoked to start the whole process. In a hosted environment (one with an operating system), the first user-written function that is invoked is called main. (Implementation-supplied functions may be executed before main is invoked.) Every program running in a hosted environment must have a main function.

In a free-standing environment (one without an operating system), the implementation may dictate some other name for the first function executed. All details concerning the way this function behaves are implementation-defined, so we will concentrate on the way hosted environments use `main`.

The operating system begins executing the program with the equivalent of a function call to `main`. When `main` reaches its final statement or issues a **return**, program execution terminates. Another way of terminating execution is to call the library function `exit` anywhere in the program (see Part IV).

Any function can call any other function in the program (except for static functions that appear in a different source file). In particular, functions can call themselves recursively. Functions can also call `main` (in which case, completion of `main` will only return to its caller, not terminate program execution).

6.5 Program Parameters

You may define your `main` routine in two ways. The simplest is

```
int main(void)
{
    /* function block for "main" */
}
```

With this definition, `main` has no parameters. The second way is traditionally written

```
int main(int argc, char *argv[])
{
    /* function block for "main" */
}
```

or equivalently

```
int main(int argc, char **argv)
{
    /* function block for "main" */
}
```

Of course, different names may be used for the parameters `argc` and `argv`. The parameters `argc` and `argv` are known as **program parameters**.

The `argv` parameter is an array of pointers that point to strings. These strings are created by the host operating system or the implementation before `main` is invoked. In many implementations, the strings represent arguments specified on the command line that invoked this particular program, although this is not necessarily true of all implementations.

The `argc` parameter is the number of members in the `argv` array; `argc` is always greater than zero. By convention, `argv[argc]` is always a null character pointer.

The string `argv[0]` represents the **program name**, if it can be supplied. If the host environment cannot supply a program name, `argv[0]` points to a NUL character (`'\0'`).

The strings pointed to by `argv[1]` through `argv[argc-1]` are called `program arguments`. These can be used to set options for the program and to provide other kinds of information. The method by which these strings are created is implementation-defined.

All the strings pointed to by the members of `argv` are modifiable by the program. The standard requires that the underlying environment should not change the `argv` strings between program start-up and termination.

6.6 Program Status

As noted above, `main` is declared as a function that returns an **int** value. If the program actually terminates by `main` executing a **return** statement that returns an **int** value, the value is returned to the host operating system as the "status" of the program. The meaning and use of this status are implementation-defined.

chapter 7   Source Code Preprocessing

C's preprocessing facilities modify C source code in the translation phase. These facilities allow for text and macro substitution, conditional translation, and the inclusion of other source files.

7.1 Preprocessor Symbols

The preprocessor facilities make use of several special identifiers. These names are replaced with other values in preprocessing phases.

The identifier _ _LINE_ _ stands for the line number of the current source file line. The _ _LINE_ _ symbol will be replaced by the decimal integer constant that is one greater than the number of new-line characters read up to the point where _ _LINE_ _ appears. The value of _ _LINE_ _ is automatically set by the preprocessor as it reads the source file. It can also be set artificially by the **#line** directive (see Section 7.2.6).

The identifier _ _FILE_ _ stands for the name of the current source file. Wherever it appears in the source code, _ _FILE_ _ will be replaced by a string literal containing the appropriate file name. The file name can be changed artificially with the **#line** directive.

The identifier _ _DATE_ _ stands for a string literal of the form

```
"Mmm DD YYYY"
```

giving the date of translation. Mmm is the first three letters of the month, as in Jan, Feb, and so on. DD is the current day of the month; if this number is less than 10, the first character is a blank. YYYY is the current year.

The identifier _ _TIME_ _ stands for a string literal of the form

```
"hh:mm:ss"
```

representing the time of translation of the source file (on a 24-hour clock).

The identifier _ _STDC_ _ is the decimal constant 1. It indicates that a particular implementation of C conforms with the **ANSI** standard.

None of these symbols may be defined with **#define** or undefined with **#undef** (see Section 7.2.1 and Section 7.2.2).

7.2 Preprocessor Directives

Preprocessing directives control C's preprocessing facilities. These directives appear as single lines in the C source code (although there is a way to extend a directive to more than one line, as described shortly). These lines are independent of the rest of the source code, and can be inserted in the middle of other lines containing normal source code. Conceptually, they are executed before parsing the source code, although some implementations may perform preprocessing and parsing at the same time.

Directive lines may begin with any number of white space characters, but the first character that is not white space must be #. After the # may come more white space, then a keyword indicating what kind of directive it is. The accepted keywords are

```
define    endif    ifdef      line
elif      error    ifndef     pragma
else      if       include    undef
```

Some directives take more information after the keyword, while others do not. Details will be given in the directive descriptions in later sections.

Preprocessing directives normally end at the first new-line character after the #. If you wish to break a directive over one or more source lines, put a backslash character (\) immediately before each new-line character inside the directive. A backslash before a new-line tells the preprocessor to discard both the backslash and the new-line. For example,

```
#define printint(A) printf("%d\n",\
                            A)
```

is equivalent to

```
#define printint(A) printf("%d\n",A)
```

The same principle applies to normal code as well.

```
x = "abc\
def";
```

is equivalent to

```
x = "abcdef";
```

To let you make source files more readable, **ANSI** C lets you have source lines that only contain the # character and white space. These are called **null directives**. For example, you might write

```
#
# define ...
#
```

to make the **#define** directive stand out more clearly. Null directives are simply discarded during preprocessing.

7.2.1 The #define Directive

The simplest form of the **#define** directive is

#define *identifier char-sequence*

where *identifier* is a normal C identifier and *char-sequence* is any character sequence that does not contain a new-line. Note that there is no semicolon; the directive is terminated by the new-line character at the end of the line. White space surrounding the *char-sequence* is not considered part of the replacement text.

The **#define** directive instructs the preprocessor to replace the specified identifier with the given string wherever the identifier appears in the source file. We will call this sort of identifier a **manifest**. As an example,

```
#define VECSIZE 20
```

defines a manifest named VECSIZE. After this has been defined, we may use the identifier in source code, as in

```
float vector[VECSIZE];
```

During preprocessing, the identifier VECSIZE will be replaced by the text 20. The preprocessor does not interpret this text as a number—it is only a sequence of characters. It is a later parsing phase that recognizes 20 as an integer constant.

The **#define** directive can also have the form

#define *name(name, ..., name) char-sequence*

where each *name* is a valid C identifier and *char-sequence* is any character sequence not including a new-line. There must not be white space between the first *name* and the opening parenthesis "(." White space surrounding the *char-sequence* is not considered part of the replacement text. This list of *name*s may be empty.

This form of the directive defines a **macro**. The name of the macro is the name immediately before the "(." The names listed inside the parentheses are the **parameters** of the macro. The character sequence after the parentheses is the **body** of the macro.

Macros are used much like function calls. The source code gives the name of the macro, followed by argument values enclosed in parentheses. The preprocessor will replace this **macro call** with the body of the macro, as given in the **#define** statement that created the macro. Occurrences of macro parameters in the body of the macro are replaced by the corresponding argument values given in the macro call. For example,

```
#define DIAG(A,B)  {A,0},  {0,B}
int iden[2][2] = {DIAG(1,1)};
int negi[2][2] = {DIAG(-1,-1)},
int zero[2][2] = {DIAG(0,0)};
```

shows the definition of a macro named `DIAG` and its use. The preprocessor changes the above code to

```
int iden[2][2] = { {1,0}, {0,1} },
int negi[2][2] = { {-1,0}, {0,-1} },
int zero[2][2] = { {0,0}, {0,0} };
```

The number of arguments specified in the macro call must match the number specified in the macro definition. Arguments in the macro call are merely token strings separated by commas. Arguments may contain their own parentheses. If a token contains commas, the token should be enclosed in double quotes or parentheses to make sure that the comma is not taken as a delimiter for the argument list.

The arguments passed to a macro may contain manifests or macro calls. These will be expanded *before* the arguments are used in the macro expansion. In other words, the arguments are fully expanded and then the macro is.

After a macro or manifest has been expanded, the result is scanned again to see whether it contains other manifests or macros. This allows you to **#define** something in terms of other **#define**d items. However, if the text that replaces a macro or manifest contains a reference to the same macro or manifest, the reference is *not* replaced. In other words, you cannot **#define** macros or manifests to act recursively. If you try

```
#define MAC(X) MAC(X+5)
    . . .
MAC(3)
```

the preprocessor will make one replacement, to get

```
MAC(3+5)
```

but will not try to expand `MAC` again.

Character constants and string literals are not scanned for manifests or macros. In

```
#define CAT 9
    . . .
char s[] = "A cat has CAT lives";
```

the `CAT` inside the string literal will not be changed. Similarly, strings that are given in a macro body are *not* examined for formal parameter names. In

```
#define LIVES(WHO,HOWMANY) "A WHO has HOWMANY lives"
```

the `WHO` and `HOWMANY` inside the string will not be changed.

Because macro parameters are not recognized inside strings that appear in macro definitions, a special notation is needed if you want a macro argument value to be placed inside a string. When the body of a macro contains a # character followed by a parameter name, the sequence will be replaced by a string literal containing the value of the corresponding macro argument. For example, if we define

```
#define SAMPLE(A)  #A
```

then the macro call

```
SAMPLE(xyz)
```

will change into

```
"xyz"
```

The #A construct is replaced by the macro argument enclosed in double quotes. Whenever the original argument A contains one or more whitespace characters separating tokens, the string that results from #A will have a single space character in the same position. White space before the first token and after the last is deleted. If the original argument A contains double quotes or backslashes, backslashes will be inserted into #A to preserve the characters. For example, if A is

```
He said, "Hello!"
```

#A would be

```
"He said, \"Hello!\""
```

The scope of a macro or manifest extends from the end of the **#define** directive to the end of the translation unit. However, the manifest can be "undefined" with the **#undef** directive (described in Section 7.2.2).

An identifier that has been defined as a macro or manifest may not be redefined with another **#define** directive, unless the second definition is identical to the first. If you want to change the meaning of a **#define**d item, you must first use **#undef** to undefine the identifier; after this, a new **#define** directive is valid.

The result of replacing a macro or manifest is never treated as a preprocessing directive. If code contains a # followed by an identifier in a place where a preprocessing directive could begin, the identifier does not undergo manifest or macro expansion.

The **ANSI** standard uses "macro" both for macros that are defined with parameters and for manifests. We prefer to distinguish the two because they are used in different ways.

7.2.2 The #undef Directive

The directive

#undef *identifier*

"undefines" the given identifier. This means that any previous meaning set by a **#define** is discarded. The scope of the identifier ends at the **#undef** directive instead of continuing to the end of the translation unit. You may undefine an identifier that has not been defined.

7.2.3 The #if Directive

The **#if** directive tells the translation phase of C to discard a section of source code if a particular condition does not hold. It is commonly used as shown below:

```
#if constant-expression
   /* one set of statements */
#else
   /* another set of statements */
#endif
```

If the constant expression given in the **#if** directive is nonzero, the translation phase will use the source code between the **#if** and **#else**; the source code between the **#else** and **#endif** is discarded. If the constant expression is zero, the translation phase will discard the source code between the **#if** and **#else** and will translate the statements between the **#else** and the **#endif**. For example,

```
#define SITE_A 1
#if SITE_A
char site_name[] = "SITE_A Name";
#else
char site_name[] = "***Unknown Site***";
#endif
```

The string site_name is initialized to different values depending on the value of the manifest SITE_A. This lets you write a program's source code to apply to various sites, and all you have to change is the preprocessor definition of SITE_A.

The **#else** directive may be omitted after an **#if**. In this case, the statements between the **#if** and **#endif** will only be translated if the constant expression in the **#if** directive is nonzero.

You may nest **#if** constructions, as in

```
#if exp1
   /*stuff1*/

#if exp2
   /*stuff2*/
#else
   /*stuff3*/
#endif

   /*stuff4*/
#else
   /*stuff5*/
#endif
```

The directive

> **#elif** *constant-expression*

may be used in place of

> **#else**
> **#if** *constant-expression*

in nested **#if** constructions. This usually makes the code more readable, and the whole construction only needs one **#endif**, as in

```
#if A
  . . .
#elif B
  . . .
#elif C
  . . .
#elif D
  . . .
#endif
```

When evaluating the constant expressions in **#if** and **#elif** directives, all arithmetic is performed as if the operands had the **long** or **unsigned long** type in the *translation* environment. The expression must be an integral constant expression that does not contain cast operations or enumerated constants. In addition, keywords are not recognized in this context; specifically, **sizeof** doesn't work. The constant expression may contain **defined** expressions (as explained in the next section). Individual implementations may decide if it is valid to have a character constant with a negative value.

If the constant expression contains manifests or macros, they are replaced with their defined values before the expression is evaluated. Identifiers that have not been defined using **#define** are replaced with the text 0.

7.2.4 The defined Expression

The expressions

> **defined** *identifier*
> **defined** (*identifier*)

can be used in preprocessor directives to determine if an identifier has been defined as a macro or manifest.

```
defined(X)
```

has the value 1 if the name X is currently defined as a macro or manifest, and has the value 0 if X has never been defined with **#define**, or if it has been undefined with **#undef** since its last definition.

7.2.5 The #ifdef and #ifndef Directives

The directive

#ifdef *identifier*

is equivalent to

#if defined(*identifier*)

The code following the **#ifdef** will be translated if the given *identifier* is defined. The directive

#ifndef *identifier*

is equivalent to

#if ! **defined**(*identifier*)

and is therefore the opposite of **ifndef**.

You may freely nest **#if**, **#ifdef**, and **#ifndef** constructions. Similarly, **#else** and **#elif** directives may follow **#ifdef** and **#ifndef** in the same way they are used with **#if**. Both **#ifdef** and **#ifndef** constructions end at an **#endif**.

7.2.6 The #include Directive

When the preprocessing facilities find a directive of the form

#include "*filename*"

the line is replaced by the entire contents of the specified file. For example,

```
#include "xxx"
```

will be replaced by the contents of a file named xxx. The implementation searches for this file in places associated with the source file that contains the **#include** directive. This search procedure is implementation-defined, but the usual approach is to begin the search in the directory that contains the original source file. If the file is not found there, the implementation will continue the search in a sequence of implementation-defined locations (generally under directories of standard "inclusion" files).

If the directive takes the form

#include *<filename>*

as in

```
#include <stdio.h>
```

the implementation immediately searches through the standard sequence of implementation-defined locations, without searching for the file relative to the original source file.

It is valid to have a directive of the form

#include *manifest*

provided that the defined meaning of the *manifest* has one of the two previous forms of **#include**. For example, you could have

```
#define FILENAME "myfile"
#include FILENAME
```

Similarly, you may write

#include *macro(arg,arg,...)*

if the final result has one of the two accepted forms of the **#include** directive.

A file that is obtained via **#include** may itself contain **#include** directives. In this way, **#include** directives may be nested, up to a maximum of at least eight files. Some implementations may accept deeper levels of nested inclusions.

The last line in an included file must end in a new-line.

7.2.7 The #line Directive

A directive of the form

#line *number string*

sets the value of $\_\_LINE\_\_$ to the given number and $\_\_FILE\_\_$ to the given *string*. This effectively makes the translation phase begin numbering lines at the given number, and makes it believe that the name of the source file is the one given by *string*. For example,

```
#line 30 "newfile"
```

makes the translation phase believe that the next source line is line 30 and the current input file name is newfile.

The *string* argument may be omitted; if so, $\_\_FILE\_\_$ is not changed.

The arguments of **#line** can be manifests or macros, provided that the result of expansion gives the expected format.

7.2.8 The #error Directive

A directive of the form

#error *message*

issues the given *message* as part of a diagnostic message for the translation phase. For example,

```
#ifndef A
#error A is undefined
#endif
```

issues an error message if the macro or manifest A is not defined.

7.2.9 The #pragma Directive

The **#pragma** directive is provided so that implementations may support implementation-specific directives. The directive has the form

#pragma *text*

The *text* following **#pragma** may have any format required by a particular implementation. If an implementation does not recognize a particular **#pragma** directive, it is ignored.

7.3 *Input Concatenation*

When two or more string literals appear in input, separated only by white space, they are concatenated into a single string constant. For example,

```
x = "a" "b" "c";
```

is equivalent to

```
x = "abc";
```

The same type of concatenation takes place with wide string literals.

When **##** is found in the body of a **#define** directive, the two tokens on either side of the symbol are concatenated into one token, if possible. For example, if you have

```
#define POINT(A) 0. ## A
```

the macro call POINT(6) turns into 0.6.

If the two tokens cannot be concatenated into a single valid token, the concatenation will not take place. For example, if a **#define** directive contains 1 ## x, the result is undefined because 1x is not a valid token. However, x ## 1 yields the identifier x1.

7.4 *Translation Phases*

The order in which preprocessing operations are carried out has a significant effect on the translation of source code. The translation stage is divided into the following phases:

(a)   Characters in the physical source file are mapped into the translation character set, if necessary. Trigraphs are replaced by single-character internal representations.

(b)   Wherever a backslash is immediately followed by a new-line, the two characters are deleted, joining physical source lines into logical ones. The resulting source file must end in a new-line character.

(c)   The source text is decomposed into tokens and sequences of white space characters. Every comment is replaced by a single space character. New-line characters remain as they are, but other white space characters may be replaced by a single space.

(d)   Preprocessing directives are executed, and macros and manifests are expanded. If files are included through **#include** directives, they go through translation phases (a) to (d), recursively.

(e)   Escape sequences in character constants and string literals are converted to single characters (for the execution environment).

(f)   The ## operation is performed. Adjacent string literals and wide string literals are also concatenated.

(g)   Preprocessing tokens are converted into normal tokens. All remaining tokens are analyzed and translated, syntactically and semantically. This is the parsing phase.

(h)   All external data and function references are resolved. This is the linking stage. Library elements are obtained to satisfy external references to functions and objects not defined in the module being translated. The translated parts of the program are joined to form a single program "image" that contains all the information required for execution of the program in the execution environment.

Error messages may be issued at any point in translation. Implementations are required to give at least one diagnostic message for each translation unit that contains an error.

PART IV
ANSI C: The Standard Library

The C language as described in Part III of this book is not sufficient for writing useful programs. For example, the definition of the language has no facilities for input or output. Implementations of C must therefore supplement the abilities of the language itself with a library of functions to perform various operations. Some of these functions do work that could not otherwise be done in C (for example, I/O, dynamic memory allocation, interfacing with the operating system). Others are just supplied to save programmers the trouble of writing the functions (for example, string manipulation routines, calculation of mathematical functions).

The **ANSI** standard specifies a set of functions and/or macros that must be present in a hosted implementation of C. Implementations usually have many other supplied functions and macros that are not described by the standard.

The **ANSI** standard does not state any library requirements for freestanding implementations (implementations where programs do not run under an operating system). However, freestanding implementations will certainly supply library functions of their own, and may also supply some or all of the functions associated with hosted implementations.

We will often use the generic term **routine** to refer to a function or macro supplied as part of a C implementation.

chapter 1   Library Concepts

In order to describe how C library routines work, we must begin by explaining some of the fundamental concepts that underlie the C library.

1.1 Headers

A **header** is a collection of declarations and definitions supplied as part of an implementation of C. A typical header contains any or all of the following:

(a)   Prototype declarations for library functions.

(b)   Macro or manifest definitions using **#define**.

(c)   Special types defined with **typedef**.

(d)   Declarations of other data types (structures, unions, or enumerated types).

(e)   Declarations to describe **extern** data objects that may be used or defined by the library.

A set of **standard headers** are required by the **ANSI** standard. The information stored in a standard header is obtained with an **#include** directive of the form

```
#include <name>
```

where *name* is the name of the header whose information you want. For example,

```
#include <stdio.h>
```

obtains the information from the standard header named "stdio.h" (which is needed when you want to perform I/O operations). All of the headers required by the **ANSI** standard have names that end in ".h."

Usually, we picture each standard header as a file containing C code. Normal **#include** directives apparently obtain code from these header files and insert it in program source files that need the information. However, an implementation does not actually have to obtain standard header information in this way; it just has to appear as if the information is obtained like this.

In a source file, an **#include** directive for a standard header should appear outside all external declarations or definitions, and before the use of any of the functions, objects, types, macros, or manifests that the header declares. This usually means that all such **#include** directives should be put at the beginning of the source file so that the information is available to all the code in the file.

Standard headers may be included in any order. Including the same header more than once in a scope is valid, but the effect is no different from including the header a single time. The exception to this is the header <assert.h>. Each time you include this header, the behavior depends on the current definition of the manifest NDEBUG as described in the description of assert in Section 4.

1.1.1 Functions and Macros

The prototype of any library function is declared in one and only one standard header. For this reason, if you want to call a particular library function, you should **#include** the standard header that declares the function's prototype.

In the interests of efficiency, an implementation is allowed to define any library routine as a macro. When this is the case, the program may *not* declare the routine as if it were a function—that will cause an error. Because of this possibility, programs should *never* contain explicit declarations for library routines. Instead, they should **#include** the appropriate header.

Except in cases that will be noted explicitly in Section 4, macros that implement library routines are written to avoid the side effect problems that macros can have (discussed in Section I.8.3.3). This means that the macro arguments are protected with parentheses, they are only evaluated once, and so on.

You may issue an **#undef** directive that "undefines" the name of most library routines, as in

```
#undef getchar
```

This discards any macro definition for the routine name. If you now call the routine, you will get a version that is implemented as a function. In other words, every library routine is implemented as a function; but some headers may define more efficient macros to override these function implementations. If you **#undef** the overriding macro, your program will obtain the underlying function.

As another way of getting around the macro definition, you may enclose the symbol name in parentheses, as in

```
(abs)(x)
```

Since the name is not immediately followed by a left parenthesis ′ (′, it is not recognized as a macro; instead, it will be taken to refer to the appropriate external name.

NOTE: A few routines are *only* defined as macros—there is no corresponding function. These will be noted in the routine descriptions given later.

1.1.2 Standard Headers

The following list gives the names and descriptions of each of the **ANSI** standard headers:

`<assert.h>`   declares information used by the `assert` macro (described in Section 4).

`<ctype.h>`   declares a number of routines for testing characters (for example, is this an uppercase letter?) and for converting characters (for example, letters from upper- to lowercase).

`<errno.h>`   declares information used in handling errors detected by library routines.

`<float.h>`   defines a number of manifests that describe the way the implementation handles floating point numbers.

`<limits.h>`   defines a number of manifests describing aspects of the hardware (for example, how many bits in a byte).

`<locale.h>`   defines functions and other information used to support features that can vary from place to place: conventions for writing monetary amounts, extensions that allow for non-English alphabets, and so on.

`<math.h>`   declares a number of mathematical functions (for example, `sin`, `log`, `sqrt`).

`<setjmp.h>`   declares functions and data types that can jump out of one function and into another.

`<signal.h>`   declares functions and other symbols for exception handling. For example, `<signal.h>` is needed by interactive programs that want to handle user interrupts.

`<stdarg.h>`   declares macros and data types used by functions that take variable argument lists.

`<stddef.h>`   declares commonly used symbols (for example, `NULL`).

`<stdio.h>`   declares routines and types used in input and output.

`<stdlib.h>`   declares miscellaneous routines and symbols.

`<string.h>`   declares routines for string manipulation.

`<time.h>`   declares routines and symbols for obtaining the time and date in various forms.

1.2 Errors in Library Functions _____

Many programmers claim that error handling is one of the weakest aspects of conventional C libraries. C library routines have a reputation for being designed on the *garbage in, garbage out* principle: if the arguments passed to a function are invalid, the function will return a meaningless result, with little or no indication that anything is wrong.

To some extent, this criticism is justified, especially in older C packages. In the interests of fast performance, some library routines do not check for errors in the arguments that the caller passes. Error reporting can also be inadequate: some functions inform the caller when an operation fails, but give no indication of the cause of failure.

These design weaknesses date back to the earliest implementations of C, and improvements have been made by most vendors over the years. All the same, no current solution is totally satisfactory. The onus is still on the programmer to intercept errors *before* calling a particular library routine, since the routine may not be able to handle problems itself.

1.2.1 Error Return Values

When a library function does not succeed in performing a requested operation, it usually indicates that something has gone wrong by returning a value that could not be obtained from a successful operation. For example, when the `getchar` function is unable to read a character for some reason, it returns a value that is not a valid character in the execution character set. The calling function can test the return value to determine whether or not the library routine succeeded in its job.

1.2.2 The Errno Symbol

An error return value from a library routine tells the caller that an error was discovered. However, it usually doesn't tell the caller what *kind* of error was found. For this reason, **ANSI** C uses an external symbol named `errno` to provide additional information about errors detected by library functions.

The `errno` symbol behaves as if it were an **int** variable. It does not have to be implemented this way; for example, it could be implemented as a macro that expands to an **int** expression—but it must give a modifiable Lvalue. An appropriate declaration for `errno` is obtained with

```
#include <errno.h>
```

All source files that refer to `errno` should have this **#include** directive.

When a library function encounters an error, `errno` is assigned a positive integer value indicating what kind of error was found. For example, when a program attempts to take the square root of a negative number, the library routine asked to find the square root sets `errno` to a value that indicates "invalid argument value."

When a program begins execution, `errno` is initialized to zero. From this point on, library routines do not touch `errno` except to assign error values. Note especially that they do not set `errno` to zero if an operation is successful. If a user program calls a library function which sets `errno` to a nonzero value, the program should set `errno` back to zero before going on.

1.2.3 Error Names

Programs use symbolic names to refer to the possible values of `errno`. These symbolic names are defined in `<errno.h>`.

The **ANSI** standard only defines two possible symbolic values for `errno`. The symbol `EDOM` is used when a library function receives an invalid argument value (for example, a negative value passed to the `sqrt` function). The symbol `ERANGE` is used when the result of a library function cannot be determined validly (for example, when the `exp` function generates a result that is too big to be represented as a **double** value).

Specific implementations of C often define additional values that `errno` can take, so that library routines can indicate the error conditions that may exist on a particular machine.

1.3 I/O Concepts

C attempts to make I/O look the same, regardless of the device involved. This means that the same I/O functions are used for I/O on disk files, tapes, terminals, and so on. C uses the generic term **I/O stream** for any file, device, or facility on which a program may perform I/O.

I/O streams must be *opened* before you can perform I/O on them. The actions taken by the opening operation depend on what kind of I/O device is being opened: opening a disk file accesses the file and determines whether the user has appropriate permissions to read or write the file; opening a tape file may issue a request to a computer operator to mount the tape and may wait until the tape is mounted; opening a terminal may establish a communication link with the terminal; and so on.

The work involved in opening a stream is usually transparent to the user program: the program calls the appropriate library function to perform an opening action, and the library function decides what work has to be done to prepare the stream for I/O.

When a stream has been opened successfully, the library routine that opened the stream returns a pointer to a block of information that is needed for performing I/O on the stream. This information is stored in a data object whose type is `FILE`. The `FILE` type is defined with a **typedef** statement in `<stdio.h>`.

The internal nature of the `FILE` type varies from system to system; most programmers need not be concerned about the precise definition of `FILE` on their machine, since the library routines take care of everything. Functions that perform I/O on a stream almost always need to be passed a pointer to the `FILE` block describing the stream.

When a program is finished with a file, the file may be **closed**. From this point on, the associated `FILE` information block may not be used in I/O operations. However, the program may reopen files that have been closed, thereby creating new `FILE` information blocks that can be used for I/O.

When a program terminates normally, it automatically closes any files that are still open. If a program terminates abnormally (for example, with the `abort` function), files may not be closed; the behavior is implementation-defined.

1.3.1 Standard Streams

Some streams are opened automatically when a C program begins execution. The library also defines manifests that point to the `FILE` information blocks associated with these streams. Below we list the predefined manifests and the streams with which they are associated.

`stdin`   is associated with the **standard input stream**.
`stdout` is associated with the **standard output stream**.
`stderr` is associated with the **standard error stream**.

Historically, all three of these streams were associated with an interactive user's terminal. The `stdin` and `stdout` streams could be **redirected** and associated with files instead of the terminal. The `stderr` stream could not be redirected, so that error diagnostics written to `stderr` always appeared on the user's terminal.

As C has travelled to more machines, `stdin`, `stdout`, and `stderr` have become more abstract concepts. The **ANSI** standard simply says that these symbols will be associated with I/O streams in an implementation-defined manner.

1.3.2 Buffering

The C I/O routines often **buffer** input and output. When input is buffered, the library routine which reads input actually reads many input characters at once, even if it only returns a single character to the calling program. The remaining characters are stored in a chunk of memory called a *buffer*.

Each time the input routine is called, it returns a new character from the buffer. It does *not* have to read more input from the actual I/O device. In this way, the C program may make many calls to the input routine, but the only physical input operation is the first one (the one that fills the buffer).

Buffering output works in a similar way: the library routines you call to write out characters actually accumulate the material in a memory buffer until the buffer is full. When the buffer is full, a single physical write operation performs the actual output.

In somes cases, buffered output may be written before the buffer is full. For example, the program may explicitly *flush* an output buffer (that is, the program may ask that the buffer contents be written out whether or not the buffer is full). Section 4 describes several functions that flush buffers before they are full.

The `setbuf` and `setvbuf` routines are used to control stream buffering. These routines are also described in Section 4.

1.3.3 Text and Binary Streams

C recognizes two types of I/O streams: *text streams* and *binary streams*.

Text Streams
A text stream is an ordered sequence of bytes organized into *lines*. Each line ends in a new-line character (with the possible exception of the last line in the stream).

Conceptually, I/O takes place character-by-character, although data is often buffered and some routines can read or write many bytes at a time.

A text stream's data may be translated during the I/O process. For example, when the program asks to write a new-line character, the output function may write a carriage return followed by a new-line (linefeed) character to get the effect of going to a new line on a terminal screen. Because of this translation process, the characters that are read from a file may not be exactly the same as the characters written to the file.

If a program wants data read from a text stream to be identical to the data written, it should follow these rules:

(a)   The data should only consist of printable characters, the new-line, and the horizontal tab.

(b)   There should not be spaces immediately preceding a new-line.

(c)   The last character written to the stream should be a new-line.

Binary Streams

A binary stream is also an ordered sequence of bytes. If a program writes data to a file and reads it back, the data that the program receives is *exactly* what was written. However, implementations are allowed to add an arbitrary number of null characters on the end of the stream.

1.4 Using Variable Argument Lists

Variable argument lists let you define a function whose arguments are not fixed. Each time the function is called, there may be a different number of arguments and the arguments may have different types.

If a source code file contains the definition of a variable argument function, the directive

```
#include <stdarg.h>
```

should appear sometime before the beginning of the function definition.

In prototypes for a variable argument function (including the one at the beginning of the function's definition), all the fixed arguments must be given before the "..." that represents the variable argument list. For example, we might declare a function f with the heading

```
int f(char *str,int count, ...)
```

In order to access the values in the variable argument list, your C program must define a variable to represent the list. To do this, you declare a variable of the type `va_list`, as in

        va_list ap;

The `va_list` type is defined in `<stdarg.h>`.

Next you must associate this variable with the variable argument list. This is done with a call to the macro `va_start`. It can be represented by the prototype

        void va_start(va_list ap,lastparm);

where `lastparm` is the last fixed parameter for the function. (Since `va_start` is a macro, you can't actually declare it with a prototype; however, the prototype above should help to convey how the macro works.) In our example of `f`, we would say

        va_start(ap,count);

because `count` is the parameter preceding the ellipsis in the function prototype.

After the call to `va_start`, a macro named `va_arg` lets you obtain arguments one by one from the variable list. The macro is invoked with calls of the form

        arg = va_arg(ap,type);

where `ap` is the variable that represents the variable argument list, `type` is the type of the next argument in the list, and `arg` is a variable of that type. The assignment statement above obtains the value of the next argument on the list and assigns it to `arg`.

When you are through obtaining values from the variable argument list, you must indicate that you are finished looking at the list. You do this with a routine named `va_end`.

        va_end(ap);

indicates that you are done with the `ap` variable. Future calls to `va_arg` will not work properly unless you initialize `ap` again with a call to `va_start`.

Note that you can "walk" through the variable list several times. To end a walk, use `va_end`. To start a new walk, use `va_start`.

The variable `ap` may be passed as an argument to other functions. Therefore, your calls to `va_arg` may be spread over many functions. You must always call `va_end` when you have finished using the list (and before the variable argument function returns).

If a `va_list` object `ap` is passed to a function that uses `va_arg` on `ap`, the caller's version of `ap` may not be valid any longer. It must be passed to `va_end` before it can be used in any other way.

Example:

```
/*
 * This function determines the maximum integer
 * in a list of numbers.  It should be called with
 *      max = maxint(count,value,value,value,...)
 * where "count" is the number of "values" given.
 */
#include <stdarg.h>
int maxint(int N,...)
{
    va_list ap;
    int arg,ourmax;
    va_start(ap,N);
    if (N--) ourmax = va_arg(ap,int);
    while (N--) {
        arg = va_arg(ap,int);
        ourmax = (ourmax > arg) ? ourmax : arg;
    }
    va_end(ap);
    return(ourmax);
}
```

1.5 Signals

Signals are issued when special events occur. For example, if a C program attempts an illegal operation like dividing by zero, the hardware or software that detects the error will send an appropriate signal to the program. There are different signals for different kinds of events.

When a program receives a signal, normal execution is interrupted and a function known as a **signal handler** is invoked. A program can have a different signal handler for every type of signal, or it may use the same handler to deal with several different signals. A program uses the `signal` function to name the signal handler function that should be invoked if a particular signal occurs.

Signal handler functions should be short. This minimizes the likelihood of a new signal arriving while a signal handler is dealing with the previous signal.

Even if the handler function is short, there is still a chance a new signal may come in while the handler is executing. For example, a user may press an interrupt key several times in succession. As a result, signal handler functions must be written so they can be interrupted and start over again from the top. Using computer science terminology, signal handlers must be **re-entrant**.

To be re-entrant, signal handlers must abide by the following rules:

(a)   They may not define local variables that have the **static** storage class.

(b)   They may not use any library routines, with the exception of abort, exit, longjmp, and/or signal. (NOTE: there may be other library routines that can be used with some implementations. However, the routines just listed are the only ones that the **ANSI** standard requires to be usable.)

(c)   They may not change the value of any external data object, except for data objects with the type sig_atomic_t. This is an integral data type defined in <signal.h>. It is the only type that is guaranteed "safe" to change. Note that the function can *examine* the value of any external object of any type; the function is only prohibited from *changing* values unless they have the right type.

As is obvious from this list, a signal handler function has a limited set of actions that it can perform safely. It can terminate the program using abort or exit; it can jump to another function using longjmp; or it can assign a value to a sig_atomic_t object and return.

When a signal handler function returns, it normally returns to the instruction that was executing at the time the signal was received and execution resumes from that point. However, if the signal was SIGFPE (described in Section 3) or an implementation-defined signal related to an expression that could not be evaluated, the effect of returning from a signal handler is undefined.

If a program does not use signal to set up a handler function for a particular signal, the signal will be handled by a default handler. Some signals use a default handler named SIG_DFL. The behavior of SIG_DFL is implementation-defined; commonly, it will just terminate the program with an error message. Other signals use a default handler named SIG_IGN. This just ignores the signal. The sets of signals that use SIG_DFL and signals that use SIG_IGN are implementation-defined.

Except for the SIGILL signal (described in Section 3), the first thing that happens when a signal is raised is that the implementation issues the function call

```
signal(sig,SIF_DFL)
```

for the signal. As a result, the next time the signal occurs, it will be handled by the default handler. A user signal handler is thus set up for only one occurrence of the related signal. Often then, a signal handler function will call signal to set itself up to handle the next occurrence of the signal (as well as the occurrence that just took place).

Every type of signal corresponds to an unusual event that may occur during program execution. However, an implementation is not required to issue a signal if that even actually occurs. With some implementations, signals may never occur except when they are specifically issued with the raise routine.

In addition to the signals specified by the standard, an implementation may create implementation-defined signals. These will all have associated manifest names beginning with SIG. User code should therefore avoid creating identifiers that start with SIG.

As this brief introduction shows, signal handling is a conceptually difficult subject. For more information, see the descriptions of longjmp, signal, and raise in Section 4 and the discussion of error handling in Parts I and II.

chapter 2   Data Type Names

Many library routines use arguments or return values of special types. These are named data types created with **typedef** or **#define** instructions in the standard headers. The most familiar example of a named data type is FILE defined in <stdio.h>; FILE pointers are passed to most of the standard I/O functions.

Below we list each data type recognized by the **ANSI** standard, and the header in which the type is defined:

clock_t (found in <time.h>)
> is an arithmetic type representing a length of time in "clock ticks." A clock tick is a fraction of a second. There are CLK_TCK ticks in a second (where CLK_TCK is an implementation-defined manifest, defined in <time.h>).

div_t (found in <stdlib.h>)
> is a structure type with members

```
        int quot;
        int rem;
```

> (in either order). Such a structure is returned as the result of the div function. See the explanation of div in Section 4 for more details.

FILE (found in <stdio.h>)
> is an object type providing information about an I/O stream. Pointers to FILE are used by any library routine that performs an I/O operation on the stream.

fpos_t (found in <stdio.h>)
> is an object type that can uniquely specify any position in any file. It is used by fgetpos and fsetpos.

jmp_buf (found in <setjmp.h>)
> is an array type used by the setjmp and longjmp routines to let programs perform **goto**like operations from one function to another.

struct lconv (found in <locale.h>)
> is a structure type which specifies a number of locale-specific values. Some of these values may not be relevant to some locales. In such cases, the locale specifies a null string for members that are string-valued and the CHAR_MAX value for members whose type is **char**. Members of the structure are described below.

`char *decimal_point;`
> character used to separate integer part from fractional part in formatted quantities that do not represent money values. In the `"C"` locale, this is `"."`.

`char *thousands_sep;`
> character used to separate groups of digits to the left of the decimal point in formatted quantities that do not represent money values. For example, if the string is a comma, `printf` might print `100,000`. In the `"C"` locale, this is the null string.

`char *grouping;`
> character string indicating how to group digits to the left of the decimal point in formatted quantities that do not represent money values. Each character in the string is a positive integral quantity (expressed as a **char**) telling how many characters should be in a group; the first character indicates the size of the first group to the left of the decimal, the second character indicates the size of the second group, and so on. If the last character in the string is the MAX_CHAR value (the largest integer that can be expressed as a **char**), it indicates no further grouping. If the string ends at a `'\0'` without a MAX_CHAR character, all remaining digits are grouped using the value of the last character in the string. For example, the string `"\3"` indicates that digits should appear in groups of three, separated by the `thousands_sep` character. In the `"C"` locale, `grouping` is just associated with the null string.

`char *int_curr_symbol;`
> character string to be used as international currency symbol for the locale. This consists of four characters, followed by the usual `'\0'`. The first three give the alphabetic international currency symbol in accordance with the document *ISO 4217 Codes for the Representation of Currency and Funds*. The fourth character will be used to separate the international currency symbol from the monetary quantity.

`char *currency_symbol;`
> character string to be used as locale's currency symbol (for example, `"$"`). In the `"C"` locale, this is the null string.

`char *mon_decimal_point;`
> character used to separate integer part from fractional part in formatted quantities representing money values. In the `"C"` locale, this is the null string.

`char *mon_thousands_sep;`
> character used to separate groups of digits to the left of the decimal point in formatted quantities that represent money values. In the `"C"` locale, this is the null string.

```
char *mon_grouping;
```
character string that indicates the grouping of digits to the left of the decimal point in formatted quantities that represent money values. This is similar to the `grouping` string. In the `"C"` locale, this is the null string.

```
char *positive_sign;
```
character string used to indicate a non-negative money value. In the `"C"` locale, this is the null string.

```
char *negative_sign;
```
character string used to indicate a negative money value. In the `"C"` locale, this is the null string.

```
char int_frac_digits;
```
the number of digits to be displayed to the right of the decimal point in an internationally formatted money quantity. In the `"C"` locale, this is `CHAR_MAX`.

```
char frac_digits;
```
the number of digits to be displayed to the right of the decimal point in a formatted money value. In the `"C"` local, this is `CHAR_MAX`.

```
char p_cs_precedes;
```
is 0 if the `currency_symbol` should be written after the numeric part in a non-negative money value, and is 1 if the `currency_symbol` should be written before. In the `"C"` local, this is `CHAR_MAX`.

```
char p_sep_by_space;
```
is 1 if there should be a space between the `currency_symbol` and the numeric part of a non-negative money value, and is 0 if there should not be a space. In the `"C"` local, this is `CHAR_MAX`.

```
char n_cs_precedes;
```
is 0 if the `currency_symbol` should be written after the numeric part in a negative money value, and is 1 if the `currency_symbol` should be written before. In the `"C"` local, this is `CHAR_MAX`.

```
char n_sep_by_space;
```
is 1 if there should be a space between the `currency_symbol` and the numeric part of a negative money value, and is 0 if there should not be a space. In the `"C"` local, this is `CHAR_MAX`.

```
char p_sign_posn;
```
contains a value indicating the position of the `positive_sign` in a non-negative money value. Below we list possible values of `p_sign_posn` and their meanings:

0 parentheses around number and `currency_symbol`
1 sign string precedes number and `currency_symbol`
2 sign string follows number and `currency_symbol`
3 sign string immediately precedes `currency_symbol`
4 sign string immediately follows `currency_symbol`

In the `"C"` local, this is `CHAR_MAX`.

`char n_sign_posn;`

contains a value indicating the position of the `negative_sign` in a negative money value. Possible values are the same as those for `p_sign_posn`. In the `"C"` local, this is `CHAR_MAX`.

`ldiv_t` (found in `<stdlib.h>`)
is a structure type defined with members

```
long quot;
long rem;
```

(in either order). Such a structure is returned as the result of the `ldiv` function. See the explanation of `ldiv` in Section 4 for more details.

`ptrdiff_t` (found in `<stddef.h>`)
is a signed integral type that is the type of the result of subtracting two pointer values.

`sig_atomic_t` (found in `<signal.h>`)
is an integral type. An object of the `sig_atomic_t` type can be assigned a value in a manner that is guaranteed to be "safe" from asynchronous interrupts. In technical terms, this usually means that it only takes a single machine instruction to assign a value to such an object. If it takes more than one machine instruction to assign a value to an object, there is a chance that an interrupt will occur between machine instructions, part way through the assignment, when the value is only partly correct. With one machine instruction, interrupts cannot come in the middle of an assignment.

`size_t` (found in `<stddef.h>`)
is an unsigned integral type that is the type of the result of **`sizeof`**.

`time_t` (found in `<time.h>`)
is an arithmetic type representing a date and time in some implementation-defined form. A typical method is to give the number of seconds that have passed since a particular date and time. However, you should not assume that this is the case in all implementations. Indeed, a `time_t` value may not be directly meaningful at all.

`tm` (found in `<time.h>`)
is a structure type used by `asctime`, `gmtime`, and `localtime` to store time information. It has the format

```
struct tm {
    int tm_sec;    /* seconds (0-60)     */
    int tm_min;    /* minutes (0-59)     */
    int tm_hour;   /* hours (0-23)       */
    int tm_mday;   /* month day (1-31)   */
    int tm_mon;    /* month (0-11)       */
    int tm_year;   /* year - 1900        */
    int tm_wday;   /* day of week (0-6)  */
    int tm_yday;   /* year day (0-365)   */
    int tm_isdst;  /* daylight savings?  */
};
```

The tm_isdst field is positive if daylight savings time is in effect, zero if standard time is in effect, and negative if this information cannot be determined.

va_list (found in <stdarg.h>)

is a type that can contain the information needed by va_start, va_arg, and va_end to handle a variable argument list. A value of this type can be passed as an argument to other functions.

wchar_t (found in <stddef.h>)

is an integral type whose range can represent distinct values for all members of the largest extended character set of all the locales supported by this implementation. The '\0' character corresponds to the value 0 of the wchar_t type. The wchar_t type will also be able to represent the EOF value, as distinct from the value of any character of the extended character set. A character in the minimum character set will have a corresponding wchar_t value equal to the **int** value of the character as the only character in an integer character constant.

chapter 3   Library Manifests

C library manifests are defined in the standard headers. When a source file makes use of a library manifest, the file should **#include** the appropriate header. Manifests should *not* be defined explicitly by user-written code.

Below we list the manifests recognized by the **ANSI** standard and the headers in which they are declared:

BUFSIZ (found in <stdio.h>)
> is an integral constant expression specifying the size of buffers used by setbuf. See the explanation of setbuf in Section 4 for more details.

CLK_TCK (found in <time.h>)
> is a constant expression giving the number of "clock ticks" in a second. See the explanation of the clock function in Section 4 for more details.

EDOM (found in <errno.h>)
> is a nonzero integral constant expression assigned to errno to indicate an invalid argument value.

EOF (found in <stdio.h>)
> is a negative integral constant expression returned by input functions when end-of-file is reached. It may also be returned if an error takes place during an I/O operation.

ERANGE (found in <errno.h>)
> is a nonzero integral constant expression assigned to errno when a function result falls outside the range of values that can be represented by the result type.

EXIT_FAILURE (found in <stdlib.h>)
> is an integral expression that may be passed as the argument to exit to indicate unsuccessful program termination. See the explanation of exit in Section 4 for more details.

EXIT_SUCCESS (found in <stdlib.h>)
> is an integral expression that may be passed as the argument to exit to indicate successful program completion. See the explanation of exit in Section 4 for more details.

FILENAME_MAX (found in <stdio.h>)
> is an integral constant expression that gives the number of characters in the longest file name string that the implementation is sure to be able to open (provided that the given string meets all the other requirements that the system imposes on file names).

FOPEN_MAX (found in `<stdio.h>`)
>   is an integral constant expression giving the minimum number of files that the implementation guarantees can be open simultaneously. This will be at least eight.

HUGE_VAL (found in `<math.h>`)
>   is a large positive **double** constant expression, usually the largest that can be represented on the system. It is returned by some math functions when an overflow occurs (for example, if you apply the `exp` function to too large a value).

LC_ALL (found in `<locale.h>`)
>   is used by the `setlocale` function. See Section 4 for more details.

LC_COLLATE (found in `<locale.h>`)
>   is used by the `setlocale` function. See Section 4 for more details.

LC_CTYPE (found in `<locale.h>`)
>   is used by the `setlocale` function. See Section 4 for more details.

LC_MONETARY (found in `<locale.h>`)
>   is used by the `setlocale` function. See Section 4 for more details.

LC_NUMERIC (found in `<locale.h>`)
>   is used by the `setlocale` function. See Section 4 for more details.

LC_TIME (found in `<locale.h>`)
>   is used by the `setlocale` function. See Section 4 for more details.

L_tmpnam (found in `<stdio.h>`)
>   is an integral constant expression giving the size of a **char** array large enough to hold a temporary file name string produced by the `tmpnam` function. For more details, see the explanation of `tmpnam` in Section 4.

MB_CUR_MAX (found in `<limits.h>`)
>   is an integer expression giving the number of bytes in the longest multibyte character in the current locale's extended character set. This will be less than or equal to MB_LEN_MAX.

MB_LEN_MAX (found in `<limits.h>`)
>   is an integral constant expression giving the number of bytes in the longest multibyte character in any locale supported by the implementation.

NDEBUG (affects the behavior of `<assert.h>`)
>   controls the behavior of `assert` (see Section 4). If you **#define** NDEBUG as in

```
#define NDEBUG 1
```

Any subsequent calls to the `assert` macro will do nothing.

NULL (found in `<stddef.h>`)
>   is an implementation-defined null pointer constant.

RAND_MAX (found in `<stdlib.h>`)
>   is an integral constant expression giving the largest random number that the `rand` function can generate. This will be at least `32767`. See the explanation of `rand` in Section 4 for more details.

SEEK_CUR (found in `<stdio.h>`)
>   is an integral constant expression argument for `fseek` representing the current read/write position in a file. See the explanation of `fseek` in Section 4 for more details.

SEEK_END (found in `<stdio.h>`)
>   is an integral constant expression argument for `fseek` representing the end of a file. See the explanation of `fseek` for more details.

SEEK_SET (found in `<stdio.h>`)
>   is an integral constant expression argument for `fseek` representing the beginning of a file. See the explanation of `fseek` for more details.

SIGABRT (found in `<signal.h>`)
>   is a positive integral constant expression representing the signal for abnormal program termination. This signal value is sent by the `abort` function. See the explanation of `abort` in Section 4 for more details.

SIGFPE (found in `<signal.h>`)
>   is a positive integral constant expression representing the signal issued for an invalid arithmetic operation (for example, dividing by zero).

SIGILL (found in `<signal.h>`)
>   is a positive integral constant expression representing the signal issued for an invalid machine code construct. For example, SIGILL is raised if a function contains an illegal hardware instruction.

SIGINT (found in `<signal.h>`)
>   is a positive integral constant expression representing the signal issued for a user interrupt (for example, the user pressing the BREAK key on an interactive terminal).

SIGSEGV (found in `<signal.h>`)
>   is a positive integral constant expression representing the signal issued for invalid memory access (for example, using a pointer value that points outside the memory available to your program).

SIGTERM (found in <signal.h>)
> is a positive integral constant expression representing the signal issued for termination requests sent to your program (for example, by the operating system).

SIG_DFL (found in <signal.h>)
> is a pointer to a function returning **void** *. SIG_DFL indicates the default signal handler.

SIG_ERR (found in <signal.h>)
> is a pointer to a function returning **void** *. This value is returned by the signal function when the request to signal cannot be honored (for example, if you specify a signal number that is not recognized by the implementation).

SIG_IGN (found in <signal.h>)
> is a pointer to a function returning **void** *. SIG_IGN indicates a signal handler that just ignores signals.

stderr (found in <stdio.h>)
> is a FILE * expression representing the standard error stream.

stdin (found in <stdio.h>)
> is a FILE * expression representing the standard input stream.

stdout (found in <stdio.h>)
> is a FILE * expression representing the standard output stream.

TMP_MAX (found in <stdio.h>)
> is an integral constant expression giving the minimum number of unique file names that can be generated by the tmpnam function. See the explanation of tmpnam in Section 4 for more details.

_IOFBF (found in <stdio.h>)
> is an integral constant expression used by the setvbuf function. See the explanation of setvbuf in Section 4 for more details.

_IOLBF (found in <stdio.h>)
> is an integral constant expression used by the setvbuf function. See the explanation of setvbuf for more details.

_IONBF (found in <stdio.h>)
> is an integral constant expression used by the setvbuf function. See the explanation of setvbuf for more details.

chapter 4   Library Routines

Below we list the functions and macros of the **ANSI** C library in alphabetical order:

abort _____ *terminate a program*

Usage:
```
#include <stdlib.h>
void abort(void);
```

Description:
The `abort` function issues a `SIGABRT` signal. The default handler for this signal will abort the program. The **ANSI** standard purposefully does not dictate whether open I/O streams are closed or temporary files are removed—this is implementation-defined.

A program may use the `signal` function to set a different handler so that the `SIGABRT` is ignored or dealt with in some other way. The `abort` function can never return to its caller.

See Also:
```
exit, raise, signal
```

abs _____ *absolute value*

Usage:
```
#include <stdlib.h>
int abs(int i);
```

Where:
```
int i;
```
        is any signed integer.

Description:
The `abs` function returns the absolute value of its integer argument. If the result cannot be represented, the behavior is undefined.

See Also:
```
fabs, labs
```

acos _____ *arccos function*

Usage:
```
#include <math.h>
double acos(double x);
```

Where:
```
double x;
```
      is a value in the range -1.0 through $+1.0$.

Description:
      The `acos` function returns the arc cosine of x. This will be in the range 0.0 through π. If the argument is less than -1.0 or greater than $+1.0$, `acos` sets `errno` to EDOM and returns an implementation-defined value. With **C2C**, this is 0.0.

See Also:
      `asin, atan, atan2, cos, sin, tan`

asctime _____ *convert time structure into time string*

Usage:
```
#include <time.h>
char *asctime(const struct tm *loctim);
```

Where:
```
const struct tm *loctim;
```
      points to a time structure as returned by the `localtime` function. See Section 2 for more details.

Description:
      The `asctime` function returns a pointer to a 26-character string containing the date and time represented by the `loctim` structure. The format of this string is

```
Wed Apr 20 15:34:55 1992\n\0
```

In other words, the string gives the first three letters of the weekday, the first three letters of the month, the date in the month (with the first character blank for dates less than 10), the current time, and the year, followed by a new-line. The **ANSI** standard makes no allowance for non-English representations of the date.
      Since `asctime` may write its result string to the same memory location, every call to `asctime` may overwrite the old string. Calls to `ctime` may also overwrite the string.

See Also:
      `ctime, localtime, time`

asin _____ _arcsin function_

Usage:
```
#include <math.h>
double asin(double x);
```

Where:
```
double x;
```
      is a value in the range -1.0 through $+1.0$.

Description:
     The `asin` function returns the arc sine of x. This will be in the range $-\pi/2$ through $+\pi/2$. If the argument is less than -1.0 or greater than 1.0, `acos` sets `errno` to `EDOM` and returns an implementation-defined value. In **C2C**, this is 0.0.

See Also:
     `acos, atan, atan2, cos, sin, tan`

assert _____ _program verification_

Usage:
```
#include <assert.h>
void assert(int expression);   /* Macro */
```

Where:
```
int expression;
```
      is any integral expression.

Description:
     The `assert` macro determines whether the given expression is nonzero (true). If the expression is nonzero, `assert` takes no action and returns no value. If the expression is zero (false), `assert` prepares a message that contains the _expression_ as well as the name of the source file and line number where the `assert` macro appears. (The source file name and the line number used will be the current values of `__FILE__` and `__LINE__`, respectively.) The `assert` macro prints this message to `stderr`, then calls `abort` to terminate the program.
     The `assert` macro is used in debugging, to check for conditions that should not happen if your program is working correctly. Once you have debugged the program, you may get rid of all assertions by putting

```
#define NDEBUG 1
```

at the beginning of source files that use `assert`. This definition turns `assert` into a null macro (one that does nothing). This effectively removes the `assert` calls from your source code. In this way, you streamline the machine code produced for your program without actually removing your assertions. If it turns out that more debugging is necessary, you can easily activate your assertions again by removing the definition for NDEBUG.

See Also:
```
abort
```

atan _____ *arctan function*

Usage:
```
#include <math.h>
double atan(double x);
```

Where:
```
double x;
```
   can have any value.

Description:
   The atan function returns the principal value of the arc tangent of x. This will be in the range $-\pi/2$ to $+\pi/2$.

See Also:
```
acos, asin, atan2, cos, sin, tan
```

atan2 _____ *arctan function*

Usage:
```
#include <math.h>
double atan2(double y,double x);
```

Where:
```
double y,x;
```
   cannot both be zero.

Description:
   The atan2 function returns the principal value of the arc tangent of y/x. The signs of x and y are used to determine the quadrant of the return value. This is in the range $-\pi$ to $+\pi$. If x and y are 0.0, atan2 sets errno to EDOM and returns an implementation-defined value. With **C2C**, this is 0.0.

See Also:
```
acos, asin, atan, cos, sin, tan
```

atexit _____ *specify wrap-up function*

Usage:
```
#include <stdlib.h>
int atexit(void (*wrapfunc)(void));
```

Where:
```
void (*wrapfunc)(void);
```
    points to a "wrap-up" function.

Description:
    The argument of `atexit` is a pointer to a function that takes no arguments and returns no value. This function is called a **wrap-up function**. It will be invoked when your program terminates by calling `exit` or by returning from `main`. Wrap-up functions are not invoked if your program aborts (for example, by calling `abort`).

    Wrap-up functions are invoked in the reverse of the order in which they were set up with `atexit`. For example, if you set up wrap-up functions with

```
atexit(wrap1);
atexit(wrap2);
```

the function `wrap2` will be executed before `wrap1`.

    Wrap-up functions behave as if `main` has just returned, even if the program is actually terminating through a call to `exit`. As a result, it is an error for a wrap-up function to perform a `longjmp` or to attempt to access objects created with automatic storage duration in another function.

    Wrap-up functions are executed *before* the usual process of flushing and closing files that are still open when the program terminates. Thus, they may make use of these open files. Wrap-up functions are often used to perform special processing on these open files before they are automatically closed. Wrap-up functions are also used to perform miscellaneous "clean-up" operations.

    If `atexit` succeeds in setting up the wrap-up function, it returns zero; otherwise, it returns a nonzero value. Implementations must let you set up at least 32 wrap-up functions.

See Also:
    `exit`

atof _____ *convert string to floating point*

Usage:
```
#include <stdlib.h>
double atof(const char *s);
```

Where:
```
const char *s;
```
> points to a character string whose contents represent a floating point number, for example, `"1.23"`.

Description:
> The `atof` function converts the contents of `s` into a **double** value. The result of `atof` is the resulting **double** value.
>
> The string `s` may consist of any number of whitespace characters, possibly followed by a plus or minus sign, followed by a string of digits that may contain a decimal point (as recognized in the current locale), then an optional `'e'` or `'E'` possibly followed by a sign, followed by an integer. Conversion stops with the first character that cannot belong to such a number. A call to `atof` is equivalent to

```
strtod( s, (char **)NULL )
```

except for the way the two functions handle errors. If `atof` encounters an error, the value of `errno` is not changed and the program's behavior is undefined; if `strtod` encounters an error, it sets `errno` and returns an appropriate value.

See Also:
```
strtod, scanf
```

atoi _____ *convert string to integer*

Usage:
```
#include <stdlib.h>
int atoi(const char *s);
```

Where:
```
const char *s;
```
> points to a character string whose contents represent an integer, for example, `"-325"`.

Description:
> The `atoi` function converts the contents of `s` into an **int** value and returns this number. The string may consist of any number of whitespace characters, possibly followed by a plus or minus sign, followed by a string of digits. Conversion stops when the first inappropriate character is encountered. A call to `atoi` is equivalent to

```
(int) strtol( s, (char **)NULL, 10)
```

except for the way the two functions handle errors. If `atoi` encounters an error, the value of `errno` is not changed and the program's behavior is undefined; if `strtol` encounters an error, it sets `errno` and returns an appropriate value.

See Also:
        `atol, strtol, scanf`

atol _____ *convert string to long integer*

Usage:
```
#include <stdlib.h>
long atol(const char *s);
```

Where:
        `const char *s;`
                points to a character string whose contents represent a long integer, for
                example, `"-325"`.

Description:
        The `atol` function converts the contents of s into a **long** value and returns
this number. The string may consist of any number of whitespace characters, possibly
followed by a plus or minus sign, followed by a string of digits. Conversion stops
when the first inappropriate character is encountered. A call to `atol` is equivalent to

```
strtol( s, (char **)NULL, 10)
```

except for the way the two functions handle errors. If `atol` encounters an error, the
value of `errno` is not changed and the program's behavior is undefined; if `strtol`
encounters an error, it sets `errno` and returns an appropriate value.

See Also:
        `atoi, strtol, scanf`

bsearch _____ *search through table*

Usage:
```
#include <stdlib.h>
void * bsearch(const void *key,
            const void *table,
            size_t N, size_t keysize,
            int (*compar)(const void *, const void *));
```

Where:
        `const void *key;`
                points to the key you are searching for.
        `const void *table;`
                points to the beginning of a table that contains information to search.
                This table must be sorted in increasing order (according to the *compar*
                function—see below).

```
size_t N;
```
    is the number of entries in the table.
```
size_t keysize;
```
    is equal to `sizeof(*key)` (the size of the key you want to find).
```
int (*compar)();
```
    is a pointer to a function that determines whether or not two keys are equal. One of the function's arguments will point to the key you want to find and the other will point to a key in the table. The function should return a negative integer if the first argument is less than the second; it should return a positive integer if the first argument is greater than the second; and it should return zero if the two arguments are equal.

Description:

The `bsearch` function searches through the entries of a table sorted in ascending order. It uses your `compar` function to compare the `key` to entries in the table. If no entry matches the `key`, `bsearch` returns a null pointer. Otherwise, it returns a pointer to an entry in the table that matches the `key`. If several entries in the table match the key, `bsearch` is allowed to return any one of them.

Note that your `compar` function does not have to do a byte-by-byte comparison between the key and the table entries. For example, the table may be an array of structures and `compar` may only look at a particular field when comparing two structures. In this case, the original search key might just be a dummy, with only the significant field filled in.

Historically, `bsearch` performed a binary search through the table (which is why the routine is called `bsearch`). However, the **ANSI** standard does not require a binary search technique, so individual implementations may use different algorithms.

See Also:

    qsort

calloc _____ *allocate storage for array*

Usage:
```
#include <stdlib.h>
void *calloc(size_t N,size_t size);
```

Where:
```
size_t N;
```
    is the number of members in the array.
```
size_t size;
```
    is the size of each member.

Description:

The `calloc` function returns a pointer to space for an array of N members, each of the given size. The beginning of the array will be suitably aligned to hold any data object.

If appropriate memory cannot be obtained, `calloc` returns a `NULL` pointer. If the requested size is zero, the behavior is implementation-defined.

Each bit in the acquired space is initialized to zero. This is not necessarily the same as initializing the array members to zero. In particular, most machines do not represent the floating point `0.0` with all zero bits. More importantly, initializing a pointer to zero bits may not yield a valid pointer value. This can lead to undefined behavior if the program tries to use the pointer before giving it a valid pointer value.

See Also:
        free, malloc, realloc

ceil _____ *ceiling function*

Usage:
        #include <math.h>
        double ceil(double x);

Where:
        double x;
                is any value.

Description:
        The `ceil` function returns a **double** result representing the smallest integral value greater than or equal to `x`.

See Also:
        floor, fmod

clearerr _____ *clear error flag on stream*

Usage:
        #include <stdio.h>
        void clearerr(FILE *stream);

Where:
        FILE *stream;
                indicates the I/O stream whose error flag is to be cleared.

Description:
        The `clearerr` function clears the error indication flag for the specified stream. This is one of the few ways to clear an error indication flag once an error is detected. If `clearerr` is not called, I/O operations on the stream will keep returning an error value until the stream is closed (with `fclose`) or rewound (with `rewind`).

See Also:
        ferror, feof, fclose, rewind

clock _____ *determine processor time*

Usage:
```
#include <time.h>
clock_t clock(void);
```

Description:
The `clock` function returns the implementation's best approximation of the processor time used since some implementation-defined point in program execution. In some sense, this is the processor time used by the program thus far, although the starting point for timing may not be precisely the start of program execution.

The time is expressed in "clock ticks." There are `CLK_TCK` ticks per second, where `CLK_TCK` is a manifest defined in `<time.h>`. The `clock_t` type is an integral type defined in `<time.h>`—see Section 2 for more details.

If a time cannot be determined or represented, `clock` returns `-1` cast to the `clock_t` type.

cos _____ *cosine function*

Usage:
```
#include <math.h>
double cos(double x);
```

Where:
```
double x;
```
represents an angle expressed in radians.

Description:
The `cos` function returns the cosine of `x`. If `x` is large, the result may lose some or all of its significance.

See Also:
`acos, asin, atan, atan2, sin, tan`

cosh _____ *hyperbolic cosine function*

Usage:
```
#include <math.h>
double cosh(double x);
```

Where:
```
double x;
```
can be any value.

Description:
The cosh function returns the hyperbolic cosine of x. If the result is too large to represent as a **double** value, cosh sets errno to ERANGE and returns the number HUGE_VAL (defined in <math.h>).

See Also:
sinh, tanh, cos

ctime _____ *convert time into a string*

Usage:
```
#include <time.h>
char *ctime(const time_t *time_num);
```

Where:
```
const time_t *time_num;
```
points to a time number, as returned by the time function.

Description:
The ctime function returns a pointer to a date-and-time string that corresponds to the time number given in *time_num. The format of the date-and-time string is the same as that returned by asctime.
The ctime function may write its result string to the same memory location every time it is called, overwriting the old string. The asctime function may also overwrite this string.

See Also:
asctime, localtime, time

difftime _____ *difference between two times*

Usage:
```
#include <time.h>
double difftime(time_t time2, time_t time1);
```

Where:
```
time_t time1, time2;
```
are time numbers as returned by the time function.

Description:
The difftime function returns a **double** value giving the number of seconds that passed from time1 to time2. This will be negative if time2 came before time1.

See Also:
ctime, mktime, time

div _____ *system-independent integer division*

Usage:
```
#include <stdlib.h>
div_t div(int top,int bottom);
```

Where:
    `int top;`
        is the numerator of the division.
    `int bottom;`
        is the denominator of the division.

Description:
    The `div` function performs the integer division of `top` divided by `bottom`. The result of `div` has a structure type named `div_t`, defined in `<stdlib.h>` with the members

```
int quot;   /*quotient*/
int rem;    /*remainder*/
```

(in either order). The `quot` element is the integer quotient of the division and the `rem` element is the remainder. The remainder always has the same sign as the result of the division (which is not true of `A%B` in some implementations). The quotient is defined so that

```
top == quot*bottom + rem
```

When the division is inexact, this means that the quotient is always adjusted towards 0. Thus

```
div(9,5).quot  == +1
div(-9,5).quot == -1
```

If the result of the division cannot be represented, the behavior is undefined.

See Also:
    `ldiv`

exit _____ *terminate program execution*

Usage:
```
#include <stdlib.h>
void exit(int status);
```

Where:
```
int status;
```
> is a status that will be returned to the host environment. A status of EXIT_SUCCESS indicates normal program termination. A status of EXIT_FAILURE indicates program failure. Other status values may be supported by some implementations.

Description:

The exit function terminates program execution and returns the status value to the host environment.

The function begins its work by calling all the clean-up functions specified by atexit routines, in the reverse order that the functions were specified (so that the most recently specified clean-up function is executed first). These clean-up functions are executed in an environment that makes it look as if main has just returned. This means that automatic storage duration objects created by the program may not be accessed legally.

Next, exit flushes all I/O buffers and closes any streams that are currently open. Files created with the tmpfile function are removed.

Lastly, control is returned to the host environment. The environment receives the status value indicating the success of the program. Nonzero status values have implementation-defined meanings.

See Also:
```
abort, atexit, tmpfile
```

exp _____ *exponential function*

Usage:
```
#include <math.h>
double exp(double x);
```

Where:
```
double x;
```
> is any floating point value.

Description:

The exp function returns the exponential of x (**e** to the power of x). If the result is too large to represent as a **double** value, exp sets errno to ERANGE and returns HUGE_VAL (defined in <math.h>).

See Also:
```
log, log10, pow
```

fabs _____ *floating point absolute value*

Usage:
```
#include <math.h>
double fabs(double x);
```

Where:
```
double x;
```
>   is any floating point number.

Description:
>   The fabs function returns the absolute value of x.

See Also:
```
abs, labs
```

fclose _____ *flush and close a stream*

Usage:
```
#include <stdio.h>
int fclose(FILE *stream);
```

Where:
```
FILE *stream;
```
>   indicates the I/O stream to be closed.

Description:
>   The fclose function flushes all buffers associated with the given stream, then closes the associated file. In the process, any unwritten buffered output is written to the associated file; any unread buffered input is discarded. If the associated buffers were automatically allocated, they are freed.
>   The function returns a 0 if the stream is closed successfully, and a nonzero value otherwise.

See Also:
```
fopen, fflush
```

feof _____ *check for end-of-file on stream*

Usage:
```
#include <stdio.h>
int feof(FILE *stream);
```

Where:
```
FILE *stream;
```
>   indicates the I/O stream to be checked.

Description:
    The `feof` function returns a nonzero value if the indicated stream is at end-of-file, and 0 otherwise.

See Also:
    `ferror`

ferror _____ *check for error on stream*

Usage:
```
#include <stdio.h>
int ferror(FILE *stream);
```

Where:
    `FILE *stream;`
        indicates the I/O stream to be checked.

Description:
    The `ferror` function returns a nonzero value if the error indicator is set for the specified stream. Otherwise, it returns 0.

See Also:
    `clearerr, feof`

fflush _____ *flush an output or update stream*

Usage:
```
#include <stdio.h>
int fflush(FILE *stream);
```

Where:
    `FILE *stream;`
        indicates the I/O stream to be flushed.

Description:
    When `fflush` is applied to an output or update stream, any buffered output is delivered to the execution environment so it can actually be written to the output device. The stream remains open after the flushing operation.
    When `fflush` is applied to an input stream, the behavior is undefined.
    If a write error occurs, `fflush` returns EOF; otherwise, it returns 0.
    See Section 1.3.2 for more information about buffers.

See Also:
    `fclose, setbuf, setvbuf, ungetc`

fgetc _____ _get a character from input_

Usage:
```
#include <stdio.h>
int fgetc(FILE *stream);
```

Where:
```
FILE *stream;
```
indicates the stream you want to read.

Description:
The fgetc function obtains the next character from an input stream. The character is obtained as **unsigned char**, then converted to **int**.

If the stream is at end-of-file or if there is a read error when obtaining the character, fgetc returns EOF. The feof and ferror functions can be used to distinguish between a read error and end-of-file.

See Also:
```
feof, ferror, fputc, getc, getchar
```

fgetpos _____ _get current read/write position_

Usage:
```
#include <stdio.h>
int fgetpos(FILE *stream,fpos_t *pos);
```

Where:
```
FILE *stream;
```
indicates the stream whose position you wish to determine.
```
fpos_t *pos;
```
points to a location where fgetpos can store the position information.

Description:
The fgetpos function notes the current read/write position of stream and stores this information in the object indicated by pos. Information obtained through fgetpos can be used by the fsetpos function to return to this same position.

The result of fgetpos is zero if the read/write position is successfully saved. If the operation fails, fgetpos returns a nonzero value and stores an implementation-defined positive value in errno.

The information stored by fgetpos has an implementation-defined format. There is no guarantee that this information may be useful in any other way except as an argument to fsetpos.

The fgetpos function is similar to ftell. The difference is that ftell must represent the current read/write position as a **long** value, whereas fgetpos uses the implementation-defined fpos_t type. Since fpos_t presumably represents the read/write position in a form that is specifically tailored to the execution environment, fgetpos and its partner fsetpos are usually preferable to ftell and fseek.

See Also:
        fsetpos, ftell

fgets _____ *get a string from input*

Usage:
        #include <stdio.h>
        char *fgets(char *string,int N,FILE *stream);

Where:
        char *string;
                points to an area of memory that will receive the string you read.
        int N;
                is the maximum length of the input string, in bytes.
        FILE *stream;
                indicates the stream you want to read.

Description:
        The fgets function reads up to N-1 characters from an input stream and stores them in the memory indicated by string. The function will stop reading if it encounters end-of-file or a new-line character before N-1 characters have been read. The last character read into string will be followed by the usual ' \0'.
        If the string is read successfully, fgets returns the string pointer value . It also returns the string pointer value if end-of-file is reached after reading in some characters.
        If end-of-file is reached before any characters have been read into *string, fgets returns a null pointer and the existing contents of *string are unchanged.
        If a read error takes place, fgets also returns a null pointer. In this case, the contents of *string are indeterminate.

See Also:
        fgetc, fputs

floor _____ *floor function*

Usage:
        #include <math.h>
        double floor(double x);

Where:
        double x;
                is any value.

Description:
The floor function returns a **double** result representing the largest integral value less than or equal to x.

See Also:
ceil, fmod

fmod _____ *floating point remainder*

Usage:
```
#include <math.h>
double fmod(double x,double y);
```

Where:
```
double x,y;
```
can be any floating point values.

Description:
The fmod function is the floating point analog of the % integer remainder operation. If y is zero, the situation is implementation-defined: fmod may set errno to EDOM or it may return 0.0. In y is nonzero, fmod returns a **double** value z such that

$$x \ == \ z \ + \ N*y$$

for some integral value N. The magnitude of z will be less than the magnitude of y, and z will have the same sign as x. (This means the division that fmod performs is truncated towards zero.) Some examples of fmod are given below:

```
fmod( 7.0, 3.0)     ==  1.0
fmod(-7.0, 3.0)     == -1.0
fmod(-7.0,-3.0)     == -1.0
fmod( 7.0,-3.0)     ==  1.0
```

fopen _____ *open a file for I/O*

Usage:
```
#include <stdio.h>
FILE *fopen(const char *name,const char *options);
```

Where:
```
const char *name;
```
is a string giving the name of the file you want to open.

```
const char *options;
```
is a string specifying whether the file should be opened for reading, writing, or update (see below).

Description:

The `fopen` function opens a file for subsequent reading, writing, or update. If the open operation is successful, `fopen` returns a pointer to a `FILE` information block for the stream. If the open operation fails, `fopen` returns a null `FILE` pointer.

If you try to open a file for output but the file does not exist, `fopen` will create the file; however, `fopen` will not create a file that is being opened for reading.

The `options` argument is a string telling how the file should be opened. The following option strings are recognized by the **ANSI** standard:

`"r"`   open text stream for reading.

`"w"`   open text stream for writing. Data written to the file will overwrite the file's current contents (if any).

`"a"`   open text stream for appending. Data written to the file will be added onto the end of the file's current contents (if any).

`"r+"`   open text stream for both reading and writing. This is called an **update** option because it can be used to examine and modify a file's current contents. When the file has been opened, the stream will be positioned so that a read operation will read the first data in the file. The file must already exist; it will not be created.

`"w+"`   open text stream for reading and writing. With this mode, the current contents of the file are effectively destroyed at the time that the file is opened. Therefore you will only be able to read from the file after you have written some data there. If the file does not already exist, it will be created.

`"a+"`   open text stream for reading and appending. The stream is positioned at the end of the file's current contents. If the file does not exist, it will be created.

`"rb"`   open binary stream for reading.

`"wb"`   open binary stream for writing.

`"ab"`   open binary stream for appending.

`"rb+"`   open binary stream for update (reading and writing). Also written `"r+b"`.

`"wb+"`   open binary stream for update and discard current file contents. Also written `"w+b"`.

`"ab+"`   open binary stream for reading and appending. Also written `"a+b"`.

With "a" and "a+" modes, the current contents of the file cannot be overwritten. Even if you perform an I/O operation that moves backwards in the file (for example, fseek), the output routines will move to the end of the file before writing data.

When using one of the + modes, you may both read and write on the file. However, if you want to switch from writing to reading, you must call fflush, fseek, fsetpos, or rewind first. If you want to switch from reading to writing, you must also call one of these functions unless the last read operation encountered end-of-file.

A stream will always be fully buffered when it is opened, except when the stream may be associated with an interactive device (for example, a terminal).

Individual implementations may accept additional options. Such options will consist of one of the options given above, followed by additional characters.

See Also:
    fclose, fflush, freopen, fseek, rewind

fprintf _____ *formatted output to a file*

Usage:
```
#include <stdio.h>
int fprintf(FILE *stream,const char *format, ...);
```

Where:
    FILE *stream;
        indicates the stream to which output should be written.
    const char *format;
        is a printf-style format string.
    ...
        is a variable argument list giving the values to be written.

Description:
The fprintf function writes a formatted string to the specified stream. Arguments are converted, formatted, and printed under control of the string format. For a full description of this formatting, see the description of printf.

The result of fprintf is the number of characters written. A negative number is returned if an output error occurs.

See Also:
    fopen, fclose, fscanf, sprintf, vfprintf

fputc _____ *output a character to stream*

Usage:
```
#include <stdio.h>
int fputc(int c,FILE *stream);
```

Where:
>   int c;
>> is the character to be written out.
>   FILE *stream;
>> is the output stream where the character should be written.

Description:
> The fputc function converts c to **unsigned char** and writes it to the indicated stream. The result of fputc is the character that is written out. If a write error occurs, fputc returns EOF.

See Also:
>   fgetc, putc

---

fputs _____ *output a string*

Usage:
>   #include <stdio.h>
>   int fputs(const char *string,FILE *stream);

Where:
>   const char *string;
>> is the string you want to write out.
>   FILE *stream;
>> is the stream where the string should be written.

Description:
> The fputs function outputs a string to a file. The string must end with the usual '\0', but this character is not written out. If the write fails, fputs returns EOF; otherwise, it returns a non-negative value.

See Also:
>   fgets, fputc

---

fread _____ *read an array from a stream*

Usage:
>   #include <stdio.h>
>   size_t fread(void *ptr,size_t size,
>   size_t count,FILE *stream);

Where:
>   void *ptr;
>> points to an area of memory that is large enough to hold the data read.

```
size_t size;
```
     is the size of one array member.
```
size_t count;
```
     is the number of members in the array.
```
FILE *stream;
```
     is the input stream that should be read.

Description:
     The `fread` function reads an array into the memory indicated by `ptr`. The result of `fread` is the number of array members read. This will be equal to `count` unless a read error occurs or end-of-file is reached before reading the desired number of members. In this case, use `ferror` and/or `feof` to determine which of the two possibilities took place. If `size` or `count` is zero, `fread` returns `0` and does not change the contents of the memory indicated by `ptr`.

See Also:
     `fwrite, feof, ferror`

free   *free allocated space*

Usage:
```
#include <stdlib.h>
void free(void *ptr);
```

Where:
```
void *ptr;
```
        points to memory previously allocated by `malloc`, `calloc`, or `realloc`. If `ptr` does not refer to memory allocated by these functions, the behavior is undefined. If `ptr` is `NULL`, `free` takes no action.

Description:
     The `free` function releases a dynamically allocated chunk of memory. Once memory has been freed, the program may no longer use the contents of the memory. If you use `malloc`, `calloc`, or `realloc` to obtain space, they may give you space that was freed earlier.

See Also:
     `calloc, malloc, realloc`

freopen   *reopen a previously opened file*

Usage:
```
#include <stdio.h>
FILE *freopen(const char *name,
              const char *options,
              FILE *stream);
```

Where:
```
const char *name;
```
>   is a string giving the name of the file you want to open.
```
const char *options;
```
>   is a string specifying whether the file should be opened for reading or writing. The options for freopen are the same as those for fopen.
```
FILE *stream;
```
>   is an existing stream pointer that already points to a FILE information block for the stream you are reopening.

Description:

The freopen function closes any file currently associated with stream, then opens the file specified by the name argument using the given options. The old information block is lost in the process, so the old stream can no longer be used.

The result of freopen is the FILE pointer returned when the file is opened. If the open operation fails, this will be a null pointer.

The most common use of freopen is to redirect the standard units stdin, stdout, and stderr. For example,

```
stdin = freopen("xxx","r",stdin);
```

closes the current stdin stream, opens the file xxx for reading, then assigns the new stream pointer back to the stdin variable.

Calling freopen clears the error and end-of-file indicators for the stream.

See Also:
>   fopen, fclose

frexp _____ *obtain mantissa and base 2 exponent*

Usage:
```
#include <math.h>
double frexp(double x,int *expptr);
```

Where:
```
double x;
```
>   is a floating point number.
```
int *expptr;
```
>   points to an integer. The integer exponent will be stored in this location.

Description:

The frexp function factors x into the form $y*2^N$ where y is a **double** number greater than or equal to 0.5 and strictly less than 1.0. The integer exponent N is stored in the location indicated by expptr. The mantissa y is returned as the result of frexp.

If x is zero, frexp will set *expptr to 0 and will return 0.0.

See Also:
> ldexp, modf

fscanf _____*formatted input conversion*

Usage:
```
#include <stdio.h>
int fscanf(FILE *stream,const char *format, ...);
```

Where:
> FILE *stream;
>> is the stream from which you want to read.
>
> const char *format;
>> is a format string similar to that for scanf.
>
> ...
>> is a variable argument list of pointers to data objects.

Description:
> The fscanf function reads from an input stream, converts the data according to the given format string, and assigns the results to the locations in memory indicated by the pointers in the variable argument list. For a full description of fscanf format strings, see the explanation of scanf.
>
> The result of fscanf is the number of input items successfully matched and assigned. This may be less than the number of placeholders in the format string, if there is a conflict between the format string and the actual input. If end-of-file is encountered before a format conflict occurs or before an input item can be read, fscanf returns EOF.

See Also:
> fprintf, scanf, sscanf

fseek _____*reposition I/O stream*

Usage:
```
#include <stdio.h>
int fseek(FILE *stream,long offset,int origin);
```

Where:
> FILE *stream;
>> refers to the stream you want to reposition.
>
> long offset;
>> is a measure of distance, as returned by ftell. See below for further discussion.

```
int origin;
```
      is a manifest telling `fseek` where to start moving: the beginning of the file, the current read/write location, or the end of the file (see below).

Description:
      The `fseek` function repositions the read/write location for `stream`. After an `fseek`, input or output operations will likely take place at a different position in the associated file.
      The `origin` argument indicates the point from which `fseek` should begin its operation. There are three possible values, represented by manifests defined in `<stdio.h>`:

SEEK_SET
      moves a distance of `offset` from the beginning of the file. In this case, `offset` must be positive or zero.

SEEK_CUR
      moves a distance of `offset` from the current position in the file. `offset` may be positive or negative or zero.

SEEK_END
      moves a distance of `offset` from the end of the file. The `offset` may have any value, but positive values move the read/write position beyond the current end of the file. Implementations need not support seek operations that use SEEK_END on binary streams.

With binary streams, `offset` represents a byte offset from `origin`. With text streams, the `offset` value may only be `0L` or a value returned by an earlier call to `ftell` (in which case the `origin` must be SEEK_SET).
      The `fseek` function undoes any effects of `ungetc`. The result of `fseek` is 0 if the operation is successful, and nonzero if the request fails for any reason. A successful call to `fseek` clears the end-of-file indicator on `stream`.

See Also:
      `fsetpos, ftell, ungetc`

fsetpos _____ *seek to new read/write position*

Usage:
```
#include <stdio.h>
int fsetpos(FILE *stream,const fpos_t *pos);
```

Where:
```
FILE *stream;
```
      indicates the stream that you wish to reposition.
```
const fpos_t *pos;
```
      points to positioning information as returned by `fgetpos`.

Description:
The fsetpos function moves the read/write position of stream to the location indicated by the information in pos. The information in pos must have been obtained by a previous call to fgetpos.

Using fsetpos on a stream automatically clears the end-of-file indicator on that stream. It also undoes the effects of any calls to ungetc on that stream. After a call to fsetpos on an update stream, the program may read or write the stream.

If fsetpos is successful, it returns zero. If the operation fails, it returns a nonzero value and stores an implementation-defined positive value in errno.

See Also:
fgetpos, fseek

ftell _____ *determine read/write position*

Usage:
```
#include <stdio.h>
long ftell(FILE *stream);
```

Where:
```
FILE *stream;
```
is the stream whose read/write position you want to determine.

Description:
The ftell function returns a measure of the distance between the beginning of a file and the current read/write position. For a binary stream, this is the number of characters from the beginning of the file. For a text stream, this is an implementation-defined value that may only be meaningful to fseek. The difference between two ftell values in a text stream may not be a meaningful measure of the number of characters between the two stream positions.

If ftell cannot determine the current read/write position (or cannot represent the position meaningfully), it sets errno to an implementation-defined value and returns −1L.

See Also:
fgetpos, fseek

fwrite _____ *write array members to a stream*

Usage:
```
#include <stdio.h>
size_t fwrite(const void *ptr,
              size_t size,size_t count,
              FILE *stream);
```

Where:
```
const void *ptr;
```
points to the array whose contents you wish to write out.
```
size_t size;
```
is the size of a single array member.
```
size_t count;
```
is the number of array members you want to write.
```
FILE *stream;
```
is the stream to which the data should be written.

Description:

The `fwrite` function writes out a number of array members. The result of `fwrite` is the number of members written. This will be equal to `count` unless a write error occurs during the operation.

See Also:
```
fread, fseek, ftell
```

getc _____ *get a character from an input stream*

Usage:
```
#include <stdio.h>
int getc(FILE *stream);
```

Where:
```
FILE *stream;
```
is the stream to be read.

Description:

The `getc` function obtains the next character from an input stream. It behaves like `fgetc`, except that `getc` might be implemented as a macro which evaluates `stream` more than one, while `fgetc` will not be.

If the input stream is at end-of-file or there is a read error, `getc` returns EOF.

See Also:
```
fgetc, getchar, putc
```

getchar _____ *get a character from standard input*

Usage:
```
#include <stdio.h>
int getchar(void);
```

Description:

The `getchar` function is equivalent to `getc(stdin)`.

See Also:
        getc, putchar

getenv _____ *get value of environment variable*

Usage:
        #include <stdlib.h>
        char *getenv(const char *name);

Where:
        const char *name;
            is the name of an environment variable.

Description:
        The getenv function searches an **environment variable list** to determine the value associated with the environment variable whose name is given by the name argument. The way in which environment variables are created, stored, and assigned values is implementation-defined.
        The result of getenv is a pointer to a character string that holds the value associated with name. If there is no environment variable with the given name, getenv returns a null pointer.
        Calls to getenv may overwrite strings returned by previous calls to getenv.

gets _____ *get a string from standard input*

Usage:
        #include <stdio.h>
        char *gets(char *string);

Where:
        char *string;
            points to an area of memory that will hold the input string.

Description:
        The gets function reads a string into *string and returns a pointer to this string. Collection of the string begins at the current read/write location for stdin and ends when gets encounters a new-line character ('\n') or end-of-file. The string is terminated with '\0' (replacing the new-line character, if there was one).
        If end-of-file is encountered before any characters have been read in, gets returns a null pointer and the contents of *string remain unchanged. If a read error is encountered, gets also returns a null pointer and the contents of *string will be indeterminate.

See Also:
        fgets, fputs, puts

gmtime _____ *obtain Coordinated Universal Time (UTC)*

Usage:
```
#include <time.h>
struct tm *gmtime(const time_t *time_num);
```

Where:
```
const time_t *time_num;
```
  points to a time number as returned by the `time` function.

Description:
  The `gmtime` function returns a pointer to a time structure that expresses the Coordinated Universal Time (UTC) equivalent of the time number in `*time_num`. The layout of a time structure is given in Section 2.
  Both `gmtime` and `localtime` may use the same static buffer to hold the `tm` structure. Thus each call to `gmtime` and `localtime` may overwrite the results of the previous call.
  If UTC time cannot be determined, `gmtime` returns a null pointer.

See Also:
  `asctime, localtime, mktime, time`

isalnum _____ *is this an alphanumeric character*

Usage:
```
#include <ctype.h>
int isalnum(int c);
```

Where:
```
int c;
```
  is the character to be tested. It may be derived from an **unsigned char** value in the current locale's extended character set, or else it may be equal to the EOF manifest.

Description:
  The `isalnum` function returns a nonzero value if c is a digit or a letter (as defined in the current locale), and returns 0 otherwise.

See Also:
  `isalpha, isdigit`

isalpha _____ *is this an alphabetic character*

Usage:
```
#include <ctype.h>
int isalpha(int c);
```

Where:
```
int c;
```
> is the character to be tested. It may be derived from an **unsigned char** value in the current locale's extended character set, or else it may be equal to the EOF manifest.

Description:
   The isalpha function returns a nonzero value if c is a letter (as defined in the current locale); otherwise, it returns zero. In the "C" locale, the letters consist of the upper- and lowercase letters of the minimum character set.

See Also:
   isalnum, islower, isupper

---

iscntrl _____ *is this a control character*

Usage:
```
#include <ctype.h>
int iscntrl(int c);
```

Where:
```
int c;
```
> is the character to be tested. It may be derived from an **unsigned char** value in the current locale's extended character set, or else it may be equal to the EOF manifest.

Description:
   The iscntrl function returns a nonzero value if c is a control character, and returns 0 otherwise. The control characters are a locale-specific set of characters that are not printable characters. In the "C" locale, the set of control characters is implementation-defined.

isdigit _____ *is this a digit*

Usage:
```
#include <ctype.h>
int isdigit(int c);
```

Where:
```
int c;
```
> is the character to be tested. It may be derived from an **unsigned char** value in the current locale's extended character set, or else it may be equal to the EOF manifest.

Description:

The `isdigit` function returns a nonzero value if c is one of the digits `'0'` through `'9'`, and returns 0 otherwise.

See Also:

`isalnum, isxdigit`

`isgraph` _____ *is this a printable nonblank character*

Usage:

```
#include <ctype.h>
int isgraph(int c);
```

Where:

`int c;`

is the character to be tested. It may be derived from an **unsigned char** value in the current locale's extended character set, or else it may be equal to the EOF manifest.

Description:

The `isgraph` function returns a nonzero value if c is printable but is not a space; otherwise, it returns 0.

See Also:

`isprint`

`islower` _____ *is this a lowercase letter*

Usage:

```
#include <ctype.h>
int islower(int c);
```

Where:

`int c;`

is the character to be tested. It may be derived from an **unsigned char** value in the current locale's extended character set, or else it may be equal to the EOF manifest.

Description:

The `islower` function returns a nonzero value if c is a lowercase letter, and returns 0 otherwise. The set of characters that are considered lowercase letters is locale-specific. In the "C" locale, the set consists of the 26 lowercase letters of the English alphabet.

See Also:

`isupper, tolower, toupper`

isprint _____ *is this a printable character*

Usage:
```
#include <ctype.h>
int isprint(int c);
```

Where:
```
int c;
```
        is the character to be tested. It may be derived from an **unsigned char** value in the current locale's extended character set, or else it may be equal to the EOF manifest.

Description:
        The isprint function returns a nonzero value if c is printable; otherwise, it returns 0. For the purposes of isprint, a space is a printable character.

See Also:
```
isgraph
```

ispunct _____ *is this a punctuation character*

Usage:
```
#include <ctype.h>
int ispunct(int c);
```

Where:
```
int c;
```
        is the character to be tested. It may be derived from an **unsigned char** value in the current locale's extended character set, or else it may be equal to the EOF manifest.

Description:
        The ispunct function returns a nonzero value if c is a punctuation character, and returns 0 otherwise. A punctuation character is a printable character that is not a space, and is not alphanumeric.

See Also:
```
isalnum, isspace
```

isspace _____ *is this a whitespace character*

Usage:
```
#include <ctype.h>
int isspace(int c);
```

Where:
```
int c;
```
> is the character to be tested. It may be derived from an **unsigned char** value in the current locale's extended character set, or else it may be equal to the EOF manifest.

Description:
> The isspace function returns a nonzero value if c is a whitespace character, and returns 0 otherwise. In the "C" locale, the whitespace characters are the space, formfeed ′\f′, new-line ′\n′, carriage return ′\r′, horizontal tab ′\t′, and vertical tab ′\v′. In other locales, the whitespace characters must include the whitespace characters of the "C" locale; in addition, they may include an implementation-defined set of characters for which isalnum returns false.

See Also:
```
isalnum
```

isupper _____ *is this an uppercase letter*

Usage:
```
#include <ctype.h>
int isupper(int c);
```

Where:
```
int c;
```
> is the character to be tested. It may be derived from an **unsigned char** value in the current locale's extended character set, or else it may be equal to the EOF manifest.

Description:
> The isupper function returns a nonzero value if c is an uppercase letter, and returns 0 otherwise. The set of characters that are considered uppercase letters is locale-specific. In the "C" locale, the set consists of the 26 uppercase letters of the English alphabet.

See Also:
```
islower, tolower, toupper
```

isxdigit _____ *is this a hexadecimal digit*

Usage:
```
#include <ctype.h>
int isxdigit(int c);
```

Where:
```
int c;
```
    is the character to be tested. It may be derived from an **unsigned char** value in the current locale's extended character set, or else it may be equal to the EOF manifest.

Description:
    The isxdigit function returns a nonzero value if c is one of the digits ' 0 ' through ' 9 ', or one of the letters ' a ' through ' f ' or ' A ' through ' F '.

See Also:
```
isdigit
```

labs _____ *absolute value of long integer*

Usage:
```
#include <stdlib.h>
long labs(long n);
```

Where:
```
long n;
```
    is any long integer.

Description:
    The labs function returns the absolute value of n. If the result cannot be represented as a **long** integer, the behavior is undefined.

See Also:
```
abs, fabs
```

ldexp _____ *multiply double by power of 2*

Usage:
```
#include <math.h>
double ldexp(double x,int N);
```

Where:
```
double x;
```
    is any floating point value.
```
int N;
```
    is an integer.

Description:
    The ldexp function returns the quantity $x*2^N$. If the result of this calculation is too large to represent as **double**, ldexp sets errno to ERANGE and returns positive or negative HUGE_VAL (depending on the sign of x).

See Also:
        frexp, modf, pow

ldiv _____ *system-independent long integer division*

Usage:
        #include <stdlib.h>
        ldiv_t ldiv(long top, long bottom);

Where:
        long top;
                is the numerator of the division.
        long bottom;
                is the denominator of the division.

Description:
        The ldiv function performs the long integer division of top divided by bottom. The result of ldiv has a structure type named ldiv_t, defined in <stdlib.h> with the members

                long quot;   /*quotient*/
                long rem;   /*remainder*/

(in either order). The quot element is the integer quotient of the division and the rem element is the remainder. The remainder always has the same sign as the result of the division (which is not true of A%B in some implementations). The quotient is defined so that

                top == quot*bottom + rem

When the division is inexact, this means that the quotient is always adjusted towards 0L. Thus

                ldiv(9,5).quot   ==   1L
                ldiv(-9,5).quot == -1L

If the result of the division cannot be represented, the result of ldiv is undefined.

See Also:
        div

localeconv _____ *determine formatting conventions*

Usage:
```
#include <locale.h>
struct lconv *localeconv(void);
```

Description:
The localeconv function returns a pointer to an lconv structure describing the numeric and monetary formatting conventions currently active. Numeric conventions are set with the setlocale function and the LC_NUMERIC class argument. Monetary conventions are set with the setlocale function and the LC_MONETARY class argument. The contents of an lconv structure are described in Section 2.

User code may not change the contents of the lconv structure pointed to by the pointer returned by localeconv. Calls to setlocale with the LC_NUMERIC, LC_MONETARY or LC_ALL class may overwrite the contents of this lconv structure. Calls to localeconv may also overwrite the contents of this structure.

See Also:
```
setlocale
```

localtime _____ *obtain local time*

Usage:
```
#include <time.h>
struct tm *localtime(const time_t *time_num);
```

Where:
```
const time_t *time_num;
```
points to a time number as returned by the time function.

Description:
The localtime function returns a pointer to a time structure that corresponds to the local equivalent of the time number in *time_num. The layout of a time structure is given in Section 2.

Both localtime and gmtime may use the same static buffer to hold the tm structure. Thus each call to localtime and gmtime may overwrite the results of the previous call.

See Also:
```
gmtime, mktime, time
```

log _____ *natural logarithm function*

Usage:
```
#include <math.h>
double log(double x);
```

Where:
```
double x;
```
> is a positive floating point number.

Description:
> The log function returns the natural logarithm of x. If x is negative, log sets errno to EDOM. If x is zero, log sets errno to ERANGE.

See Also:
```
exp, log10
```

log10 _____ *base ten logarithm function*

Usage:
```
#include <math.h>
double log10(double x);
```

Where:
```
double x;
```
> is a positive floating point number.

Description:
> The log10 function returns the base ten logarithm of x. If x is negative, log10 sets errno to EDOM. If x is zero, log10 sets errno to ERANGE.

See Also:
```
exp, log
```

longjmp _____ *nonlocal goto*

Usage:
```
#include <setjmp.h>
void longjmp(jmp_buf snapshot,int value);
```

Where:
```
jmp_buf snapshot;
```
> is an information block that must have been previously initialized by a call to setjmp.

```
int value;
```
is returned as the value of the set jmp routine that took the snapshot. If the given value is 0, the corresponding set jmp routine will actually return the value 1.

Description:
    The longjmp function is used in conjunction with the setjmp routine to jump from one block into another, possibly from one function into another. The first step in the process is to call setjmp, as in

```
jmp_buf snapshot;
     ...
switch (setjmp(snapshot)) {
  case 0: /* Set up call */
  case 1: /* Non-local goto */
     ...
```

The set jmp routine saves the current state of the program in the information block referred to as snapshot. It then returns the value 0.
    Later in program execution, possibly in another function, you can make the call

```
longjmp(snapshot,value);
```

This jumps back to the point where set jmp was used to take the snapshot. From the program's point of view, it looks like set jmp has returned again, only this time its result is the given value instead of 0. If the value argument of the longjmp was 0, set jmp returns 1, to make sure that the program can distinguish between the set jmp that takes the snapshot and the simulated return that happens after a longjmp.
    The longjmp call must appear in the same function as the set jmp call, in a child function, in a grandchild function, or in a later descendant. You cannot longjmp to a function that has finished execution.
    When execution picks up after a longjmp, all accessible data objects will have their values at the time of the longjmp. There is one exception to this: the value of objects with automatic storage duration which do not have a **volatile** type and which have been changed between the original set jmp and the longjmp will be indeterminate.
    If you try to perform a longjmp without first using set jmp to take a snapshot, the behavior is undefined. However, you can perform set jmp calls without ever long-jumping to them.
    The **ANSI** standard guarantees that longjmp will work correctly in contexts of interrupts, signals, and associated functions. This means that longjmp is safe to use in handling single signals. However, there is no guarantee that longjmp will work correctly if execution of a signal handler is interrupted by a second signal.

See Also:
    set jmp

malloc _____ *dynamic storage allocation*

Usage:
```
#include <stdlib.h>
void *malloc(size_t size);
```

Where:
```
size_t size;
```
     specifies the number of bytes of memory you want to obtain.

Description:
     The malloc function returns a pointer to the beginning of a block of memory of the given size. This memory is aligned in such a way that it can hold any type of object.
     If memory cannot be allocated, malloc returns a NULL pointer. If the size argument is zero, the behavior is implementation-defined.

See Also:
```
calloc, free, realloc
```

mblen _____ *length of multibyte character*

Usage:
```
#include <stdlib.h>
int mblen(const char *mb,size_t N);
```

Where:
```
const char *mb;
```
     is either a null pointer or a pointer to a character string containing the multibyte character to be examined.
```
size_t N;
```
     gives a length, in bytes.

Description:
     The mblen function checks to see whether there is a valid multibyte character (in the current locale) beginning at the location indicated by mb. The function only checks the first N bytes; therefore, it will only recognize multibyte characters whose length is less than or equal to N.
     If *mb contains a valid multibyte character, mblen returns the number of bytes making up the character. This could be zero, if the string begins with ' \0'. If the first N bytes of mb do not contain a valid multibyte character from the current locale, mblen returns −1.
     Note that mblen returns a signed integer instead of an (unsigned) size_t value, as is usually used for measuring lengths.

If the mb argument is a null pointer, mblen returns 0 if multibyte characters do not have shift-dependencies, and a nonzero value otherwise.

NOTE: if the current locale has shift dependencies, mblen keeps track of the current shift state. Calling mblen with a null pointer for mb puts mblen into the initial shift state. Otherwise, the function will start out in whatever shift state it had at the end of the previous call.

See Also:
>   mbtowc, wctomb

mbstowcs _____ *convert multibyte character string to wide characters*

Usage:
```
#include <stdlib.h>
size_t mbstowcs(wchar_t *wcstring,
                const char *mbstring,
                size_t N);
```

Where:
>   wchar_t *wcstring;
>>   points to an area of memory where mbstowcs can store the wide character string result. This must be large enough to hold up to N wide characters.
>   const char *mbstring;
>>   points to a string of multibyte characters.
>   size_t N;
>>   is the maximum number of multibyte characters to convert from mbstring.

Description:
The mbstowcs function converts multibyte characters from mbstring into wide characters, and stores the wide characters in the memory indicated by wcstring. The multibyte string is assumed to begin in the initial shift state. Conversion stops when N wide characters have been stored or when mbstowcs converts a multibyte character into the null wide character (corresponding to '\0'). In this last case, the zero value will be stored in the wide character string (marking its end).

If mbstowcs encounters an invalid multibyte character as it is performing the conversions, it returns −1 cast to size_t. Otherwise, it returns the number of multibyte characters converted, not counting a final zero value (if one was found).

If mbstring overlaps wcstring, the behavior is undefined.

See Also:
>   mbtowc, wcstombs, wctomb

mbtowc _____ *convert multibyte character to wide character*

Usage:
```
#include <stdlib.h>
int mbtowc(wchar_t *wc,
           const char *mb,
           size_t N);
```

Where:
> `wchar_t *wc;`
>> is a null pointer or a pointer to a region of memory where the wide character may be stored.
>
> `const char *mb;`
>> is a null pointer or a pointer to a string that contains a multibyte character.
>
> `size_t N;`
>> gives a length, in bytes.

Description:
> The `mbtowc` function converts the multibyte character beginning at `mb` into a wide character and stores the wide character in the location indicated by `wc`. Multibyte and wide characters are interpreted according to current locale conventions.
> At most, `mbtowc` only looks at the first `N` bytes of `mb`. If `mb` does not begin with a valid multibyte character whose length is less than or equal to `N`, `mbtowc` returns −1. Otherwise, `mbtowc` will return the number of bytes in the multibyte character that was converted. This could be zero, if the string begins with `'\0'`. The result will always be less than or equal to `N` and to `MB_CUR_MAX`.
> If `wc` is null, `mbtowc` simply returns the length of the first multibyte character in the first `N` bytes of `mb`. It returns −1 if these bytes do not contain a valid multibyte character. Thus, with a null `wc`, `mbtowc` behaves like `mblen`.
> If the `mb` argument is a null pointer, `mbtowc` returns 0 if multibyte characters do not have shift-dependencies, and a nonzero value otherwise. In this case, `mbtowc` does not change the value of `*wc`.
> NOTE: if the current locale has shift dependencies, `mbtowc` keeps track of the current shift state. Calling `mbtowc` with a null pointer for `mb` puts `mbtowc` into the initial shift state. Otherwise, the function will start out in whatever shift state it had at the end of the previous call.

See Also:
> `mblen, mbstowcs, wcstombs, wctomb`

memchr _____ *first occurrence of character in object*

Usage:
```
#include <string.h>
void *memchr(const void *obj,int c,size_t N);
```

Where:
```
const void *obj;
```
points to an object in memory.
```
int c;
```
is the character you want to find.
```
size_t N;
```
is the size of the *obj object.

Description:

The memchr function converts c to **unsigned char** and returns a pointer to the first occurrence of this character in the object indicated by obj. If the character is not found in *obj, memchr returns a NULL pointer.

See Also:
```
strchr, strcspn
```

memcmp _____ *compare parts of two data objects*

Usage:
```
#include <string.h>
int memcmp(const void *obj1,
           const void *obj2,
           size_t N);
```

Where:
```
const void *obj1,*obj2;
```
point to the two data objects to be compared.
```
size_t N;
```
is the size of the two data objects.

Description:

The memcmp function compares the data object *obj1 with *obj2. Both are assumed to be N bytes long. Comparisons are made according to the ordering sequence of the execution character set, and bytes are treated as if they were **unsigned char**.

The memcmp function returns a 0 if the two objects are equal, a positive value if obj1 is greater than obj2, and a negative value if obj1 is less than obj2.

See Also:
```
strcmp, strncmp
```

memcpy _____ *copy memory*

Usage:
```
#include <string.h>
void *memcpy(void *dest,const void *src,size_t N);
```

Where:

```
void *dest;
```
> points to an area of memory into which data will be copied.

```
const void *src;
```
> points to an area of memory containing data to be copied.

```
size_t N;
```
> is the number of characters to copy.

Description:

The `memcpy` function copies N consecutive bytes from `*src` into `*dest`. If these two areas of memory overlap, the behavior is undefined. The result of `memcpy` is the value of `dest`.

See Also:

> `memmove, strcpy, strncpy`

memmove _____ *copy memory with overlap*

Usage:

```
#include <string.h>
void *memmove(void *dest,const void *src,size_t N);
```

Description:

The `memmove` function is identical to `memcpy`, except that `memmove` allows overlap between the areas `*src` and `*dest`. Copying takes place as if all the `*src` data is copied to memory that does not overlap either `*src` or `*dest`, and then all this data is copied into `*dest`.

Because `memmove` can deal with overlap, it may be slower than `memcpy`. Therefore, most programmers will only use `memmove` in situations where overlap is expected.

See Also:

> `memcpy, strcpy, strncpy`

memset _____ *set bytes to specific value*

Usage:

```
#include <string.h>
void *memset(void *mem,int c,size_t N);
```

Where:

```
void *mem;
```
> points to the beginning of the memory to be initialized.

```
int c;
```
> is the value that is to be assigned to each byte.

```
size_t N;
```
      is the number of bytes to be initialized.

Description:
      The memset function converts c to **unsigned char** and assigns the resulting character to the N bytes beginning at *mem. The result of memset is the mem pointer value.

mktime _____ *convert time structure to time number*

Usage:
```
#include <time.h>
time_t mktime(struct tm *timestruct);
```

Where:
```
struct tm *timestruct;
```
      points to a time structure as generated by gmtime.

Description:
      The mktime function converts a time structure into a time number and returns this number. The time structure is assumed to give a time in the local time zone. The layout of a time structure is given in Section 2.

      The time structure whose address is passed to mktime does not have to conform to the usual restrictions on time structures. The tm_wday and tm_yday elements are ignored as input, and therefore do not have to agree with the date as given by other elements in the structure. Similarly, other elements in the structure are not subject to their usual range restrictions; for example, tm_mon can be outside the range 0 through 11.

      When mktime is passed a pointer to a time structure that does not conform to the usual restrictions, it converts the elements in the structure so that they *do* conform. For example, if the structure refers to December 32 of some year, the elements are changed to refer to January 1 of the next year. The tm_wday and tm_yday elements are also adjusted if necessary. In this way, mktime can be used to determine the day of the week on which a particular date falls.

      If the time structure gives a time that cannot be represented as a time number, mktime returns –1 cast to time_t.

See Also:
      localtime, time

modf _____ *obtain fractional and integer part of number*

Usage:
```
#include <math.h>
double modf(double x,double *yp);
```

Where:
```
double x;
```
> is the floating point number that will be broken into parts.
```
double *yp;
```
> points to memory where `modf` can store the integer part of x.

Description:

The `modf` function returns the fractional part of x and stores the integer part in the memory location indicated by yp. Both the fractional and integer parts have the same sign as x. For example, in

```
double y, z;
z = modf(-2.5,&y);
```

z is assigned -0.5 and y is assigned -2.0.

See Also:
```
fmod, frexp, ldexp
```

offsetof _____ *offset of structure member*

Usage:
```
#include <stddef.h>
size_t offsetof(type,member);   /* Macro */
```

Where:
```
type
```
> refers to a structure type. This can be a name defined in a **typedef** statement, or it can have the form

```
struct TAG
```

```
member
```
> refers to a member in the given structure type (see below). If this is a bit field, the behavior is undefined.

Description:

The `offsetof` macro expands to an expression giving the offset (in bytes) of a member of a structure type. The result of the expression has the `size_t` type.

The `member` argument of the macro is typically the name of a member of the given type of structure. The precise technical requirements for `member` are these: if we were to declare a structure S with

```
static type S;
```

then the expression `&(S.member)` must evaluate to an address constant.

Example:
```
size_t offset;
offset = offsetof(struct tm,tm_year);
```

perror _____ ***print error message to stderr***

Usage:
```
#include <stdio.h>
void perror(const char *usermsg);
```

Where:
```
const char *usermsg;
```
        is a string that will be printed as the first part of the error message. A helpful sort of string might be the name of the program or some similar identifier.

Description:
    The `perror` function prints an error message to `stderr`, based on the current value of `errno`. Thus the message printed by `perror` reflects the last error encountered during a call to a library function.
    The `perror` function should be called immediately after the library routine that generated the error. If it isn't, errors in other library routines may change the value of `errno`, also changing the error message that is written out.
    The `usermsg` string is printed first, followed by a colon and a space; `perror` then prints the error message string as generated by the `strerror` function. If `usermsg` is a null pointer, `perror` just prints the `strerror` message.

See Also:
```
printf, strerror
```

pow _____ ***calculate number to some exponent***

Usage:
```
#include <math.h>
double pow(double x,double y);
```

Where:
```
double x;
```
        is any floating point number.
```
double y;
```
        is the exponent that will be used.

Description:
    The `pow` function returns the value of x raised to the yth power. If x is zero and y is less than or equal to zero, `errno` is set to `EDOM`, if the system cannot represent the result. `EDOM` is also assigned to `errno` if x is negative and y is not an

integer. ERANGE is assigned to errno if the result of the exponentiation cannot be represented as a **double** value.

See Also:
> exp, ldexp, log, log10

---

printf _____*formatted output to standard output*

Usage:
```
#include <stdio.h>
int printf(const char *format, ...);
```

Where:
> const char *format;
>> tells how to format the various arguments (see below).
>
> . . .
>> is a variable argument list of expressions whose values should be printed according to the placeholders in the format string. If there are more placeholders than supplied arguments, the result is undefined. If there are more arguments than placeholders, the excess arguments are simply ignored.

Description:
> The printf function writes formatted output to stdout. The result of printf is the number of characters written. If a write error occurs, printf returns a negative number.
> The output is formatted according to the format string. This is a multibyte character string beginning and ending in the initial shift state. The string may contain two kinds of objects:

(a)   ordinary multibyte characters which are simply copied to stdout;

(b)   placeholders, which tell printf how to format arguments in the variable argument list.

Each placeholder starts with the character % and ends with one or two letters that indicate what *type* of formatting is necessary. Between the % and the *type* field may appear *modifiers*, *width*, and *precision* fields. A complete placeholder has the form

> %[*modifiers*][*width*][*.precision*]*type*

where square brackets indicate that a field is optional.
> Because '%' has a special meaning to printf, you must use two of them to stand for a literal percent character. For example, you would use

```
printf("We had 100%% attendance!\n");
```

to print out the line

```
We had 100% attendance!
```

The Type Field:

Below we list the recognized *type* fields. Note that each *type* requires that the output value associated with the placeholder have a particular data type. Note also that the standard rules for passing arguments in a variable argument list automatically convert **char** and **short** values to **int**, and **float** values to **double**, so **char**, **short**, and **float** arguments are not possible.

c   **int** argument is converted to **unsigned char**, and then output. Note that this only writes a single character, even if the original **int** value held more than one character.

d   **int** argument is output as a signed decimal integer. If the number is positive, a `'+'` sign may or may not be output, depending on the value of the *modifiers* field.

e   **double** argument is output in scientific notation

```
[-]m.nnnnnne+xx
```

with one digit before the decimal point. This digit will be nonzero if the number is nonzero. The default number of digits after the decimal point is six, but this can be changed with a *precision* field. The **double** value is rounded to the required number of decimal places. The exponent always contains at least two digits, and will contain more if the exponent is greater than 99 or less than −99. If the value is zero, the exponent will be zero.

E   same as %e format, except that the `'E'` will be in uppercase instead of lower.

f   **double** argument is output in conventional form:

```
[-]mmmm.nnnnnn
```

The default number of digits after the decimal point is six, but this can be changed with a *precision* field. If a decimal point is printed, at least one digit will be printed before it. The **double** value is rounded to the required number of decimal places.

g   **double** argument is output in %e or %f format. The %e is only used if the exponent resulting from the conversion is less than −4 or greater than or equal to the *precision*; otherwise %f is used. Trailing zeros are removed from the result, and a decimal point only appears if it is followed by a digit.

G   same as %g format except that %E format is used instead of %e.

i   same as %d.

n   **int** * argument is taken to point to an integer; printf assigns this integer the number of characters that have been written to the output stream so far by this call to printf. No output is written for this placeholder.

o   **int** argument is output as an unsigned integer written with octal digits. This will not have a leading zero, unless the # *modifier* is used (see below).

p   corresponding argument is assumed to be a pointer to **void**. The value of the pointer is converted to a sequence of printable characters in an implementation-defined manner.

s   corresponding argument is assumed to be a pointer to a character type. Characters in this string will be output until a ' \0' character is found or the number of characters indicated by the *precision* field has been printed.

u   **int** argument is output as an unsigned decimal integer.

x   **int** argument is output as an unsigned integer written with hexadecimal digits, using the letters ' a' to ' f' for hex digits greater than 9. This will not have a leading ' 0x' unless the # *modifier* is used (see below).

X   same as %x except that the letters ' A' to ' F' are used for hex digits greater than 9.

hd   same as %d except that **int** argument is converted to **short** before formatting and printing.

hi   same as %hd.

hn   same as %n except that the argument is taken to be **short int** *.

ho   same as %o except that the **int** argument is converted to **unsigned short** before formatting and printing.

hu   same as %u except that the **int** argument is converted to **unsigned short** before formatting and printing.

hx   same as %x except that the **int** argument is converted to **unsigned short** before formatting and printing.

hX   same as %X except that the **int** argument is converted to **unsigned short** before formatting and printing.

ld   same as %d except argument is **long** integer.

li   same as %ld.

ln   same as %n except that the argument is taken to be **long int ***.

lo   same as %o except argument is **unsigned long** integer.

lu   same as %u except argument is **unsigned long** integer.

lx   same as %x except argument is **unsigned long** integer.

lX   same as %X except argument is **unsigned long** integer.

Le   same as %e except argument is **long double**.

LE   same as %E except argument is **long double**.

Lf   same as %f except argument is **long double**.

Lg   same as %g except argument is **long double**.

LG   same as %G except argument is **long double**.

The Modifiers Field:

The *modifiers* field consists of zero or more characters that indicate how output should be padded (for example, whether numbers are preceded by blanks or leading zeros), and whether or not ′+′ or ′-′ signs are printed. Below we list the possible *modifier* characters:

- (minus)   Indicates that values should be left-justified in the output field. The default action is to right-justify them.

+ (plus)   Relevant only for signed numeric output values. This *modifier* character tells printf to put a sign in front of the number, whether or not it is negative. Thus negative numbers will be preceded by ′-′ while zero and positive numbers will be preceded by ′+′. The default is to add the sign only if the number is negative.

  (blank)   Relevant only for signed numeric output values. This *modifier* character tells printf to put a sign in front of numbers only if they are negative. If the number is non-negative, printf will put in a blank instead of a sign. The default is not to put a blank in front of non-negative number. At least one space will be output, even if the argument is such that no output would normally be produced. If both ′+′ and ′ ′ are specified as *modifier* characters, the ′+′ overrides the ′ ′.

(sharp)   Relevant only for some numeric output values. If *type* is 'o', all nonzero values will have a leading 0; normally, octal output has no leading zero. If *type* is 'x' or 'X', all nonzero values will have a leading 0x or 0X respectively; normally, such prefixes are omitted. If *type* is 'e', 'E' or 'f', printf will always print out a decimal point (normally, the decimal point is omitted if the number has no fractional part). If *type* is 'g' or 'G', printf will always print out a decimal point and trailing zeros will not be removed; usually 'g' and 'G' remove trailing zeros. For other *type*s, the '#' *modifier* character is ignored.

0 (zero)   For all numeric conversions, leading zeros will be used to pad numbers instead of spaces. The zeros will follow any indication of sign or base. If both the '0' and '–' *modifiers* are used, the '0' will be ignored. If an integral *type* has a *precision*, the '0' *modifier* will be ignored.

The Width Field:

The *width* field is a non-negative decimal integer giving the minimum number of multibyte characters to be printed. If the output value is shorter than the given width, it is padded to the appropriate width by putting blanks on the right (or on the left, if the '–' *modifier* character is specified).

The *width* field can also be the character '*', in which case printf will take the next argument in the argument list and take that as the width value. For example,

```
printf("%*d",4,X);
```

prints the value of X with a *width* of 4. Note that the *width* value is obtained from the argument list *before* the output value is obtained.

The *width* field specifies the *minimum* number of characters to be output. If more characters are needed, the output will be wider than *width* (unless the *precision* value dictates otherwise).

The Precision Field:

The *precision* field is a dot '.' followed by a non-negative decimal integer. Its meaning depends on the *type* field as given below:

(a)   If the *type* is 'd', 'i', 'o', 'u', 'x' or 'X', the *precision* number is the smallest number of digits that may appear in the output value. If necessary, the number will be padded on the left with leading zeros. If the *precision* number is 0 or the field is just a '.' with no number following, an output value of 0 will result in no characters being printed.

(b)   If the *type* is 'e', 'E', or 'f', the *precision* number is the number of digits printed after the decimal point. If the *precision* number is 0 or the field is just a '.' with no number following, no decimal point is printed.

(c)   If the *type* is `'g'` or `'G'`, the *precision* number is the maximum number of significant digits to be printed. If the *precision* number is 0 or the field is just a `'.'` with no number following, no decimal point is printed.

(d)   If the *type* is `'s'`, the *precision* number gives the maximum number of characters to be printed.

(e)   If the *type* is an `'h'`, `'l'` or `'L'` type, the *precision* field has the same effect as it has for the type without the `'h'`, `'l'` or `'L'`.

The *precision* field can also be the character `'*'`, in which case `printf` will take the next argument in the argument list and take that as the precision value. For example,

```
printf("%*.*f",8,3,Y);
```

prints the value of Y with a *width* of 8 and a *precision* of 3.

Notes:
    If a decimal point is to be printed, `printf` will use the decimal point character for the current locale.
    If a call to `printf` produces more than 509 output characters, the operation may fail under some implementations.
    Below we list the defaults when width and/or precision fields are omitted:

```
"%1c"       "%1.1d"     "%6.6e"     "%6.6E"
"%6.6f"     "%6.6g"     "%6.6G"     "%1.1o"
"%1s"       "%1.1x"     "%1.1X"     "%1.1ld"
"%1.1lo"    "%1.1lx"    "%1.1lX"    "%6.6Le"
"%6.6LE"    "%6.6Lf"    "%6.6Lg"    "%6.6LG"
```

Example:
```
#include <stdio.h>
int i = 3, j = -1, k = 4;
char *s = "string";
float x = 3.14159265;
printf("j = %.*d, %.3s x = %10.*f",i,j,s,k,x);
    /* prints:  j = -001, str x =     3.1416 */
```

See Also:
    `fprintf, scanf, sprintf, vprintf`

---

putc _____ *output a character*

Usage:
```
#include <stdio.h>
int putc(int c,FILE *stream);
```

Where:
```
int c;
```
>   is the character you want to output.
```
FILE *stream;
```
>   is the stream to which output is written.

Description:
>   The `putc` function writes a character to the given stream. It behaves like `fputc`, except that `putc` may be implemented as a macro that evaluates `stream` more than once, while `fputc` will not be.
>   The result of `putc` is the character that was written. If a write error occurs, `putc` returns EOF.

See Also:
```
putchar, getc, fputc, printf
```

putchar _____ *output a character to standard output*

Usage:
```
#include <stdio.h>
int putchar(int c);
```

Where:
```
int c;
```
>   is the character you want to output.

Description:
>   The `putchar` function is defined so that `putchar(c)` is equivalent to `putc(c,stdout)`.

See Also:
```
getchar, putc, printf
```

puts _____ *output string to standard output*

Usage:
```
#include <stdio.h>
int puts(const char *string);
```

Where:
```
const char *string;
```
>   is the string you want to write out.

Description:

The `puts` function writes out a string to `stdout`. The string must end with a `'\0'`; this is converted into a new-line when the string is printed.

The result of `puts` is EOF if the write operation fails; otherwise, it is non-negative.

See Also:

`fputs`, `gets`, `printf`

---

qsort _____ *sort an array*

Usage:

```
#include <stdlib.h>
void qsort(void *table,size_t N,size_t size,
           int (*compar)(const void *,const void *));
```

Where:

`void *table;`

points to the array you want to sort.

`size_t N;`

is the number of members in the array.

`size_t size;`

is the size of an array member.

`int (*compar)();`

points to a function that determines whether or not two keys are equal. This function should take two **void** `*` arguments, both pointing to items in the table. The function should return a negative integer if the first argument is less than the second; it should return a positive integer if the first argument is greater than the second; and it should return zero if the two arguments are equal. This function lets `qsort` determine the order in which to sort the array.

Description:

The `qsort` function sorts the members of an array into ascending order using a user-specified comparison function. If two members of the array compare as equal, their order in the resulting array is unspecified.

This function is called `qsort` because its original implementation used a "quicksort" algorithm. However, the **ANSI** standard does not require that implementations of `qsort` use this particular technique; any sorting algorithm is acceptable.

See Also:

`bsearch`

raise _____ *issue signal*

Usage:
```
#include <signal.h>
int raise(int sig);
```

Where:
```
int sig;
```
    is the number of a signal recognized by the implementation.

Description:
    The `raise` function issues the given signal. For example, `raise` can be used to simulate exception conditions. The result of `raise` is zero if the signal was successfully issued. A nonzero value is returned if the signal could not be issued (for example, if the `sig` value is not a valid signal).

See Also:
```
signal
```

rand _____ *obtain pseudorandom number*

Usage:
```
#include <stdlib.h>
int rand(void);
```

Description:
    The `rand` function returns a pseudorandom integer in the range 0 to `RAND_MAX` (a manifest defined in `<stdlib.h>`). Each new call to `rand` returns a new number. The seed of the random number generator may be set with `srand`.

See Also:
```
srand
```

realloc _____ *change size of allocated space*

Usage:
```
#include <stdlib.h>
void *realloc(void *oldp, size_t size);
```

Where:
```
void *oldp;
```
    points to the beginning of a block of memory previously allocated by `malloc`, `calloc`, or `realloc`.
```
size_t size;
```
    is the new size you want for this memory block.

Description:

The `realloc` function returns a pointer to a block of memory of the given `size`. This size may be larger or smaller than the amount of memory in the block indicated by `oldp`. The contents of the block of memory indicated by the return value will be equal to the memory indicated by `oldp`, up to the lesser of the old and new sizes.

If `oldp` is a null pointer, `realloc` works like `malloc` and allocates a suitably aligned object of the given `size`. If `size` is zero and `oldp` is not null, the old object (`*oldp`) is freed, as with the `free` function.

If appropriate space cannot be allocated, `realloc` returns a null pointer and the object indicated by `oldp` is not changed.

See Also:

    calloc, free, malloc

remove _____ *remove file*

Usage:

    #include <stdio.h>
    int remove(const char *filename);

Where:

    const char *filename;
        is the name of the file you wish to remove.

Description:

The `remove` function makes it impossible to access the given file under the specified name. On many systems, this means deleting the file. If the operation succeeds, `remove` returns 0; otherwise, it returns a nonzero value.

Normally, a file that is being removed should not be open. If it is open, the behavior is implementation-defined.

See Also:

    rename

rename _____ *rename a file*

Usage:

    #include <stdio.h>
    int rename(const char *oldname,const char *newname);

Where:

    const char *oldname;
        is the old name of the file. This must already exist.

```
const char *newname;
```
        is the name you want to give to the file. If this already exists, the behavior is implementation-defined.

Description:
    The `rename` function changes the name of a file, if possible. The function returns 0 if the renaming operation is successful. Otherwise, it returns a nonzero value and the file retains its old name (if it exists).

See Also:
```
remove
```

rewind _____ *rewind a stream*

Usage:
```
#include <stdio.h>
void rewind(FILE *stream);
```

Where:
```
FILE *stream;
```
        is the stream you want to rewind.

Description:
    The `rewind` function adjusts the specified stream so that the next I/O operation on it will take place at the beginning of the file. In this respect, it is equivalent to

```
fseek(stream,0L,SEEK_SET);
```

except that `rewind` returns no value. The `rewind` function also clears the error indicator for the stream.

See Also:
```
fseek
```

scanf _____ *formatted read on standard input*

Usage:
```
#include <stdio.h>
int scanf(const char *format, ...);
```

Where:
```
const char *format;
```
        is a format string as described below.

. . .

is a variable argument list of pointers to data objects. If there are more pointers than placeholders in the `format` string, the extra pointers are ignored. If there are fewer pointers, the behavior will be undefined.

Description:

The `scanf` function reads input from `stdin` and assigns it to the data objects indicated by the pointers in the variable argument list. The result of `scanf` is the number of input items successfully matched and assigned. This may be less than the number of placeholders in the `format` string, if there is a conflict between the `format` string and the actual input.

The `format` string is a multibyte character string beginning and ending in the initial shift state. It tells how to interpret the characters that are read. For example, it tells whether digits should be treated as character data or converted as part of an integer.

The `format` string may contain the following:

(a)   Whitespace characters to match whitespace in the input. One or more whitespace characters in `format` match zero or more whitespace characters in the input.

(b)   Ordinary multibyte characters (not whitespace and not %). If an ordinary character is found in `format`, the next character in the input must match that character. Otherwise, `scanf` returns.

(c)   A placeholder that tells `scanf` how to interpret the next input field. The data will be interpreted accordingly, then assigned to the data object indicated by the corresponding pointer in the variable argument list.

An input field is defined as a string of nonwhitespace characters. It extends to the next inappropriate character or until the field width limit (if specified) is reached.

A placeholder starts with the % character and ends with one or two letters that indicate how the input field should be interpreted. This indicator is called the *type* field. Between the % and the *type* field may appear (in order) an asterisk * and a *width* field. A complete placeholder has the form

%[*][*width*]*type*

where square brackets indicate that a field is optional.

Because % has a special meaning to `scanf`, you must use two of them to stand for a literal percent character in the input. For example,

```
scanf("%%%d",&i)
```

reads a percent sign followed by an integer and assigns the result to `i`.

The Type Field:

Below we list recognized *type* fields. Note that each *type* requires that the pointer argument that corresponds to the placeholder should point to a particular data type.

c   A single character is expected, and the corresponding argument should be a pointer to **char**. If a field width is given, the corresponding argument should refer to a character array, into which the indicated number of characters will be read; a ′\0′ will *not* be added to the end of data read this way. If no width is given, the default is to read one character. NOTE: when reading a character with this construct, scanf does *not* skip over leading whitespace characters. If you want to skip over whitespace, use the sequence %*[ ]%c.

d   A (possibly signed) decimal integer is expected, and the corresponding argument should be a pointer to **int**.

e   A floating point number is expected, and the corresponding argument should be a pointer to **float**. The format for floating point numbers is a (possibly signed) string of digits possibly containing a decimal point, followed by an optional exponent field consisting of an ′E′ or ′e′ followed by a (possibly signed) integer. The *type*s %E, %f, %F, %g, and %G are all equivalent to %e.

i   An integer is expected. If it begins with ′0x′ or ′0X′, it will be assumed to be in hexadecimal format. If it begins with ′0′, it will be assumed to be in octal format. Otherwise, it will be assumed to be in decimal format. The corresponding argument should be a pointer to **int**.

n   No input is read. The corresponding should be a pointer to an **int**; scanf will assign this integer the number of characters read from stdin so far in this call to scanf. This will not be counted as a matched item in the result returned by scanf.

o   An octal integer is expected, and the corresponding argument should be a pointer to **unsigned int**.

p   A pointer value is expected. This pointer should be represented in the same format as is output with the %p placeholder by printf. The only time %p is valid in scanf is to read a value that was written by one of the printf family earlier in the execution of the same program. The corresponding argument should be a pointer to a **void *** item.

s   A character string is expected. The corresponding argument should be a pointer to an array of **char** large enough to hold the string and a terminating ′\0′; scanf adds the ′\0′ to terminate the string once it finds a whitespace character that is not part of the input field.

u   An unsigned decimal integer is expected, and the corresponding argument should be a pointer to **unsigned int**.

x   A hexadecimal integer is expected, and the corresponding argument should be a pointer to **unsigned int**.

hd   Same as %d, except that the corresponding argument should be a pointer to **short**.

hi   Same as %i, except that the corresponding argument should be a pointer to **short**.

hn   Same as %n, except that that corresponding argument should be a pointer to **short**.

ho   Same as %o, except that the corresponding argument should be a pointer to **unsigned short**.

hu   Same as %u, except that the corresponding argument should be a pointer to **unsigned short**.

hx   Same as %x, except that the corresponding argument should be a pointer to **unsigned short**.

ld   Same as %d, except that the corresponding argument should be a pointer to **long**.

le   Same as %e, except that the corresponding argument should be a pointer to **double**. The *type*s %lf and %lg are equivalent to %le.

LE   Same as %e, except that the corresponding argument should be a pointer to **long double**. The *type*s %LF and %LG are equivalent to %LE.

li   Same as %i, except that the corresponding argument should be a pointer to **long**.

ln   Same as %n, except that that corresponding argument should be a pointer to **long**.

lo   Same as %o, except that the corresponding argument should be a pointer to **unsigned long**.

lu   Same as %u, except that the corresponding argument should be a pointer to **unsigned long**.

lx   Same as %x, except that the corresponding argument should be a pointer to **unsigned long**.

[The opening square bracket begins a special placeholder called a *scanlist*. The bracket is followed by a set of characters and a closing square bracket '] '. The argument corresponding to a scanlist placeholder should be a pointer to a character array. If the first character is not a circumflex (' ^ '), the input field consists of all subsequent input characters until the function finds a character not in the character set within the brackets. For example,

```
%[0123456789]
```

will gather characters until it finds a character that is not a digit. A closing square bracket that comes immediately after the opening square bracket is considered part of the scanlist rather than the end of the list. For example,

```
%[])}]
```

is a scanlist that matches all three kinds of closing brackets.

If the first character inside the square brackets *is* a circumflex, the input field consists of all subsequent input characters until the function finds a character that *is* in the bracketed character set. For example,

```
%[^0123456789]
```

will gather characters until it finds a digit. Again, a closing square bracket that comes immediately after the circumflex is considered part of the scanlist.

If a scanlist contains a ' – ' character that is not immediately after the opening square bracket or the circumflex, the behavior is implementation-defined.

There must be at least one input character matching the scanlist, or a matching failure occurs (described below).

Assignment Suppression:

If the first character after the % of a placeholder is an asterisk *, a value of the appropriate width and type is read (if possible), but the value is then discarded (not assigned to any object). For example,

```
scanf("%*d %d",&i);
```

reads and discards an integer, then reads another integer and assigns the value to i.

The Width Field:

The width field is a non-negative value specifying the maximum number of characters in the input field. For example, with

```
fscanf("%3i%3i",&i,&j);
```

the input `123456` would be interpreted as two numbers: `123` and `456`. Normally, it would be considered a single six-digit number.

Failures:
There are two ways in which `scanf` may fail:

(a)   An *input failure* occurs when `scanf` cannot read any more input characters. If this happens before any data can be converted and assigned, `scanf` returns `EOF`.

(b)   A *matching failure* occurs if a normal character in the format string does not match the corresponding character in the input. It also happens if the first character to be read for an input field does not match the *type* of the placeholder.

If a matching failure occurs, the unmatchable character is left in the input stream. It will be the next character read from the stream (unless the stream is repositioned by a function like `fsetpos`).

Examples:
```
#include <stdio.h>
int i;
char s[100];
scanf("%o%s",&i,&s);
```

may be executed on the input line

```
    666      cheers!
```

to assign `666` to `i` and the string `"cheers!\0"` to `s`. On the input line

```
    0084    0084
```

the number `84` is assigned to `i` and the string `"0084\0"` is assigned to `s`.

See Also:
    `fscanf, printf, sscanf`

---

setbuf _____ *set buffer*

Usage:
```
#include <stdio.h>
void setbuf(FILE *stream,char *buf);
```

Where:
>   FILE *stream;
>>   indicates the stream whose buffering you want to control.
>   char *buf;
>>   is either a null pointer or a pointer to a character array of length BUFSIZ (a manifest defined in <stdio.h>).

Description:
>   The setbuf function controls buffering on streams. If the buf argument is a null pointer, I/O on stream will not be buffered. Otherwise, the stream will be fully buffered and the memory that buf points to will be used as a buffer for I/O on the given stream.

See Also:
>   fflush, setvbuf

---

setjmp _____ *take snapshot for nonlocal goto*

Usage:
>   #include <setjmp.h>
>   int setjmp(jmp_buf snapshot);   /*Macro or function?*/

Where:
>   jmp_buf snapshot;
>>   is an information block that summarizes the "state" of a program at the time setjmp is called.

Description:
>   The setjmp routine takes a "snapshot" of a program that can be used by a longjmp function later in program execution. For more information, see the explanation of longjmp.
>   Implementations need not implement setjmp as a function; it might only be a macro. Therefore it should not be undefined with **#undef**.
>   The setjmp routine can only be used in one of the following contexts:

(a)   As the entire controlling expression of a loop, an **if**, or a **switch** statement.

(b)   As one operand of a comparison operation. In this case, the other operand must be an integral constant expression. The comparison operation must be the entire controlling expression of a loop, an **if**, or a **switch** statement.

(c)   As the operand of a unary ! operation. The ! operation must be the entire controlling expression of a loop, an **if**, or a **switch** statement.

(d)   As the only operation in an expression statement. Such a statement may include an explicit cast of the setjmp result to **void**.

Some implementations may let you use set jmp in other contexts, but such usage is nonportable.

See Also:
longjmp

setlocale _____ *control locale-specific settings*

Usage:
```
#include <locale.h>
char *setlocale(int class,const char *locale);
```

Where:
int class;
> indicates which locale-specific conventions should be set. The class argument should be one of the following manifests (defined in <locale.h>:

LC_COLLATE
> says that the functions strcoll and strxfrm should use the collating sequence of the locale specified by locale.

LC_CTYPE
> says that the character-handling functions declared in <ctype.h> should use the extended character set of the locale specified by locale.

LC_MONETARY
> says that the function localeconv should format monetary values in the format of the locale specified by locale.

LC_NUMERIC
> says that the decimal point character and other nonmonetary numeric conventions should be those of the locale specified by locale. This affects localeconv and all the functions that read or write formatted floating point numbers.

LC_TIME
> says that the locale-specific formats of the strftime function should be set to those of the locale specified by locale.

LC_ALL
> says that all of the above locale-specific features should be set to those of the locale specified by locale.

```
const char *locale;
```
is a string specifying a locale supported by the current implementation. All implementations will support the "C" locale. If `locale` points to a null string, `setlocale` will use the conventions of the implementation's "native" environment; these conventions are implementation-defined. The `locale` value may also be a null pointer, as described below.

Description:

The `setlocale` function tells library functions to behave according to the conventions of a particular locale. As shown above, `setlocale` may only set up some of the conventions of a locale, and leave the others as they were. All C programs behave as if

```
setlocale(LC_ALL,"C");
```

is executed during program start-up.

If the `locale` argument is a null pointer, `setlocale` returns a pointer to a string which identifies the locale currently associated with the given `class` of conventions. In this case, the conventions of the `class` are not changed.

If the `locale` pointer is not null, `setlocale` tries to set the locale conventions as requested. If this fails, `setlocale` returns a null pointer. Otherwise, `setlocale` returns a string giving the new locale setting for the given class. This string can be used in a subsequent call to `setlocale` (with the same `class` value) to restore that part of the program's locale. A new call to `setlocale` may overwrite the contents of the string returned by the previous call to `setlocale`.

See Also:

    localeconv

---

setvbuf _____ *versatile buffer control*

Usage:
```
#include <stdio.h>
int setvbuf(FILE *stream,char *buf,
            int type,size_t size);
```

Where:

    FILE *stream;
        is the stream whose buffering you want to control.
    char *buf;
        is either a null pointer, or a pointer to a character array whose size is given by the `size` argument.
    int type;
        is a manifest indicating the type of buffering for the stream (see below). These manifests are defined in `<stdio.h>`.

```
size_t size;
```
      is the size of buffer that you will use.

Description:
      The `setvbuf` function lets you dictate how I/O on a stream will be buffered.
The value of the `type` argument may be one of the following manifest values:

`_IONBF`
      No buffering. For output streams, data written to the stream will be transmitted
      directly to the associated file. For input streams, each read operation will obtain
      data directly from the associated file.

`_IOLBF`
      Line buffering. For output streams, data written to the stream will be buffered,
      but the buffer will be flushed when a new-line character is written, when the
      buffer is full, or when input is requested. For input streams, data is read into the
      input buffer line-by-line.

`_IOFBF`
      Full buffering. For output streams, data written to the stream will be saved in a
      buffer and not written until the buffer is full or explicitly flushed with
      `fflush`. For input streams, data will be read into a buffer and read operations
      will obtain data from the buffer instead of directly from the associated file.

      If the `buf` argument is a null pointer, `setvbuf` will allocate a buffer of the
appropriate size with automatic storage duration (which means that the buffer will be
freed when the function that calls `setvbuf` returns). If `buf` is not null, `setvbuf`
will use the address in `buf` as the start of the I/O buffer. It must be possible to use
this buffer as long as the file is open, so it should not be allocated in local storage if
the file will remain open after the function returns.
      The result of `setvbuf` is zero if the buffering is set up successfully. It is
nonzero if the buffering request fails, or if `type` or `size` has an invalid value.

See Also:
      `fflush`, `setbuf`

signal _____ *set up signal handler*

Usage:
```
#include <signal.h>
void (*signal(int sig,void (*newfunc)(int)))(int);
```

Where:
      `int sig;`
            is an integer value indicating the signal that you wish to handle. Signals
            are represented by manifest names defined in `<signal.h>`. Different

implementations have different sets of recognized signals. The minimum set is

```
SIGABRT     SIGFPE      SIGILL
SIGINT      SIGSEGV     SIGTERM
```

These are described in Section 3. All of the above signals can be issued with an explicit call to `raise`. With some implementations, there may not be any other way that these signals occur.

```
void (*newfunc)(int);
```

is the function that should be invoked if the signal ever occurs. This may be a user-defined function. If the signal occurs, the function will called with a single **int** argument giving the number of the signal. When `newfunc` returns, the program will resume execution at the point that the signal was received. However, the signal-handling function for this particular signal will be reset automatically to `SIG_DFL` when the `newfunc` returns, unless the encountered signal happened to be `SIGILL`. Thus `signal` must be invoked again if the signal is to be dealt with a second time.

`SIG_DFL` is another possible choice for `newfunc`. This is the default; it handles the signal in an implementation-defined way (usually terminating the program).

The other choice for `newfunc` is `SIG_IGN`. This function simply ignores the signal.

Description:
The `signal` function tells the execution environment that a certain function should be invoked if a particular signal is issued during program execution. For example, `signal` lets you set up a function that will perform break-handling.

Most functions in the standard library are not guaranteed to be usable after a signal that was not caused by the `abort` or `raise` function. However, `signal` itself can always be called safely inside a signal-handling function.

A signal-handling function cannot refer to any object with static storage duration except by assigning a value to a volatile static variable of type `sig_atomic_t` (see Section 2).

The result of `signal` is a pointer to the function that was previously ready to handle this particular signal. This may have been set by a previous call to `signal`. It may also have been set at program start-up.

The program start-up procedure performs the equivalent of

```
signal(sig,SIG_IGN);
```

for some implementation-defined subset of possible signals. Such signals will therefore be ignored the first time they occur during program execution. For all other signals, program start-up performs

```
signal(sig,SIG_DFL);
```

These signals will be handled in the default manner.

If `signal` cannot set the given signal (for example, because the `sig` value is not a recognized signal number), the function returns a value referred to as `SIG_ERR`. For example, you might write

```
if ( signal(sig,newfunc) == SIG_ERR )
    printf("Unsuccessful signal operation");
```

If this type of error occurs, `errno` will be assigned a positive value.

See Also:
> raise

sin _____ *sine function*

Usage:
```
#include <math.h>
double sin(double x);
```

Where:
```
double x;
```
> represents an angle expressed in radians.

Description:
> The `sin` function returns the sine of `x`. If `x` is large, the result may lose some or all of its significance.

See Also:
> acos, asin, atan, atan2, cos, tan

sinh _____ *hyperbolic sine function*

Usage:
```
#include <math.h>
double sinh(double x);
```

Where:
```
double x;
```
> is any floating point number.

Description:
    The `sinh` function returns the hyperbolic sine of x. If the result is too large, `sinh` sets errno to ERANGE and returns positive or negative HUGE_VAL (depending on the sign of x).

See Also:
    `cosh, tanh, sin`

sprintf _____ *formatted output to a string*

Usage:
```
#include <stdio.h>
int sprintf(char *string,const char *format, ...);
```

Where:
```
char *string;
```
   is the string to which you want to write.
```
const char *format;
```
   is a `printf`-style `format` string.
```
...
```
   is a variable argument list giving the values you want to write.

Description:
    The `sprintf` function writes to the specified `string`. The arguments are converted, formatted, and printed under the control of the `format` string. For a full description of the formatting used by `sprintf`, see the description of `printf`.
    The result of `sprintf` is the number of characters written into `string`, not counting the `'\0'` on the end.

See Also:
    `fprintf, printf, sscanf, vsprintf`

sqrt _____ *square root function*

Usage:
```
#include <math.h>
double sqrt(double x);
```

Where:
```
double x;
```
   is a non-negative number.

Description:
    The `sqrt` function returns the (non-negative) square root of x. If x is negative, `sqrt` sets errno to EDOM.

See Also:
>   pow

srand _____ *set seed for random number generation*

Usage:
```
#include <stdlib.h>
void srand(unsigned int seed);
```

Where:
>   unsigned int seed;
>   is a starting value for a progression of random numbers.

Description:
>   The srand function sets the "seed" for a pseudorandom number generator. Once the seed has been set, you may call rand to obtain pseudorandom numbers.
>
>   If you always use the same seed, you will always obtain the same sequence of pseudorandom numbers from rand. This helps you duplicate results for debugging purposes. If you want a *random* seed, you might use a value based on the date and time.
>
>   If rand is called before srand is used to set a seed, the default seed is 1U.

See Also:
>   rand

sscanf _____ *formatted input conversion*

Usage:
```
#include <stdio.h>
int sscanf(const char *string,
           const char *format, ...);
```

Where:
>   const char *string;
>   points to the string you want to read.
>   const char *format;
>   is a format string similar to that for scanf.
>   ...
>   is a variable argument list of pointers to data objects.

Description:
>   The sscanf function reads input from the given string and assigns it to the objects indicated by the pointers in the variable argument list. The format string tells how to interpret the characters being read. For a full description of format strings used by sscanf, see the description of scanf.

The result of sscanf is the number of input items successfully matched and assigned. This may be less than the number of placeholders in the format string, if there is a conflict between the format string and the actual input. An EOF is returned if the end of the string is encountered before a format conflict occurs or an input item can be read.

If arguments refer to overlapping memory areas, the behavior is undefined.

See Also:
    fscanf, scanf, sprintf

strcat _____ *append a string to another*

Usage:
```
#include <string.h>
char *strcat(char *str1,const char *str2);
```

Where:
```
char *str1;
```
    points to a string terminated by the usual ' \0'.
```
const char *str2;
```
    points to a string whose contents will be appended to str1.

Description:
    The strcat function appends a copy of the string str2 to the end of the string str1. Both strings must be terminated by the usual ' \0' character. The first character of str2 overwrites the ' \0' of str1. If the two strings overlap, the behavior is undefined.
    The result of strcat is the value of str1.

See Also:
    strncat

strchr _____ *first occurrence of character in string*

Usage:
```
#include <string.h>
char *strchr(const char *string,int c);
```

Where:
```
const char *string;
```
    points to the string you want to examine.
```
int c;
```
    is the character you want to look for.

Description:
The strchr function converts c to **char** and returns a pointer to the first occurrence of this character in *string.

The '\0' that terminates the string is considered part of the string. Thus it is possible to find the end of the string with a call of the form

```
ptr = strchr(s,'\0');
```

If the character is not found in the string, strchr returns a null pointer.

See Also:
memchr, strrchr

---

strcmp _____ *compare two strings*

Usage:
```
#include <string.h>
int strcmp(const char *str1,const char *str2);
```

Where:
```
const char *str1,*str2;
```
are the strings to be compared.

Description:
The strcmp function compares the string str1 to the string str2. Both strings must be terminated by the usual '\0' character. Comparisons are made according to the ordering sequence of the execution character set, with characters interpreted and compared as **unsigned char**.

The function returns 0 if the strings are equal, a positive number if str1 is greater than str2, and a negative number if str1 is less than str2.

See Also:
memcmp, strcoll, strncmp

---

strcoll _____ *compare with different collating sequence*

Usage:
```
#include <string.h>
int strcoll(const char *str1,const char *str2);
```

Where:
```
const char *str1,*str2;
```
are the strings to be compared.

Description:
> The `strcoll` function is exactly like `strcmp`, except that the results of `strcoll` are locale-dependent; `strcoll` performs its comparison using the character collating sequence of the current locale. For example, a particular locale might use a collating sequence where uppercase letters compare equal to their lowercase counterparts. By contrast, `strcmp` operates strictly according to the ordering sequence of the execution character set.
>
> The `strcoll` function returns 0 if the strings are equal, a positive number if `str1` is greater than `str2`, and a negative number if `str1` is less than `str2`.

See Also:
> `memcmp`, `strcmp`, `strncmp`

---

strcpy _____ *copy one string into another*

Usage:
```
#include <string.h>
char *strcpy(char *dest,const char *src);
```

Where:
> `char *dest;`
>> is a string into which characters will be copied.
> `const char *src;`
>> is the string you want to copy. This must end with the usual `'\0'`.

Description:
> The `strcpy` function copies the `src` string into the `dest` string. The `dest` string must be big enough to hold the contents of `src`. Since `strcpy` copies the `'\0'` from the end of `src`, the new string `dest` will have the usual terminating `'\0'`. If the two strings overlap, the behavior is undefined. The result of `strcpy` is the value of `dest`.

See Also:
> `memcpy`, `memmove`, `strncpy`

---

strcspn _____ *offset of first character not in set*

Usage:
```
#include <string.h>
size_t strcspn(const char *string,const char *set);
```

Where:
> `const char *string;`
>> is the string to be examined.
> `const char *set;`
>> is a string containing zero or more characters.

Description:
> The `strcspn` function returns the number of characters at the beginning of `string` that do not appear in the set of characters pointed to by `set`. For example, if `set` just contains a blank character, `strcspn` will return the number of characters preceding the first blank in `string`. If none of the characters in `*set` are found in `*string`, `strcspn` returns the length of `*string`.

See Also:
> `strchr, strspn`

strerror _____ *error message associated with number*

Usage:
```
#include <string.h>
char *strerror(int errnum);
```

Where:
> `int errnum;`
>> is an error number (that is, one of the recognized values that `errno` may take).

Description:
> The `strerror` function returns a string describing the error associated with the given error number. For example,

> `strerror(EDOM)`

returns a pointer to a string describing the `EDOM` error. Programs may not use this pointer to modify the returned string. However, some implementations of `strerror` may overwrite the area that contains the string each time `strerror` is called.

See Also:
> `perror`

strftime _____ *prepared formatted date/time string*

Usage:
```
#include <time.h>
size_t strftime(char *dest,size_t max,
                const char *format,
                const struct tm *timestruct);
```

Where:
    `char *dest;`
        points to a memory area where the formatted date/time string should be stored.
    `size_t max;`
        is the maximum number of bytes that `strftime` is allowed to store in `dest`.
    `const char *format;`
        is a multibyte string describing the format of the desired date/time string. Further details are given below.
    `const struct tm *timestruct;`
        points to a time structure, as created by `localtime` or `gmtime`. The date/time values in this structure will be the ones used to prepare the formatted date/time string.

Description:
    The `strftime` function prepares a formatted date/time string and writes the result into `dest`. The string contains multibyte characters, as supported in the current locale. If the locale has shift-dependencies, the date/time string will begin and end in the initial shift state.

    The `format` string is somewhat like a `printf` format string: it is a multibyte string that may contain normal multibyte characters and placeholders. The format string must begin and end in the initial shift state.

    Placeholders consist of a `%` character followed by another character. Each placeholder is replaced with values based on the date/time values stored in `*timestruct`. Other multibyte characters in the `format` string are copied directly into the `dest` string.

    Below we list the placeholders that may be used in the `format` string and what they represent:

`%a`   abbreviated weekday name (locale-specific).

`%A`   full weekday name (locale-specific).

`%b`   abbreviated month name (locale-specific).

`%B`   full month name (locale-specific).

`%c`   date and time in a locale-specific format.

`%d`   day of the month as a decimal number (`01-31`).

`%H`   hour as a decimal number (24-hour clock: `00-23`).

`%I`   hour as a decimal number (12-hour clock: `01-12`).

`%j`   day of the year as a decimal number (`001-366`).

%m   month as a decimal number (01-12).

%M   minute as a decimal number (00-59).

%p   locale's equivalent of AM or PM.

%S   second as a decimal number (00-59).

%U   number of week in the year, as a decimal number (00-53); %U takes Sunday as the first day in the week.

%w   weekday as a decimal number; Sunday is 0, Saturday is 6.

%W   number of week in the year, as a decimal number (00-53); %W takes Monday as the first day in the week.

%x   date in a locale-specific format.

%X   time in a locale-specific format.

%y   year as a decimal number (without century: 00-99).

%Y   year as a decimal number (with century, as in 2001).

%Z   time zone name or null string if no time zone can be determined (locale-specific).

As with printf, a percent sign in the format string is written as %%.

No more than max bytes are copied into dest. If the length of the formatted date/time string is less than max, strftime puts a '\0' on the end of the string.

If the length of the formatted date/time string is less than or equal to max, strftime returns the number of bytes stored in dest (not counting any terminating '\0' character). Otherwise, strftime returns zero; in this case, the contents of dest are indeterminate.

If one argument overlaps another, the behavior is undefined.

See Also:
      asctime, gmtime, localtime, printf

strlen _____*find the length of a string*

Usage:

```
#include <string.h>
size_t strlen(const char *string);
```

Where:

```
const char *string;
```
   is the string whose length is to be determined. It must end with the usual
   `'\0'`.

Description:

   The `strlen` function returns the number of characters in `string` that
precede the terminating `'\0'`.

strncat _____ *append part of a string to another*

Usage:

```
#include <string.h>
char *strncat(char *str1,const char *str2,size_t N);
```

Where:

```
char *str1;
```
   is a string terminated by the usual `'\0'`.
```
const char *str2;
```
   is a string whose characters will be appended to the end of `str1`.
```
size_t N;
```
   is the maximum number of characters from `str2` that should be
   appended to `str1`.

Description:

   The `strncat` function appends a maximum of `N` characters from `str2` to the
end of `str1`. The first character of `str2` overwrites the `'\0'` of `str1`. If `str2` has
less than `N` characters, `strncat` will stop when it encounters the terminating `'\0'`.
If `str2` has more than `N` characters, the first `N` characters will be appended and
`strncat` will add a `'\0'` character to mark the new end of `str1`. The result of
`strncat` is the value of `str1`.
   If the strings overlap, the behavior is undefined.

See Also:

```
strcat
```

strncmp _____ *compare parts of two strings*

Usage:

```
#include <string.h>
int strncmp(const char *str1,
            const char *str2,
            size_t N);
```

Where:
```
const char *str1,*str2;
```
are the strings to be compared.
```
size_t N;
```
is the maximum number of characters to compare.

Description:

The `strncmp` function compares the first N characters of `str1` to the first N characters of `str2`. If one or both of the strings is shorter than N characters (that is, if `strncmp` encounters a `'\0'`), comparisons will stop at that point.

Comparisons are made according to the ordering sequence of the execution character set, with characters interpreted and compared as **unsigned char**. The function returns 0 if the two strings are equal, a positive number if `str1` is greater than `str2`, and a negative number if `str1` is less than `str2`. If N is 0, `strncmp` will always return 0—no characters are checked, so no differences are found.

See Also:
```
memcmp, strcmp, strcoll
```

strncpy _____ *copy characters from string*

Usage:
```
#include <string.h>
char *strncpy(char *dest,const char *src,size_t N);
```

Where:
```
char *dest;
```
is the string into which characters will be copied. This must be able to hold at least N characters.
```
const char *src;
```
is the string you want to copy.
```
size_t N;
```
is the number of characters to copy.

Description:

The `strncpy` function copies at most N characters from `src` to `dest`. If `strncpy` finds a `'\0'` before it has copied N characters, it pads `dest` to N characters by adding `'\0'` characters. If `src` is more than N characters long, the first N characters will be copied as is; `dest` will *not* be given a trailing `'\0'`.

If the strings overlap, the behavior is undefined. The result of `strncpy` is the value of `dest`.

See Also:
```
memcpy, memmove, strcpy
```

strpbrk _____ *search string for first character in set*

Usage:
```
#include <string.h>
char *strpbrk(const char *string,const char *set);
```

Where:
```
const char *string;
```
  is the string you want to examine.
```
const char *set;
```
  points to an array of zero or more characters.

Description:
  The `strpbrk` function returns a pointer to the first character in `*string` that is one of the characters in `*set`. For example, if `*set` is a string consisting only of a blank (followed by the usual `'\0'`), `strpbrk` would return a pointer to the first blank in `*string`. If no characters from `set` appear in `string`, `strpbrk` returns the null pointer.

See Also:
  `strchr, strrchr, strcspn`

strrchr _____ *last occurrence of character in string*

Usage:
```
#include <string.h>
char *strrchr(const char *string,int c);
```

Where:
```
const char *string;
```
  points to the beginning of the string that is to be examined.
```
int c;
```
  is the character you want to find.

Description:
  The `strrchr` function converts `c` to a **char** and returns a pointer to the last occurrence of this character in `*string`.
  The terminating `'\0'` is considered part of `string`. This lets you find the end of the string with

```
ptr = strrchr(string,'\0');
```

If the character is not found in the string, `strrchr` returns a null pointer.

See Also:
  `strchr`

strspn _____ *scan string for set of characters*

Usage:
```
#include <string.h>
size_t strspn(const char *string,const char *set);
```

Where:
```
const char *string;
```
    is the string to be examined.
```
const char *set;
```
    is an array containing zero or more characters, with the usual `'\0'` marking the end of the string.

Description:
    The `strspn` function returns the number of characters at the beginning of `string` that also appear in the set of characters pointed to by `set`. For example, if `set` just contains a blank character, `strspn` will return the number of blanks at the beginning of `string`. If none of the characters in `*set` are found in `*string`, `strspn` returns 0.

See Also:
```
strcspn, strchr, strrchr
```

strstr _____ *first substring of string*

Usage:
```
#include <string.h>
char *strstr(const char *string,const char *substr);
```

Where:
```
const char *string;
```
    is the string to be examined.
```
const char *substr;
```
    is the substring you want to find.

Description:
    The `strstr` function returns a pointer to the first occurrence of a substring inside another string. For example,

```
strstr(line,"the")
```

returns a pointer to the first occurrence of the string `"the"` in the string indicated by `line`. If the substring is not found in the string, `strstr` returns a null pointer. If `substr` is the null string, `strstr` returns `string`.

See Also:
>   strtok

strtod _____ *convert string to double precision number*

Usage:
```
#include <stdlib.h>
double strtod(const char *s,char **ptr);
```

Where:
>   `const char *s;`
>>   is the string to be converted. It may consist of zero or more whitespace characters, possibly followed by a plus or minus sign, followed by a string of digits that may contain a decimal point (as defined in the current locale), then an optional `'e'` or `'E'` possibly followed by a sign, followed by an integer.
>
>   `char **ptr;`
>>   is the address of a **char** pointer; `strtod` will set this **char** pointer to point to the character in `string` that immediately follows the double precision number. For example, with
>>
>>```
>>        string = "1.23y";
>>        dx = strtod(string,&p);
>>```
>>
>>   `strtod` would assign p a pointer to the character `'y'` in `string`. If no floating point number can be formed from `string`, p will point to the first character of `string`. The `ptr` argument can also be `(char **)NULL`, in which case `strtod` just obtains the **double** number and does not worry about any following characters.

Description:
>   The `strtod` function obtains a number from the beginning of `string` and returns the number as a **double** value. Conversion stops with the first character that cannot be part of such a number.
>   If the first nonwhitespace character of `string` cannot start a **double** number, `strtod` returns `0.0`; if a non-null `ptr` is specified in this case, the pointer is stored in `*ptr`. If the correct value would cause an overflow, `strtod` returns plus or minus `HUGE_VAL` (defined in `<math.h>`) and sets `errno` to `ERANGE`. If the correct value would cause an underflow, `strtod` returns `0.0` and again sets `errno` to `ERANGE`.

See Also:
>   `atof, sscanf`

strtok _____ *obtain next token from string*

Usage:
```
#include <string.h>
char *strtok(char *string,const char *set);
```

Where:
    `char *string;`
> is either a null pointer or a string from which tokens will be obtained (see below). This string will be changed by the action of `strtok`, and therefore should not be a string literal.

    `const char *set;`
> is a string containing "separator characters": characters that may separate tokens in `string`. For example, if `set` is the string `" \t"`, tokens in `string` may be separated by blanks or tab characters.

Description:
> The `strtok` function returns a pointer to a "token" taken from `string`. For the purposes of `strtok`, a token is a sequence of characters that are not found in `set`.

> Only the first call to `strtok` should contain a pointer to `string`. Later calls to obtain more tokens from the string should pass a null pointer in place of the `string` argument.

> Between calls, `strtok` keeps a pointer in local static storage to remember where the last token was. The string of separators given by `set` may be changed between calls.

> When `strtok` finds a token in the string, it puts a `'\0'` in the place of the separator character at the end of the token. In this way, the token looks just like a normal null-terminated string.

> When the only characters left in the string are characters that appear in `set`, `strtok` returns a null pointer.

See Also:
    `strcspn, sscanf`

strtol _____ *convert string to long integer*

Usage:
```
#include <stdlib.h>
long strtol(const char *s,char **ptr,int base);
```

Where:
    `const char *s;`
> is the string to be converted. This string may consist of any number of whitespace characters, possibly followed by a plus or minus sign, followed by a string of digits.

```
char **ptr;
```
is the address of a **char** pointer; `strtol` will set this **char** pointer to
point to the character in s that immediately follows the long integer. For
example, with

```
string = "123y";
li = strtol(string,&p,10);
```

`strtol` will assign p a pointer to the character `'y'` in `string`. If no
integer can be formed from `string`, p will point to the first character of
`string`. The `ptr` value can also be `(char **)NULL`, in which case
`strtol` just obtains the **long** number and does not worry about any
following characters.

```
int base;
```
 is the base for the number represented in the string. For example, the
calls

```
strtol("10",&p,10);
strtol("10",&p,8);
```

convert the same string into an integer using decimal and octal
conversion, respectively. A `base` of 0 indicates that the base should be
determined from the leading digits of `string`. A leading 0 indicates an
octal number; a leading `'0x'` or `'0X'` indicates a hexadecimal number;
otherwise, the number is taken to be decimal.

Description:
 The `strtol` function converts the first part of `string` into a long integer,
and returns this integer. Conversion stops with the first character that cannot be part
of such a number.
 The string to be converted can contain the digits `'0'` to `'9'`. Depending on
the base, the string can also contain letters representing digits greater than 9. The best
known example is hexadecimal which uses `'0'` to `'9'` and `'A'` to `'F'` as digits. An
uppercase letter has the same value as a lowercase one, so abc is the same number as
ABC.
 The set of letters which can be part of a number are determined by the `base`.
Since you have 10 possible digits and 26 letters, the maximum value for the `base`
argument is 36. A leading `0X` or `0x` is ignored if the `base` is 16.
 If the first nonwhitespace character of `string` is not appropriate for an integer
with the given base, `strtol` returns `0L`; in this case, the value of s is stored in
`*ptr` (if `ptr` is not null). If the correct value would cause an overflow, `strtol`
returns `LONG_MAX` or `LONG_MIN` (defined in `<limits.h>`) depending on the sign
and sets `errno` to ERANGE.

See Also:
 `atol, strtoul`

strtoul _____ *convert string to unsigned long*

Usage:
```
#include <stdlib.h>
unsigned long strtoul(const char *s,
                      char **ptr,
                      int base);
```

Description:
   The strtoul function is identical to strtol except in two respects. First, strtoul returns an **unsigned long** instead of a **long**. Second, if the correct value would cause an overflow, strtol returns ULONG_MAX (defined in <limits.h>) and sets errno to ERANGE.

See Also:
```
strtol
```

strxfrm _____ *transform string for comparison*

Usage:
```
#include <string.h>
size_t strxfrm(char *modstr,
               const char *orig,
               size_t N);
```

Where:
```
char *modstr;
```
   points to an area of memory where the transformed string may be placed. This must be at least N characters long.
```
const char *orig;
```
   points to the string you want to transform.
```
size_t N;
```
   is the maximum number of characters that should be transformed.

Description:
   The strxfrm function converts a string into a form that might be called the "lowest common denominator" in the current locale. If orig1 and orig2 are transformed into modstr1 and modstr2 using strxfrm, then the result of

```
strcmp(modstr1,modstr2)
```

is equal to the result of

```
strcoll(orig1,orig2)
```

   As an example, suppose that in a particular locale, strcoll uses a collating sequence where uppercase letters compare equal to lowercase ones. Then strxfrm might convert all letters in all strings into lowercase. In this way, if the original strings compare equal with `strcoll` (which ignores case distinction), the transformed strings will compare equal with `strcmp` (because all letters in the transformed strings are in the same case).

The `strxfrm` function stops converting characters when it encounters a `'\0'` or when it has stored N characters in `*modstr`. The result of `strxfrm` is the length of the transformed string, not counting any `'\0'` at the end.

The `modstr` argument need not have the same number of characters as `orig`. There may not be a way to derive the original `orig` string from the resulting `modstr`. If `modstr` and `orig` overlap, the behavior is undefined.

If N is zero, `modstr` may be NULL; in this case, `strxfrm` returns the number of bytes needed to hold the transformed `orig` (not counting the `'\0'` on the end).

See Also:
>   `strcmp, strcoll`

---

system _____ *execute a system command*

Usage:
```
#include <stdlib.h>
int system(const char *command);
```

Where:
>   `const char *command;`
>>   is either a null pointer or a string containing a command that should be submitted to the host operating system.

Description:
The `system` function submits a command to a command processor. The way that this command is executed is implementation-defined. The return value is also implementation-defined.

If the `command` argument is a null pointer, `system` determines whether there is a command processor to which commands may be passed. A 0 is returned if there is no such processor; otherwise, `system` returns a nonzero implementation-defined value.

---

tan _____ *tangent function*

Usage:
```
#include <math.h>
double tan(double x);
```

Where:
>   `double x;`
>>   represents an angle expressed in radians.

Description:
> The `tan` function returns the tangent of x. If x is large, the result may lose some or all of its significance.

See Also:
> `acos, asin, atan, atan2, cos, sin`

tanh _____ *hyperbolic tangent function*

Usage:
```
#include <math.h>
double tanh(double x);
```

Where:
> `double x;`
>> is any number.

Description:
> The `tanh` function returns the hyperbolic tangent of x.

See Also:
> `cosh, sinh, tan`

time _____ *obtain time of day as time number*

Usage:
```
#include <time.h>
time_t time(time_t *time_num);
```

Where:
> `time_t *time_num;`
>> may be a null pointer or a pointer to a memory location where a time number may be stored.

Description:
> The `time` function returns the current date and time expressed as a number. For a description of time numbers and the `time_t` type, see Section 2.
> If `time_num` is not a null pointer, the time number is also stored in `*time_num`.
> If a time number cannot be calculated, `time` returns −1 cast to the `time_t` type.

See Also:
> `ctime, difftime, gmtime, localtime`

tmpfile _____ *create a temporary file*

Usage:
```
#include <stdio.h>
FILE *tmpfile(void);
```

Description:
The `tmpfile` function creates and opens a temporary binary file for updating (corresponding to the `"wb+"` option of `fopen`). When the file is closed, it will automatically be removed.

The function returns a null pointer if an appropriate temporary file cannot be created and opened. Otherwise, it returns a pointer to the stream information block for the file.

See Also:
```
tmpnam, fopen
```

tmpnam _____ *create name for temporary file*

Usage:
```
#include <stdio.h>
char *tmpnam(char *name);
```

Where:
```
char *name;
```
is either a null pointer or a pointer to a character array. If it points to an array, the array must be able to hold at least `L_tmpnam` characters (where `L_tmpnam` is a manifest defined in `<stdio.h>`).

Description:
The `tmpnam` function creates a file name that is not the same as any file that exists at the time of the call. If the `name` pointer argument is not null, `tmpnam` stores the created file name in the character array beginning at `*name`. In this case, `tmpnam` returns the `name` pointer.

If `name` is null, `tmpnam` stores the created file name in a static character array and returns a pointer to the beginning of this array. The same static array may be used every time `tmpnam` is called, which means that each call that passes a null `name` pointer may overwrite the name created by the previous call.

The `tmpnam` function may be called up to `TMP_MAX` times (where `TMP_MAX` is a manifest defined in `<stdio.h>` and guaranteed to be at least 25). If it is called more often than this, the behavior is implementation-defined.

Notice that `tmpnam` does not create or open a file with the new name. To do that, you need to use `fopen` or `tmpfile`.

See Also:
```
fopen, tmpfile
```

tolower _____ *convert uppercase letter to lower*

Usage:
```
#include <ctype.h>
int tolower(int c);
```

Where:
```
int c;
```
is the character to be converted. It may be derived from an **unsigned char** value in the current locale's extended character set, or else it may be equal to the EOF manifest.

Description:
If c is an uppercase letter, tolower returns the corresponding lowercase letter (if there is one in the current locale). Otherwise, tolower just returns the value of c itself. In the "C" locale, tolower only works on the 26 lowercase English letters.

See Also:
```
toupper
```

toupper _____ *convert lowercase letter to upper*

Usage:
```
#include <ctype.h>
int toupper(int c);
```

Where:
```
int c;
```
is the character to be converted. It may be derived from an **unsigned char** value in the current locale's extended character set, or else it may be equal to the EOF manifest.

Description:
If c is a lowercase letter, toupper returns the corresponding uppercase letter (if there is one in the current locale). Otherwise, toupper just returns the value of c itself. In the "C" locale, toupper only works on the 26 uppercase English letters.

See Also:
```
tolower
```

ungetc _____ *push character back into input stream*

Usage:
```
#include <stdio.h>
int ungetc(int c,FILE *stream);
```

Where:
```
int c;
```
        is the character to be pushed back. This cannot be equal to EOF.
```
FILE *stream;
```
        is the input stream that receives the pushed back character.

Description:

    The ungetc function converts c to an **unsigned char** and pushes it back into the specified input stream. The next time this stream is read, the first character read will be c.

    The result of ungetc is the character that was pushed back. If the operation fails, the result is EOF.

    Trying to push back several characters in succession may not work with some implementations.

    On an input stream, fseek, fsetpos, and rewind discard characters that have been pushed back.

    The end-of-file indicator on a stream is cleared by a successful ungetc.

See Also:
```
fflush, fseek, rewind, scanf
```

---

va_arg _____ *obtain argument from variable list*

Usage:
```
#include <stdarg.h>
type va_arg(va_list ap,type);   /* Macro */
```

Where:
```
va_list ap;
```
        represents a variable argument list; ap must be set up with a call to va_start before calling va_arg.

```
type
```
        is the type of argument being obtained.

Description:

    The va_arg macro obtains the value of an argument from a variable argument list. For more information, see Section 1.4.

See Also:
```
va_start, va_end, vfprintf, vprintf, vsprintf
```

va_end _____ *end variable list*

Usage:
```
#include <stdarg.h>
void va_end(va_list ap);   /* Macro or function? */
```

Where:
```
va_list ap;
```
represents a variable argument list; `ap` must be set up with a call to `va_start` before calling `va_end`.

Description:
The `va_end` routine is used to indicate that you have reached the end of a variable argument list. For more information, see Section 1.4.

Implementations need not implement `va_end` as a function; it might only be a macro. Therefore it should not be undefined with **#undef**.

See Also:
va_start, va_arg, vfprintf, vprintf, vsprintf

va_start _____ *start variable list*

Usage:
```
#include <stdarg.h>
void va_start(va_list ap,lastparm);   /* Macro */
```

Where:
```
va_list ap;
```
represents a variable argument list.
```
lastparm
```
is the name of the last parameter specified in the function's prototype (that is, the one that immediately precedes the ellipsis "..."). This should not have the **register** storage class, it should not have a function or array type, and it should not have a type that is incompatible with the type that results after the default argument conversions are applied.

Description:
The `va_start` macro may be used in variable argument functions. For more information, see Section 1.4.

See Also:
va_arg, va_end, vfprintf, vprintf, vsprintf

vfprintf _____ *print variable argument list*

Usage:
```
#include <stdio.h>
#include <stdarg.h>
int vfprintf(FILE *stream,
             const char *format,
             va_list ap);
```

Where:
> `FILE *stream;`
>> is the stream to which you want to write.
>
> `const char *format;`
>> is a `printf`-style format string.
>
> `va_list ap;`
>> represents a variable argument list containing the values you want to print.

Description:
> The `vfprintf` function is the same as `fprintf` except that it prints out values from a variable argument list. The `ap` variable must have been initialized with the `va_start` macro. If there have already been calls to `va_arg` to obtain arguments from the variable list, `vfprintf` will start at the first argument that has not yet been obtained through `va_arg`. The `vfprintf` function effectively uses `va_arg` to obtain arguments from the variable list.
>
> The result of `vfprintf` is the number of characters printed out. A negative number is returned if an output error occurs.
>
> The state of `ap` is indeterminate after `vfprintf` has returned.

See Also:
> `fprintf, printf, vprintf, vsprintf`

vprintf _____ *print variable list on standard output*

Usage:
```
#include <stdio.h>
#include <stdarg.h>
int vprintf(const char *format,va_list ap);
```

Where:
> `const char *format;`
>> is a `printf`-style format string.
>
> `va_list ap;`
>> represents a variable argument list containing the values you want to print.

Description:
    The vprintf function is the same as printf except that it prints out a number of values from a variable argument list. The ap variable must have been initialized with the va_start macro. If there have already been calls to va_arg to obtain arguments from the variable list, vprintf will start at the first argument that has not yet been obtained through va_arg. The vprintf function effectively uses va_arg to obtain arguments from the variable list; therefore a call to va_arg after vprintf will obtain the argument *after* the last argument printed.
    The result of vprintf is the number of characters printed out. A negative number is returned if an output error occurs.
    The state of ap is indeterminate after vprintf has returned.

See Also:
    printf, vfprintf, vsprintf

vsprintf _____ *print variable list into string*

Usage:
```
#include <stdio.h>
#include <stdarg.h>
int vsprintf(char *string,
             const char *format,
             va_list ap);
```

Where:
    char *string;
        points to the string where the output will be written.
    const char *format;
        is a printf-style format string.
    va_list ap;
        represents a variable argument list with the values you want to print.

Description:
    The vsprintf function is the same as sprintf except that it prints out a number of values from a variable argument list. The ap variable must have been initialized with the va_start macro. If there have already been calls to va_arg to obtain arguments from the variable list, vsprintf will start at the first argument that has not yet been obtained through va_arg. The vsprintf function effectively uses va_arg to obtain arguments from the variable list; therefore a call to va_arg after vsprintf will obtain the argument *after* the last argument printed.
    The result of vsprintf is the number of characters printed out, not counting the trailing '\0'.
    The state of ap is indeterminate after vsprintf has returned.

See Also:
    printf, sprintf, vfprintf, vprintf

wcstombs _____ *convert wide character string to multibyte*

Usage:
```
#include <stdlib.h>
size_t wcstombs(char *mbstring,
                const wchar_t *wcstring,
                size_t N);
```

Where:
>   `char *mbstring;`
>>   points to an area of memory where `wcstombs` can store the resulting multibyte character string.
>
>   `const wchar_t *wcstring;`
>>   points to the wide character string that is to be converted.
>
>   `size_t N;`
>>   gives the maximum number of bytes that can be held by the multibyte string.

Description:
>   The `wcstombs` function converts wide characters from `wcstring` and stores them as multibyte characters in the memory indicated by `mbstring`. If the locale has shift-dependencies, the multibyte string will begin in the initial shift state.
>   The function will stop if it encounters the null wide character. In this case, the null character will be converted and stored in `mbstring`. The function will also stop if it cannot add the next converted multibyte character to `mbstring` without going over the limit of `N` bytes.
>   If `wcstombs` encounters a wide character value that has no corresponding multibyte character representation, it returns -1 cast to the `size_t` type. Otherwise, it returns the number of bytes stored in `mbstring`, not counting a final zero character (if any).

See Also:
>   `mbstowcs, mbtowc, wctomb`

wctomb _____ *convert wide character to multibyte*

Usage:
```
#include <stdlib.h>
int wctomb(char *mb,wchar_t wc);
```

Where:
>   `char *mb;`
>>   is either a null pointer or a pointer to a memory area where a multibyte character may be stored. Such a memory area should be large enough to store a character that is `MB_CUR_MAX` bytes long (the length of the longest multibyte character in the current locale).

```
wchar_t wc;
```
     is a wide character.

Description:

    The `wctomb` function converts the wide character `wc` into a multibyte character and stores it in the memory indicated by `mb`. If the `wc` value cannot be converted into a valid multibyte character for the current locale, `wctomb` returns `-1`. Otherwise, it returns the number of bytes in the multibyte character stored in `*mb`. This could be zero if `wc` is zero. It is always less than or equal to `MB_CUR_MAX`.

    If the `mb` argument is a null pointer, `wctomb` returns `0` if multibyte characters do not have shift-dependencies, and a nonzero value otherwise.

    NOTE: if the current locale has shift dependencies, `wctomb` keeps track of the current shift state. Calling `wctomb` with a null pointer for `mb` puts `wctomb` into the initial shift state. Otherwise, `wctomb` assumes that it should write out the multibyte character beginning with the shift state that `wctomb` had at the end of its last call. After converting a `wc` value of zero, `wctomb` goes back to the initial shift state.

See Also:

    `mblen, mbstowcs, mbtowc, wcstombs`

appendix A Glossary

This appendix summarizes most of the definitions that appear in this book. When a definition contains a term that is itself defined in this glossary, the term will be put in *italics*.

Active Position
> For a text output device, the place where the next output character will be printed. For example, on a display terminal, the active position is often represented by the position of the terminal's cursor.

Additive Expression
> An expression with one of the following forms:

> ```
> A + B
> A - B
> ```

Address Operator
> The & operator, used to obtain a *pointer* to a *data object*.

Alert Character
> A special character that produces an audible or visual effect when written to an output device. For example, the alert character might cause an interactive terminal to "beep." Represented by the *escape sequence* ' \a' .

Alignment
> A hardware requirement on some machines that places restrictions on the memory locations where certain types of data may be stored. For example, an **int** value may have to begin (that is, be aligned) at the beginning of a *word*, not at some *byte* in the middle of a word.

Angle Bracket
> One of the characters < and >.

Argument
> A value passed to a function as "input." For example, the argument of the square root function is the number whose root you want calculated.

Argument Conversion Rules
> Rules that convert argument values to different types. They are used when C cannot use a *function prototype* to determine the appropriate data types to pass. This happens when the function call takes place outside the *scope* of a prototype for the function. It

also happens when the prototype contains an ellipsis signifying a *variable argument list*. The **char** and **short** types undergo the *integral promotions*, **float** is converted to **double**, and other types are passed as is.

Array
> An ordered collection of *data objects* that all have the same type.

Assignment Expression
> An expression that assigns a value to a variable, array member, structure member, or union interpretation.

Auto-Decrement Expression
> An arithmetic expression containing the -- operator. The value of X-- is the current value of X. After this value is obtained (for use in another expression), the current value of X is decremented by 1 (1 is subtracted from X). In evaluating --X, X is first decremented by 1, and this new value is the value of the expression.

Auto-Increment Expression
> An arithmetic expression containing the ++ operator. The value of X++ is the current value of X. After this value is obtained (for use in another expression). the current value of X is incremented by 1 (1 is added to X). In evaluating ++X, X is first incremented by 1, and this new value is the value of the expression.

Automatic Storage Duration
> The storage duration of *block scope* data declared **auto** or **register**, or without a *storage class specifier*. Such data objects are created every time execution enters the *block* in which they are declared. They are discarded every time execution leaves this block.

Backspace Character
> A special character represented by the *escape sequence* '\b'. When written to an output device, the backspace moves the *active position* backwards one character.

Binary File
> A file whose contents are written and read as a *binary stream*.

Binary Number System
> A method of representing numbers with only the digits zero and one. This is the method used inside every computer running C.

Binary Search Method
> A way to search through a sorted list of data objects in order to locate a particular object. A binary search begins by looking at the object in the middle of the list. If this is the desired item, the search is over. If the desired item comes before the middle item, the search continues by eliminating the last half of the list and examining the middle item of the first half; if the desired item comes after the middle item, the search continues by eliminating the first half of the list and examining the middle

item of the last half. The search continues in this way, eliminating half of the remaining list at each step.

Binary Stream

A sequence of bits read from or written to an I/O device. When a program reads data that was written as a binary stream, the program gets *exactly* the same sequence of bits that was written.

Bit

The smallest piece of data in a computer. It can have the value 0 or 1.

Bit Field

An element of a *structure* that is declared as a sequence of one or more bits. Bit fields are either **int** or **unsigned int**.

Bitwise AND Expression

An expression of the form A&B, where A and B have *integral type*. The result is an **int** which has a 1-bit in every position where both A and B have a 1-bit, and 0-bits everywhere else.

Bitwise Complement

An expression of the form ~X, where X has *integral type*. The result has a 1-bit everywhere X has a 0-bit, and a 0-bit everywhere X has a 1-bit.

Bitwise Exclusive OR Expression

An expression of the form A^B, where A and B have *integral type*. The result has a 1-bit in every position where one operand has a 1-bit and the other has a 0-bit, and a 0-bit everywhere else.

Bitwise Inclusive OR Expression

An expression of the form A|B, where A and B have *integral type*. The result has a 0-bit where both operands have a 0-bit, and 1-bits everywhere else.

Bitwise Shift Expression

An expression of the form A>>B or A<<B, where A and B have *integral type*. The result is the value of A with its bits shifted right or left B positions.

Black Box

A phrase used to describe how *functions* should usually work. From the point of view of a function's caller, it should only be necessary to know *what* the function does, not *how* it does it.

Block

A collection of zero or more declarations followed by one or more statements, all enclosed in *brace brackets*.

Block Scope

The scope of symbols declared by declarations at the beginning of a *block*. A symbol with block scope is recognized from the end of the symbol's *declarator* to the end of the block that contains the symbol's declaration.

Body

The body of a *function* consists of the declarations and statements that define the function's actions. The body of a loop is the collection of declarations and statements (if any) that are used in each execution of the loop.

Brace Bracket

One of the characters { and }.

Buffer

An intermediate holding area in memory for input or output.

Bug

An error in a program.

Byte

The amount of memory required to hold a single character. In implementations of **ANSI** standard C, this must be at least eight *bits*.

Callee

In a *function call*, the function that is called.

Caller

In a *function call*, the function that makes the call.

Carriage Return

A special character represented by the *escape sequence* `'\r'`. When written to an output device, the carriage return moves the *active position* to the beginning of the current line.

Case Clause

A section of code following a *case label* inside a **switch** *statement*.

Case Label

A label of the form

> **case** *constant-expression* :

inside a **switch** statement.

Cast Expression

An operation for converting one type of value to another. A cast expression has the form *(type) expression*

where *type* is a valid C type. The result of the cast expression is the result of *expression* converted to the given *type*.

Character Constant
　An **int** value consisting of one or more multibyte characters enclosed by single quotes (').

Character Set
　A scheme for representing text characters with numeric values. The most common character sets for **ANSI** C are called ASCII, EBCDIC, and ISO 646.

Collating Sequence
　The order in which the characters of the *character set* are numbered. The collating sequence determines every character's numerical value. It has an effect on such functions as strcmp and strcoll.

Comma Expression
　An expression of the form A, B where A and B are other expressions of any type. A is evaluated, and then B is evaluated. The result of the expression is the value of B.

Command Line
　The instruction that tells a computer to run a particular program. The format of such an instruction depends on the computer system being used.

Compatible Types
　Two types that are similar enough to be considered "the same" for the purposes of various operations. For a precise definition, see Section III.2.11.

Compiler
　A program that translates *source code* into *machine code*.

Compound Assignment
　An expression that combines *assignment* with some other operation. For example, A+=B combines assignment and addition; it is equivalent to A=A+B.

Compound Statement
　Another term for *block*.

Condition
　An integral expression used in **if**, **while**, and **do-while** statements (amongst others). If the value of the expression is nonzero, the condition is considered *true*. If the value is zero, the condition is considered *false*.

Constant Expression

Loosely speaking, an expression whose operand values are either constants or subexpressions whose values do not change during execution (for example, the **sizeof** a data type or the address of an object with *static storage duration*). For a more precise definition, see Section III.3.19.

Control Expression

The expression that appears at the beginning of a **switch** statement.

Cover Function

A user-written *function* whose main job is to call a *library function*. The cover function also takes care of anything special that might be associated with using the library function. For example, it may check that arguments are valid before calling the library function, and may check errno after calling the library function. Other functions in the program should call the cover function rather than calling the library function directly.

Cross-Compiling

Translating a program on one type of computer, for execution on a different type of computer.

Data Object

A piece of information stored in a particular memory location.

Decimal Integer Constant

A number without a decimal point or exponent, written using the digits 0 through 9.

Declaration

A piece of source code that tells what one or more identifier names will mean in a C program.

Declarator

The part of a *declaration* that follows the *type* and *storage class specifiers*. This always includes the name of the symbol being declared; it may also include other symbols (for example, a number in square brackets to indicate an *array*) and an *initializer*.

Declarator List

A comma-separated list of *declarators*.

Default Argument Conversion

See *argument conversion rules* above.

Definition

A *declaration* that reserves memory space for a data object. Also, the source code for a function.

Directive
> Short for *preprocessing directive*.

Domain Error
> An error that occurs because an invalid argument value is passed to a function (for example, a negative value to the square root function). When this error occurs in a *library function*, the library function assigns the EDOM value to errno.

Element
> An object contained in a *structure*.

Enumerated Type
> An **int** type created by an **enum** declaration.

Enumerated Value
> An *identifier* which stands for a value of an *enumerated type*.

Enumeration List
> The list of *enumerated values* that make up an *enumerated type*.

Environment
> The hardware and support software under which an implementation of C runs. An implementation uses two environments (which may or may not be the same): the translation environment (in which C source code is translated) and the execution environment (where a translated program actually runs).

Environment Variable List
> A list from which getenv may obtain a value. All other details of this list depend on the particular computer system being used.

Equality Expression
> An expression of the form A==B. The value of the expression will be 1 if A and B are equal, and 0 otherwise.

Escape Sequence
> A way to represent characters that would otherwise be difficult to show in source code. Escape sequences may appear in *character constants* and *string literals*. Escape sequences begin with the backslash character (\) followed by one-to-four other characters. Standard escape sequences are listed in the endpapers.

Execution Environment
> The *environment* in which a C program executes.

Execution Error
> An error that occurs while a program is executing (for example, division by zero).

Exponent

Part of a floating point number. In `1.04E2`, the exponent is `2`.

Expression

A construct that can be evaluated to obtain a value. The simplest expressions just consist of a constant or a variable. More complicated expressions involve one or more operations (for example, additions, comparisons, subscripting, function calls, assignments). By extension, **void** functions and operations are considered expressions, even though they do not obtain values.

Expression Statement

A statement consisting only of a C expression. The most common kinds of expression statements are assignment expressions and function calls, but any kind of expression is valid. The result of the expression is discarded.

Extended Character Set

The largest set of characters that is recognized by a particular implementation in a specific *locale*. This will include the *minimum character set*. It may also include *wide characters* or *multibyte characters*.

External Definition

A declaration for a function that includes the body of a function. Also a declaration for a *file scope* data object that allocates space for the object (for example, one that contains an *initializer*).

External Definition File

A *source file* whose contents are mostly *external definitions* for data objects.

External Function Prototype Declaration

A *declaration* giving the types (and possibly names) for a function's arguments and its return value. In the Learner's Guide, we recommend that these declarations should always start with the word **extern**, although this is not strictly necessary.

External Linkage

A characteristic of a particular symbol that allows the symbol to be referenced in more than one *source file*.

External Variable

A *file scope* variable whose *external data definition* does not have a *storage class specifier* or has the **extern** specifier.

False

In C programs, represented by a zero value.

File Scope

The *scope* of symbols declared by declarations that do not appear inside function definitions. A symbol with file scope is recognized from the end of the symbol's *declarator* to the end of the file that contains the declaration, plus all files that are included or include the given file.

Fixed Arguments
In a function that takes a variable number of arguments, the set of arguments that *must* be specified.

Floating Point Constant
A number that has a decimal point and/or exponent.

Folding
Splitting a single long line of text into two or more lines.

Formal Parameter
See *parameter*.

Format String
A string literal or character array passed to functions like `printf` and `scanf` to indicate how values should be printed out or read in.

Formfeed Character
A special character represented by the *escape sequence* `'\f'`. When written to an output device, the formfeed moves the *active position* to the start of the next logical page.

Freestanding Implementation
An implementation of C where programs do not run under an operating system.

Function
Part of a C program. The functions of a C program make up the executable part of the program, that is, the description of the actions that the program should take.

Function Call
An *expression* that calls on a *function* to obtain a value, based on arguments passed to the function. For example, a square root function call asks the square root function to obtain the square root of a number that is specified as an argument.

Function Declaration
A *declaration* stating that a particular name refers to a function that returns a particular type of value. If the declaration is given in prototype form, it also gives the types (and perhaps the names) of the function's parameters.

Function Definition
Source code describing a *function*. A typical definition consists of a *function prototype*, followed by a *block* containing *declarations* and *statements* telling the actions that the function should take.

Function Locator

An *expression* that refers to a *function*: either the name of the function or `*fp` where `fp` is a pointer to a function.

Function Prototype

A *declaration* that gives the name of a *function*, the type of result returned by the function, the types of arguments that should be passed to the function, and perhaps parameter names for these arguments. Function prototypes may appear at the beginning of a *function definition* or in other declarations.

Function Scope

The *scope* of identifiers that serve as statement labels. Any such identifier is recognized in any **goto** statement in the function that contains the label.

Global

A word used to describe any function or data object that can be used by any source file in a C program.

Hardware

The actual machinery of a computer system. See also *Software*.

Header

A collection of information describing library functions, data types, manifests, and macros. Header information is obtained with a *preprocessing directive* of the form

#include <*name*>

where *name* is the name of the header. See also *Standard Header*.

Horizontal Tab Character

A special character represented by the *escape sequence* `'\t'`. The horizontal tab is also a *whitespace character* that may be used to indent sections of source code. The effect of a tab is to move the *active position* to the next "tab stop" on the current line.

Hosted Implementation

An implementation of C where programs run under an operating system (or similar software).

I/O Stream

Conceptually, a sequence of *bytes* that have been read from an input device or are being written to an output device. The term is also used to refer to input or output devices themselves, and to the various constructs that C programs use to keep track of I/O.

Identifier

A name used in a C program. Identifiers may name functions, variables, data types, and so on. Identifiers can contain uppercase letters, lowercase letters, digits, and the underscore character (_). The first character may not be a digit.

Implementation

A "package" containing the software needed to translate C programs and prepare them for execution (including the required set of *library functions*). The package should also contain documentation, explaining how to use the software and describing the behavior of *implementation-defined* features.

Implementation-Defined Behavior

Behavior of a particular C construct that may be different under different *implementations* of C. For example, if A is a negative integer and B is positive, the result of A/B may be different on different machines. The behavior of this expression is therefore implementation-defined.

Incomplete Type

A *type* that has not yet been fully declared. For example, an array type that was declared without stating the array size is an incomplete type. By convention, **void *** is always regarded as an incomplete type.

Indirection Operation

An expression of the form *P, where P is a *pointer* value. The result of the expression is an *Lvalue* referring to the memory location to which P points.

Initialization

The process of assigning a value to an object before using it. Initialization can be performed by the *declaration* that declares the object, or by an *assignment expression*.

Initializer

A value or list of values appearing in a *declarator*. The object being declared will be assigned the value(s) specified by the initializer.

Input

Information that a program reads during execution. Input may come from a terminal keyboard, from a variety of devices (for example, disks or tapes), or from other computers.

Integer

A whole number (a number with no fractional part).

Integral Constant Expression

Loosely speaking, a *constant expression* whose operands have *integral type*. For a more precise definition, see Section III.3.19.

Integral Promotion

The process that converts a signed or unsigned `char`, `short`, or *bit field* to `int` or `unsigned int`.

Integral Type

One of the signed or unsigned data types `char`, `short`, `int`, or `long`.

Internal Linkage

A characteristic of a particular symbol that allows the symbol to be referenced in more than one *scope* in the same *source file*.

Interpretation

One of the possible meanings of a *union* data type.

Interpreter

An *implementation* of C that simultaneously translates and executes a C program, statement by statement.

Isolating Functionality

Making sure that each task a program does is only done by one function in a program. This makes it easier to improve the way that the task is done, since you only have to change a single function.

Keyword

A word with a special meaning in a programming language. For example, `int` is a keyword in C.

Library Function

Any one of a set of functions that are supplied as part of an *implementation* of C. The other kind of function is a user-written function, a function written by the person who wrote the rest of the program.

Linear Search

Searching through a list of items, beginning at the start of the list and moving forward item by item until you find the one you want.

Linked List

In C, a list made up of structures. Each structure in the list contains a *pointer* to the next structure in the list.

Linker

A program that performs *linking*.

Linking

A process that binds together the results of separately translated *translation units* into a single executable program.

Loader

A piece of software that actually initiates execution of a program. Loaders are closely associated with *linkers*; on some systems, linking and loading is done by the same piece of software.

Locale

A C construct which is intended to accommodate different languages, alphabets, and typographic conventions. The `setlocale` function lets you tell C to behave in accordance with the conventions of a particular locale. Every locale has its own name. By default, C compilers use the conventions of the `"C"` locale. These are the conventions used throughout this book.

Locale-Specific Behavior

Behavior of a specific C construct that may vary from *locale* to locale. For example, date formats produced by the `strftime` function depend on the current locale.

Logic Error

An error which results in incorrect program behavior, but which does not cause an error message. In other words, the instructions of your program are valid C instructions, but they do not have the effect you want.

Logical AND Expression

An expression of the form `A&&B`, where `A` and `B` have *scalar type*. The result is `1` if both `A` and `B` are nonzero, and `0` otherwise. `B` is not evaluated if `A` is found to be zero.

Logical OR Expression

An expression of the form `A||B`, where `A` and `B` have *scalar type*. The result is `0` if both `A` and `B` are zero, and `1` otherwise. `B` is not evaluated if `A` is found to be nonzero.

Looping Statement

A statement that can repeatedly execute zero or more other statements. The looping statements of C are **for**, **while**, and **do-while**.

Lvalue

An expression that refers to a particular function or a data object stored in memory. Historically, an Lvalue was the only kind of expression that could appear on the Left of an assignment operation.

Machine Code

Instructions expressed in a form that a particular computer understands.

Macro

A symbol defined with the **#define** directive and intended to be used in *macro calls*. The word "macro" is sometimes used to refer to *manifests* as well as true macros.

Macro Call

A construct resembling a *function call* but evaluated at translation time rather than execution time. The result of a macro call is C source code that replaces the macro call and is then translated.

Manifest

A symbol defined with the **#define** directive but not called as a macro. Manifest symbols in source code are replaced by the text associated with the symbol by the **#define** directive. The difference between a macro and a manifest is that a macro is given arguments when it is called, while a manifest takes no arguments.

Mantissa

A part of a floating point number. In `1.04E2`, the mantissa is `1.04`.

Member

A part of a larger data object (for example, a single object contained by a structure or array).

Memory

That portion of the computer's hardware which is used to store information.

Memory Address

A value that refers to a particular location in the computer's memory.

Memory Allocation

The process whereby a program declares that a particular area in the computer's memory will be used to hold the value of a specified data object.

Minimum Character Set

The set of characters that must be present to support C source code. These are the English alphabet (upper- and lowercase), the digits, the underscore, and the following punctuation characters:

```
!    #    "    '    %    ^    &    *    /
(    )    [    ]    {    }    \    +    -
<    >    .    ,    ?    ;    :    |    =
```

Each of these must be able to be represented as a single-byte character.

Modifiable Lvalue

An *Lvalue* whose contents may be changed. For example, a variable that is not **const** is a modifiable Lvalue.

Multibyte Character

A character in an *extended character set*, expressed as a string of one or more single-byte characters. Different multibyte characters in an extended character set may be made up of different numbers of single-byte characters.

Multidimensional Array

    An *array* whose members are referenced using two or more subscripts.

Multiplicative Expression

    An arithmetic expression with one of the following forms:

```
A * B
A / B
A % B
```

Name Space

    A context in which identifiers can be used. It must be possible to distinguish this context from other possible contexts. For example, statement labels form a name space because they are only used as labels and in **goto** statements (so they cannot be confused with variables, types, and so on).

New-line Character

    A special character represented by the *escape sequence* `'\n'`. When written as output, the new-line causes the *active position* to move to the beginning of the line following the current one.

NUL

    A special character represented by the *escape sequence* `'\0'`. When expanded to **int**, it is equal to zero. NUL is used to mark the end of strings.

Null Directive

    A *preprocessing directive* that consists only of the # character. It has no effect.

Null Pointer

    A *pointer* value that does not point to any object or function.

Object Code

    Code that results from translating *source code*. This may be true *machine code* or an intermediate stage between source code and machine code.

Object Library

    A collection of functions and other code in *object code* format. Code in an object library can be *linked* with other code to form a complete program.

Object Module

    A file containing *object code*. Also, any item in an *object library*.

Object Pointer

    A *pointer value* that points to a *data object* (as opposed to one that points to a *function*).

One-dimensional Array

An *array* whose members are referenced using a single subscript.

Operating System

Software that provides various kinds of services to other programs. The operating system also "supervises" what programs do.

Output

Information produced by a program. Output may be written on a terminal, to a printer or some other device (for example, disk or tape), or to another computer.

Overflow

An error that results when a program attempts to use a particular data type to hold a value that falls outside the range of values the type can represent.

Parameter

A symbol used by a *function* to refer to argument values passed by the function's caller. In effect, an argument value is "assigned" to the parameter when the function is called. From that point on, the parameter can be used as if it were a variable that contained the argument value. The value of the parameter can be changed if desired.

Placeholder

A construct in a *format string* representing a value to be printed out or read in.

Pointer Value

A value that refers to a memory location. It can be used in *indirection operations* to inspect or change the data object stored in the referenced memory location.

Pointer Variable

A *variable* that holds a *pointer value*.

Precedence

A characteristic of an operation that dictates when it will be performed in comparison to other operations. For example, multiplication has a higher precedence than addition, so multiplication operations take place before addition operations in the same expression.

Precedence Class

A set of operations that all have the same *precedence*. For example, addition and subtraction have the same precedence and therefore form a precedence class.

Precision

A value specified in a *placeholder*. The effect of a precision value depends on the placeholder that contains it. See the descriptions of `printf` and `scanf` in Part IV.4 for full details.

Preprocessing Directive

An instruction to the C translator. This may tell the translator to skip sections of source code, to change the source code, to add source code from other files, and so on.

Program

A collection of definitions and instructions telling a computer how to perform a particular task.

Program Maintenance

The process of making small changes to an existing program in order to make the program more useful.

Program Name

A way for other pieces of software to identify a particular program. The name of a C program does not (in general) appear in the source code of the program.

Program Parameter

One of the arguments `argc` and `argv` passed to the `main` function where a program begins execution. See Section I.10 for more details.

Programming Language

A way of expressing instructions for a computer. Programming languages are closer to human language than the form in which computer instructions are expressed inside the computer.

Prototype

See "function prototype."

Prototype Scope

The *scope* of a *parameter* name which appears in a *function prototype* that does not begin a function definition. A symbol with prototype scope is only recognized up to the end of the prototype in which the symbol appears.

Qualified Type

A type containing one or more of the *qualifiers* **const** or **volatile**.

Query Function

A *function* designed to look up a piece of information and return this information to the *caller*.

Range Error

An error that occurs because the result of a function cannot be represented as a value of the correct type (for example, because the result of an **int** function is too big to represent as an **int**. When this error occurs in a library function, the function assigns the ERANGE value to `errno`.

Recursion
> The process of a function A calling itself, or calling another function B which eventually calls A again.

Redirection
> Associating `stdin` or `stdout` with a file instead of the terminal.

Re-Entrant Function
> A function that will work properly if it is called recursively (see *recursion*).

Relational Operator
> One of the operators > (greater than), < (less than), >= (greater than or equal to), and <= (less than or equal to).

Reserved Name
> A name that should not be used as an *identifier* by any user program. All *keywords* are reserved, as are the names of *library functions* and names beginning with any of the following:
>
>   E   is   mem   str   to   __
>
> or an underscore followed by an uppercase letter.

Result
> The final value produced by a function. For example, the result of the square root function is the number that is the square root of the function's argument.

Round-off Error
> A small numeric discrepancy which arises because fractions cannot be represented with infinite precision inside the computer.

Routine
> A *function* or *macro*. More generally, any piece of code that does a specific task.

Satisfied Case
> In a **switch** statement, a **case** whose case label matches the value of the *control expression*.

Scope
> A characteristic of an identifier, indicating the region of source code in which the identifier will be recognized. For example, the scope of a *function parameter* is the function that contains the parameter. Outside the function, the parameter name will not be recognized.

Signal

An indication that a special event has occurred. For example, a signal is issued if a program attempts to divide by zero. The signal is transmitted to the program itself, which then activates the *signal handler function* associated with that signal.

Signal Handler Function

A function intended to handle the occurrence of a particular *signal*. See Section II.8 for more details.

Software

A set of instructions that tell a computer how to perform certain jobs. The collection of programs on a computer system.

Source Code

All or part of a program written in a programming language, before the program is translated.

Source File

A file containing *source code*.

Source Module

Another name for a *source file*.

Specifier

A *keyword* used in a declaration.

Standard Error Stream

A *text stream* where programs traditionally write error messages. When a program begins execution, the standard error stream is associated with the symbol `stderr`.

Standard Header

One of a set of *headers* required by the **ANSI** standard. Standard headers declare standard *library functions*, *types*, *macros*, and *manifests*.

Standard Input Stream

A *text stream* through which programs read input. When a program begins execution, the standard input stream is associated with the symbol `stdin`.

Standard Output Stream

A *text stream* to which programs write output. When a program begins execution, the standard output stream is associated with the symbol `stdout`.

Statement

An executable instruction in a C program.

Static Storage Duration

The *storage duration* of *block scope* data declared to be **static** and of all *file scope* data objects. Such data objects are created and initialized before the program begins running and are present throughout the entire execution of the program.

Stepwise Refinement

A process to arrive at a sequence of detailed instructions that will perform a particular task. The task is broken into a series of general steps, which are then broken up into more detailed steps, and so on.

Storage Class Specifier

One of the words **auto**, **extern**, **static**, or **register**, used to indicate *storage duration* in a declaration.

Storage Duration

The period of time that a *data object* exists. Data objects with static storage duration exist through the entire execution of a program. Data objects with auto storage duration only exist while a particular *function* is executing; they cannot be used once the function finishes.

String Literal

A sequence of zero or more *multibyte characters* enclosed in double quotes (").

Structure

A data object that contains several subobjects or *members*. The members of a structure may have different types.

Structure Tag

A name used in **struct** declarations to describe a particular *structure* type. For example, in

```
struct COMPLEX {
    double re,im;
};
```

the structure tag is COMPLEX.

Subscript

A value or expression used to refer to a member of an *array*. Subscripts are always enclosed in square brackets, as in a[10].

Suffix

One or more characters added to a constant to specify a *type* for that constant. A tag of U or u specifies an unsigned type, and a tag of L or l specifies a long type. Such tags can be combined. For example,

```
1U    /* unsigned */
1L    /* long */
1UL   /* unsigned long */
```

Text Editor

A program for creating *text files*. The *source code* for a program is usually created with a text editor.

Text File

A file whose contents are written and read as a *text stream*.

Text Stream

A sequence of characters read from or written to an I/O device. These characters represent text lines. Because text may be converted to a "standard" format, data read from a *text file* may not be exactly the same as the data originally written to the file.

Token

A single word, constant, name, operator, or punctuation mark in a program.

Top Type

The "main" type of a more complex type. For example, the top type of a "pointer to `int`" is "pointer", and the type would be called a "pointer type."

Topdown Decomposition

Another name for *Stepwise Refinement*.

Translation

The process of converting a program written in a programming language into *machine code*.

Translation Environment

The *environment* in which a C program is translated.

Translation Error

An error found when a program is being translated. For example, a statement like

```
A +/ B
```

will result in a translation error because it is not valid C code.

Translation Unit

The *source code* that results after all preprocessing has taken place. The translation unit contains the source code from the original *source file*, plus source code from any files obtained through `#include` directives, minus any code skipped because of `#if` and other directives.

Trigraph

A way to represent characters that are not found in the *character set* used in the *translation environment*. Trigraphs may be used anywhere in C source code. Trigraphs consist of two question marks (??) followed by another character. Standard trigraphs are listed in the endpapers.

True

In C programs, represented by any nonzero value.

Truncation

Chopping off the last part of something. For example, C converts positive floating point values to integers by truncating the fractional part: 3.7 is truncated to 3. Some implementations of C may also truncate long variable names.

Type

A characteristic of all data objects and functions. The type of a data object tells what kind of information is stored in the object (for example, a number, a character, a pointer value). The type of a function tells what kind of value it returns.

Type Declaration

A declaration that associates a name with a particular type.

Type Qualifier

One of the following keywords: **const**, **volatile**.

Type Specifier

One of the following keywords: **char**, **double**, **float**, **int**, **long**, **short**, **signed**, **unsigned**.

Unary Expression

An *expression* that only uses one operand. The unary expressions of C are:

```
*A   &A   +A   -A   !A   ~A   ++A   A++   --A   A--   sizeof
```

Union

A data type that allows the contents of a particular memory area to be interpreted in several different ways.

Union Tag

A name used in **union** declarations to describe a particular union type. See also *structure tag*.

Unqualified Type

A *type* that does not have any *type qualifiers*.

User Interface

The way in which a program presents itself to the person using it. This includes such matters as the way in which the program phrases messages to the user, the way in which the user enters input and commands, the format in which information is displayed, and much more.

User Library

A library of functions and other software, created by a user. Similar to the standard *library functions*, but built by the user to meet the user's own needs.

Usual Arithmetic Conversions

The rules by which the types of arithmetic data objects are converted when the objects are used in expressions. The rules are given in Section III.2.12.3.

Variable

A data object that can be assigned a value. Every variable has a name, a *type*, and a *storage duration*.

Variable Argument List

Used by a function that can take a variable number of *arguments*. In a *function prototype*, the variable part of an argument list is written as . . . as in

```
int printf(char *format,...);
```

Variable Declaration

A *declaration* that gives the name, *type*, and *storage duration* of a *variable*. It may also initialize the variable to a value.

Vector

A *one-dimensional array*.

Vertical Tab

A special character represented by the *escape sequence* ' \v'. When a vertical tab is output, it moves the *active position* to the next vertical tab stop position.

White Space

A sequence of one or more *whitespace characters*.

Whitespace Character

One of the following characters: the space, the horizontal tab (' \t'), the formfeed (' \f'), the new-line (' \n'), the carriage return (' \r'), and the vertical tab (' \v').

Wide Character

A character of the *extended character set*. Such characters are represented by integers of the type wchar_t, defined in <stddef.h>.

Wide String Literal

> An `L` followed by a sequence of zero or more *multibyte characters* enclosed in double quotes (`"`). The multibyte characters will be converted into *wide characters*, making an array of `wchar_t` integers.

Width

> A value specified in a *placeholder*. In a `printf` call, the width gives the minimum number of characters that should be used in printing out a value. In a `scanf` call, the width gives the number of characters in the input field.

Word

> The amount of memory required to hold an **int** value. In implementations of **ANSI** standard C, this must be at least 16 bits. A word must consist of a whole number of *bytes*.

Wrap-Up

> A stage of program termination. Wrap-up takes place when the `exit` function is called, or when the first invocation of `main` terminates. During wrap-up, the program will execute any wrap-up functions that have been recorded by previous calls to the `atexit` library function.

appendix B   Comparison to Earlier Versions

This appendix briefly discusses a number of ways in which **ANSI** C differs from earlier versions of C. We will not discuss every feature, but we will try to direct attention to those features that have changed.

Note that we will discuss some changes that have little practical effect on the behavior of a program on this system, because the changes have a marked impact on program portability.

B.1 Prototypes

The most dramatic difference between the current version and older versions is the use of prototypes in function declarations and definitions. While the older form is still supported, it should no longer be used for new functions. The use of prototypes has several consequences.

(a) When calling a function, it is no longer necessary to cast arguments when a prototype is in scope. Indeed, you should *not* cast arguments. Arguments will be converted to the correct type based on the prototype. Explicitly casting arguments just subverts built-in error-checking facilities that make sure argument values are appropriate to the expected argument types.

(b) It is now possible to pass **char** and **float** arguments to functions. In earlier implementations of C, these types were always cast to **int** and **double** (respectively). Similarly, functions can return **char** and **float** values.

(c) The variable argument list facilities (. . .) provide a more uniform approach to defining variable argument functions.

(d) If there is a prototype declaration of a function in scope, all declarations of the function must use prototypes. As a result, you should remove all old-style declarations of library functions from your source code (since they will conflict with prototype declarations found in header files like <stdio.h>.

B.2 Names

Names beginning with an underscore or with

```
     E    is    mem    SIG    str    to
```

are effectively reserved to allow for expansion of the library. The keywords

```
const    enum    signed    void    volatile
```

are recent additions.

B.3 Type Changes

A number of new types have been added, and old data types sometimes behave differently. These are discussed in the sections that follow.

B.3.1 Void and Void *

The **void** keyword is used in declaring functions that take no arguments, as in

```
int rand(void);
```

and functions that return no value, as in

```
void exit(int status);
```

It can also be used as an explicit cast when you want to discard a value. When the result of an expression is cast to **void**, it is discarded.

The **void *** type is a "generic" object pointer type, and should be used for all "typeless" object pointers. Internally, the type is the same as the old **char *** but different type-checking rules are applied to its use. Many of the functions that used to accept or return **char *** pointers now use **void *** (`malloc`, `bsearch`, `qsort`, and so on).

Any object pointer value may be converted to **void *** and vice versa. Going to **void *** and back again to the original type preserves the original pointer value.

In general, function pointers may not be converted to **void ***, although we expect that many implementations will allow this as an extension.

B.3.2 Character Data

The introduction of **signed char** and **unsigned char** give ways to declare explicitly how **char** values will be used. You should use **unsigned char** except where you explicitly want **signed char**.

For the sake of portability, you should never use **char** itself. This is because the standard lets **char** be **signed** on some systems and **unsigned** on others. Thus the behavior of **char** objects will vary from system to system.

The situation is complicated by the historic use of **char**. Most library functions use **char *** pointers, as opposed to **unsigned char *** which is to be preferred for the sake of portability. The use of cover functions can remove some of the ambiguity here.

Note that character constants are defined to be **int** quantities. There is therefore an implicit conversion when assigning them to any kind of **char** object.

The **ANSI** standard has also introduced **multibyte characters** and **wide characters**. These are intended to meet the requirements of international alphabets and character sets. If an implementation chooses to support an extended character set, it does so in two ways:

(a)   Each character in the extended set can be represented as a multibyte character. This is a sequence of one or more **char** values.

(b)   Each character can also be represented as a wide character. A wide character value is an integer of some signed or unsigned type. The wide character type is given the name wchar_t in the <stddef.h> header.

Comments, string literals, character constants, and header names may contain multibyte characters. There are also ways to define wide character constants and wide string literals. For further information on these new kinds of characters, see Section III.1.5.1.

B.3.3 Floating Point Types

The type **long double** has been introduced to support machines that have extended precision floating point types. The type **long float** is no longer supported—use **double**.

B.3.4 Const and Volatile

The **const** and **volatile** type qualifiers have been added. The value of an object declared **const** cannot be changed by the source code in the declaration's scope. If **const** is applied to a function parameter, the corresponding object will be given a value when a corresponding argument is passed to the function. If **const** is applied to any other data object, the object must be initialized when declared. Typically, **const** is used for constant data objects, as in

```
const double pi = 3.14159;
```

It is also used when a function parameter is a pointer, but when the function will not use that pointer to change the value of the object pointed to, as in

```
int printf(const char *format,...);
```

An object that is declared **volatile** may change its value without the program's "knowledge." For example, a system clock maintained by the hardware will change value without the program taking any explicit action. The use of **volatile** puts limits on the amount of optimization a program may do when manipulating such objects; the program is not allowed to assume that a **volatile** object retains its value for any length of time.

C has a number of rules that prevent you from subverting the intent of **const** and **volatile**. For example, a pointer to a **const** object can be assigned a pointer to a non-

const object, but not vice versa. In other words, you can pretend that a non-**const** object is **const**, but you can't pretend that a **const** object is non-**const**. The same goes for **volatile**.

The **volatile** qualifier is seldom used in application code; it is more suited to low level systems programming. The **const** qualifier is used extensively, especially in function prototypes.

B.4 Constants and Arithmetic

A number of changes have been made in the behavior of constants and the manipulation of numbers.

B.4.1 Numeric Constants

It is now possible to specify a floating point constant that is **float**, by adding an F or f as a suffix to the number. In previous implementations, all floating point constants were **double**.

Unsigned integral constants may be specified by adding U or u as a suffix to the number.

Adding L or l to a floating point constant gives a number whose type is **long double**. Similarly, **long** and **unsigned long** constants may be created by adding L or l to an integer or unsigned integer.

When an integer constant does not have a suffix, the rules determining the type of the constant have changed. A decimal integer constant is either **int**, **long**, or **unsigned long**, depending on which type is big enough to hold the number. Octal or hexadecimal constants can also be **unsigned int** (if they are too big for an **int** but will fit into **unsigned**).

B.4.2 Unsigned Arithmetic

Arithmetic with unsigned quantities will never overflow. If a value is too large to be represented as the appropriate unsigned quantity, it is reduced modulo the largest value of that unsigned type, plus one.

B.4.3 String Literals

String literals are no longer modifiable. For example,

```
cp = "abcd";
cp[2] = 'x';
```

is now invalid.

B.4.4 Conversion Rules

The rules for converting data from one type to another have been reformulated. Generally speaking, conversions attempt to retain the *value* of original objects whenever possible. If this is not possible, conversions try to be simple and logical (for example, preserving the bit pattern if the value itself cannot be preserved). Here are some of the most important points.

(a) Bit fields (**signed** or **unsigned**) and **char** and **short** quantities (**signed** or **unsigned**) are now converted to **int**. The exception is **unsigned** quantities which have the same number of bits as an **int**; these are converted to **unsigned int**. Thus, all **char** values and all bit fields shorter than the size of an **int** will be treated as signed **int** values when used in expressions. This may be confusing, particularly when a **char** object or bit field starts out as **unsigned**.

(b) When converting a signed value to the unsigned type of the same length, the two's complement bit pattern is preserved. Mathematically, the result is the non-negative remainder obtained when dividing the original number by the number that is one greater than the largest unsigned number that can be represented by the unsigned type.

(c) When an unsigned value is converted to a signed value of the same length, the result is implementation-defined.

(d) When a floating type is converted to an integer type, the fractional part is discarded (truncation towards zero).

(e) An explicit cast operation is required to convert a pointer of one type to a pointer of another type, unless one of the types is **void ***. It is always invalid to convert a function pointer type to an object pointer type, or vice versa.

The usual arithmetic conversions allow arithmetic to be performed in single precision if both operands are **float**. Previously, all arithmetic was double precision, regardless of the type of the operands.

B.5 *Expressions*

Some Lvalues may not appear on the left hand side of an assignment, notably those declared with the **const** attribute.

If pf is a pointer to a function, it may be used in function calls as

```
(*pf)()      or      pf()
```

The **sizeof** operator may be applied to the name of an array to obtain the size of the entire array. However, this does not apply to arrays that are passed as arguments to functions (since the function is actually passed a pointer to the array, so **sizeof** will just determine the size of the pointer). The value of **sizeof** has the type `size_t` (defined in `<stddef.h>`) which is an **unsigned** type. Thus any expression that includes **sizeof** operations will use unsigned arithmetic.

The integer division and remainder operations are system-dependent when one or both of the operands are negative. For system-independent division and remainder operations with negative numbers, you must use the `div` library routine.

Pointer arithmetic may not be performed on **void *** quantities. When one pointer is subtracted from another, both must be pointers into the same array. The result has a signed integral type called `ptrdiff_t`, defined in `<stddef.h>`.

The pointer value `P+1` can be used in some types of expressions, even when P points to the last element of an array. In particular, `P+1` can always be compared to other pointers into the array, and other pointers may be subtracted from `P+1`.

A **void *** pointer can be compared for equality or inequality with any other object pointer value.

A compound assignment like

```
A /= B
```

is now precisely equivalent to

```
A = A / B
```

except that the A is only evaluated once. In some previous implementations,

```
int A = 8;
    ...
A /= 3.0;
```

was implemented by converting the `3.0` to **int** and then performing integer division. It will now use floating point division.

The rules governing constant expressions have been reformulated. Constant expressions are evaluated in the *translation* environment, which can affect results on cross-compilers.

The definition of constant expressions has been made more rigorous. See Section III.3.19 for details.

B.6 Declarations

A special meaning has been introduced for the statement

```
struct tag;
```

See Section II.5.5.1 for details.

Union objects may now be initialized. The initialization process always uses the *first* interpretation of the union.

Scalar data objects with block scope may be initialized with any values that can be calculated at the time of the initialization. In particular, they may be initialized with variable values, including local variables that were declared and initialized earlier in the same block, as in

```
void func(void)
{
    int a = 1;
    int b = a + 3;
    . . .
```

Auto arrays and structures may now be initialized. The initialization values must be constant expressions, however. They do not have the freedom that scalar data objects have.

When an object with static storage duration (**static** or **extern**) has no explicit initializer, it is initialized as if it were assigned the constant 0. For some data types on some machines, this is *not* the same as filling in the object with 0-bits.

B.6.1 Scopes and Linkage

The rules governing scope and linkage have changed slightly. The most important is the handling of the **static** keyword. In the old C, code like

```
extern int var_name;
        . . .
static int var_name;
```

would change var_name from external linkage to internal linkage when the keyword **static** was encountered. Now, this is considered an error. The **static** must appear on the first declaration of the object within the scope.

There are now four scopes.

Function Scope
> This is only applicable to statement labels. They can be used anywhere inside the function where they are defined.

Block Scope
> This is used for any name declared inside a block and for parameters declared at the beginning of a function definition. The name will be known from the end of the declarator to the end of the block.

File Scope
> This is used for any name declared outside of all blocks. The scope of the name extends from the end of the declarator to the end of the file, plus any files that are included by the file, plus any files that include the file.

Prototype Scope

This is only pertinent inside function prototype declarations. The scope of the names declared inside the prototype extends only to the end of the prototype declaration. For example, there is no conflict if the name of a parameter in a prototype is the same as a name outside the prototype (although there is a conflict if two parameters in the prototype have the same name).

B.6.2 Name Spaces

The ways in which names can be used divide into separate name spaces. For example, names used as statement labels can be distinguished from other names because labels are only used in **goto** statements and in labels. Therefore, C lets you use the same name for a statement label and for a variable in the same scope.

The possible name spaces are:

Labels

As just described.

Tags

Tags for structures, unions, and enumerated types form a single name space. Thus a structure tag cannot be the same as a union tag in the same scope, but it can be the same as a variable name.

Structures and Unions

Structure members and union interpretations each form a separate name space. Thus a member of one structure type can have the same name as a member of another structure or an interpretation of a union.

Other

All other names are grouped together in a single name space.

B.6.3 External Object Definitions

In most old versions of C, an external data object had precisely one declaration that did not have the **extern** specifier; all other declarations had to have the **extern** keyword. The declaration without the keyword was the *definition*. It was the only declaration that could have an initialization value.

In **ANSI** C, a declaration which is outside of all functions and which has an initialization value is a definition of the object, whether or not the declaration contains the keyword **extern**. Thus

```
extern int i = 1;
```

is a valid external definition. If none of the program's source files contains a declaration that gives an initialization value, the old rule applies: one declaration must omit the keyword **extern** and all the others must have it.

B.7 Preprocessor Features _____

The **#elseif** directive of some previous implementations has been renamed **#elif**.

The **#** and **##** operators have been added for the definitions of manifests and macros. The **##** operator concatenates two tokens into a single token; for example,

```
    x ## 1      ⇒     x1
```

The **#** operator followed by a macro parameter produces a string containing the corresponding argument, as in

```
        #define string(A)    #A
            ...
        string(xyz)   ⇒   "xyz"
```

When the preprocessor encounters two adjacent string literals, they are concatenated in source code. For example,

```
        "abc" "def"   ⇒   "abcdef"
```

A program may now have two **#define** statements for the same manifest or macro (without an intervening **#undef**), provided that the definitions are identical.

The **#error** directive has been introduced to allow for error messages generated during preprocessing.

The **ANSI** standard has provided the **#pragma** directive to allow for the addition of nonstandard preprocessing directives. In this version of C, **#pragma** is used to implement directives of interest to the LINT program checker.

Trigraphs are unique to the **ANSI** standard. If an old program has a string constant containing two question marks followed by another character, the sequence may now be interpreted as a trigraph.

B.8 Library Routines _____

The standard C library has undergone a number of changes, mostly in response to changes in the language itself. The following general principles should be observed.

(a)   Every library routine is associated with a *header* file. For example, the I/O routines are associated with <stdio.h>. Whenever a source file uses a library routine, it should **#include** the associated header. The header contains prototype declarations for all associated routines with that, as well as definitions for types, macros, and manifests that are used by the routines.

(b)   Every library routine is implemented by a function. A header may also contain a macro implementation of any routine. To obtain the function, **#undef** the macro.

(c)   Because some routines may be implemented as macros, you may obtain errors if you try to declare the routines in your own code. Therefore, user code should *never* contain declarations of library routines. If old code contains explicit declarations, they will often be flagged as errors (since many library functions have changed argument and/or result types).

B.8.1 New Header Files

Several new header files have been defined.

`<stddef.h>`
contains standard definitions like `NULL`, `size_t`, `ptrdiff_t`. Will be included in many source files.

`<limits.h>` and `<float.h>`
contain definitions describing machine characteristics. See Appendices C and D.

`<stdarg.h>`
contains type and macro definitions for manipulating variable argument lists.

`<stdlib.h>`
contains a miscellany of definitions (for example, `malloc`).

`<string.h>`
contains definitions for string and `mem` functions.

B.8.2 Use of Void * Pointers

Many routines that formerly used **char** ***** pointers now use **void** ***** pointers. This includes the following:

```
bsearch     free        memchr      memset
calloc      fwrite      memcmp      qsort
fread       malloc      memcpy      realloc
```

B.8.3 Use of the Size_t Type

The following routines use `size_t` where earlier versions may have used **int** or **unsigned int**:

```
bsearch     malloc      memmove     strcmp
calloc      memchr      memset      strncat
fread       memcmp      qsort       strncmp
fwrite      memcpy      realloc     strncpy
```

B.8.4 Use of Const Arguments

The following routines use **const** arguments:

asctime	getenv	sscanf	strspn
atof	gmtime	strcat	strstr
atoi	localtime	strchr	strtod
atol	memchr	strcmp	strtok
bsearch	memcmp	strcpy	strtol
ctime	memcpy	strcspn	strtoul
fopen	memmove	strlen	system
fprintf	printf	strncat	vfprintf
fputs	remove	strncmp	vprintf
freopen	rename	strncpy	vsprintf
fscanf	scanf	strpbrk	

B.8.5 Locales

The concept of *locales* has been introduced to allow support for differing international conventions. Through the setlocale function, a program indicates what *locale-specific* conventions various library functions should follow.

Most of the <ctype.h> functions are now locale-specific. For example, consider isalpha: the characters it recognizes as "letters" will vary depending on the current locale settings.

Locale settings also control functions that read and write numbers (printf, scanf, strtod, and so on). The settings indicate the format of numbers (for example, what character string should be interpreted or used as a decimal point).

For more about locales, see Section III.1.5.

B.8.6 Miscellaneous Changes

The value that used to be called HUGE is now called HUGE_VAL.

The only two standard values for errno are EDOM and ERANGE. Additional values are extensions to the standard.

appendix C Floating Point Definitions

The `<float.h>` header contains definitions that describe the nature of floating point numbers in a particular implementation. Several parameters are used to describe such numbers.

s   stands for the sign of the number. This will be -1 or $+1$.

b   is the base of the number, also known as the radix of exponentiation representation. This will be an integer greater than 1.

e   is the exponential part of the number. This will be an integer that is found in the range (*emin,emax*) where these two values are implementation-defined.

p   is the precision of the number. This gives the number of digits in the mantissa of the floating point number. Each digit will be given in base *b*.

f   represents a non-negative integer less than *b*.

A nonzero normalized floating point number x can be expressed as

$$s \times b^e \times \sum_{k=1}^{p} (f_k \times b^{-k})$$

The `<float.h>` header defines manifests which refer to the parts of a floating point number mentioned above. As with the manifests in `<limits.h>` (described in Appendix D), each manifest in `<float.h>` must be greater than or equal to some minimum acceptable value given by the **ANSI** standard. Below we list the manifests and their minimum accepted values.

`FLT_RADIX (2)`
   minimum value of *b*.

`FLT_ROUNDS`
   indicates how addition operations round off values when the precision of a floating point number is not large enough to store the actual value. If `FLT_ROUNDS` is greater than zero, the machine rounds results to the appropriate precision. If `FLT_ROUNDS` is 0, the machine truncates results to the appropriate precision. If `FLT_ROUNDS` is -1, the machine's actions cannot be determined (which means that it sometimes rounds and sometimes truncates).

FLT_MANT_DIG
   is the number of base *b* digits in the mantissa of a **float** value.

DBL_MANT_DIG
   is the number of base *b* digits in the mantissa of a **double** value.

LDBL_MANT_DIG
   is the number of base *b* digits in the mantissa of a **long double** value.

FLT_EPSILON (1E-5)
   size of the smallest **float** number such that FLT_EPSILON plus 1.0 is not equal
   to 1.0.

DBL_EPSILON (1E-9)
   size of the smallest **double** number such that DBL_EPSILON plus 1.0 is not equal
   to 1.0.

LDBL_EPSILON (1E-9)
   size of the smallest **long double** number such that LDBL_EPSILON plus 1.0L
   is not equal to 1.0L.

FLT_DIG (6)
   number of decimal digits of precision in a **float** value. This will be *p* if *b* equals
   10. Otherwise it is the value

$$(p - 1) \times \log10(b)$$

DBL_DIG (10)
   number of decimal digits of precision in a **double** value. This is defined in a similar
   way to FLT_DIG.

LDBL_DIG (10)
   number of decimal digits of precision in a **long double** value. This is defined in a
   similar way to FLT_DIG.

FLT_MIN_EXP
   smallest possible value of *e* (*emin*) for a **float** value.

DBL_MIN_EXP
   smallest possible value of *e* for a **double** value.

LDBL_MIN_EXP
   smallest possible value of *e* for a **long double** value.

FLT_MIN (1E-37)
   smallest normalized positive **float** value.

`DBL_MIN (1E-37)`
> smallest normalized positive **double** value.

`LDBL_MIN (1E-37)`
> smallest normalized positive **long double** value.

`FLT_MIN_10_EXP (-37)`
> base 10 exponent of `FLT_MIN`.

`DBL_MIN_10_EXP (-37)`
> base 10 exponent of `DBL_MIN`.

`LDBL_MIN_10_EXP (-37)`
> base 10 exponent of `LDBL_MIN`.

`FLT_MAX_EXP`
> largest possible value of e (*emax*) for a **float** value.

`DBL_MAX_EXP`
> largest possible value of e for a **double** value.

`LDBL_MAX_EXP`
> largest possible value of e for a **long double** value.

`FLT_MAX (1E+37)`
> largest normalized positive **float** value.

`DBL_MAX (1E+37)`
> largest normalized positive **double** value.

`LDBL_MAX (1E+37)`
> largest normalized positive **long double** value.

`FLT_MAX_10_EXP (+37)`
> base 10 exponent of `FLT_MAX`.

`DBL_MAX_10_EXP (+37)`
> base 10 exponent of `DBL_MAX`.

`LDBL_MAX_10_EXP (+37)`
> base 10 exponent of `LDBL_MAX`.

appendix D Contents of <limits.h>

The <limits.h> header contains a variety of manifests describing data types on a particular machine. The **ANSI** standard places minimum values on each of these manifests. For example, the CHAR_BIT manifest (which tells how many bits there are in a byte) must be at least eight. Individual implementations might have larger values for any of these manifests. For example, on machines where a byte contains nine bits, CHAR_BIT will have the value nine.

Below we list the manifests defined in <limits.h>. The parenthesized number after each is the minimum value accepted by the **ANSI** standard.

CHAR_BIT (8)
> number of bits in a byte.

SCHAR_MIN (-127)
> minimum value of a **signed char** object.

SCHAR_MAX (+127)
> maximum value of a **signed char** object.

UCHAR_MAX (255U)
> maximum value of an **unsigned char** object.

CHAR_MIN
> minimum value for a **char** object. This will be 0 if **char** is an unsigned type, and SCHAR_MIN otherwise.

CHAR_MAX
> maximum value for a **char** object. This will be either SCHAR_MAX or UCHAR_MAX.

SHRT_MIN (-32767)
> minimum value for a **short int** object.

SHRT_MAX (+32767)
> maximum value for a **short int** object.

USHRT_MAX (65535U)
> maximum value for an **unsigned short** object.

INT_MIN (-32767)
> minimum value for an **int** object.

INT_MAX (+32767)
    maximum value for an **int** object.

UINT_MAX (65535U)
    maximum value for an **unsigned int** object.

LONG_MIN (-2147483647)
    minimum value for a **long int** object.

LONG_MAX (+2147483647)
    maximum value for a **long int** object.

ULONG_MAX (4294967295U)
    maximum value for an **unsigned long** object.

appendix E Standard Headers

Below we list the symbols defined in the standard headers of the **ANSI** standard. For functions, we show complete prototypes; for macros, we show prototype forms that suggest how the macro is used; for other symbols, we give brief descriptions.

```
<assert.h>:
        NDEBUG  /* is debugging on? */
        void assert(int expression);   /* Macro */

<ctype.h>:
        int isalnum(int c);
        int isalpha(int c);
        int iscntrl(int c);
        int isdigit(int c);
        int isgraph(int c);
        int islower(int c);
        int isprint(int c);
        int ispunct(int c);
        int isspace(int c);
        int isupper(int c);
        int isxdigit(int c);
        int tolower(int c);
        int toupper(int c);

<errno.h>:
        EDOM    /* int constant, domain error */
        ERANGE  /* int constant, range error  */
        errno   /* int, error number */

<locale.h>:
        LC_ALL      /* set all locale conventions  */
        LC_COLLATE  /* set collating conventions   */
        LC_CTYPE    /* set <ctype.h> behavior      */
        LC_MONETARY /* set monetary conventions    */
        LC_NUMERIC  /* set numeric conventions     */
        LC_TIME     /* set standard date/time form */
        NULL        /* null pointer constant       */
        struct lconv /* locale conventions         */
        struct lconv *localeconv(void);
        char *setlocale(int class,
                const char *locale);
```

```
<math.h>:
        HUGE_VAL      /* large double value */
        double acos(double x);
        double asin(double x);
        double atan(double x);
        double atan2(double y,double x);
        double ceil(double x);
        double cos(double x);
        double cosh(double x);
        double exp(double x);
        double fabs(double x);
        double floor(double x);
        double fmod(double x,double y);
        double frexp(double x,int *expptr);
        double ldexp(double x,int N);
        double log(double x);
        double log10(double x);
        double modf(double x,double *yp);
        double pow(double x,double y);
        double sin(double x);
        double sinh(double x);
        double sqrt(double x);
        double tan(double x);
        double tanh(double x);

<setjmp.h>:
        jmp_buf       /* type to hold snapshots */
        void longjmp(jmp_buf snapshot,int value);
        int setjmp(jmp_buf snapshot);

<signal.h>:
        sig_atomic_t   /* safe type for assignments */
        SIG_DFL        /* default signal handler   */
        SIG_ERR        /* "signal" error return    */
        SIG_IGN        /* ignores signals          */
        SIGABRT        /* abort program signal     */
        SIGFPE         /* invalid arithmetic op.   */
        SIGILL         /* invalid machine op.      */
        SIGINT         /* user interrupt           */
        SIGSEGV        /* invalid memory access    */
        SIGTERM        /* external program
                                    termination    */
        int raise(int sig);
        void (*signal(int sig,void (*newfunc)(int)))(int);
```

```
<stdarg.h>:
        va_list         /* type for variable arg. list */
        type va_arg(va_list ap, type);       /* Macro */
        void va_end(va_list ap);
        void va_start(va_list ap, lastparm);  /* Macro */

<stddef.h>
        ptrdiff_t    /* type, difference of pointers */
        size_t       /* unsigned type, sizeof result */
        wchar_t      /* type, wide characters        */
        NULL         /* null pointer constant        */
        size_t offsetof(type,structure_member);   /* Macro */

<stdio.h>:
        FILE          /* type for I/0 streams   */
        fpos_t        /* type, file position    */
        size_t        /* sizeof result          */
        _IOFBF        /* for setvbuf            */
        _IOLBF        /* for setvbuf            */
        _IONBF        /* for setvbuf            */
        BUFSIZ        /* buffer size, setbuf    */
        EOF           /* end of file            */
        FILENAME_MAX  /* max file name size     */
        FOPEN_MAX     /* max files open         */
        L_tmpnam      /* max name for tmpnam    */
        NULL          /* null pointer constant  */
        SEEK_CUR      /* for fseek              */
        SEEK_END      /* for fseek              */
        SEEK_SET      /* for fseek              */
        stderr        /* standard error stream  */
        stdin         /* standard input stream  */
        stdout        /* standard output stream */
        TMP_MAX       /* max tmpnam files       */
        void clearerr(FILE *stream);
        int fclose(FILE *stream);
        int feof(FILE *stream);
        int ferror(FILE *stream);
        int fflush(FILE *stream);
        int fgetc(FILE *stream);
        int fgetpos(FILE *stream,fpos_t *pos);
        char *fgets(char *string,int n,FILE *stream);
        FILE *fopen(const char *name,const char *options);
        int fprintf(FILE *stream,const char *format, ...);
        int fputc(int c,FILE *stream);
        int fputs(const char *string,FILE *stream);
        size_t fread(void *ptr,size_t size,
                     size_t count,FILE *stream);
```

```
        FILE *freopen(const char *name,
                      const char *options,
                      FILE *stream);
        int fscanf(FILE *stream,const char *format, ...);
        int fseek(FILE *stream,long offset,int origin);
        int fsetpos(FILE *stream,const fpos_t *pos);
        long ftell(FILE *stream);
        size_t fwrite(const void *ptr,size_t size,
                      size_t count,FILE *stream);
        int getc(FILE *stream);
        int getchar(void);
        char *gets(char *string);
        void perror(const char *usermsg);
        int printf(const char *format, ...);
        int putc(int c,FILE *stream);
        int putchar(int c);
        int puts(const char *string);
        int remove(const char *filename);
        int rename(const char *oldname,const char *newname);
        void rewind(FILE *stream);
        int scanf(const char *format, ...);
        void setbuf(FILE *stream,char *buf);
        int setvbuf(FILE *stream,char *buf,
                    int type,size_t size);
        int sprintf(char *string,
                    const char *format, ...);
        int sscanf(const char *string,
                   const char *format, ...);
        FILE *tmpfile(void);
        char *tmpnam(char *name);
        int ungetc(int c,FILE *stream);
        int vfprintf(FILE *stream,const char *format,
                    va_list ap);
        int vprintf(const char *format,va_list ap);
        int vsprintf(char *string,const char *format,
                    va_list ap);

<stdlib.h>:
        div_t          /* type from div              */
        ldiv_t         /* type from ldiv             */
        size_t         /* sizeof result              */
        wchar_t        /* wide character type        */
        EXIT_FAILURE   /* indicates program failure  */
        EXIT_SUCCESS   /* indicates program success  */
        MB_CUR_MAX     /* largest current MB char    */
        NULL           /* null pointer constant      */
        RAND_MAX       /* largest number from rand   */
```

```
        void abort(void);
        int abs(int i);
        int atexit(void (*wrapfunc)(void));
        double atof(const char *s);
        int atoi(const char *s);
        long atol(const char *s);
        void * bsearch(const void *key,
                    const void *table,
                    size_t N, size_t keysize,
                    int (*compar)(const void *,
                                  const void *));
        void *calloc(size_t N,size_t size);
        div_t div(int top,int bottom);
        void exit(int status);
        void free(void *ptr);
        char *getenv(const char *name);
        long labs(long n);
        ldiv_t ldiv(long top,long bottom);
        void *malloc(size_t size);
        int mblen(const char *mb,size_t N);
        size_t mbstowcs(wchar_t *wcstring,
                    const char *mbstring,
                    size_t N);
        int mbtowc(wchar_t *wc,const char *mb,size_t N);
        void qsort(void *table,size_t N,size_t size,
                int (*compar)(const void *,
                              const void *));
        int rand(void);
        void *realloc(void *oldp,size_t size);
        void srand(unsigned seed);
        double strtod(const char *s,char **ptr);
        long strtol(const char *s,char **ptr,int base);
        unsigned long strtoul(const char *s,
                            char **ptr,int base);
        int system(const char *command);
        size_t wcstombs(char *mbstring,
                    const wchar_t *wcstring,
                    size_t N);
        int wctomb(char *mb, wchar_t wc);

<string.h>:
        NULL        /* null pointer constant */
        size_t      /* sizeof result          */
        void *memchr(const void *obj,int c,size_t N);
        int memcmp(const void *obj1,
                const void *obj2,size_t N);
        void *memcpy(void *dest,const void *src,size_t N);
```

```
        void *memmove(void *dest,const void *src,size_t N);
        void *memset(void *mem,int c,size_t N);
        char *strcat(char *str1,const char *str2);
        char *strchr(const char *string,int c);
        int strcmp(const char *str1,const char *str2);
        int strcoll(const char *str1,const char *str2);
        char *strcpy(char *dest,const char *src);
        size_t strcspn(const char *string,const char *set);
        char *strerror(int errnum);
        size_t strlen(const char *string);
        char *strncat(char *str1,const char *str2,size_t N);
        int strncmp(const char *str1,const char *str2,
                    size_t N);
        char *strncpy(char *dest,const char *src,size_t N);
        char *strpbrk(const char *string,const char *set);
        char *strrchr(const char *string,int c);
        size_t strspn(const char *string,const char *set);
        char *strstr(const char *string,const char *substr);
        char *strtok(char *string,const char *set);
        size_t strxfrm(char *modstr,const char *orig,
                        size_t N);

<time.h>:
        clock_t    /* time measured in clock ticks    */
        size_t     /* sizeof result                   */
        time_t     /* integer representing date-time  */
        struct tm  /* time structure                  */
        CLK_TCK    /* number of clock ticks in second */
        NULL       /* null pointer constant           */
        char *asctime(const struct tm *loctim);
        clock_t clock(void);
        char *ctime(const time_t *time_num);
        double difftime(time_t time2,time_t time1);
        struct tm *gmtime(const time_t *time_num);
        struct tm *localtime(const time_t *time_num);
        time_t mktime(struct tm *timestruct);
        size_t strftime(char *dest,size_t max,
                        const char *format,
                        const struct tm *timestruct);
        time_t time(time_t *time_num);
```

appendix F   ASCII Character Set

This table gives all 128 ASCII transmission codes and the characters that correspond to them. Codes 000-037 and 177 are not printable.

000 nul	020 dle	040 sp	060 0	100 @	120 P	140 '	160 p
001 soh	021 dc1	041 !	061 1	101 A	121 Q	141 a	161 q
002 stx	022 dc2	042 "	062 2	102 B	122 R	142 b	162 r
003 etx	023 dc3	043 #	063 3	103 C	123 S	143 c	163 s
004 eot	024 dc4	044 $	064 4	104 D	124 T	144 d	164 t
005 enq	025 nak	045 %	065 5	105 E	125 U	145 e	165 u
006 ack	026 syn	046 &	066 6	106 F	126 V	146 f	166 v
007 bel	027 etb	047 '	067 7	107 G	127 W	147 g	167 w
010 bs	030 can	050 (	070 8	110 H	130 X	150 h	170 x
011 ht	031 em	051)	071 9	111 I	131 Y	151 i	171 y
012 lf	032 sub	052 *	072 :	112 J	132 Z	152 j	172 z
013 vt	033 esc	053 +	073 ;	113 K	133 [	153 k	173 {
014 ff	034 fs	054 ,	074 <	114 L	134 \	154 l	174	
015 cr	035 gs	055 -	075 =	115 M	135]	155 m	175 }
016 so	036 rs	056 .	076 >	116 N	136 ^	156 n	176 ~
017 si	037 us	057 /	077 ?	117 O	137 _	157 o	177 del

appendix G The C2C Compiler

The **C2C** compiler was written by the Software Development Group of the University of Waterloo, as an aid to writing programs in **ANSI** standard C. We do not claim that it conforms to the **ANSI** standard; at the time of publication, the standard had yet to be adopted officially. However, **C2C** will let you run programs that have been written with the C language as described in this book.

C2C runs on IBM PC computers and true compatibles, under MS-DOS 3.0 and later.

G.1 Documentation

Companies that sell software often find it difficult to ensure that the software matches its documentation. Frequently, the schedules for producing documentation and software are different, and last minute changes in software may not be noted in the documentation. In addition, programmers have a tendency to keep old books and manuals around long after they have gone out of date, causing more confusion.

One common solution to this problem is commonly called a **read.me** file. This file describes any changes in software that might have happened between the time that the documentation went to the printers and the time that the software itself began distribution. The file is distributed on the same disk or tape that contains the software, so that the read.me file is directly associated with the software itself.

The **C2C** package has adopted this strategy. On the disks that contain the software, you will find a file named `read.me` that describes any differences between the software and this appendix. Make sure you read the file before trying to use **C2C**; it may contain very important information. The `read.me` file will be more up-to-date than this appendix, and takes precedence over what we say here.

The `read.me` file contains instructions for installing the **C2C** package. In the rest of this appendix, we will assume that you have installed the package in accordance with those instructions.

G.2.1 Documentation Conventions

The **C2C** command compiles C source code. Command lines will usually have options telling **C2C** how to behave. There are three option forms:

`+Name`	turns on an option.
`-Name`	turns off an option.
`Name=value`	specifies a value for an option that takes a value.

In our documentation, all option names are written with some letters in uppercase and some in lowercase. In the interest of abbreviation, any or all of the letters shown in lowercase may be omitted. For example, if the documentation writes an option as

```
-LoaD
```

the option can be written as

```
-load    -lod    -lad    -ld
```

and so on. When you type in commands, letters can be entered in either upper- or lowercase; **C2C** does not distinguish between cases in option names. The special use of case is just a documentation convention.

G.2 Single File Compilation

Suppose that you have stored the source code of your entire program in a file named `prog.c`. To compile the program, type the command

```
c2c prog.c Output=prog.exe
```

This translates the program and stores the executable result in a file named `prog.exe`. To run the translated program, you can just type

```
prog
```

provided that your current directory has been specified in your MS-DOS search rules. For more on search rules, see the description of the **PATH** command in your MS-DOS documentation.

When compiling a program, the position of items on the command line is not important. For example, you could have compiled the program with

```
c2c o=prog.exe prog.c
```

and got exactly the same results. Note that this version of the command uses the abbreviation `o=` for `Output=` in accordance with the abbreviation convention discussed earlier.

G.3 Use of Object Libraries

When a program is split over several source files, it becomes convenient to use **object libraries**. An object library can hold a number of object modules (translated source files) in an easy-to-use form.

Typically, you would create an object library by translating each source file except the one containing `main`, and storing the translated result (the object module) in the object library. You would then compile the source file containing `main`. The command that compiles `main` would contain an option saying that all the other functions are stored in the object library you have created. **C2C** will then translate `main` and link in all the other object modules from the object library in order to produce a complete program.

If you make a change in any source module, you would translate the source module and *update* the object library to contain the new object module. The new module replaces the old one. In this way, the object library always contains the most up-to-date versions of the object modules.

By keeping up-to-date object modules in an object library, you can avoid translating your whole program every time you make a change—you only have to translate the parts that you've changed. In addition, storing object code in an object library takes less space than storing each object module as a separate file.

G.3.1 Creating an Object Library

Suppose that your program is split over the source files `filea.c`, `fileb.c`, `filec.c`, and so on, plus the file `main.c` that contains the `main` function. The command

```
c2c filea.c Update=prog.lib +Clear
```

translates the source code in `filea.c` and stores the resulting object module in an object library named `prog.lib`. (Of course, you could use any name you want for the object library.) The `+Clear` option is only used when you want to start a new object library; it "clears" out anything that the file currently contains and sets up the file to be a new object library. Note that `+Clear` is *required* whenever you want to create a new library file.

You can continue adding object modules to the library with similar commands, as in

```
c2c fileb.c u=prog.lib
c2c filec.c u=prog.lib
```

and so on. Each time, the new object module is added to the existing library.

G.3.2 Obtaining Object Modules from a Library

Once you have stored all your object modules in the library, you can compile `main`. To do this, use the command

```
c2c main.c Library=prog.lib Output=prog.exe
```

This compiles `main.c`. Whenever `main` refers to a function or external variable that is not in `main.c` itself, **C2C** will look for that function or variable in the library that is named in the `Library=` option. If a function that is obtained in this way refers to other functions or external variables, they will also be obtained from `prog.lib`. Everything will then be linked together, and written to `prog.exe` as an executable program.

Note that **C2C** only obtains functions and variables from the library when they are referenced in `main.c` or in code that `main.c` references. In other words, **C2C** only gets what it needs; the library may contain functions and/or variables that go unused.

G.3.3 Multiple Libraries

People tend to build up personal libraries of functions that they use in many different programs. If you are working on a specific project, you may want to obtain object code from a library associated with a specific project and also from your own personal library. **C2C** lets you do this by specifying more than one library on a command line, as in

```
c2c main.c l=project.lib l=personal.lib o=project.exe
```

This command line has two (abbreviated) `Library=` options. When trying to resolve a reference, **C2C** will search `project.lib` first (because it is specified first on the command line). If `project.lib` does not contain the required function or variable, **C2C** will search `personal.lib`.

C2C searches through libraries in the order they are given on the command line, and does *not* go backwards. In the example above, `personal.lib` should not contain any references to material in `project.lib`, because **C2C** will not go back to look for them. If necessary, you must type

```
l=project.lib l=personal.lib l=project.lib
```

so that **C2C** goes back to searching `project.lib` after `personal.lib`.

The last library to be searched is always the *standard library*, containing the usual library functions (`printf`, `scanf`, and so on). This library does not have to be specified on the command line; **C2C** searches it automatically. If any of the libraries on the command line contain functions with the same name as standard library functions, **C2C** will link in the version from the command line library rather than the one from the standard library. You should avoid this situation, since it often leads to puzzling bugs.

G.3.4 Making Changes

Now, suppose that you change `filea.c` and want to remake the program to run with this change. The command

```
c2c filea.c Update=prog.lib
```

updates the library to contain new versions of all the material in `filea.c`. Other material remains unchanged. You can then relink the program with the command

```
c2c main.c l=prog.lib o=prog.exe
```

But there's another approach you can take that may save work. You begin by compiling `main.c` and adding the resulting object module to the library too, as in

```
c2c main.c u=prog.lib
```

After you make your change to `filea.c`, you update the library with the usual

```
c2c filea.c u=prog.lib
```

Then you issue the command

```
c2c l=prog.lib use=main o=prog.exe
```

The `Library=` option tells **C2C** to look up references in `prog.lib`. The option `USe=main` tells **C2C** to get the compiled `main` routine out of the library and to link in everything that `main` references. This brings in the whole program, so that the whole program is linked together appropriately. The `Output=` option tells **C2C** to write the linked program into `prog.exe`.

If we now make a change in `fileb.c`, we can remake the whole program with the commands

```
c2c fileb.c u=prog.lib
c2c l=prog.lib o=prog.exe USe=main
```

We don't have to recompile `main` because it's already in the library; we just have to specify the `USe=main` option to *get* `main` from the library. We changed the order of the options on the command line just to show that order doesn't matter.

G.4 Summary of the C2C Command

Below we summarize the options of the **C2C** command. Note that several options were not discussed in preceding sections.

`+Clear`

Used to initialize or create an object library. Any existing contents of the library are discarded. The library to be initialized must be specified with an `Update=library` option.

`Define=name=value`

Defines a manifest with the given `name` and `value`. For example, the command line option

```
Define=NDEBUG=1
```

has the same effect as putting

```
#define NDEBUG 1
```

at the beginning of the source file.

Include=directory

Is used when you are using **#include** to obtain files that are not standard headers. When this option is present, **C2C** will search for include files under the given directory. For example, if a file contains

```
#include "file.h"
```

and the command line specifies `I=\dir`, **C2C** will begin its search for the desired include file under the directory that contains the source file. If the include file is not found there, **C2C** searches for

```
\dir\file.h
```

If the include file is still not found, **C2C** will search under the directory that includes the standard headers, and finally under the current directory. A command line may have more than one `Include=` option, in which case, directories are searched in the order specified.

Library=file

Indicates that the given `file` is an object library. **C2C** will search this library to resolve references. If a command line contains more than one `Library=` option, libraries are searched in the order they appear on the command line.

-LoaD

Does not create a linked executable file. For example, in

```
c2c file.c -ld output=file.ld
```

the output will be written as an object file instead of an executable `.exe` file. Note that the object file format is unique to **C2C**.

Map=file

Writes a load map to the specified file. This tells the memory location of every function and external variable in the linked program.

Output=file

Specifies a file to which output should be written. This will be an object module if `-Load` is specified; otherwise, it will be an executable `.exe` file. If no `Output=` option is specified, object modules are written to `a.ld` and executable files to `a.exe`.

`Update=library`
> Indicates that the object module should be written to the given library. The translated material will replace any functions/variables with the same names.

`USe=name`
> Forces **C2C** to link in the object module that contains the function or variable with the given `name`, plus all other functions or variables that the module references. You can also write
>
>   USe=name,name,name,...
>
> to force in several different names.

Other options may be supported. See the `read.me` file for details.

Bibliography

Draft Proposed American National Standard for Information Systems—Programming Language C, American National Standards Institute, X3J11/88-090, May 13, 1988.

The C Programming Language, by Brian W. Kernighan and Dennis M. Ritchie, Prentice-Hall, 1978.

American National Dictionary for Information Processing Systems, Information Processing Systems Technical Report ANSI X3/TR-1-82, 1982.

ISO 4217 Codes for the Representation of Currency and Funds

ISO 646-1983 Invariant Code Set

Index

A 9
B 0
C 1
D 2
E 3
F 4
G 5
H 6
I 7
J 8

Library Routines (continued)

```
<stdio.h>   int       sscanf(const char *string,const char *format, ...);
<string.h>  char *    strcat(char *str1,const char *str2);
<string.h>  char *    strchr(const char *string,int c);
<string.h>  int       strcmp(const char *str1,const char *str2);
<string.h>  int       strcoll(const char *str1,const char *str2);
<string.h>  char *    strcpy(char *dest,const char *src);
<string.h>  size_t    strcspn(const char *string,const char *set);
<string.h>  char *    strerror(int errnum);
<time.h>    size_t    strftime(char *dest,size_t max,const char *format,
                          const struct tm *timestruct);
<string.h>  size_t    strlen(const char *string);
<string.h>  char *    strncat(char *str1,const char *str2,size_t N);
<string.h>  int       strncmp(const char *str1,const char *str2,size_t N);
<string.h>  char *    strncpy(char *dest,const char *src,size_t N);
<string.h>  char *    strpbrk(const char *string,const char *set);
<string.h>  char *    strrchr(const char *string,int c);
<string.h>  size_t    strspn(const char *string,const char *set);
<string.h>  char *    strstr(const char *string,const char *substr);
<stdlib.h>  double    strtod(const char *s,char **ptr);
<string.h>  char *    strtok(char *string,const char *set);
<stdlib.h>  long      strtol(const char *s,char **ptr,int base);
<stdlib.h>  unsigned long strtoul(const char *s,char **ptr,int base);
<string.h>  size_t    strxfrm(char *modstr,const char *orig,size_t N);
<stdlib.h>  int       system(const char *command);
<math.h>    double    tan(double x);
<math.h>    double    tanh(double x);
<time.h>    time_t    time(time_t *time_num);
<stdio.h>   FILE *    tmpfile(void);
<stdio.h>   char *    tmpnam(char *name);
<ctype.h>   int       tolower(int c);
<ctype.h>   int       toupper(int c);
<stdio.h>   int       ungetc(int c,FILE *stream);
<stdarg.h>  type      va_arg(va_list ap, type);
<stdarg.h>  void      va_end(va_list ap);
<stdarg.h>  void      va_start(va_list ap, lastparm);
<stdio.h>   int       vfprintf(FILE *stream,const char *format,va_list ap);
<stdio.h>   int       vprintf(const char *format,va_list ap);
<stdio.h>   int       vsprintf(char *string,const char *format,va_list ap);
<stdlib.h>  size_t    wcstombs(char *mbstr,const wchar_t *wcstr,size_t N);
<stdlib.h>  int       wctomb(char *mb, wchar_t wc);
```

Keywords

auto	double	int	struct
break	else	long	switch
case	enum	register	typedef
char	extern	return	union
const	float	short	unsigned
continue	for	signed	void
default	goto	sizeof	volatile
do	if	static	while